DESTROYING
THE WORLD
TO SAVE IT

DESTROYING
THE WORLD
TO SAVE IT

Aum Shinrikyō, Apocalyptic Violence,
and the New Global Terrorism

Robert Jay Lifton

Metropolitan Books
Henry Holt and Company | New York

Metropolitan Books
Henry Holt and Company, LLC
Publishers since 1866
115 West 18th Street
New York, New York 10011

Metropolitan Books is a registered trademark
of Henry Holt and Company, LLC.

Published in Canada by Fitzhenry & Whiteside Ltd.,
195 Allstate Parkway, Markham, Ontario L3R 4T8

Library of Congress Cataloging-in-Publication Data
Lifton, Robert Jay, 1926–
Destroying the world to save it : Aum Shinrikyō, apocalyptic violence,
and the new global terrorism / Robert Jay Lifton.—1st ed.
p.   cm.
Includes bibliographical references and index.
ISBN 0-8050-5290-9 (hb : alk. paper)
1. Oumu Shinrikyō (Religious organization)   2. Asahara, Shōkō.
I. Title.
BP605.088L54   1999   99-23905
299'.93—dc21   CIP

Henry Holt books are available for special promotions
and premiums. For details contact: Director, Special Markets.

First Edition 1999

Designed by Michelle McMillian

Printed in the United States of America
All first editions are printed on acid-free paper. ∞

1   3   5   7   9   10   8   6   4   2

FOR NATASHA

Contents

DESTROYING THE WORLD TO SAVE IT

Introduction: Ends and Beginnings

I t is not true that there is nothing new under the sun. To be sure, the oldest human emotions continue to haunt us. But they do so in new settings with new technology, and that changes everything.

On March 20, 1995, Aum Shinrikyō, a fanatical Japanese religious cult, released sarin, a deadly nerve gas, on five subway trains during Tokyo's early-morning rush hour. A male cult member boarded each of the trains carrying two or three small plastic bags covered with newspaper and, at an agreed-upon time, removed the newspaper and punctured the bags with a sharpened umbrella tip. On the trains, in the stations where they stopped, and at the station exits, people coughed, choked, experienced convulsions, and collapsed. Eleven were killed and up to five thousand injured. Had Aum succeeded in producing a purer form of the gas, the deaths could have been in the thousands or hundreds of thousands. For sarin, produced originally by the Nazis, is among the most lethal of chemical weapons. Those releasing it on the trains understood themselves to be acting on behalf of their guru and his vast plan for human salvation.

Aum and its leader, Shōkō Asahara, were possessed by visions of the end of the world that are probably as old as death itself. Asahara also held in common with many present-day Christian prophets of biblical world-ending events a belief that Armageddon would be connected to those most secular of "end-time" agents, nuclear warheads or chemical and biological weapons of mass destruction.

But his cult went a step further. It undertook serious efforts to acquire and produce these weapons as part of a self-assigned project of making Armageddon happen. For the first time in history, end-time religious fanaticism allied itself with weapons capable of destroying the world and a group embarked on the mad project of doing just that. Fortunately, much went wrong. After all, it is not so easy to destroy the world. But we have a lot to learn from the attempt.

The impulses that drove Asahara and Aum are by no means unique to him and his group. Rather, Aum was part of a loosely connected, still-developing global subculture of apocalyptic violence—of violence conceived in sweeping terms as a purification and renewal of humankind through the total or near-total destruction of the planet. One can observe these inclinations in varied groups on every continent. Their specific transformative projects may be conceived as religious or political, the violence to be employed either externally directed or suicidal or both at once. One can find certain psychological parallels to Aum Shinrikyō in, for instance, the Jewish fundamentalists who encouraged the assassination of Israeli Prime Minister Yitzhak Rabin, in Palestinian Hamas suicide bombers, and in Hindu and Muslim fundamentalists who act violently on behalf of claims to ancient sacred places on the Indian subcontinent. But my exploration of Aum led me particularly to the apocalyptic inclinations of American groups like the Charles Manson Family, Heaven's Gate, and Peoples Temple, as well as the Oklahoma City bombers, Aryan supremacists, and paramilitary survivalists on the radical right. Just as we now take for granted the interconnectedness of the global economic system, so must we learn to do the same for the growing global system of apocalyptic violence. Outbreaks anywhere reverberate everywhere.

Increasingly widespread among ordinary people is the feeling of things going so wrong that only extreme measures can restore virtue and righteousness to society. When the world comes to be experienced as both hateful and dead or dying, a visionary guru can seize on such feelings while promising to replace them with equally absolute love and life-power. Nor are any of us completely free of those inner struggles. The sentiments that created Aum Shinrikyō are part of the spiritual and psychological ambience each of us inhabits day by day.

Apocalyptic violence has been building worldwide over the last half of the twentieth century. Having studied some of the most destructive events of this era, I found much of what Aum did familiar, echoing the totalistic belief systems and end-of-the-world aspirations I had encountered in other versions of the fundamentalist self. I came to see these, in turn, as uneasy reactions to the openness and potential confusions of the "protean" self that history has bequeathed us. I had been concerned with these matters since the mid-1950s, when I first studied "thought reform" (or "brainwashing") in Communist China and then among American cultic religious groups. I came to recognize the power of a totalized environment for mobilizing individual passions in the creation of fierce, often deeply satisfying expressions of collective energy.

Aum's obsession with nuclear weapons and with the atomic destruction of Hiroshima in particular connected with interview work I had done in that city in the early 1960s on the psychological effects of the atomic bomb and on the psychology of the survivor. In subsequent work I had explored the dangers of "nuclearism," the embrace and even deification of nuclear weaponry so that potential agents of mass destruction become a source of security, life-power, and even at times salvation. My work in the early 1970s with Vietnam veterans who told of destroying a village—indeed, much of a country—in order to save it had reverberations in Aum, where the ambition was considerably greater: destroying a world in order to save it. There were striking parallels in Aum to behavior I encountered in the 1970s and 1980s while studying the Nazis' utilization not only of professional killers but also of killing professionals—in this case, doctors. In Aum, too, doctors were central to the cult's reversal of healing and killing. They participated in individual murders and had an important role, together with other scientists, in producing and releasing deadly chemical and biological weapons.

Aum is now viewed throughout the world as the primary example of the extraordinary dangers posed by private terrorist groups arming themselves with versions of "the poor man's atomic bomb." For Aum was a small antigovernment group claiming ten thousand followers in Japan, about fourteen hundred of whom were renunciants, or monks, at thirty facilities across the country; thirty thousand in Russia (a figure that has been disputed); and a handful in West Germany, Sri Lanka, and the United States. Yet this relatively tiny organization managed to manufacture, stockpile, and release deadly sarin gas first in the city of Matsumoto, northwest of Tokyo, and then in Tokyo itself. It also prepared equally deadly anthrax bacillus and botulinus toxin, releasing them several times in Tokyo and nearby areas (including in the vicinity of two American military bases), largely unsuccessfully but with effects not yet fully known. Between 1990 and 1995 the cult staged at least fourteen chemical and biological attacks of varying dimensions. Aum also made inquiries, particularly in Russia, into acquiring or producing nuclear weapons. It was the grandiose plan of Shōkō Asahara to employ this weaponry to initiate World War III, a global holocaust of unprecedented proportions that would in turn trigger a hoped-for Armageddon. In his fantasies he saw the United States as a major military participant in this apocalyptic project.

But plans and fantasies, however earnest and elaborate, are not the same as action. A simple but terrible question therefore haunts this study: How did Aum Shinrikyō come to cross the crucial threshold from merely anticipating Armageddon to taking active steps to bring it about?

My way of going about answering this question was, as always, to talk to people—to interview those involved. I have been doing that for decades in applying a psychological perspective to historical problems. Here, during five trips to Japan between 1995 and 1997, I was able to conduct intensive interviews with ten former members of Aum, eight men and two women, averaging more than five hours with each person. Since the guru himself and most of his leading disciples were in prison and inaccessible, the people I interviewed tended to be at either the lower or the mid echelons of a very hierarchical organization. Only a privileged inner circle of Asahara's highest-ranking followers were told of the more violent aspects of the guru's visionary plans, and even then often incompletely. Most of those I interviewed had little or no knowledge of the various facets of Aum violence. But while part of Aum they had to do considerable psychological work to fend off that knowledge in the face of the evidence around them.

I was also able to have discussions, though less structured, with two additional former members and one present member as well as with many close observers of Aum. I spent several particularly valuable days with one of the people most intensely involved in helping former Aum members extricate themselves psychologically from the cult and find alternative forms of spiritual expression. Because my Japanese is limited, I required interpreters for all these exchanges. I was extremely fortunate to have the close collaboration of an eminent scholar of Japanese religion, Manabu Watanabe, in this project. He interpreted for me in many of these interviews and meetings and consulted on various issues having to do with present and past patterns in Japanese religion, history, and psychology. Almost all the interviews were tape-recorded and then transcribed and retranslated by young bilingual scholars, providing a further opportunity to explore nuanced meanings.

Several of the former Aum members I spoke to were introduced to me by scholars and journalists they had been in touch with. Having found some value in the interviews, these former members introduced me to friends who had also been part of Aum. Much of their motivation had to do with their need to understand more about what had happened to them in the cult, how they had become so profoundly involved with a group they and others came to see as criminal, and how they could extricate themselves from their tie to a guru who still had a considerable psychological hold on them. I felt a certain sympathy for their efforts, while remaining aware, as were most of them, of their moral complicity in Aum. To protect their anonymity, I have used pseudonyms consisting only of family names for those I interviewed. In addition, I have altered certain identifying details that do not affect the substance of our exchanges.

I supplemented my interviews with efforts to learn all I could about historical and cultural influences on Aum—from writings by and discussions with scholars concerned with Japanese religion and society,

Japanese journalists who had covered or followed the story of the cult, and Europeans and Americans familiar with Japan's religious climate. I utilized the Japanese and American Internets for early reports on Aum and details of the ongoing trials of its leaders, especially that of its guru. And I drew upon my past work on Japan, including studies of its youth and of prominent figures of the modern era.

I focused on the inner life of Aum members and above all on the extraordinary ramifications of the guru-disciple relationship. Most of Aum's wildly destructive visions came from its guru, but he in turn was completely dependent upon his disciples to sustain those visions and act upon them—indeed, for his own psychological function. One can understand little about Aum without probing the extremity of what can be called its guruism, and that guruism helps us to grasp certain essential aspects of the leader-follower interaction in much of the extreme behavior taking place elsewhere. Included in Aum's guruism was a bizarre embrace of science to "prove" Aum's religious truths and to provide Asahara with the kinds of ultimate weapons that might bring such "truths" to fruition.

No truth was more central to Aum than the principle that world salvation could be achieved only by bringing about the deaths of just about everyone on this earth. Disciples described their embrace of this vision and their understanding of its evolution from Hindu, Buddhist, and Christian doctrine, but they always assumed that the world-ending violence would be initiated by others, not by the cult itself. Yet Asahara's idiosyncratic version of these traditions came to focus on the Buddhist concept of *poa*, which, in his distorted use, meant killing for the sake of your victims: that is, to provide them with a favorable rebirth. One can speak, then, of a weapons-hungry cult with a doctrine of altruistic murder—murder ostensibly intended to enhance a victim's immortality. The doctrine sanctified not only violence against the world at large but the killing of numerous individuals who ran afoul of the guru's aspirations.

At the heart of Aum's violence—and its violent world-ending fantasies—was the interaction of a megalomanic guru with ultimate weapons of annihilation. Such weapons were profoundly attractive precisely because they enabled him to feel that he alone had the power to destroy the world. The existence of the weapons, then, effaces age-old distinctions between world-destroying fantasy (whether of paranoid schizophrenics, religious visionaries, or even ordinary people in their dreams) and the capability of actualizing that fantasy. That blurring of categories was noted by a thoughtful psychoanalyst, Edward Glover, within months of the atomic destruction of Hiroshima and Nagasaki. He spoke of the atomic bomb as "less a weapon of war than a weapon of extermination [and therefore] well adapted to the more bloodthirsty fantasies with which man is secretly preoccupied during phases of acute frustration." He concluded, "The capacity so painfully acquired by normal men to distinguish between sleep, delusion, hallucination and the objective reality of waking life has for the first time in human history been seriously weakened."

In sustaining his ties to ultimate weapons, Asahara brought to bear highly varied, seemingly contradictory personal characteristics: a genuine religious talent, a form of paranoia that enabled him to function at a rather high intellectual level, a con-man style that involved continuous falsification (both conscious lying and self-deception), a grandiosity of moral claim that justified unlimited mass murder, and a tendency, when control over his environment was threatened, to succumb to paranoid psychosis. His obsession with weapons of mass destruction aside, Asahara was hardly unique. All megalomanic gurus are likely to be some such psychological composite—hence the confusion of observers who focus on just one or two of these characteristics. Certainly, all of them operated in Aum as the guru and his closest disciples, struggling with internal and external crises, managed to generate a powerful momentum toward mass killing and eventually crossed a threshold that allowed for no turning back.

Aum is a Japanese phenomenon but a more general one as well. To begin to explain its emergence we must look at various psychological and historical currents in contemporary and modern Japan, which are replete with violence, national guruism, and apocalyptic temptation. But we are, of course, only dealing with a Japanese expression of our universal psychological repertoire, with feelings now being experienced everywhere, perhaps most strongly in the United States. We all have to face Aum's significance for the human future and to ponder the question of how to deal with, and what alternatives there might be to, its vision of apocalyptic violence.

For Aum is about death in the nuclear age, about a distorted passion for survival, and about an ever more desperate quest for immortality. It is also about despising the world so much that one feels impelled to destroy it. In these ways, Aum encompassed the most destructive forces of the century just passing.

1 | The Guru and His Cult

One can look at the guru of a fanatical new religion or cult* as either everything or nothing. The everything would acknowledge the guru's creation of his group and its belief system, as well as his sustained control over it—in which case the bizarre behavior of Aum Shinrikyō could be understood as little more than a reflection of Shōkō Asahara's own bizarre ideas and emotions. The nothing would suggest that the guru is simply a creation of the hungers of his disciples, that he has no existence apart from his disciples, that any culture can produce psychological types like him, that without disciples, there is no guru. Both views have elements of truth, but the deeper truth lies in combining them, in seizing upon the paradox.

---

*I am aware of the controversy surrounding the use of the word *cult* because of its pejorative connotation, as opposed to the more neutral *new religion*. I use both terms in this book, but as in past work I confine the use of *cult* to groups that display three characteristics: totalistic or thought-reform-like practices, a shift from worship of spiritual principles to worship of the person of the guru or leader, and a combination of spiritual quest from below and exploitation, usually economic or sexual, from above.

Gurus and disciples are inevitably products of a particular historical moment. They represent a specific time and place, even as they draw upon ancient psychological and theological themes. As our contemporaries, they are, like the rest of us, psychologically unmoored, adrift from and often confused about older value systems and traditions. That unmoored state has great importance. Here I would stress only that a guru's complete structural and psychological separateness from a traditional cultural institution—in Asahara's case an established religion—permits him to improvise wildly in both his theology and his personal behavior, to become a "floating guru." Disciples in turn are open to any strange direction he may lead them and contribute their own unmoored fantasies without the restraining force that a religious or institutional hierarchy might provide.

The guru narrative is always elusive. The guru appears to us full-blown, catches our attention because of what he, with disciples, has done—all the more so when that is associated with any kind of violence, no less mass murder. We then look back on the guru's life history to try to understand his part in this culminating act. But while we should learn all we can about him, we are mistaken if we believe that his childhood—or his past in general—will provide a full explanation of that act.

No adult is a mere product of childhood. There is always a forward momentum to the self that does not follow simple cause and effect. Each self becomes a constellation or a collage that is ever in motion, a "self-system" or "self-process." There are, of course, powerful early influences on that self, but outcomes depend upon evolving combinations of experience and motivation that are never entirely predictable. This is especially clear with exceptional people: one would be hard put to explain the extraordinary actions of either a Picasso or a Hitler on the basis of childhood experience alone. With anyone, we can at best connect that childhood to later inclinations, attitudes, or passions, finding certain continuities of talent, destructiveness, or both. But precisely the quality that claims our interest here—what we usually call charisma—tends to leap out of the life narrative and create a special realm of its own.

The British psychoanalyst Anthony Storr offers a useful description of a guru type: a spiritual teacher whose insight is based on personal revelation, often taking the form of a vision understood to come directly from a deity. The revelation, which has transformed his life, generally follows upon a period of distress or illness in his thirties or forties. There is suddenly a sense of certainty, of having found "the truth," creating a general aura around him that *"he knows."* The emerging guru can then promise, as Asahara did, "new ways of self-development, new paths to salvation, always generalizing from [his] own experience."

But the guru, in turn, needs disciples not only to become and remain a guru but to hold himself together psychologically. For the guru self often teeters on the edge of fragmentation, paranoia, and overall psychological breakdown. We will observe a particularly bizarre and violent version of this in Asahara, and in the manner in which he disintegrated when his closest disciples turned against him. Disciples are crucial to all dimensions of a guru's psychological struggles in ways that are seldom fully grasped.

What has also been insufficiently recognized is the life-death dimension that pervades the guru-disciple tie, a dimension I have stressed throughout my work. Moving away from the classical Freudian model of instinct, mostly sexual, and defense, mostly repression, I emphasize our struggles with the continuity of life and our ways of symbolizing life and death. At an immediate level these include experiences of vitality as opposed to numbing and inner deadness. But I also include an ultimate level of universal need for human connectedness, for a sense of being part of a great chain of being that long preceded, and will continue endlessly after, one's own limited life span. This sense of immortality encompasses feelings of living on in our children and their children, in our influences on other human beings, in our "works," in a particular set of spiritual or religious beliefs, in what we perceive as eternal nature, or in the oneness of transcendent experiences.

In the cult, the guru becomes a crucible for life-power. That life-power is experienced as a surge of vitality, or what was constantly spoken of in Aum as "energy." One's previously deadened life now has vigor and purpose, even if the vigor and purpose are borrowed from the guru. That life-power becomes bound up with larger spiritual forces, that is, with a fierce sense of death-defying immortality. This aspect was the most compelling feature of Asahara's hold on his disciples. The charisma that a guru like him is always said to possess is usually described with phrases like "magnetic attractiveness" or a "naked capacity of mustering assent." But at the heart of charisma is the leader's ability to instill and sustain feelings of vitality and immortality, feelings that reach into the core of each disciple's often wounded, always questing self, while propelling that self beyond itself. Such feelings can be as fragile as they are psychologically explosive.

In this book Asahara, the guru, will be everywhere, most of all inhabiting, even in the wake of Aum's violence, the minds of the disciples I interviewed. At the same time he will be nowhere, his guruism a phantom force, wavering between hyperreality and nothingness.

One-Eyed Child

Shōkō Asahara's childhood brings to mind Erasmus's aphorism "In the country of the blind the one-eyed man is king." But this particular one-eyed child was apparently an odd and uneasy king. Born in 1955 into the impoverished family of a tatami craftsman in a provincial area of Kyūshū, the southernmost of Japan's main islands, he was the sixth of seven children and the fourth of five boys. Chizuo Matsumoto (Asahara's birth name), afflicted with congenital glaucoma, was without sight in one eye and had severely impaired vision in the other. Because he did have some vision he was eligible to attend an ordinary school, but his parents chose to send him to a special school for the blind. It had the advantage of providing free tuition and board, and a completely sightless older brother was already enrolled there.

Having some vision while his fellow students had none, and being bigger and stronger than most of them, he could be a dominating, manipulative, bullying, and sometimes violent figure in the school, where he would remain until he was twenty years old. He would, for instance, force his roommates to strike one another in a contest he called "pro wrestling," and when he found their efforts unsatisfactory he would himself demonstrate how it should be done. He could be rebellious to the point of threatening teachers but, if challenged, would back down and deny any provocation. He always had a few completely blind followers toward whom he could at times exhibit great kindness, and his teachers observed that he was also capable of tenderness toward his older brother and a younger brother who later became a student at the school. But he was generally coercive, gave evidence of resentment over having been forced to attend this special school, and was prone to quick changes in attitude and demands.

In his early ventures into proto-guruism, this one-eyed "king" did not command wide allegiance. He unsuccessfully ran for class head on several occasions, and each failure left him dejected. Once, after being voted down by fellow students despite an attempt to bribe them with sweets, he accused a teacher of influencing the election by saying bad things about him, but the teacher pointed out to him that the other students were simply afraid of him.

While his actual background was humble enough, there were rumors of a further taint—that his family came from the outcast group known by the euphemism *burakumin* (literally "village people") or that they were Korean, also a victimized group in Japan. These rumors, though false, suggest something of others' attitudes toward him. Yet later he would sometimes himself imply that he was *burakumin*, in order to identify himself with a despised and victimized group and so to claim extraordinary triumph over adversity.

Most accounts of Asahara's early years emphasize his preoccupation with money. He would charge other students for favors his partial sight allowed him to accomplish and insist upon being treated by them when he took them to food shops or restaurants. He is said to have accumulated a considerable sum of money this way by the time of his graduation. But whatever the complexities of his school life, he apparently obtained rather good grades as a student and achieved a black-belt ranking in judo.

One aspect of Asahara's childhood is not frequently mentioned. He was attracted to drama of all kinds. From an early age, he loved to watch melodramas on television; later he acted in various school plays and as a high school senior wrote a play of his own about Prince Genji, a great romantic figure, taking the exalted leading role for himself. His stated ambition was to become prime minister of Japan. (One teacher remembered him avidly absorbing a biography of Kakuei Tanaka, the new prime minister in 1972.) He even reportedly said in those years that he wished to be "the head of a robot kingdom" (although in the context of the popular science-fiction culture of his adolescence, this fantasy might not have been as strange as it may now sound). His teachers generally came to think of him as someone who wished to "extend his own image into someone strong or heroic." A former classmate made the interesting observation that as the school for the blind was a closed society, so in Aum Asahara would try "to create the same kind of closed society in which he could be the head."

None of this can account for what he did later. Moreover, retrospective reconstructions always run the risk of evoking the past selectively in the light of subsequent behavior, particularly when that behavior is extreme. But every guru begins somewhere. Asahara's childhood undoubtedly contributed to his sense of alienation, of otherness, to his generalized hatred of the world, to his tendency toward paranoia, to what was to become a habit of violence, to his cultivation of the art of performance, and to his aspirations toward the heroic and transcendent. Overall, he developed in childhood an inclination toward controlling and manipulating other people, and perhaps the beginnings of an identity as a "blind seer."

The Guru Myth: Beginnings

The narrative of the guru—of the religious founder in general—can be seen as a version of the myth of the hero. That myth involves a mysterious birth and early childhood, a call to greatness, and a series of ordeals and trials culminating in heroic achievement. I believe that this culmination lies not, as Freud claimed, in the resolution of the Oedipus complex and symbolic reconciliation with the father but rather in the hero's achievement of special knowledge of, or mastery over, death, which can in turn enhance the life of his people. In the case of the religious hero—the guru—the ordeals faced must be moral and spiritual; the crux of the guru biography, therefore, is the overcoming of moral failure by means of spiritual rebirth.

Asahara entered readily into that myth by means of conscious manipulation as well as unconscious inclination. After graduating from a special extension course at the high school for the blind in 1975, he moved to the Kyūshū city of Kumamoto, where he became, at the age of twenty, an acupuncturist and masseur (the latter a traditional occupation for the blind in Japan). But in 1976 he was convicted by a Kyūshū court of causing bodily injury to another person (one report suggests that he misused the judo he had studied) and was fined 15,000 yen ($150). In 1977 he moved to Tokyo, largely because of that incident. He was said to have at times expressed an ambition to enter either the law or the medical school of Tokyo University, Japan's most elite educational institution. According to the narrative of his life (largely supplied by him), an important reason for his move was to attend a preparatory, or "cram," school in order to take that university's extremely difficult entrance examinations, which he then failed. Since there are no clear records connecting him with either the examinations or a cram school, it is possible, as some observers have speculated, that Asahara invented that sequence of events as part of his mythic tale.

In any case, in Tokyo he resumed his work as an acupuncturist and masseur, while at the same time immersing himself in the revolutionary writings of Mao Zedong. In 1978, he met, impregnated, and married Tomoko Ishii, who gave birth to a daughter and would eventually bear their five other children. That same year, with the financial support of his wife's family, he opened a Chinese herbal-medicine pharmacy, which made a great deal of money. But in 1982, at the age of twenty-seven, he was arrested for selling fake Chinese medicines, convicted, fined 200,000 yen (about $2,000), and given a brief jail sentence. He went into bankruptcy, experienced a profound sense of humiliation, and plunged more deeply into studies he had already begun of various forms of traditional fortune-telling, Taoist medicine, and related expressions of divination and mysticism.

This pre-Aum experience suggests that Asahara (then still going by the name of Matsumoto) wavered between fantasies of mainstream power (entering Tokyo law school or becoming prime minister) and radical rebelliousness (lawbreaking and a fascination with Mao). He did the same in his preoccupation with healing: the vision of Tokyo

University medical college giving way to fringe expressions of spiritual healing that relied on con-man tactics. His trajectory went from grandiose plans to conquer society from within to embittered failure to idiosyncratic healing enterprises.

He would later place all of his experience within a guru myth. He described himself as having been "mentally unstable" and full of "doubts about my life." In connection with such doubts, he described "a conflict between self-confidence and an inferiority complex." Then came his heroic spiritual quest: "One day I stopped fooling myself altogether and thought: 'What am I living for? Is there anything absolute, does true happiness really exist in this world? If so, can I get it?' I did not realize at this point that what my soul was looking for was enlightenment. But I couldn't sit still. Urged by such restlessness, I started a blind search. It was an intense feeling; it was a faith."

Many people in such situations, he further explained, would simply change jobs or "just disappear." In him, however, there "awoke . . . the desire to seek after the ultimate, the unchanging, and I began groping for an answer." His spiritual journey, he tells us, meant "discarding everything . . . everything that I had" and required "great courage and faith, and great resolution." The emerging guru had found a way to heal himself and could embark on "a long and arduous eight years of practice" on the road to enlightenment.

In 1981, at age twenty-six, during his troubled Tokyo days, he joined Agonshū, one of the most successful of Japan's "new religions." (The term refers to religious sects that have arisen since the late nineteenth century, often beginning with the vision of an ordinary person who becomes the sect's founder and borrowing eclectically from various religious traditions.) Although he was later to disparage Agonshū and even claim that it had been spiritually harmful to him during his three years of membership, there is every evidence that he derived from it many of his subsequent religious principles. Indeed, he found there a powerful guru model, sixty-year-old Seiyū Kiriyama, a highly charismatic figure. Kiriyama claimed, as the British scholar Ian Reader tells us, "miraculous and extraordinary happenings, visitations, and other occurrences that create[d] a sense of dramatic vigor and expectation around the religion and its leader, endow[ed] them with a legitimacy and suggest[ed] that they possess[ed] a special, chosen nature." In those three years Asahara was in effect apprenticing for joining the ranks of the "dynamic, charismatically powerful . . . religious figures" who, Reader says, "have frequently, by their very natures, upset or challenged [Japanese] social harmony and norms."

From Kiriyama and Agonshū, Asahara also drew upon a variety of ideas and practices that would become important in Aum: expressions of esoteric Buddhism, mystical forms of yoga, and forms of self-purification aimed at freeing oneself from bad karma. He was also much influenced by Agonshū's use of American New Age elements from the human-potential movement, individual psychology, and applied neurology. It was here as well that he first encountered the writings of Nostradamus, the sixteenth-century French astrologer and physician who predicted the end of the world with the coming of the year 2000. Asahara, who was to radically alter, supplement, and totalize these influences, soon became a fledgling guru, acquiring a few disciples by the time he left Agonshū.

The emerging guru may have a number of visions, but one in particular usually serves as a crucial illumination and a sacred mandate for a special spiritual mission. This should not be seen as simply a matter of calculation or fakery: intense personal conviction is essential to the guru's success. But that conviction can be helped considerably by grandiose ambitions and manipulative inclinations, which themselves can be enhanced by impressive demonstrations of superhuman powers. Prior to his main vision, Asahara claimed to have experienced during his early period in Agonshū an "awakening of Kundalinī"—a concept of mystical yoga in which one gains access to the cosmic energy that ordinarily lies "sleeping" at the base of the spine. An accomplished practitioner, he opened a yoga school in Tokyo at about this time and was to gain many early converts through the skills he demonstrated.

In 1984 Asahara founded Aum Shinsen no Kai. Aum (often rendered in English as Om or Ohm), a Sanskrit word that represents the most primal powers of creation and destruction in the universe, is often chanted in Buddhism as part of a mantra or personal incantation. Shinsen no Kai means "circle of divine hermits" or "wizards" and has a strong suggestion of esoteric supernatural power. Asahara also created a commercial enterprise, the Aum Corporation. It was to have the important function of publishing his books.

In 1985 Asahara became famous when a photograph of him "levitating" appeared in a popular occult magazine, *Twilight Zone,* identifying him as the "Aum Society representative." The ability to levitate is considered to reflect extraordinarily high spiritual attainment. In his case it was apparently simulated by means of an upward leap from the lotus position along with a bit of trick photography. The placing of the picture in such a visible outlet was an early example of Asahara's strong sense of the importance of the media.

That same year, at the age of thirty, Asahara experienced his central, self-defining vision. While he was wandering as a "homeless monk" near the ocean in northern Japan, a deity appeared before him and ordained him as Abiraketsu no Mikoto, "the god of light who leads the armies of the gods" in an ultimate war to destroy darkness and bring about the kingdom of Shambhala—in Tibetan and other Buddhist traditions, a utopian society of spiritually realized people. The vision was announced to the world in a Japanese New Age magazine in the form of an interview with Asahara.

In the original report of the vision, the god who manifested himself was nameless, but in later versions of it Asahara identified the god as Shiva, the Hindu deity who by then had become his ultimate spiritual authority (or his guru, as he sometimes put it). It was somewhat odd for Asahara to invoke a Hindu god in the creation of an essentially Buddhist group, even if the esoteric Buddhism he drew upon stayed close to its Hindu roots. His choice of Shiva (as opposed to Vishnu or Brahma, the other great Hindu gods) probably had two important determinants. First, Shiva is specifically identified as the god of yoga. Second, while all Hindu gods have destructive as well as beneficent tendencies, Shiva is specifically associated with salvation through world destruction. Asahara was later to claim that Aum Shinrikyō emerged directly from this vision, but he was rewriting history a bit since he had formed Aum Shinsen no Kai the previous year. In 1987, two years after his vision, he renamed the group Aum Shinrikyō, the Shinrikyō meaning "teaching of the supreme truth." Very likely the change reflected his desire for a name that was less obscure, more accessible, and more absolute.

The context in which Asahara placed the vision set the tone for what could be called Aum's New Age Buddhism. Aum did not employ traditional Japanese Buddhist terms, which originated in China and are expressed in Chinese characters, but instead used early Buddhist terms from Sanskrit, Tibetan, and Pali and expressed them in kata-kana, a Japanese phonetic system employed for retained foreign words. These terms were combined with American New Age ones like *empowerment* (rendered in katakana as *empawahmento*). This application of a New Age sensibility to ancient Buddhist and Hindu mysticism was to have great appeal for many young people.

In 1986 Asahara claimed another transcendent religious experience, a "final enlightenment," achieved while meditating in the Himalayas—perhaps the world's ideal place for such visions. A New Delhi holy man whom Asahara sometimes referred to as his master and a "great saint" later told a Japanese reporter that he referred a supplicant Asahara to monks in the Himalayas and was "surprised" when he reappeared four or five days later with a claim to enlightenment, as the master had always assumed that such spiritual achievement required a lifetime. Yet Asahara seems to have been convinced, in at least a part of his mind, that he had indeed become enlightened and that his spiritual achievement entitled—even required—him to be a great guru or perhaps a deity.

Asahara would soon combine such spiritual grandiosity and his organizational and financial skills with endless self-promotion. He would make a point of meeting with prominent Buddhist figures in various parts of the world—most notably the Dalai Lama in India—and of having photographs taken with them, which would then be displayed in Aum publications together with his hosts' lavish expressions of praise for him and his spiritual quest. Here the emerging guru undoubtedly took liberties in converting spiritual hospitality into self-advertisement.

"Guru" is not a title that is used in much Japanese religious practice. It is a Sanskrit word meaning "heavy," suggesting a person of special weight. The guru's authority is such that he is sometimes described as "Father-Mother." In the original Hindu tradition he is more important to the Brahman (a member of the Hindu priestly cast) than the Brahman's actual parents because the latter merely "bring him into existence" while "the birth of a Brahman to a Veda (sacred knowledge) lasts forever." *The Tibetan Book of the Dead* describes three kinds of gurus: ordinary religious teachers who are part of the "human line"; more extraordinary human beings possessed of special spiritual powers; and "superhuman" beings of the "heavenly (or 'divine') line." Asahara was to claim to be all three.

But the guru represents "an ambivalent tradition from the start," the Hindu scholar Wendy Doniger tells us; he is never without conflicts concerning the reach of his guruism and the discipleship that comes to surround it. Asahara reflected some of that ambiguity in saying to a disciple, "If one pretends all of his life to be a saint, he is a saint." To which it should be added that one has to have some belief in one's sainthood to create the pretense in the first place.

The Emergence of Aum Shinrikyō

By the mid-1980s, Chizuo Matsumoto, a name suggesting nothing but ordinariness, had become Shōkō Asahara, a much more striking and unusual name. (Shōkō means "bright light," and the characters he chose for Asahara suggest a field of hemp, a plant associated with the Buddhist idea of connection.) The respected yoga practitioner and teacher (or *sensei*) became the charismatic guru with long, flowing hair and beard. As time went on, he would also begin to dress in the flowing purple robes that suggested a Hindu holy man. Asahara was skillful in his eclecticism, enlarging his teachings to include the Mahāyāna Buddhist theme of the salvation of all beings—salvation here suggesting happiness, welfare, emancipation, and enlightenment—and developing a "Shambhala plan" for the peaceful salvation of all of Japan by means of Aum communes to be set up everywhere.

In his pre-Aum days, Asahara had focused on nonreligious ways of attaining supernatural power, advocating the exploitation of sexual partners along with frequent masturbation as means of achieving transcendence and enlightenment. In Aum he instead preached sexual abstinence while continuing to emphasize that superhuman powers could be achieved, though now by spiritual means. He used his own "levitation" as proof of this, claiming as well that advanced Aum practitioners were capable of remaining underwater up to fifteen minutes or in an airtight box immersed in water for twelve hours. As guru, moreover, Asahara retained his own sexual privileges in what was in principle an otherwise celibate community, continuing to live with his wife and family, taking on long-term mistresses from among Aum disciples, and offering Tantric sexual initiations, or "transfers of energy," to various female followers.

Even in its early years, Aum Shinrikyō showed signs of extreme guruism, intense apocalypticism, and the violent potential in both. Asahara was spoken of and addressed as *Sonshi*, meaning "revered master" or "exalted one," a highly worshipful term not ordinarily used in Japanese Buddhism. A disciple came to understand that without the guru nothing was possible, but with him there opened up a path to perfection and to reincarnations in higher realms. It was expected that the disciple would not only surrender himself to the guru but "merge" or "fuse" with him. He was to become what Asahara in one of his sermons spoke of as a "clone" of the guru. As early as 1986, Asahara declared in another sermon that Japan would sink into the ocean, there would be a third great war, and the world would end. He initially claimed that by creating thirty thousand enlightened beings Aum could prevent Armageddon, but he came to emphasize its inevitability and Aum's role in the final battle.

Asahara recruited scientists more actively than he did any other group. His enthusiasm about science undoubtedly was connected with his lust for murderous weapons. But the guru also wished to consider himself a scientist and once declared, "A religion which cannot be scientifically proven is fake." He was especially interested in brainwaves and claimed that by studying them Aum could establish a scientific basis for the stages of spiritual attainment described by past Buddhist saints. With the help of Hideo Murai, his chief scientist, Aum introduced the use of a headset that purportedly contained the guru's brain waves, which it transmitted to the disciple in a procedure known as the "perfect salvation initiation" (or PSI). The PSI, much revered in

Aum, was meant to bring about the desired "cloning" of the guru by means of technology and science. In this way science readily became pseudoscience, or simply fantasy. There was also a strong element of science fiction in the PSI and other Aum projects, much of it actively fed by television. What took shape in Aum was a blending of science, occultism, and science fiction, with little distinction between the fictional and the actual.

Among Asahara's most crucial early decisions was the creation of *shukke*, or renunciants. *Shukke* means "leaving home" and is a traditional term for monks or nuns who give up the world. Aum's message was that if one really wished to follow the guru and join in his full spiritual project, one had to become a *shukke*, removing oneself completely from one's family and one's prior work or study and turning all one's resources—money, property, and self—over to Aum and its guru. Even one's name was to be abandoned, replaced by a Sanskrit one. Such a renunciation of the world in favor of life in a small, closed society is the antithesis of the this-worldly emphasis of most Japanese religious practice and a repudiation of the still powerful hold the Japanese family has over its members. As a family-like alternative to an actual family's conflicts and confusions, however, it proved a definite attraction to many young people.

Living together in Aum facilities, *shukke* underwent severe forms of ascetic practice, including celibacy and a prohibition against ejaculation, fasting, long hours of meditation, intense breathing exercises, and vigorous sequences of prostration combined with demanding work assignments and irregular sleep (often only a few hours a night). Their existence was a spartan one—two meals a day of extremely simple "Aum food" (rice and vegetables), tiny sleeping spaces, and no personal possessions. The fervent atmosphere was further heightened by Aum's gradual adoption of a series of initiations. In addition to PSI, there was *skaktipat*, in which the guru mobilized a disciple's energy by touching his chakra points, or energy centers, on the forehead or top of the head; there was a "*bardo* initiation" (named for the "in-between state" connecting death and rebirth), in which the initiate was brought before the "Lord of Hell" to hear accusations about his life-long misbehaviors (the accusations sometimes rendered more specific by information previously obtained with the help of narcotic drugs); a

"Christ initiation," in which the guru or a high disciple would personally offer the initiate a liquid containing LSD to help evoke visions; a "narco initiation," in which a narcotic drug was used to extract a confession; and a "resolve initiation," in which, again with the use of a narcotic drug, the initiate was required to chant repeatedly his failure to absorb Aum's full message and his determination to make greater efforts to do so in the future.

The Totalistic Community

Aum's environment became one of intense *ideological totalism*, in which everything had to be experienced on an all-or-nothing basis. A number of psychological patterns characterize such an environment. Most basic is *milieu control*, in which all communication, including even an individual's inner communication, is monopolized and orchestrated, so that reality becomes the group's exclusive possession. Aum's closed subculture of guru and renunciants lent itself to an all-encompassing form of milieu control, though no such control can ever be complete or foolproof. Another pattern of the totalistic environment is *mystical manipulation*, systematic hidden maneuvers legitimating all sorts of deceptions and lies in the service of higher mystical truths. Aum had a hierarchy of mystical manipulators, each disciple being under another's authority, reaching up to the guru himself.

In such a closed world, there is often a *demand for purity*, an insistence upon an absolute separation of the pure and the impure, good and evil, in the world in general and inside each person. In Aum, only the guru could be said to be completely pure. Disciples, even the highest ones, engaged in a perpetual, Sisyphean struggle for purity, their guilt and shame mechanisms taken over by the cult if not by the guru himself. An *ethos of confession* can provide a continuing mechanism for negative self-evaluation. In Aum, abject confession became a form of shared group arrogance in the name of humility—so that each member (and Aum as a whole) would, in Albert Camus's words, "practice the profession of penitence, to be able to end up as a judge," since "the more I accuse myself, the more I have the right to judge you."

Contemporary totalistic communities like Aum claim special access to a *sacred science*, so that what are understood to be ultimate spiritual truths also become part of an ultimate science of human behavior. There is a *loading of the language*, in which words become limited to those that affirm the prevailing ideological claims (Aum "truth" versus outside "defilement"). At the same time a principle of *doctrine over person* requires all private perceptions to be subordinated to those ideological claims. In Aum, that meant that doubts of any kind about the guru, or about his or Aum's beliefs or actions, were attributed to a disciple's residual defilement.

Finally, in their most draconian manifestation, totalistic environments tend to press toward the *dispensing of existence*, an absolute division between those who have a right to exist and those who possess no such right. That division can remain merely judgmental or ideological, but it can also become murderous, as in Aum, which rendered such a "dispensation" altruistic by offering a "higher existence" to those it killed. Aum ultimately became convinced that no one outside the cult had the right to exist because all others, unrelated as they were to the guru, remained hopelessly defiled.

Within that totalism Aum disciples could thrive. They could embrace the extremity of the cult's asceticism as a proud discipline that gave new meaning to their lives. Above all, they could repeatedly experience altered states of consciousness, what in Aum were known as "mystical experiences." These too had a characteristic pattern: light-headedness followed by a sense of the mind leaving the body, the appearance of white or colored lights, and sometimes images either of the Buddha or of the guru. Such altered states resulted from intense forms of religious practice—especially from the oxygen deprivation brought about by yogic rapid-breathing exercises—and, later on, from the use of drugs like LSD. But they were all attributed to the guru's unique spiritual power and so were considered indicators of one's own spiritual progress. There was nothing more important to disciples than to hold on to these mystical experiences, for which purpose they could numb themselves to immediate evidence of violence around them—or join in that violence.

There was considerable violence even in the training procedures to which disciples could be subjected: protracted immersion in extremely hot or cold water, hanging by one's feet for hours at a time, or solitary confinement for days in a tiny cell-like room that had no facilities and could become unbearably hot. Though the distinction between training and punishment often blurred, these procedures were justified by the need of the disciple to overcome the bad karma he brought to Aum or, in the phrase commonly used in the cult, to "drop karma."

To justify further violent actions, Asahara drew upon, and distorted, militant forms of Tibetan Buddhism. He embraced *Vajrayāna* (or "Diamond Vehicle") Buddhism, which stressed the power of the guru and provided him with useful parables of violence by disciples on behalf of their guru. To this he added Tantric Buddhism, which elevates the worship of the god Shiva. Asahara loosely combined them into a highly personalized mix that he called Tantra Vajrayāna.

Asahara also drew from Vajrayāna the concept of *poa*. In esoteric Buddhism, *poa* is a spiritual exercise performed when one is dying, sometimes with the aid of a guru, a "transference of consciousness" from the bodily "earth plane" to the "after-death plane" that enables one to achieve a higher realm in the next rebirth or even passage to the Pure Land, the step prior to nirvana. Asahara came to equate murders with a highly idiosyncratic interpretation of *poa*, in which the killer was offering a benefit to the victim in a form of an improved rebirth. *Poa* became for him a core ideological principle, a theological lever for the dispensing of all existence.

Asahara's tendencies toward megalomania required, and were fed by, his disciples' infinite adulation. Over the years that the interaction was sustained, one can speak of the guru's *functional megalomania*. He presented himself to the world as civilization's greatest spiritual figure—an embodiment of Shiva, the Buddha, and Christ—and as a genius in virtually every field of human endeavor. In addition, there were claims that he possessed nirvana-like brain waves, blood with special properties that could be transmitted to disciples who drank it, and a unique and distinctive form of DNA. Within the cult his megalomania was made manifest through his claim to spiritual omniscience and to control over everyone's bad karma. The megalomania also drew Asahara to weapons of ultimate destruction, the possession of which in turn fed and enhanced that mental state.

The High Disciples

Though many Aum members were middle-aged and not particularly well educated, the cult had a higher percentage of university students and young university graduates than any of the other new religions in Japan, of which there are thousands. Noting that many of Aum's crimes were committed by young people from leading universities, some Japanese journalists spoke of its disciples as "the best and the brightest." But that characterization is somewhat misleading. While a few Aum leaders were highly trained professionals, most high disciples were bright people with university backgrounds who were nonetheless only half-educated, uncertain of the meaning of what they had learned and unsure of the value of what they were doing when they first encountered Aum Shinrikyō. The people I interviewed (who were in less exalted positions in Aum) tended to be alienated from their society, somewhat isolated from others, drawn to occult forms of religious experience, and struggling to extricate themselves from strong feelings of dependency toward their families. They were often at a confusing point of transition in their lives.

Shōkō Asahara's highest disciples, too, had come to Aum as part of a spiritual quest, although theirs led them to criminal behavior. I briefly introduce a few of them here as they will play important roles in subsequent chapters.

Hideo Murai joined Aum in 1987 at the age of twenty-nine. He had an undergraduate degree in science, had done graduate work in astrophysics at Osaka University, and held a job in the research department of a large steel corporation. Long preoccupied with transcending ordinary human existence, he was a particularly fanatical disciple of Asahara, who made him "minister of science and technology" and put him in charge of Aum's manufacture and use of deadly weapons. He became a mad scientist in his zealous efforts to actualize his guru's wildest scientific and technological fantasies. In April 1995, a month after the Tokyo sarin attack, he was stabbed to death by a member of the *yakuza*, the Japanese mafia. The murder was generally believed to have been ordered by Asahara.

Kiyohide Hayakawa, six years older than Asahara, joined in 1986 at the age of thirty-seven. He differed from most other Aum recruits in that he had earlier been a leader, in his case in the leftist student movement. He was to become in many people's eyes the second-most-powerful person in Aum. Having studied architecture and engineering but drawn to Aum by a passion for science fiction, he became "minister of construction." While he did take part in building and in Aum's aggressive acquisition of land, he was mainly known as a dark figure who developed a strong interest in ultimate weapons and made extensive trips to Russia, where he used every means, including bribery, to make military and scientific contacts and acquire weapons of mass destruction and related technology. He was directly involved in a number of murders committed by the cult. At this writing, he is in prison, where, like most other Aum leaders, he has turned against his guru. He is also on trial, as the Japanese judicial system is such that the trial process can go on for a number of years, during which a defendant may have periodic hearings on his case and also testify in related ones.

Ikuo Hayashi was Aum's most accomplished doctor, a cardiac surgeon who had spent a year of training in the United States. Long attracted to various forms of New Age Buddhism and a former member of Agonshū, Hayashi left an important hospital position to join Aum in 1988 at the age of forty-two. Declaring Aum's asceticism to be spiritually superior to medical work, he brought his family and a lover with him into the cult and became its "minister of healing." He was involved in every kind of medical abuse, including extensive druggings of Aum members and designated enemies that sometimes resulted in deaths. He also participated in the Tokyo sarin attack. He was convicted of murder but because of his contrition, as well as his candid exposure of Aum's, Asahara's, and his own crimes, was spared the death penalty and sentenced to life imprisonment.

Tomomasa Nakagawa was the other prominent doctor in Aum. He joined in 1988 while still a medical student in Kyoto and became the guru's personal physician. He was sufficiently enthusiastic in his subservience to the guru to be chosen as part of a murder team just two months after becoming a renunciant. Nakagawa became more involved than Hayashi in hands-on killing. He also did much to produce the last-minute batch of sarin gas used for the Tokyo attack. In addition, as head of the so-called household agency (also known as the secretariat of the sacred emperor), a special group that was particularly close to the guru, he became a visionary planner of large-scale killing. He, too, is in prison and on trial.

Yoshihiro Inoue was in essence educated by the cult itself, embracing its teachings while still in high school and becoming a renunciant in 1988 at the age of eighteen. He was often considered the guru's closest disciple and came to have a powerful mystical presence of his own that contributed to his effectiveness in recruiting. One former member told me in awe how the lightbulbs went out when Inoue entered his room. As "minister of intelligence" he was involved in many kidnappings and murders as well as in various attempts at industrial espionage aimed at acquiring information useful to weapons making. Currently in prison and on trial, he has provided in his testimony against the guru a dramatic account of Aum's behavior.

Hisako Ishii, who left Agonshū with Asahara, was his longest-term and perhaps most fanatical disciple. She was thought of as Asahara's first *shukke*, or renunciant. A graduate of a junior college, she had been an office worker but in Aum, as "minister of finance," achieved considerable power in administrative terms second only to the guru's. She presided aggressively over Aum's amassing of wealth, whether through the personal and family holdings of members, extortion from patients in Aum's "hospital" facilities and from others, or illegal land acquisition. She was also implicated in helping other Aum members escape after the sarin attack. In May 1997, she made a belated public confession, which many thought halfhearted, though she disparaged Asahara's claim to infallibility. She remains in prison and on trial.

Seiichi Endō joined Aum in 1989 at the age of twenty-eight, having been a veterinarian and then a graduate student in virology. Though he worked on the production of the cult's drugs, he was primarily involved as "minister of health and welfare" in the making and use of biological and chemical weapons. His scientific shortcomings and miscalculations greatly hindered the effectiveness of Aum's biological weapons and perhaps its chemical weapons as well. Sharing Asahara's obsession with these during his years in the cult, he was nonetheless quick to condemn the guru when captured, to seek "atonement," and to dismiss Aum's religious experiences as largely drug-induced. Like others, he is in prison and on trial.

Masami Tsuchiya, in contrast to Endō, was a talented chemist who joined the cult in 1989 at the age of twenty-four shortly after receiving an advanced degree from Tsukuba University, known for its scientific standing. Tsuchiya was a dedicated and effective worker in Aum and the first to succeed in making sarin gas. He also harbored wildly apocalyptic fantasies and wrote in his diary of how someday soon Aum would supercede the Japanese state and make its way to Jerusalem. He was at times so immersed in spiritual meditation, and possibly so psychologically dissociated, that he became unavailable for weapons work. In prison he was one of the few Aum leaders to continue to embrace both cult and guru, reasserting the perfection of "the great, perfect, absolute guru Sonshi Asahara" and claiming himself to have entered the spiritual realm of nirvana.

Fumihiro Jōyū left a position with Japan's space agency (he had majored in telecommunications) to pursue his passion for yoga by joining Aum in 1989 at the age of twenty-six. Appointed "minister of foreign affairs," he was made the head of the large Aum operation in Russia, where he was said to have become something of a guru himself. He returned to Japan to serve as Aum's public spokesman, displaying poise in disseminating falsehoods and skill at manipulating the media. Handsome and appealing to many, he became a matinee idol for quite a few Japanese women and girls. (When I visited an Aum bookstore months after the sarin attack, his picture seemed to be the hottest sales item.) Managing to avoid involvement in Asahara's violence, he was convicted only of fraud in land dealings and sentenced to a brief jail term, thereby becoming the first and perhaps only high-ranking Aum leader expected to leave prison within a few years of the Tokyo attack. For that reason and because he continues to refer to Asahara as his "spiritual leader and savior," there is a widespread feeling that Jōyū will become the new head of Aum Shinrikyō.

The Geography of Aum

By the standards of Japanese new religions, Aum was not large. Yet it seemed to be everywhere, doing everything. Its headquarters was in Fujinomiya, a small city near Mount Fuji, about one hundred kilometers from Tokyo; its principal facility was just a few miles away in a village called Kamikuishiki. There were additional facilities, twenty in all, throughout urban Japan, mostly concentrated around Tokyo, Yokohama, and other cities in central Honshu, the main Japanese island.

A large percentage of Aum's renunciants lived in the ten buildings known as Satyam (or "truth") in Kamikuishiki or the two located in Fujinomiya. The buildings contained large dormitories where Aum members slept, each in a cubicle barely big enough for one person in a prone position, and large areas known as *dōjō*, a term used for places of Zen or other spiritual practice, literally meaning "halls of the way." These living quarters were kept in a filthy state, partly because it was Aum's Buddhist policy to kill no living creatures, including ants, bedbugs, or rats; partly because Aum had not officially registered in either location and was therefore not entitled to garbage collection; and partly as a form of radical spiritualism involving disdain for such external, middle-class matters as cleanliness or ordinary hygienic measures. The guru's living area was more spacious, including rooms for his wife and children and a separate kitchen, as well as an area for religious practice, but was luxurious only in comparison with the cubicles assigned to ordinary members.

In among the other buildings was Satyam 7, a large three-story prefabricated structure for the "secret work" of the ministry of science and technology that ordinary members were forbidden to enter. The building contained Aum's main laboratories and plants for chemical and biological weapons. There was an additional secret botulinus laboratory in an Aum facility in central Kyūshū, and a special laboratory and plant for producing anthrax spores on the top floor of an eight-story building owned by the cult in Tokyo. These laboratories and plants contained millions of dollars of highly advanced equipment (not all of it properly utilized) purchased from various parts of the world, much of it from the United States.

In early 1995, Satyam 7 was involved in a sequence of events that said much about Aum's blend of religion and lethal weaponry. Alarmed by newspaper reports of evidence of sarin in the soil near the Kamikuishiki facility and fearful of being discovered, Asahara ordered the building's laboratories and plants shut down and its interior made to look like a place of religious worship. At the entrance to what had been the sarin laboratory was placed an enormous statue of Shiva and a smaller gold statue of the Buddha. Aum proudly displayed these two statues to visitors as proof of the cult's innocence but never permitted them to enter the closed area beyond the statues, where there remained considerable residual evidence of sarin production. In one notorious case, a Tokyo professor generally sympathetic to Aum and other new religions, asked by a magazine to make an "inspection," was shown the room with the statues and reported Aum to be solely a religious organization. Later, when Aum was revealed to be responsible for the sarin attack, public outrage was such that the professor was forced to resign from his university.

Another secret component of Aum's weapons-making facilities was a large factory located near a river just a few miles from the Mount Fuji compounds. Run by the ministry of science and technology, it was called Clear Stream Temple but sometimes known as the Supreme Science Institute. Its main function was to manufacture Russian AK-74 automatic rifles, but it also produced needed parts for the Satyam 7 sarin plant, a spraying device for the gas, and supposed prototypes of laser weapons.

Separate from all other Aum facilities was its Astral Hospital Institute, a small nine-bed suite on the second floor of a four-story commercial building on a busy Tokyo street. The unit engaged more in medical abuse and extortion than in healing. There were also medical units in the regular Aum facilities as well as tiny tatami cells known as "shield rooms," sometimes on a special floor or in small units outside the main buildings where Aum members and others could be sent while being drugged and detained by medical personnel. Murders were committed in these cells and in larger nearby rooms beyond the view of ordinary members.

There were many ways in which Aum spread its net beyond its physical facilities. It was not hard to find out about the group, as Asahara quickly became a very public personality. His subordinates systematically approached television stations to arrange appearances, and magazines to suggest interviews and articles. Asahara became for many a compelling television performer and a dramatic figure in occult publications. Aum had an important if convoluted radio arrangement that was very useful for the spread of its ideas. From early 1992 on, Aum rented airtime from Radio Moscow for two daily half-hour programs, at an estimated cost of $700,000 a year. The guru's words were broadcast there and relayed back to Japan, where they could be picked up on certain frequencies, with the help of a transmitter in Vladivostok. In this way "Radio Aum Shinrikyō" gained a regular outlet. Aum also leased Russian television time to make videotapes that could be shown for recruiting purposes in Japan.

Asahara was a prolific writer, though disciples undoubtedly wrote many of the books and pamphlets published under his name. These written works, widely distributed through Aum bookstores and ordinary ones, could be compelling in their declarative claims and promises. Aum also gained great visibility by running candidates for the Japanese Diet in the election campaign of 1990. Though Asahara and other Aum leaders were ignominiously defeated and much ridiculed for Aum's style of electioneering—members wearing Asahara masks, singing the cult's songs, and dancing its dances—the cult managed to distribute millions of leaflets and its presence was made strikingly visible in ways that evoked sympathetic interest in many young spiritual seekers.

Aum cultivated not only the media but also universities, arranging for Asahara to be invited to speak at many of them. Several former students I interviewed told me of having first become interested in the group through the guru's appearance at their campuses. Aum was welcomed because it was soon seen as one of the more interesting new religions in its intellectual reach, its focus on renouncing the world, and what some have described as its members' hippielike demeanor. In addition, the cult sometimes took advantage of the Japanese proclivity for groups, organizing small "circles" of people interested in such things as "Indian philosophy," without initially identifying the connection to Aum.

There was also a sexual aspect to Aum's recruiting. Its publicity publications featured pictures of attractive women with soulful expressions and beautiful long hair. When a man telephoned an Aum facility for information, he might be greeted by a lilting, even flirtatious female voice. The Aum female persona, often exemplified by

Hisako Ishii, seemed to radiate a mixture of old-fashioned Japanese beauty, an appealing version of female spiritual realization, and a gently erotic promise of individual solace and intimate new ties. However misleading the persona—disguising as it did the fierce belligerence set loose in women like Ishii—it undoubtedly aided in the recruiting of young men.

Within Aum there was a strict spiritual hierarchy. Simply joining the group made one a *zaike*, or lay member; then the pressure was immediately on to become a *shukke*. There was a special *"Poa* Course" for members unable to become *shukke* but motivated toward attaining the status of bodhisattvas, those who practice spiritual virtues in this world and thereby move close to Buddhahood. But only a *shukke*, one was told, could truly merge with the guru and experience the deep satisfactions he made available, whether in the form of supernatural power, mystical states, or immortalizing promises of better rebirths. Aum's energies came mainly from *shukke*, who, although they numbered only about fourteen hundred at the height of Aum's power, expressed those energies in such intense and varied ways as to seem a far larger contingent. As Aum's founder and guru who had achieved final enlightenment, Asahara of course was at the top. Only he was considered what in Aum was called a "victor of truth" (from the Buddhist concept of "one who on the way of truth has attained supreme enlightenment"). The next-highest spiritual level was that of "great master" (or *seitaishi*), a category that included Asahara's wife, Tomoko Matsumoto, his third daughter, Ācharii; Hideo Murai; Fumihiro Jōyū; and Hisako Ishii. The rank just below that—"truly enlightened master" (or *seigoshi*)—included Endō and Hayakawa, among others. These spiritual categories, decided upon by the guru himself, were taken very seriously in Aum. The prospect of moving up a category could motivate a disciple to do almost anything.

Aum Shinrikyō's leaders also took seriously its extraordinary division into "ministries" and "agencies," as though it were a vast governmental structure. These divisions were ostensibly a form of preparation for the post-Armageddon world. A number of people have commented, however, on the broad resemblance of Aum's structure to that of Japan's World War II–era government and emperor system, including a version of the imperial household. While each of Asahara's ministries and agencies had specific functions, they can be understood psychologically as grandiose projections of an individual and collective megalomania.

Another expression of that megalomania was Aum's expansion into a corporate empire. It made enormous amounts of money from the business of religion, not in itself unusual for Japanese new religions, but with particular mercenary ferocity. Through the Aum Publishing Company and its printing presses, located at the Fujinomiya headquarters, the cult churned out and sold vast numbers of books, magazines, pamphlets, videotapes, *manga* (comic strips or graphic novels, an extremely popular form in Japan), and religious pictures and objects. Religious experience did not come cheap. A *shaktipat* by the guru cost $500 for everyone but a renunciant (who would already have given Aum all his money and holdings); a liter of the guru's bathwater, which one could drink for its special effects, was $1,000; a month's rental of a Perfect Salvation Initiation headset was $10,000; for a "blood initiation" (drinking the guru's blood), one also paid $10,000.

Aum soon extended its corporate interests in highly secular directions. One of its most lucrative enterprises was the assembling and marketing of computers; the cult's negligible labor costs enabled it to undersell competitors throughout Japan. Its far-flung business activities included noodle shops and other restaurants in many Japanese cities, a fitness club, baby-sitting and dating services, travel agencies, real estate interests, as well as a variety of "dummy companies" not identified as part of Aum that dealt in chemicals, pharmaceuticals, and technical equipment of various kinds and frequently served as fronts for the acquisition of weapons-related material.

Aum also had overseas holdings: a tea plantation in Sri Lanka, an import-export company in Taiwan, and a huge sheep ranch in Australia (obtained mainly as a site for the cult's weapons experiments and for possible uranium deposits on the property). There was even an Aum corporate presence in New York City, established in 1987, used mostly to purchase books and high-tech equipment that could contribute to its weapons-making activities.

Aum's enormous accumulation of money made possible its outrageous actions. Its assets by early 1995 were said to be as high as a billion dollars. Whether or not that figure is accurate, the full story of Aum's finances has not yet been told. For instance, rumors have circulated about Aum's selling its illegally produced drugs on the black market with the help of the Japanese mafia, an endeavor that would have brought in huge amounts of money.

Violations and Violence

Aum's societal and legal violations began early. More than other cults, it recruited very young people—sometimes even children in their early teens—who would disappear into Aum facilities as renunciants. Concerned parents and parental groups were rebuffed in every possible fashion. In its land acquisitions Aum did not hesitate to use fraudulent methods, falsifying documents and the identity of the buyer. All this could be seen by the outside world as no more than the behavior of an aggressively expanding religious group. Yet, from late 1988 on, people were being killed in Aum.

The first death is generally described as having been "accidental," but the word is misleading. A disciple was killed during one of Aum's violent training procedures: prolonged upside-down hanging followed by immersion into extremely cold water with resulting shock. Such procedures were prescribed by the guru for what he judged to be bad behavior—sexual urges, insufficient submissiveness, or—as in this case—desire to leave the cult. The process was considered therapeutic in the sense of forcibly removing bad karma.

There followed the clear-cut murder of Shūji Taguchi, a friend of the victim who was deeply upset by his death and by Aum's intention to cover it up. He spoke of leaving the group and, under threatening interrogation, admitted that the idea of killing the guru had entered his mind. Upon learning this, Asahara made it clear that Taguchi should be "poa'd." The murder was committed in a small cell in February 1989 by Hideo Murai and four other male disciples, who strangled their victim with a rope. Part of the motive for the murder was Asahara's determination to prevent any information from getting out that might interfere with Aum's achieving official recognition as a religion—so crucial to its prestige and, through tax advantages, to its economic potential. That status was granted the same year.

There are estimates of as many as eighty individual murders committed by Aum members. A young lawyer named Tsutsumi Sakamoto, his wife, and their fourteen-month-old son were murdered in their home by an Aum team in early November 1989. Representing parents and lawyers' groups who were protesting Aum's methods, Sakamoto was in the process of exposing fraudulent claims about the genetic uniqueness of the guru's blood and DNA. Asahara's instructions were to kill only Sakamoto himself with an injection of potassium chloride to be administered by Dr. Nakagawa, but apparently those orders were extended to include the wife and child when the team bungled its mission by failing to confront Sakamoto alone. The lawyer and his wife were strangled and their young son was suffocated, the bodies then buried in out-of-the-way places so that the full story did not become known until six years later, though many suspected Aum at the time.

Dr. Nakagawa also participated in the January 1994 murder of Kōtarō Ochida, a pharmacist who had defected from Aum and later tried to rescue from the cult a sick woman from whom the group had extorted a great deal of money. Ochida had enlisted the help of the woman's son, also an Aum member, in the rescue attempt. Asahara forced the son to carry out the killing, making it clear that he would meet the same fate if he failed to do so.

In late February 1995, Aum members finally committed a murder that had dire legal consequences for the cult. Kiyoshi Kariya, an elderly notary public, had refused to reveal to Aum the location of his sister, who had fled the cult; she had already donated hundreds of thousands of dollars but Aum wanted still more of her considerable wealth. The intent had apparently been only to have Dr. Hayashi and Dr. Nakagawa inject Kariya with the barbiturate thiopental, a "truth serum" that Aum commonly used, in order to obtain information about his sister. But something went wrong—probably the dosage was miscalculated—and Kariya died. Asahara ordered the body cremated in the basement of Satyam 2, where a microwave incinerator had been installed for precisely that purpose. By then there was much reason to suspect Aum, and the investigation of the murder became the justification for vast police raids on Aum's facilities on March 22—by which time the police had finally come to suspect Aum's connection with sarin gas production and use as well.

Over time Asahara and his closest disciples came to think of Aum as a military organization. They sought to acquire weapons of every variety on behalf of the guru's visions of either a triumphant Armageddon or a this-worldly political and military coup d'état that would enable him to take over Japan. In early 1990 Aum began working on its first weapons of mass destruction, which were biological. In April of that year, the cult attempted to release botulinus toxin from trucks first in central Tokyo, then near American naval installations at Yokohama and Yokosuka, and finally at Narita Airport, the largest in Japan. But biological weapons are easier to produce than to release; repeated technical problems interfered with the viability of the released toxin and nothing much happened. Three years later, Endō presided over another effort to release botulinus toxin, this one near the imperial palace at the time of the royal wedding of the crown prince and Masako Owada. Again nothing happened. Three weeks after, Aum released anthrax spores from the roof of its Tokyo headquarters; once more no one was killed or, as far as is known, injured. In March 1995 Aum made one more attempt to release botulinus toxin, this time in a large Tokyo subway station by means of briefcases containing dispensers. It turned out that no botulinus toxin had been put in the briefcases.

The story with sarin nerve gas was quite different. Although Aum may not have embarked seriously on its production until 1993, there were casualties from the beginning, first among Aum members at Kamikuishiki from leakage within that facility. Aum then made two test runs of releasing the gas. The initial one was directed at sheep on its large ranch in Australia. A subsequent sarin release in June 1994 from an Aum truck in the city of Matsumoto, about a hundred miles from Tokyo, was partly experimental but specifically directed at the apartment building of three judges who were presiding over a trial involving Aum's fraudulent behavior in connection with land purchases. All three became ill from the gas, one seriously, while seven other people were killed. The attack interrupted the trial and postponed indefinitely the negative decision anticipated by Aum. It was the first large-scale nonmilitary use of a nerve gas anywhere on earth. The police did not suspect the cult of the attack.

The Tokyo subway attack on March 20, 1995, was a response to information Aum obtained about the upcoming large-scale police raids. It was meant to be diversionary, to confuse the police and convince them that someone else was responsible and that Aum itself was being victimized. The gas for the Tokyo attack, hurriedly prepared, was impure and its effectiveness relatively limited. The ultimate Aum sarin project was supposed to be a November 1995 attack, for which a large helicopter had been purchased in Russia and a leading Aum member trained in the United States to fly it. As that attack was to initiate Armageddon, the guru had issued the grandiose order to Murai to produce "seventy tons of sarin."

Aum also experimented with sarin and other gases in targeting individuals. It twice used sarin in unsuccessful attempts to assassinate Daisaku Ikeda, the head of the largest of Japan's new religions, Sōka Gakkai, and Asahara's hated rival. Four attacks were made using VX (a nerve gas even more deadly than sarin), killing a young man believed to be a police informer and injuring the head of an anti-Aum parents' group, who went into a coma but survived. Another attack was made in September 1994 with phosgene (a gas used in World War I that severely irritates the respiratory system) on the leading journalistic critic of Aum, Shōko Egawa; she experienced throat and bronchial symptoms and required hospitalization. By that time, the police had received a number of complaints about Aum kidnappings and drug abuse and had gathered soil samples near its main facility containing traces of compounds that result from the disintegration of sarin. Eager to obtain more information, they are said to have made the foolish move of sending an undercover agent into the cult, who is believed to have been murdered by Aum.

Asahara was fascinated by the possibility of advanced laser weapons (as yet nonexistent), which he often portrayed as "death rays," and ordered his scientists to produce them. His "minister of intelligence" organized attempts at industrial espionage that included surreptitious entry into the laser-research lab of NEC (an enormous computer and electronics firm) and into Nippon Oil, Mitsubishi, and other electronics and chemical firms. On some occasions Aum members were caught and arrested without the police grasping the nature of their fantasy-driven spying. Aum actually carried out an experimental laser test, projecting a beam of red light across the sky from Satyam 5 at the main facility, but the test had little to do with actual weaponry.

Aum's scientists did come to understand that lasers could enhance the development of nuclear weapons by helping to enrich mined natural uranium—and nuclear weapons provided Aum's ultimate model for the technology of world destruction. Asahara and Aum never ceased their search for nuclear materials—whether in Japan, uranium-rich Australia, or in Russia, where Hayakawa recorded in his diary a question that has now become famous in Japan: "How much is a nuclear warhead?"

Following the Tokyo sarin attack, the guru ordered that Aum resort to acts of terrorism in order to prevent his capture. Aum members were suspected (without clear evidence) of attempting, on March 30, to assassinate Takaji Kunimatsu, head of the National Police Agency and the person responsible for investigating Aum. On April 15, the entire city of Tokyo was put on alert because Asahara had predicted that a major disaster would take place on that date. On May 5, an Aum team deposited plastic bags containing cyanide gas in the Shinjuku subway station, an enormously crowded area, and only the alertness of a few station attendants prevented tens of thousands of deaths. On May 16, which turned out to be the day Asahara was captured, Aum sent a parcel bomb to the Tokyo city hall in an attempt to kill the governor, Yukio Aoshima, who had declared that he would revoke Aum's status as a religion; the parcel was opened by a municipal worker who lost several fingers. The cult had run a trajectory from one "accidental" killing to ultimate terror. Its pursuit of violence, too, made this small cult seem ubiquitous.

The Culture of Violence

Aum created a spiritual atmosphere of violence that affected all of its renunciants, even those who had little knowledge of its violent intent or acts. Closed off from the rest of society, they absorbed the guru's message that their life purpose was to participate somehow in the ultimate violence of world destruction. They came to embrace Asahara's message that extreme actions might be necessary and that their own violent impulses were both noble and desirable because they were associated with a mission of spiritual salvation. Focusing on their individual states of consciousness, on the "truth" of their "mystical experiences," they were able to abandon empathy for the outside world. What was happening inside their own heads—and that of the guru— was all that mattered.

Yet the high energy of Aum members was never separate from a sense of pressure. Guru and disciples could attribute that pressure to the outside world, which the hidden manipulations of the cult's ultimate enemies, identified by Asahara as the Freemasons and the Jews, had rendered evil and polluted. But the inside world of Aum also generated considerable anxiety, frustration, and anger. The guru himself was caught on the treadmill of his unceasing but unachievable visions and found it increasingly difficult to sustain his absolute control over his own created environment. Hence he was enraged by defections, which came to symbolize his inevitable failure. Disciples in turn were frustrated by their inability to achieve the absolute state of subjugation to the guru required of ideal clones. Both guru and disciples recast these inner conflicts into rage toward Aum's designated enemies—not only the Freemasons and the Jews but also the Japanese and American governments and their military and intelligence agencies.

The first words the Japanese public heard from the guru about sarin gas were his claim that enemies were using it to attack him and his followers. The claim could seem very real to Aum members, and even perhaps to the guru himself, because it was consistent with their sense of being a noble spiritual enclave in an otherwise evil world. And Aum members did actually suffer the effects of sarin—from unintentional leakage and quite probably as well from intentional releases meant to "prove" their victimization. At a press conference in early 1995, Aum claimed that Japanese or American aircraft had been attacking its facilities with sarin as a form of religious persecution and spoke of deaths and illnesses among its members, releasing a video, *Slaughtered*

Lambs, showing Dr. Hayashi injecting sick Aum members with atropine, an antidote to sarin poisoning. Asahara frequently spoke of himself as being close to death—sometimes from sarin, sometimes from mustard gas, sometimes from Q fever or heart disease. His cry was that the Japanese government was "oppressing a prophet."

The only possible response was "war," a vague and all-encompassing image that included everything from individual murder to actively bringing about Armageddon, which in early Jewish writings is called "forcing the end." To survive this war Aum had to destroy its enemies. Thus, a ninety-five-page "Manual of Fear" in the January 1995 issue of the Aum publication *Vajrayāna* declared war on the Jews, whose "world shadow government" was said to murder "untold numbers of people." Violence, of course, could be justified by the various strands of Buddhist, Hindu, and Christian thought Asahara had tied together, especially his version of *poa*, which enabled Aum to pursue violence on all levels, its war, while holding to a claim of nonviolent virtue.

As paranoia and projection intensified, Aum moved closer to forcing the end. Ever more desperate to realize his prophecies, Asahara ordered the Tokyo sarin attack not only to divert the police but to break out of a psychological sense of entrapment, hit out at society in general, and activate the energy of world destruction.

2 | Imagining the End

About the inevitability of World War III and Armageddon, Shōkō Asahara once declared: "I stake my religious future on this prediction." We may assume that he was unaware of the irony of that statement. (Who, after all, would be around to affirm his "religious future"?) But in his own theological terms the statement had a certain logic. As he saw it, Armageddon, the final global conflagration, would be survived only by himself and a small band of followers, who would then create the world's "religious future." His religious standing—his status as a guru—was absolutely inseparable from this vision. Since *everything* was staked on it, the inference was that *anything*—including violence—might be called upon to ensure its arrival.

Aum's attempts at world destruction were not, however, simply an effort to confirm the guru's prophecy (though that was indeed a factor). Rather, Asahara's shifting predictions and lurid descriptions of the sequence of events by which the world would end became Aum's controlling narrative, the story that subsumed all else and into which every struggle had to fit. The narrative provided a fierce dynamic that fed hope, fear, and paranoia, while never allowing either guru or disciples to rest.

The Narrative of Armaggedon

To be sure, Asahara was hardly alone in his preoccupation with a cataclysmic end to the world. His embrace of the Christian image of Armageddon from the Book of Revelation indicated as much. Not only is a world-ending event a widespread contemporary motif for religious and political groups everywhere, but some version of it has apparently been present from the beginning of history. Imagining a world cleansing and a new beginning, it has the appeal of making death both less fearful and more significant. For Aum, it meant that the world could be seen as so hopelessly polluted, so suffused with evil, as to preclude half measures.

The writings of Nostradamus that so obsessed Asahara had also long been embraced by others, especially New Age writers in America. Loose Japanese translations by Ben Gotō have gone through more than four hundred printings since 1973 and have sold in the millions. Like a number of other leaders of Japanese new religions, Asahara understood these translations to suggest that, following Armageddon, a savior would come from "the East." To support his claim to be that savior, Asahara even sent a "group of translators" to France to conduct research on the original texts.

Asahara was profligate in his borrowings when it came to Armageddon, combining his interpretations of Nostradamus and the Book of Revelation (from which Nostradamus took his apocalyptic predictions) with world-ending imagery from Hindu and Buddhist texts. He became so compelling a narrator of end-of-the-world scenarios that, as one former disciple put it, listening to those stories was "like standing on top of a hill and looking down in the valley far below—and having somebody push you off." But many disciples, it could be said, had already made their own way to that cliff. Immersed as they were in the apocalyptic imagery so prominent in postwar Japanese popular culture, some of them were more or less waiting for an Asahara to give them that shove. In a society that only decades earlier had undergone an equivalent of world destruction in its abject defeat in war and its experience of having two of its cities atomically annihilated, there was a vast flow of apocalyptic narratives. Most Aum disciples, for instance, had grown up viewing a variety of futuristic daily animated television shows and reading *manga* dramatically focused on world destruction and daring rescue missions undertaken by heroic Japanese. The most influential of these was the animated television series *The Voyage of the Space Battleship Yamato*, about a massive spaceship named after a huge imperial navy battleship that in the last days of World War II made an essentially suicidal foray against the American fleet. The show was set in the year 2199, when the earth, already inundated with radiation pollution in the wake of a nuclear holocaust, is being bombarded by meteors and attacked by evil aliens from the mysterious planet Gamilus. Earth's only hope is for the *Yamato* and its crew to venture into space to obtain a "cosmo cleaner," a technological wonder device to counter nuclear pollution. In a final, Armageddon-like battle they defeat the forces of Gamalus, obtain the cosmo cleaner, and return triumphantly to an earth ready to undergo renewal.

Such highly popular stories contributed to a psychological climate in which Asahara could claim absolute virtue in his war against absolute evil. Aum went so far as to use the name "cosmo cleaners" for decontamination devices it installed to protect cult members from chemical and biological weapon attacks.

The "pollution" that Asahara stressed, however, was spiritual and took the form of "bad karma," which was said to afflict just about everyone on earth, including Aum members. Large disasters like the Kobe earthquake of January 1995, which destroyed much of that city and killed five thousand people, were but "signs" of the coming end, indications that World War III had already begun; the decline of the Japanese economy, too, was a sign. Asahara did offer his Shambhala plan, in which a proliferation of Aum communes, or "Lotus Villages," would ensure the peaceful salvation of Japan (and eventually humankind), but this vision of religious utopia became intertwined with one of prior world destruction. As the religious scholar Manabu Watanabe puts it, these Lotus Villages "would be possible only when there were no other people except Aum believers."

In 1990, after Aum's bid to have Asahara and other of its candidates elected to the diet failed dismally, Asahara assembled most of Aum's members on Ishigaki, a small southern island near Okinawa, for what was called an "Armageddon seminar." During that meeting he relentlessly preached the inevitability and imminence of the world's end in the face of its mounting evil; all Aum members, he insisted, would need to defend their guru and join him in his noble struggle against evil by becoming renunciants. Indeed, the guru's persistent sense that not enough people were doing so was undoubtedly a factor in his escalating Armageddon rhetoric. In the wake of the seminar, Asahara drew increasingly upon his religious source books for world-ending imagery and quite literally injected himself into the Book of Revelation, claiming the role of the "blind savior" with "a long beard and long hair" who would appear, according to his interpretation of that text, at the time of Armageddon. While Asahara would only intensify his Armageddon narrative in the coming years, he had long prepared himself to do so.

A preoccupation with world-ending events, including an expectation of nuclear war, had been present in his teachings almost from the beginning as Asahara drew links between the most violent and apocalyptic elements of the world's religious texts and actual events. All this was reflected in a *manga* Aum published in 1989 entitled *The Day of Perishing*. The cartoon story begins with a number of Aum disciples receiving an urgent call to join the guru in his room, where they hear him declare: "My guru, the god Shiva, suddenly said to me: 'Now is the time to decode the Book of Revelation, receive its message, and start Aum's salvation work.'" Asahara then quotes a passage from Revelation about the appearance of a divine being who sits on a throne and resembles "the Son of Man," adding: "When I read this, I was astonished, because this 'Son of Man' is exactly like the god Shiva, whom I met in the astral world." The *manga* Asahara—like the real Asahara—then goes on to interpret some of the more arcane imagery of that arcane book, linking the "opening" of various "seals" mentioned in the text with worldly occurrences. The opening of the sixth seal, for instance, means the eruption of volcanos, and he notes that Mount Fuji has become active again. He adds that the time is coming when such natural disasters can "no more purify the evil karma of the human race," when God will "make us purify our karma through the 'artificial fire' of nuclear wars," which could be Armageddon. The guru's further "decoding" reveals that the people of God upon whose foreheads the angels place seals are Aum followers; that the white robes they wear are Aum uniforms; that the seals themselves refer to the Hindu *shaktipat*, which in Aum meant the transfer of energy from the guru to the disciple; and that the washing of the robes with blood represents Aum's "blood initiation," drinking of the blood of the guru.

In the cartoon Asahara states that Armageddon is inevitable, though Aum followers can reduce the number of its victims through their spiritual practice. He then turns to *The Tibetan Book of the Dead* for a distinction between "gods of peace" and "gods of terror," relating the latter to the Hindu era of *kaliyuga*, or destruction of the cosmos, and declares: "Our time is the era when salvation is done by gods of terror." Human beings are so dominated by desire that they are largely beyond saving and, according to the law of karma, "when our bad karma accumulates, gods of terror . . . force us to realize this truth . . . [and] their severe, wrathful judgment is actually a manifestation of love." Finally, he offers a concrete prediction: "The U.S. president in office in 1995 and the Soviet chairman will lead the world to Armageddon."

In this single Revelation-based narrative, Asahara managed to connect Armageddon not only with his own Hindu god Shiva, the Old Testament, the New Testament, and the figure of Jesus but also with religious martyrs in general, nuclear holocaust, and *The Tibetan Book of the Dead*. This was a remarkable religious and secular stew, even for an eclectic Japanese new religion. But in that 1989 vision, though end-time violence was to be dreadful in every way, none of it was to come from Aum.

"Armageddon" then was transformed within the confines of Aum from a name for a final battlefield derived from Christian eschatology into a symbol for an expectation of destruction fed by all the major religions. Asahara strongly emphasized that ours is the era Hindus call *kaliyuga*, an age dominated by cosmos-undermining evil dating back more than five thousand years. It is also, he claimed, the Buddhist *mappō*, a period of great spiritual decline said to have begun in about the twelfth century, fifteen hundred years after the death of the Buddha.

Kaliyuga and *mappo* were originally imagined as gradual but devastating eras of moral decline, not of world-ending struggle, though *kaliyuga* was sometimes expected to culminate in the destruction of the cosmos. But in the minds of Asahara and his followers, these two divergent traditions blended with Christian eschatology into a fierce psychological expectation of the end. Asahara fueled that sense of expectation with an ever-widening set of apocalyptic references from the Old Testament, Zoroastrianism, and even an obscure turn-of-the-century Japanese prophet whose world-ending vision drew upon an unlikely combination of Shinto and Christianity.

In the world of Aum, Asahara's endism became all-pervasive. His many-sided Armageddon constellation was the only prism through which to view the world and give it meaning, and it was increasingly bound up with Aum's immediate and growing problems. Beleaguered by mounting opposition and multiplying legal battles (mostly brought about by its own coercive and fraudulent activities), Aum struggled to hold on to its membership, and Asahara's world-ending prophecies grew ever more urgent. Armageddon became the center of a vicious circle: a sense of the end of the world impelled Aum toward, and in its eyes justified, extreme behavior of many kinds; this extreme behavior led to inner conflict and sometimes resistance among members that threatened the life of the cult; that in turn brought on Aum's persecutory version of Armageddon prophecy.

Asahara's growing world-ending frenzy as well as his inner turmoil played themselves out in the experiences of cult members. Among his disciples were many for whom the prospect of Armaggedon was the most compelling aspect of membership in Aum. Driven to more and more extreme feelings and actions, though, some of them struggled with disturbing impulses to leave the cult. But even among those who wavered, their bond with the guru kept alive their fervent anticipation of Armageddon.

The Gentle Armageddonist

Matsui is a tall but delicately built, soft-spoken young man with an aura of gentleness, even lostness about him. When he joined Aum in 1993, he had just graduated from a leading university in central Japan but had failed his graduate school examinations and was unemployed. He was, as he put it, not only a *rōnin* (originally a samurai without a master, now a student without a university) but a *takurō* (a *rōnin* who stays at home). He was initially attracted to Aum by a yoga course the cult offered, but what really drew him to the group was its preoccupation with Armageddon.

From his secondary school years, Matsui had been both frightened and excited by all sorts of prophecies of Armageddon, especially those of Nostradamus and of the American mystic Edgar Cayce, an early-twentieth-century folk healer and "psychic diagnostician" whose writings were rediscovered by American advocates of New Age spirituality. Matsui was at various times attracted to New Age versions of Paracelsus, the sixteenth-century Swiss physician and alchemist credited with important medical observations despite his extravagant occult claims, and to a number of expressions of Eastern and Western spiritualism. At one point he became involved with the Jehovah's Witnesses, the proselytizing sect of Christian pacifists, for whom meetings and study groups about Armageddon loomed large. For years, then, Matsui's religious search combined a millennial preoccupation with a hunger for absolute spiritual truth.

Both needs were powerfully answered by Aum. He began reading its materials as a teenager in the late 1980s, finding that Aum "from its very beginning" strongly stressed *katasutorofu*, or "catastrophe," and *shūmatsu*, "the end." Matsui became fascinated by Asahara's apocalyptic eclecticism. He liked the blend of Christianity and Buddhism, and, even more, Aum's being "very New Age."

All that Matsui came to feel in Aum about world endings would be bound up with his transcendent experiences and his involvement with the guru. Indeed, on first stepping into the Aum facility, he experienced "something physiological, . . . a sensation I had not had before." He saw "clear white lights," and when he viewed Asahara's picture on an altar, "the word *guru* came to mind. I felt energy emanating from it, . . . coming from the altar, and all through the space there were extraordinary vibrations." More advanced Aum members explained to him that this was a "normal" reaction to the guru or his image and that it had to do with one's "inner mind seeking the truth."

In the months after his first yoga class, as he gave ever-larger portions of his time and life to Aum, Matsui seemed to thrive on the cult's ascetic practices (yoga, meditation, breathing exercises). At the same time he felt threatened by the very immersion he was experiencing. When pressured to become a renunciant, he began to waver and "slowly realized that this was not a good idea." Like some others, he tried to run away from the Aum facility where he had agreed to stay temporarily but was quickly intercepted by Aum members who combined force and what he called "persuasion" to bring him back. Realizing that "they were receiving their orders from above," that is, from the guru, Matsui felt that there was no way out. He became a renunciant, after all, and soon his own enthusiasm was reignited. For him, as for many others, that enthusiasm was apocalyptic in spirit, as evidenced by his reaction to a Christ initiation. A drug (probably LSD) was used, "so I had a lot of hallucinations and my body jumped," and the experience was "more real than a dream." The first part of it entered into the mystery of rebirth:

> I had a vision of myself actually going through reincarnation. I had never before understood what reincarnation really was. I did not understand the true nature of one's self. Now I thought something like [the self going through reincarnation] is my true self. It is a borrowed, ephemeral thing. Not this physical body that I now have. My true self is something pure, childlike, really like a baby.

The second part of the vision involved a literal merging with the guru. As Asahara appeared in the vision, Matsui felt himself "in a trance, suddenly doing certain practices I had never learned and chanting weird mantras." The rest of the vision literalized the merging:

> The connections I had to Asahara—in Aum we call it a spiritual pipeline—became concrete in this vision. There were various other individuals and at the center was Asahara, who was shining

brightly. . . . I was at the bottom but the people at the bottom were being pulled up, and then I was pulled up. It was a force that could not be resisted. As I was pulled up, the surroundings slowly got brighter. I asked Asahara, "What am I?" As I was pulled up, I became one with Asahara—all the chains and links that connected me with him suddenly disappeared and I was surrounded by light. Everything became bright white.

Ultimately the hallucination disappeared and there was nothing. There was nothingness. I lost the sense of my physical body and I had only my consciousness, a marvelous feeling. And then, strangely, there were things I wanted to ask Asahara. And when I thought of a question, the answer came right back. I was Asahara at that point. Then I, also Asahara, asked, "Is this what is called nothingness?" Then he, also myself, answered, "Yes, you are experiencing this for the first time, aren't you?" He answered very informally.

Matsui here followed Aum's practice of blending the concepts of nothingness and emptiness (often used interchangeably in East Asian Buddhism) into a single concept of an empty mind that receives everything from the guru. Like so many other disciples of Asahara, he experienced a dissolving of the self, physically and spiritually, into that of the guru. This merging, rendered especially vivid but not created by the LSD, took Matsui ever more deeply into the guru's world-ending projections.

For Matsui, Asahara's "way of thinking" was "extremely valuable" in clarifying for him his place in a world headed for doom. Particularly compelling was the guru's tendency to address his predictions to the actual world: "He read the Book of Revelation politically, as part of real history. So the First World War was this way, the Second World War was that way, and the Third will be like this." Whenever there was any significant political change or upheaval like the Gulf War, "he gave many sermons and talked more about his prophecies"; he would "agitate" his followers and insist that, with Armageddon coming soon, "time was short."

As Matsui's Armageddon mind-set deepened, his only reservation had to do with when events were likely to occur. Asahara, in his own agitation, kept pushing the date for World War III forward, finally insisting that Armageddon would occur in 1997, indeed "that the end had already begun." But as Matsui remembered his own beliefs, "I was of the opinion that this would require time, that there was no need to be that urgent, that things just won't collapse and the world become a terrible place so suddenly." Nor did Matsui think only of a "terrible outcome." In fact, the idea of Armageddon made him feel pleased and excited "that I was born in such a great age." He contrasted the "relatively peaceful years [between 1950 and 1989] with the present time of more chaotic events. I find this situation to be more intriguing. It's a time when we cannot tell the future."

Matsui believed that the outcome was "in the hands of the gods and Buddha." Asahara loomed large for him not only as a guru "providing guidance and protection through religion," but also because he seemed to be planning "a practical way" to deal with Armageddon, "a practical means of survival," even if he had not yet evolved "a clear, solid plan." Matsui and other disciples were also impressed with their leader's overall principle of preparation through spiritual practice. Convinced that such vast events "can't be influenced by individuals thrashing about," Matsui wished to "prepare myself peacefully and calmly, so that I wouldn't panic, to set my mind straight and engage in training." He was moved when his guru proclaimed, "Let us welcome a death that we will not regret"—a statement that seemed profound both in its assertion of the principle of reincarnation and in its advocacy of the right kind of Armageddon-related death. Neither Matsui nor other former disciples I talked with seemed troubled by the contradictory nature of Asahara's Armageddon statements, which sometimes promised survival and at other times insisted that everyone would die.

The outcome would be "a matter of karma," Matsui thought, but he considered both possibilities. He and others, he believed, could "disappear in an instant." But his unbounded faith in Asahara led him to a powerful if vague sense of his own survival. This was conveyed in a vision he had while in Aum that remains with him to this day:

There seems to be a war, with great fires from the war in the distance. Everything is burning and parts of the earth are sinking into the ocean. It is not an urban landscape. I think it is a mountain. It seems that I was living the life of a hermit. I see myself engaged in my spiritual training, and I see comrades who are doing the same thing.

He described scenes of great suffering, of being confronted by the awesome destruction, of "entire cities swallowed up by the sea. There was not only one war, there were many. If one stopped, others would go on." Sometimes he would imagine absolute and total annihilation ("a flash of light and then everything ends") and at other times a more gradual process in which "only some of the cities are destroyed."

Asahara was not always manifest in these visions, but there was no doubt about his ultimate presence. When I asked what happened after Armageddon, Matsui described a vision he had while taking another of Aum's drugs. In it the guru led a kind of exodus: "We were all going somewhere in something like a submarine" that carried Aum members as well as a few strangers. When I asked where the submarine was going, he mentioned that others in Aum had had similar visions and in most cases the submarine was headed for Australia—"in any case, not staying in Japan." (There had, in fact, been talk in Aum toward the end, of a submarine-style escape.)

In general, Matsui's own post-Armageddon images were of pain and chaos followed by "some sort of order," involving domination by Western victors and "Asia becoming enslaved to the West." Given the Japanese defeat in World War II and the subsequent American occupation of the country, this was a projection of past experience into the future—and it was an outcome Asahara warned his disciples about. But Matsui also accepted his guru's emphasis on Armageddon as a great human "lesson" that would force people to reflect deeply about themselves and to "live as purely as possible." (Here he specifically invoked the kind of reflection Japanese were forced to undertake after World War II.)

Whatever the suffering, Matsui believed that Armageddon would be in the service of renewal, a renewal that required concrete physical preparation—"making sure that I have my clothes, food, and housing"—but was primarily spiritual. As he summed it up, "From this state of destruction of the material world, we rebuild things. We have to keep in mind that we start from the very beginning and that is where Aum Shinrikyō becomes involved. Asahara will create a new basis for civilization, a new paradise."

Partly because of his strong responses to the guru's prophecies, Matsui once more became frightened and uncertain about whether he wanted to stay in Aum. His ambivalence was recognized and for a period of time he was confined in a small cell and subjected to an initiation that took the form of coercive truth extraction:

They brainwash you by giving you the drug used for operations [probably thiopental]. When you are injected with it you start to lose consciousness, . . . not completely, but you don't remember what you said. And when you are asked questions, the answers pop out. They want to check on whether what is inputted [by Aum] has affected your overall consciousness, whether it is engraved, and whether you have any lingering attachments to the outside world. Do you really want to be a monk or not? So they ask these various things. And then you just have to answer them truthfully. I seemed really to tell the truth. Then I was to continue to chant my "resolve"—to say that nothing [of Aum truths] was as yet inputted, that it was not yet branded in my unconscious.

This was both a "narco initiation" (confession extraction) and a "resolve initiation," in which Matsui had to endlessly chant his deficiencies and his determination to overcome his failure to absorb Aum's full message. Though he added, "I knew what they were doing to me was mind control but I had no choice," at the time his predominant feelings were probably guilt over failing his guru and considerable fear. He accepted his interrogators' accusations and was aware of their absolute power over him. Yet even after he had succumbed to Aum's authority and again proclaimed his wish to advance his spiritual standing in the group, he was told by a higher-ranking member, "I think that you are not at that stage because your chakra are leaking energy."

During the period just before the sarin attack in Tokyo, Asahara's apocalypticism began to run rampant, and Matsui again became confused. The guru, he recalled, seemed "intense or perhaps even crazy."

Insisting that Aum was being attacked by poison gas and that Armageddon was imminent, Asahara declared himself to be "the greatest prophet of the twentieth century." According to Matsui, "he would say to his followers, 'Don't you realize that this is war!'" But the guru could bring "a calm side" to his prophetic frenzy, reassuring his followers that he was "happy to greet Armageddon because mankind needs to go through this in order to experience a spiritual process" and emphasizing that "to lead them we Aum members must survive." While Matsui partly sensed that there was something wrong with Asahara, he was still under the spell of the guru's prophecy and feared that in leaving Aum he would not survive the onrushing apocalyptic event.

On first learning about the Tokyo sarin attack, Matsui assumed that Aum's enemies, the Freemasons and Jews, were the perpetrators and that it was part of an assault on Aum. The large-scale police search of Aum facilities two days later seemed only to confirm that the whole incident was "a plot against us" that would lead to Asahara's arrest and to Japan's doom. At the time, he explained, "I couldn't believe that Aum committed this criminal act." The vastness of the police raids ("a *very* large number of *very* heavily armed men") seemed inappropriate for such "a small organization," and there was an added, particularly Japanese reason the raids offended him: "The police entered without taking their shoes off so the place was filled with dirt and we thought that it was all dirty and this continued for days." Though Aum was hardly known for its cleanliness, this was in his and other disciples' eyes the pollution of their spiritual home by a tainted outside world. He expected the attacks on Aum to escalate: "I was thinking that sarin was secretly used by the United States during the Gulf War and that this gas was again being used secretly in attacking Aum Shinrikyō, just as Master had said. Aum Shinrikyō would have to be suppressed before the war [World War III] could begin." In other words, he and other disciples understood these events to be part of Asahara's world-ending narrative. Armageddon was really occurring, starting with the destruction of Aum.

But in another part of his mind Matsui harbored doubts, which were increased by his own immediate perceptions. During the raids he observed "with my own eyes" that the police uncovered, in the main

Aum facility, a large quantity of illegal drugs, so that he felt himself to be "a kind of witness." He had previously suspected that Aum was armed for "self-defense," but now "my suspicions grew stronger that perhaps it was not for self-defense but for use against others, for some kind of terrorist activity, for a kind of action I was not comfortable with." He "escaped" from Aum a few weeks later, spurred not only by these suspicions but also by an increasing sense that for Aum "the future is not bright." He remained uncertain as to who had been responsible for the Tokyo subway attack until a couple of months later, when the confessions of Aum leaders began to appear in the media.

He continued to feel uneasy and in our interviews sought to explain his feelings by bringing up my work on Hiroshima, some of which he had read. Mentioning that I had observed in survivors "bad feelings toward those who were killed," he admitted having similar feelings, what amounted to guilt and shame, toward Aum members now in prison. He was saying not only that he felt guilty because people he had respected for reaching higher spiritual realms than himself were now being incarcerated while he was not but also that, in leaving, he had betrayed Aum's great mission of universal salvation via Armageddon.

In our final interview, I asked Matsui why he thought Aum had stockpiled and then used sarin gas. He first pointed to Asahara's "greedy ambition" and his ressentiment (using the Japanized word, *rusanchiman*). But he quickly softened that judgement, indeed almost reversed it, by linking the attack, however apocalyptic, to a genuine salvation project: "Deep in Asahara's heart, there was perhaps the thought of using whatever means were necessary for true salvation because essentially Asahara wanted to save people." Later he juxtaposed imagery of violence and serenity in a way that again suggested he was still drawn to Asahara's vision of Armageddon and spiritual renewal:

Ultimately it would take the form of a religious war, and from the world's three great religions and from other religions like communism, perhaps a different idea would be born and there would be a new world religion. This new doctrine would overcome all religious wars. . . . This [universal religion] will be needed for people to reflect on how the world had come to such a [degraded] state.

He summed up that sense of a new beginning by saying, "Perhaps we would become children." As we explored these matters, Matsui volunteered that it was now especially difficult for him to discuss his ideas about the end of the world. The subject "is something that I don't like to talk about," he said, quickly adding, "or rather I don't talk about it enough." He found this "really difficult to explain." My impression was that his pain had to do with a guilty sense that his own prior world-ending imagery had blended with and contributed to Asahara's world-ending vision—all the more so since he was haunted by this imagery, particularly as preached by a guru with whom he still felt to some degree merged.

Matsui resembled a number of others I interviewed in that he built his tie with Aum around his consuming hunger for Armageddon. Partly following his guru, he stressed the link between Aum—the "anti-Freemasons"—and the Freemasons themselves. For Aum and its enemy alike, that is, the highest goal remained the apocalypse itself. That mind-set could make disciples highly vulnerable to Asahara's mounting feeling, as Matsui put it, "that we should get actively involved in Armageddon soon."

3 | Forcing the End

A ny imagined Armageddon is violent, but the violence tends to be distant and mythic, to be brought about by evil forces that leave God with no other choice but a total cleansing of this world. With Aum's Armageddon the violence was close at hand and palpable. Aum was always an actor in its own Armageddon drama, whether as a target of world-destroying enemies or as a fighting force in a great battle soon to begin or already under way. As time went on, however, Aum increasingly saw itself as the initiator, the trigger of the final event.

From the beginning, Shōkō Asahara drew upon the most violent images from the traditions he claimed to represent. From the Tibetan Tantric Buddhist tradition (which he also referred to as Vajrayāna or Tantra Vajrayāna), he preached a crucial, three-sided principle: the guru may initiate violence according to his judgment; the violence must be carried out by his loyal disciples; and the recipients of that violence will benefit from it. As early as July 1987, he was already preaching that entire violent constellation to his three-year-old cult: "The teachings of esoteric Buddhism of Tibet were pretty savage. For instance, when a guru ordered a disciple to kill a thief, the disciple went ahead and did it as an act of virtue. In my previous existence, I myself have killed someone at my guru's order. When a guru orders you to take someone's life, that is an indication that the person's time is up. In other words, you are killing the person at exactly the right time and therefore letting the person have his *poa*."

The clear message even then was that a devoted disciple kills for his guru and thereby benefits everyone. Not surprisingly, Asahara, who himself looked to the Hindu god Shiva as both his personal divinity and his guru, conceived of the many-sided deity (as a number of his former disciples told me) primarily as a god of destruction. And indeed, in at least one authoritative description of Hindu tradition, Shiva comes close to resembling Asahara: "In order to save the world, Shiva in his perverse power dances the world out of existence wildly laughing, scattering ashes from his body so that the world may be renewed." Asahara's early identification with this aspect of Shiva provided him with an important model for what could be called his *world-ending guruism*. He also drew upon sacred Japanese sources of violence associated with World War II–era imperial religion, declaring himself "a divine emperor," even as he condemned the existing emperor and Japanese authority in general.

Asahara could look to New Age astrological doctrine as still another source of cosmic violence. In connection with what is usually described as a gentle astrological transition, Asahara spoke of the beginning of the Age of Aquarius as the cleansing of the evil of the Age of Pisces and indicated that the energies of the two spiritual eras would be so much in conflict that they would "consume each other and at that moment there will be many victims." At the same time, Asahara brought a quality of worship to the gods of science and high technology, especially in relation to destructive weaponry, so that they lived side by side in his mind with Shiva and the Vajrayāna-linked *poa* principle.

Armageddon gradually came to underpin all Aum's aspirations— theocratic, mystical, political, and military. Since Armageddon was also synonymous with World War III, which Asahara often claimed had already begun, the cult saw itself as existing on a "war footing."

Though a distinction was made between ordinary disciples, for whom the guru's admonition "that this is war" meant "a sense of crisis and the expectation that something horrible would happen," and trusted higher disciples, for whom it meant that they "must participate in the war and Aum must win that war," the distinction was far from absolute. Ordinary disciples I interviewed spoke of having shared Aum's war fever. Although ignorant of the buildup and planned use both of ordinary and of ultimate weapons, they viewed themselves nonetheless as foot soldiers in the final war.

All Aum members had been made to understand that war and Armageddon were necessary for overcoming the bad karma that increasingly dominated humankind. By 1992 the guru was speaking of the end of the century as a time of violent transition, which in a scientific mode he likened to a chemical process, an admixture of pressure, a catalyst, and heat. The pressure was the "unreasonable" opposition of society, the catalyst "the guru or the teaching of supreme truth," and the heat "the accumulation of good karma by Aum believers." Through these forces, he preached, "there will arise chemical phenomena that we cannot imagine . . . there will appear a new form of matter." Creating such "new matter" was seen as an even more extreme process than creating "new human beings," one requiring not just spiritual evolution but a violent explosion.

In the dynamic of murderous salvation, Asahara and his disciples lived out a three-way interaction involving a violent ideology, the violent psychological impulses of the guru himself (eventually shared by many of his followers), and external pressures and stimuli. Among the pressures were media revelations about many of Aum's fraudulent and possibly violent activities as well as legal steps against the cult by parental groups and committed lawyers. Stimuli included violent events elsewhere, like the Gulf War of 1990. The guru not only identified with the Iraqi dictator Saddam Hussein, in his eyes a nonwhite target of American perfidy, but also saw the high-tech, laser-guided weapons that defeated Saddam as a harbinger of Armageddon.

Aum's humiliating defeat in the 1990 elections for the Diet is frequently cited as the cause of subsequent Aum violence. But Aum's entry into politics and its bizarre campaign style were expressions of the kind of degeneration in Asahara that had already contributed to cult murders and weapons hunger. In general, Aum's combination of paranoia, grandiosity, and violent ideology propelled the group into confrontations of all sorts with the surrounding society—provoking fear, resentment, and bitter lawsuits. The cult had a tendency, as one observer put it, to "create problems and then try to solve them." Through the interaction of violent ideology, violent guru, and social antagonism, Aum sustained a dynamic that pressed ever more urgently toward ultimate violence, fusing of prophecy and reality, and the materializing of a fantasized world-destroying event.

Attack Guruism and Action Prophecy

A mounting paranoia is likely to transform guruism as extreme as Aum's into *attack guruism*. There are paranoid people who quietly nurse their sense of persecution and their grudges against the world. But there is another paranoid type, who, feeling himself attacked, lashes out at the world or at particular groups or people designated as enemies.

Whenever publicly criticized or exposed, whenever Aum was contested legally, Asahara immediately attacked (or counterattacked) the adversary, through the media and the courts, through threats and harassment, by kidnapping, drugging, or murder, and ultimately by attempted mass killing. Asahara's impulse to attack was always buttressed by Aum's polarizing ideology: any critic was by definition evil and manifesting bad karma; attacking him furthered Aum's mission of world salvation. Asahara's leading disciple and minister of intelligence, Yoshihiro Inoue, would later refer to paranoia and the kind of guruism that arose from it when he spoke of Asahara's "angry emotions, derived from his vices, which he called the guru's will" and of his "ordering disciples like us to kill, in the name of *poa*, in order to carry out that will."

In fact, belligerent interaction with others became such a psychological and ideological need that reality often had to be redefined to fit Aum's version of its own purity in the face of outside iniquity. Asahara's many claims that others were attacking the cult and him with sarin gas seems so badly false that one is tempted simply to accuse him of lying. But given his paranoia and need to attack he may have become inwardly convinced (at least in a part of his mind) of his victimization, for elaborate devices to combat chemical and biological attacks were placed in the guru's living area by Aum scientists and technicians, suggesting that Asahara did believe himself to be under attack. Though it is also possible that these devices were merely a manipulative pretense, it seems more likely that they were an element in an internalized persecutory narrative, in the ongoing drama of Aum's persecution by a "defiled" world.

A similar pattern can be observed in Asahara's intensifying efforts to identify and deal with "spies" in the cult, whether through the use of horoscopes, interrogations under drugs, combinations of severe spiritual practice and punishment, or murder. Asahara could not tolerate doubt or doubters, struggling as he was to sustain, against his own doubts, an environment—indeed a universe—that he could completely control. To the extent he succeeded, Aum was a world apart from any other, which is why one former disciple could call it "extraterritorial"—suggesting a walled-off enclave subject only to its own laws, rules, and violent solutions. Aum's attack stance was aimed at maintaining that extraterritoriality, indeed extending it to the entire world, and the only way such control could ultimately be exercised over the world was to destroy it.

Within Aum, Asahara's attack guruism was anchored in what was called the mahāmudrā. In Tibetan Buddhism, the term refers to a state in which a devotee achieves "the unity of emptiness and luminosity" and, thereby, "the purification . . . [of] the transitory contaminations of confusion." The concept was sometimes conceived in this way in Aum, and a few of Asahara's closest disciples were described as achieving mahāmudrā. But given Aum's atmosphere, attaining mahāmudrā came largely to mean the overcoming of all resistances to an absolute and unquestioned dedication to the guru himself. Mahāmudrā then became an ordeal or "test" prescribed by the guru to determine whether his disciples were capable of reaching the ultimate internal requirement of attack guruism. The most dedicated of his disciples were continually haunted by their inability to reach the unreachable ideal of total and unqualified devotion—complete fusion with the guru—and therefore endlessly berated themselves for their shortcomings. When the guru would make a particularly bizarre or impossible demand, they would sense that there was something wrong with it (and him) but would quickly decide that this was a mahāmudrā, a guru challenge, precisely *because* it was so absurd, bizarre, or impossible and that any negative view of the demand was nothing other than a reflection of their incomplete spiritual subservience to the guru. They would then struggle to inwardly embrace, and outwardly act upon, the bizarre demand. At the same time, they were deeply motivated to safeguard their high positions in the cult, their treasured closeness to the guru, and to avoid being severely punished or even murdered.

We may suspect that Asahara himself went through a similar psychological process, fending off his own inner suspicions that his demands were inappropriate or perhaps "crazy" by rendering them mahāmudrās for others that would advance the spiritual allegiance of true disciples and reveal the shortcomings of lesser ones. Hence, according to a close observer, "he seemed to reach the point where he could elevate any foolish or contradictory action on his part to a mahāmudrā." This use of mahāmudrā fueled Asahara's attack guruism as he prepared his disciples for participation in the project of cosmic destruction.

Asahara's *action prophecy* functioned much the same way—that is, he aggressively sought to bring about whatever he predicted. In a sense, it was a literal expression of a "self-fulfilling prophecy," a rather mild social science term aimed at research thought to be constructed so as inevitably to prove what it sets out to prove. But it may be more accurate to say that Asahara's most dire prophecies were consistent with his psychological and ideological impulses. He predicted to happen what he wanted to happen. And what he ultimately wanted to happen was the world's destruction. It is true that such destruction was necessary to him as a confirmation of his prophecy, but it is equally true that prophecy was itself a form of action, intended at some level of consciousness to contribute to an omniviolent outcome. What made Asahara an action prophet was the inseparability of prophecy and action, of what he imagined and what he did.

The Hebrew biblical concept of "forcing the end" refers to active human efforts to hasten God's pace in bringing about the destruction that must precede the yearned-for appearance of the Messiah. Traditional Jewish thought is critical of that "impatience," insisting that God moves at his own pace, needing no help in the task. Asahara differed from most ancient and contemporary prophets who have been and remain content to express combinations of fear and anticipation of a final cataclysm, even if they also believe that various human actions (ranging from moral decline in general to nuclear war in particular) may contribute in one way or another to the process that will bring it about.

Asahara seems to have been an action prophet from the beginning. Yoshihiro Inoue, his close disciple, declared that Aum was based on the guru's prophecy of Armageddon. "It was our practice [as disciples]," he said, "to fulfill his prophecy, and under his direction Aum Shinrikyō was militarized as a means of accomplishing his prophecy." Inoue could also have said that the prophecy itself was meant to bring about that militarization for the purpose of world destruction.

At least a few of Asahara's leading disciples left the cult when they became aware, as early as 1990, that the guru wished his prophecies to be realized and was taking aggressive steps in that direction. There was, in fact, a kind of self-selection ensuring that those who remained would be exclusively devoted to seeing those prophecies through to their action-oriented ends. In becoming "clones" of the guru, they came to live psychologically and spiritually within his prophecies. Asahara once declared that "Shiva wants the Tantra believers to dominate the nations" and that "if I am the prophesied Christ, World War III [and Armageddon] can be a springboard for me and for Aum Shinrikyō." As the cult tried to "realize" such predictions, Aum as an entity became a collective expression of action prophecy.

Killing the World: *Poa* for Everyone

Aum's violence could be said to begin with a dispensing of suffering: its theory and practice of removing bad karma justified training procedures sufficiently harsh as to become forms of torture and even murder. Almost immediately following the cult's first two murders, principles justifying murder were put forward actively in Aum as Vajrayāna teachings; not only was killing a person with a great accumulation of bad karma a way of "transforming" his life, but under the right circumstances, it could be considered "an act of love." The guru or high disciple who killed was seen as making a personal sacrifice by taking the other's bad karma on himself.

As Aum extended this concept to designated enemies (such as the murdered Sakamoto family), the term *poa* was increasingly brought to bear as a form of justification. The guru made clear many times what *poa* meant in Aum: "Suppose there was someone who would accumulate bad karma and go to hell if allowed to live. And suppose an enlightened individual thought that it was better to terminate the person's life and gave the person *poa*. . . . Objectively speaking, it is a destruction of life. . . . However, based on the notion of Vajrayāna, it is no other than respectable *poa*."

Although open to many different interpretations, the Tibetan Buddhist parables from which Asahara devised his version can certainly be seen as at odds with the more general Buddhist reverence for all forms of life. *Poa* is usually understood, moreover, as an act of disciplined meditation, greatly enhanced by the presence of one's guru. There are stories of gurus able to "transfer either a human soul or an animal" to higher realms. There are also parables in some traditions of Tibetan Buddhism that suggest killing at the command of one's guru, a prominent example being a talented disciple's miraculous invoking of lethal hailstones to destroy a village whose occupants were robbing the guru's other disciples. Although such parables were not associated with the concept of *poa*, Asahara drew upon them as well as upon stories of spiritually evolved persons who seem to violate Buddhist prohibitions by catching, killing, and eating fish or by hunting and killing animals—until it is explained that the evolved person is absorbing the bad karma of these creatures and so elevating their lives in death. Another favorite of Asahara's was a parable about the Buddha himself, who, while on a ship, was said to have killed a jewelry thief (in some versions a murderer), thereby protecting others on board and preventing the villain from accumulating, through further evil deeds, still more bad karma and worse retribution in the next life.

Asahara both drew upon and distorted such traditional parables as he brought to them his version of *poa*; the combination was then welded into a fixed concept of altruistic murder. Crucial to that step was the infusing of his unbounded guruism with the principle that "when your guru orders you to take someone's life . . . you are killing that person exactly at the right time and therefore letting that person have his *poa*." In such situations, he declared in one of his sermons, "any enlightened person will see at once that both the killer and the person to be killed are going to benefit from the act." Indeed, *poa* became a principle of killing that offered a form of life-power to both killer and victim. Above all, the immortality of both was to be enhanced. In this way Shōkō Asahara took Aum a conceptual step beyond any taken even by Nazi killers. The Nazis understood them-selves as killing Jews in order to heal their own people, "the Nordic race," and thereby enhance their racial immortality. They claimed no spiritual benefits for the Jews from being murdered. In Aum, the "healing" embraced both the perpetrators and their victims: they merged into an all-encompassing immortalization.

To administer *poa*, one required what was called in Aum "a sacred carefree mind," a particularly radical form of Buddhist nonattach-ment. In Aum practice, it meant an absolute separation from any con-cern about the outside world and an equally absolute focus on carrying out the will of the guru. In effect, the sacred carefree mind was a form of psychic numbing in which one freed oneself, joyfully, from all moral restraint. As one close observer explained, "It meant caring nothing if you harm me or if I harm you." In Aum, the "if I harm you" was the more significant part of this spiritual equation, one of the many ways in which disciples came to withdraw their empathy from the world outside themselves.

Observers of the cult in Japan have pointed out, quite correctly, that *poa* offered a convenient rationalization for murderous acts and that the concept was consciously manipulated to justify Aum's accelerating series of killings, first of its own members and then of designated out-side enemies. But *poa* was more than mere excuse or rationalization. As in other cases of mass killing, the back-and-forth psychological flow from murderous ideology to murderous actions was so intense that it became virtually impossible to separate conscious rationaliza-tion from compelling ideological conviction. The socialization to an environment of killing, observable in all expressions of mass murder or genocide, further blurred the distinction, but the underlying ideology of *poa* was crucial to the killing.

For Aum was killing not only to heal but also to survive. The constant imagery of being attacked by enemies was of course part of a guru-centered paranoia, but the paranoia itself was related to a sense that the life of the cult was profoundly threatened. Inoue later testified that in early 1995 Asahara juxtaposed two statements: "The bud of the supreme truth will perish in the present situation" and "We must disperse seventy tons of sarin." When asked about the connection between these two statements, Inoue explained the guru's motivation in this way: "Well, Aum is under attack by a nerve gas and Asahara will perish and the executive members of Aum will also perish, so that the teachings of Aum Shinrikyō will not survive. . . . So to protect the supreme truth we have to *poa* the persecutors." When, in February 1994, in a sermon from China, the guru reported on a vision in which the gods suggested that he would reign as emperor of Japan from 1997 on, he added, "So we must kill as soon as possible those opposed to the supreme truth." The psychological point here is that the guru's murderous paranoia covered over his terror of personal annihilation.

The step from *poa* for designated individual enemies to *poa* for an evil world had a certain ideological plausibility. It was a huge step nonetheless. Taking that step was made possible in part by the guru's increasing emphasis on the relentless accumulation of bad karma by ordinary people. Under such circumstances, he frequently implied and sometimes said directly, extreme measures were justified. Initially Asahara did not use the term *poa* in connection with mass killing, nor did he ever make public any intention on the part of Aum Shinrikyō to engage randomly in such killing or initiate violence that would bring on World War III and Armageddon. But once people everywhere were declared to be accumulators of bad karma, the *poa* ideology could be invoked for any kind of mass murder. Asahara could even come to believe (according to the testimony of high disciples) that the bad karma of ordinary people arose from their lack of "connection" with him and that his giving them *poa*—killing them—could finally bring about the necessary link.

In that way the all-important goal of "salvation" was bound up with the idea of mass violence. In Aum salvation was generally talked about in relation to "total happiness," emancipation, and compassion. But on a number of occasions Asahara made the provocative if cryptic declaration to his disciples that "one cannot choose the means of salvation." He spoke also of "drastic salvation" as being necessary under extreme conditions. So drastic did Asahara's vision of salvation become that, as the religious scholar Manabu Watanabe explains, there was "no room for people other than Shōkō Asahara to live in a world where Aum Shinrikyō reign[ed]." That was true because all Aum disciples were to become his clones and all "others" in the world were to be subjected to *poa*.

Within Aum's often haphazard environment, there was no such thing as a carefully conceived and executed plan. In retrospect, people who were close to Asahara now believe him to have been quixotic and contradictory, as well as uncertain about his own intentions. But there were many indications that he considered November 1995 the target date for the violence that would bring on World War III and Armageddon. That projection had to do, in part, with the expected readiness of a much-fantasized-about "laser beam weapon." Inoue has described a small meeting Asahara had with four of his leading disciples in early 1995 in which one of them asked, "When can we fight seriously and what will that mean?" The guru responded with the November date. Inoue said he "understood this to mean a fight with the human race and Japan, which Aum was trying to dominate and reign over." While here we enter a particularly elaborate realm of fantasy, the exchange offers a glimpse of Aum's tendency to combine its vision of genocidal salvation with a quest for weapons that could help realize that vision.

Toward the end many Aum members feared for their lives should they show any disloyalty. One high disciple described how he left the group but was brought back by Aum members and told by the guru not only that he knew too many secrets to be permitted to go back to ordinary society but also that Asahara wanted the disciple to die with him. Asahara frequently spoke of his own death, and one senses that something in him imagined a Götterdämmerung, a twilight of the gods, a world destruction that would include him, the guru-god, in the ultimate experience of salvation. But Asahara, as we know, also wished very much to survive, even as he sought to initiate a chain reaction of death. Hence a radio speech he made three days after the Tokyo sarin attack and one day after the first major police raids, in which he declared these events to have been "a step in the expansion of the Aum Shinrikyō plan of salvation." He called upon all to "awaken and help me, . . . to become my hand, foot, or head to help my salvation plan. Now let's carry out the plan for salvation—and face death without regret."

A Defender of *Poa*

Iwai was an intense spiritual seeker who also prided herself on her rationality. She had tried a number of the new religions and judged them all wanting before finding in Asahara and Aum a deep satisfaction that was both intellectual and spiritual. Encountering Asahara, she remembered, she was impressed with his ability "to analyze things, to judge things." In reading his books, she was particularly struck by his discussion of "emptiness," which other Buddhist sects seemed to shy away from. "I needed someone who was a practitioner and could teach the principles of Buddhism clearly." In this rational vein, "I came to understand the rules of karma—they are not at all supernatural."

But soon she was aware of transcending her tendency "to understand things by logic and to hold back my feelings." Thus, she described her experience of taking part in a PSI, or perfect salvation initiation, as follows:

> They applied gel to my scalp—put a sponge on it—and then sent electric power [via electrodes] into my head. It was not actual power but rather the brain waves coming into you—several patterns of brain waves, one of which, a very distinct pattern, was Asahara's. I thought that this man could really control his brain waves.

She felt enormous pleasure in "absorbing the brain waves" of the guru.

While undergoing the initiation by day she had several nights running a recurrent dream:

I went to kindergarten with my mother. It was a huge kindergarten. We took an escalator to the third or fourth floor. There was a curtain and in the back was a room with three Buddhist statues sitting on the tatami. I sat in front of the curtain. Suddenly the middle statue stood up and started walking toward me. It said, "Your way of dressing is wrong."

She understood the dream to be a significant religious experience. Perhaps unconsciously she sensed its suggestion that she was in the process of replacing her "wrong" pre-Aum existence with Aum's way of "dressing," or being. Going to a kindergarten with her mother suggests becoming a dependent child again in order to pursue her religious quest, as well perhaps as making the transition from parental authority to Aum's. In any case, after a week of the initiation process, people around her told her that she had "really changed."

Much of the change had to do with her evolving feelings toward the guru: "I had even more respect for him as a mentor, as a person far ahead of me, highly advanced in spiritual practice. I had the feeling that he was a great person. I felt happiness. He became closer to me." About the overall initiation experience, she said:

You can't put it into words. After I took off the PSI [electrodes] there was still something that remained—still touching that point. And whenever I had that perception I would automatically think of *Sonshi*. Before I took the PSI, I was still a little uneasy about living in the *dōjō*. After I took it for a week it made me very calm. I was determined to live in Aum, as *Sonshi*'s soul and my soul were now connected deep down and also *Sonshi* was always caring about me, worrying about me.

She went on to explain that the souls of ordinary people—including hers, mine, and the interpreter's—are "covered with dirt. They are polluted. But *Sonshi*'s soul is different from ours. It is open, uncovered, without any dirt."

She emphasized how happy she felt when entering the Aum building, how in Aum she was "very free." She associated that sense of freedom with such things as an absence of discrimination against women, the opportunity to leave behind the angry conflicts she had experienced both at home and at an unsatisfying job, but most of all a chance to pursue her spiritual quest without restraint. She became the staunchest defender of the concept of *poa* I was to encounter.

What propelled her toward acceptance of *poa* as a life principle was the intensity of her response to the guru, her sense of mystical tie and oneness with him. Behind that response was a pattern of antagonistic compliance, of resistance and then total submission, a pattern that reflected her explosive struggles with dependency and autonomy. In one "shouting match," she told an Aum member that she had "no patience with your stupid talk," but soon afterward she succumbed completely, became a renunciant, and demanded money for the cult from her parents.

Both her anger and her need for "logic" and a rationale contributed to her embrace of Aum's violent perceptions of bad karma. She told of an incident in which, as the leader of a small work project, she encountered a lethargic woman whose resistance to the work took the form of retreating into a large cardboard box. Iwai tried to force her out physically, but when she touched the woman she almost instantaneously experienced a "high fever" and felt ill. This happened on several occasions, and although each time immobilized by fever for a few days, she considered her reaction a fortunate one. "It was lucky that the bad karma burned," she believed, all the more so since she understood her own karma to render her susceptible: "I am burdened with bad karma from previous lives. It's kept in some sort of balance within me. But when I received karma from someone else, I couldn't handle it. So it burned and became fever."

She was living out Asahara's idea of karma as a deeply embedded badness, dangerously contagious and transferable from one person to another, that must at times be contested with force and that can also assault the body and require physiological counterviolence—a high fever—to "burn" it out. Iwai often brought up in our discussions the general need for disciples to "drop karma," a process that called for Aum's most energetic training procedures, including intense breathing exercises, and that could include the kind of fever she described. Much of her Aum practice had to do with ridding herself of her bad karma, which she experienced as personal antagonisms or violent tendencies.

Iwai at first declared that she had "no interest" in the guru's prophecies and expressed disdain for many of the male disciples because "men were very much interested in these things." She was especially contemptuous of men who became monks because of the expected Armageddon: "I thought they were stupid to be moved by such logic." She also claimed that the cult's increasing insistence on an impending Armageddon was "much exaggerated." Ever loyal to the guru, she represented him as playing down his ultimate prophecies. "Whether Armageddon comes or not is of little importance to us— whether it comes in ten years or in one year, because in any case we must all die," is how she characterized his attitude. She also approved of her guru's use of prophecy to manipulate disciples: "I simply thought that the idea of Armageddon was handy for organizing followers and I was kind of sympathetic to Master, who had so many followers to deal with."

But Iwai turned out to share much more of her guru's prophetic vision of violence than she realized. When asked about Armageddon itself, she plunged into her own personal narrative of an Armageddon-like end. Since her junior high school days, she began, she had been extremely critical of the country's educational system as it was geared toward "the education of slaves." Consequently, Japanese "cannot think on their own," and this failing affects all their relationships, especially those with people from other countries. As a result, she predicted, "Japan would decline, whether by major war, by being taken over in some way by another country, or by the collapse of Japan's economy. In one way or another, Japan would self-destruct." From that standpoint, she could admire her revered guru's "analytical ability and boldness" in speaking of imminent Japanese decline. Put another way, her deep antagonism toward Japanese society found convincing expression in the guru's world-ending prophecies, whatever her stated antipathy toward such prophecy in general.

The idea of Armageddon became "more real" to her—in fact, "the story of Armageddon took over my mind"—immediately following the Tokyo sarin attack. She and other members thought Aum was being falsely accused of the attack by a "society [that] seemed to have no sense of human rights" and whose use of police power—that is, the raids on Aum—"was nothing more than a revival of the secret police [tokkō keisatsu]" of the World War II era. Japan's economic and social problems, she believed, had led it to "turn to a war" against Aum, in which the cult "would be more and more hunted." She even imagined a kind of genocidal state campaign against Aum: "All the remaining followers would have to get together somewhere, very likely at Mount Fuji. Sarin would then be sprayed on us and they would claim that we had committed mass suicide, even though we were actually murdered."

As Armageddon came to dominate her thoughts, she had a second vision, this time of a violent Aum purification. "Suppose Armageddon does not come but Aum is crushed," she said. "Those people who came to Aum because they didn't like society and wanted to escape from it or because they wanted to have supernatural power—there were many such people who came to Aum for wrong and misguided reasons—they would all disappear. Then only the great spiritual achievers [subarashii jōjusha] would remain. With or without Aum, they would together carry out their practices and seek truth as a small group." She was not entirely clear whether "disappearance" meant annihilation and death or merely leaving the cult because of persecution, but there was little doubt about the overall violence of the image. She was very pleased with this vision, saying that it was "not a bad image," indeed it was a "wishful" one of a welcome "time of selection." What is most significant here is the totalistic nature of the violence she imagined—either the absolute martyrdom of Aum by evil outside forces or a purification process that would permit only a handful of Asahara's most dedicated disciples (herself included) to survive.

If her own violent angers, her blend of rage and dependency, connected her psychologically to the guru's world-ending projections, they also connected her to the violent theory he put forward. Here Iwai made particular reference to the guru's rendering of a parable that she understood to be taken from Tantric Buddhist writings: "There is a story about a highly evolved spiritual being who grilled and ate a fish. While eating the fish on the riverbank he was asked, 'Why do you, such an advanced being, kill and eat a living fish?' He answered that by eating a living fish, he *poa*'d that fish and sent it to a better world in its next life." This parable, she made clear, was often discussed in Aum and she had no doubt that it was meant as a justification for killing.

From his sermons and writings, Iwai understood her guru to teach the principle that "those in a higher stage elevate and save those in a lower stage [by killing them]. If there is little time [for salvation], it is necessary to select who is to be saved." The implication was that those "selected" to be killed were fortunate because they would achieve salvation. She was moved and convinced by the guru's teachings that to kill in this way was to "transform" a life and enable the person killed to be born again in a human world rather than in the lower animal world to which bad karma would assign one. Iwai vividly remembered various parables from her guru's sermons in which enlightened people apply *poa* to people who are "accumulating bad karma" and would otherwise "end up in hell."

In their hermetic, guru-saturated environment, Iwai and other disciples internalized this vision of virtuous killing that immortalized both killer and victim. For Iwai Asahara was the unerring conduit between mythic narrative and murderous action. Having gradually come to understand that Aum had initiated the sarin killings, she offered a vigorous theological defense based on her guru's sermons. "There are," she stated, "two ways of thinking." On the one hand, "the victims of sarin were killed for the sake of highly evolved spiritual beings, so they will be awarded virtue. These victims contributed their lives to the further development of highly evolved beings and in being killed by sarin were sacrificed for the sake of protecting Aum. So, without any will to do so, they protected Aum." On the other hand, "those people on whom sarin was spread suffered harm. But they were people who were not happy—or maybe happy is not a good word. People who are at a low spiritual level lead a worthless existence and continue to live in a way that causes trouble to others. At a certain point they may have greatly suffered, but they have now gone beyond suffering and raised their spirituality and by doing so can [in subsequent lives] bring greater merit to other people instead of the suffering they themselves experienced."

These two versions of *poa*—that of victims nurturing the development of evolved beings and that of themselves being spiritually enhanced—converged in Asahara's principle that "making an evolved spiritual being is a wonderful thing. For it is said that the merit that is generated will extend over seven generations. If someone is sacrificed for such a wonderful outcome, merit will certainly be returned to that person." Good karma, Iwai added, thus increases and cancels out bad karma. "When the evolved being eats fish, they become his flesh and blood, nourishing him and benefiting him. This makes good karma, which overcomes bad karma.... The fish's own karma improves when it benefits the evolved being." She then quoted another way Aum had of explaining the karma exchange: "Suppose you are in debt for one million yen. When you save five hundred thousand yen—or do good—then your debt will decrease to five hundred thousand yen. Suppose you have a debt of five hundred thousand yen. When you save one million yen, your debt will be erased and you will have a saving of five hundred thousand yen."

There was something about the sarin killings, however, that did trouble Iwai. In the days after the attack, she happened to be living outside of cult facilities with Aum members from the ministry of science and technology and was "shocked" by their "deteriorated spiritual behavior." Instead of pursuing Aum's ascetic existence, they lived what was in her eyes a dissipated life, "eating bowls of noodles, chatting idly about unnecessary things, and sleeping rather than engaging in religious practice"—that is, "leading a life in no way different from that of ordinary people." Consequently, "I could not explain to myself, as hard as I tried, why people were killed by sarin for the sake of these [dissolute] individuals."

The experience was deeply disturbing to her because the disciples in question were part of the ministry responsible for making, stockpiling, and in some cases using the weaponry. According to Iwai's moral calculus, if those who killed others (or for whose sake others were killed) were on a low spiritual level, then "Aum simply murdered people"— just as a low-level person eating fish would "only be performing a bad deed." Yet in making that distinction, she reaffirmed her belief in a *proper* version of the *poa* principle. She reminded me that "practitioners in Aum performed highly demanding exercises, which meant that the people they killed could receive special virtue. The practices we did were much harder than death." That is, enlightened Aum practitioners *earned* their right to kill.

During our talks Iwai kept struggling to differentiate between virtuous transformation and plain murder. About the sarin attack, she told me that she believed it had been wrong to kill the subway riders, but she defended her guru by pointing out that "he was in a panic because he felt so hunted down." Similarly, Aum members had no choice but to follow him because "everybody wanted to believe Master." She said these things in our last interview, partly in an attempt to soften the harshness of her position on *poa*. She also sought to soften Asahara's words, by quoting a statement she claimed was his (though it was never mentioned by other Aum members I encountered and seemed both out of character for Asahara and a contradiction of *poa*): "Suppose a soul in heaven sees souls in the human world and says, 'You should not be performing such bad deeds, you should die,' and kills them. This [heavenly] soul is bad, has a misplaced anger, and deviates from the truth." She was seeking to stay connected to her guru by claiming that he had offered a humane alternative to his statements on *poa* and to his own murderous actions. She could then argue, "What Asahara did was wrong according to what he himself said," and add hopefully, "Asahara's thinking may have been changing in connection with that point." She could also speak of uncertainties or "contradictions" in connection with *poa*, adding, "Physically he murdered people. That is wrong." But the word "physically" was a hedge, implying as it did that spiritually he was doing something else. Certainly, the matter was far from clear in her mind.

Asahara, she concluded, was seeking to "negate the karma" of disciples like her, just as he thought "that *poa* would change the karma of those murdered," but in actuality, she emphasized, "Asahara himself is under the law of karma. He cannot transcend it." As she now saw it, the real mistake on Asahara's part—and on hers as well—was to press to make people "perfect" in a way that took insufficient account of their karma, of the iron law of cause and effect that had to govern their lives.

One year after the sarin attack, she had finally achieved enough distance from Aum to express feelings she associated with "responsibility" but that were also related to a sense of guilt. First, she now realized that "I worked very hard to earn money for them to make sarin." Second, "I tried to negate the karma given to me as a Japanese and a human being born to my parents. I tried so hard to escape it. This caused people around me much pain." Third, she showed "weakness of self." That weakness, she felt, caused her to have an exaggerated need for a guru and to seek in Aum strong support from others and "a wall of protection."

Speaking as well of a larger problem of Japanese society "that surfaced through me, a weak being," she offered a generational analysis of Aum's attractions that was by no means without compassion or insight. Her parents, now in their seventh decade, having witnessed the failure of all attempts at constructive social change during the 1960s, had embraced a path of materialism, economic success, and narrow "my home-ism"; her generation was dissatisfied with mere economic privilege and, at a time when the family and other institutions seemed to be breaking down, "longed for the ideal father or ideal mother." She spoke of "the gap between the way society actually works and the way the immature mind perceives it" as a factor in creating the Aum phenomenon. She then offered a litany of recent Japanese social problems, most of them highlighted in the media: bullying among children (which in Japan can be violent as well as psychologically devastating and is viewed as a major problem), murders committed by high school students, children's refusal to go to school, a similar, sudden refusal by men over forty to go to work, and outbursts of family violence, such as a woman's beating her stepchild to death or parents' abusing children. Given these disturbances in society, she declared, Japanese should ask "*why* we joined Aum and not *how* we were brainwashed in Aum."

But her sensitive social perspective only led her back to moral equivocation about Aum and the killings:

It is no use saying that the Aum incident should not have happened. A lion kills a zebra or a grass field becomes forest and then woods, which may eventually wither—all this follows the law of karma. Without the Aum incident, the problem of mind, the problem of the individual Japanese mind, could have become much worse. . . . I don't know whether the Japanese people realize this or not, but Japan has reached this critical point. If you catch a cold without knowing it and have a fever, you may take your temperature or you may continue working, neglect the fever, and so suffer from cancer in the future. It is similar to that. Whether people realize it or not, Japan is signaling that it has reached that critical point.

In our final discussion of *poa* and her view of Aum's path of murderous salvation, she said:

It is very difficult to explain or describe. The killing soul and the killed soul are somehow connected in terms of the larger self. So an individual called Matsumoto [Asahara] was wrong, I think, but in terms of society as a whole Aum was inevitable. The entire Aum incident happened for a good reason. . . . Asahara was raised to a level from which he was worshiped. He misunderstood that position and did these things. It's sad for him but it happened as it had to. Suppose a soul like Asahara appears again and does these things again. I would not want to join him, but doing those things would have some significance. Not that I want a great soul to appear and do *poa* . . .

Violent Salvation

Most renunciants experienced fierce emotions when it came to defending their guru's salvational project from powerful and unrelenting enemies. That combination of feelings led them to embrace a concept of violent salvation that, though vague, was all-encompassing and passionate.

Harada, who was in her late twenties when I met her, had spent more that five years as a *shukke*, or Aum nun. A valued and trusted believer absolutely dedicated to the guru, she had never been a member of Shōkō Asahara's inner circle. In our discussions, she kept returning to Asahara's end-of-the-world preaching at his Armageddon seminar on Ishigaki Island and on the boat over. She described a kind of Ship of Fools, a scene of terror, expectation, and gaiety, "like a big party." Already feeling vulnerable because of the boat's violent rocking ("Everybody was very sick"), the disciples were warned by the guru that "this was their last chance," as a "big disaster" would destroy the earth. "We don't have much time left and you must follow me to survive." Like others on board, Harada worried about her karma because "if you have bad karma you die. It was like a time of selection." She felt she was putting her life in the hands of the guru: "Master acts like a lawyer for us before a judge."

In the years that followed, she was aware that the guru's words became ever more ominous. She understood him to be saying, "It is too difficult to help all people, so sometimes we have to use force to accelerate salvation. . . . It's all right to sacrifice some people, to steal or kill or commit adultery or tell a lie, because that can be a shortcut to salvation." Aum's teaching, as she came to understand it, was that "we don't have a human conscience, since human judgment is different from that of God or of a higher being."

There was a parallel justification for coercing Aum members or enacting violence against them. She remembered seeing an ordained member (who had apparently violated the cult's prohibition on sexual activity) confined "in a single cell with handcuffs" and also heard stories of people being hung upside down—all of which she interpreted as "Master trying to wash off their bad karma with strong treatment." She felt similarly about being confined herself for a week to a tiny cell in brutal summer heat while being exposed day and night to the words and images of the guru. She was told that this was a necessary procedure to repurify her from "alien influences" to which she had been exposed. At the time she psychologically fended off evidence before her, and thoughts within her, of Aum wrongdoing. Since any doubts about Aum behavior were considered expressions of "defilement," she consciously as well as unconsciously invoked patterns of numbing and denial: "I would try to shut out, eradicate, forget these thoughts."

She knew about certain people doing "secret work" and thought this "could be dangerous" but justified it by telling herself, "Master says it's our mission to prepare for Armageddon." She came to realize that those involved in producing sarin and other potential weapons were the ones who felt most "pressed by Armageddon." She added candidly, "I'm glad that Master didn't ask me to do things like that," which was her way of telling me that she would have followed any order he gave her. As she explained, "I tried to be an innocent child who absorbed what he said and what he did. He assured us that this was the fastest way to achieve enlightenment." In everything, the guru made it repetitiously clear that "your work is your spiritual practice." What Harada was struggling to convey to me was the manner in which Aum violence became spiritualized.

Harada assumed that as a lower-level disciple she might not grasp Asahara's thought or meaning, but she was convinced that "he had to have deep meaning to do or say these things. Even if it was a mistake, that was all right. Or perhaps he took such extreme steps purposely to wake people up." She shared in Aum's grandiose projections that "only we could survive and help people after that because we were a special people." Disciples like Harada sensed, however obscurely at times, that it was the cult's sacred mission to preside over the destruction and re-creation of humankind—and that this was not just a matter of prediction, that actions would be involved. This half knowledge, in turn, contributed to retrospective feelings of guilt, in Harada and other disciples, over acts of violence like the Tokyo attack, about which they had been completely ignorant.

At the time Harada completely accepted Aum's definition of *poa*. People of high spiritual attainment could and should "for the sake of salvation kill those beings who commit bad deeds and who [if within Aum] cause Aum to commit bad deeds. . . . A spiritual achiever can *poa* another being to a higher world. That's why it's all right and a merit for him." But she also distanced herself, partly retrospectively, from this principle in two ways. First, *poa* actions were to be undertaken solely by those who came close to being saviors and had very special spiritual attributes: "I thought only very selected saints who have supernatural powers, only Buddha could do that." Second, she believed that *poa* was to be understood as a theoretical principle and that "Master would never actually do this kind of thing." But such distancing was never fully effective. Another side of her believed that "Master is a messiah and God—Buddha—so he can really *poa*."

Long after leaving Aum she continued to be drawn to the guru and had difficulty accepting what she essentially knew to be true: that Aum was responsible for the sarin attack. Most of all she wanted the guru to offer an explanation for the killings. "If he really thought he could *poa* people, he should say, 'According to this teaching, I *poa*'d these people.' I expected Master to give specific reasons why he did it." As she gradually separated herself from Asahara psychologically, she was still searching for a way to exonerate him and to reactivate her connection to him. In a sense she was still searching for a justification for *poa*.

She also struggled with a sense of guilt—expressed in recurring self-accusatory dreams—for having left Aum and broken the "pipeline to the guru." She was strongly affected by letters from friends still in Aum that declared, "You cannot understand a higher being. You can't judge every incident from the viewpoint of a human. You can't judge God's mind or decisions made by God."

Harada imagined herself going over the guru's head to the god Shiva, the highest authority Asahara invoked on the issue of *poa*. "I wish I could connect with Lord Shiva and ask him everything." At times she would find herself thinking, "If the Master is the Messiah, maybe he did the right thing to *poa* the people." At times she wished to numb herself completely to Aum's many killings in order to recover her beloved guru. Quite ingenuously, she said to me, "If you put killing matters aside, maybe he is a great leader, a true guru."

Kuno, a young student of Buddhism, at first thought he found in Aum a unique realization of that religion. Through intense spiritual practice, he not only had strong mystical experiences but seemed to undergo a welcome personality change. In the past fearful and subjected to bullying by other boys because of his delicacy and "female language" (the softer, more compliant words and tones that Japanese girls and women are expected to employ), he came to feel more confident and bold in Aum.

Kuno understood Armageddon as an actual military engagement in which he would fight: "I will be a warrior in the battle between good and evil, between the Freemasons' evil secret army and Aum's good army." He would combine "spiritual fighting" with physical combat to counter "evil energy." Although he had a vision in which "tanks and soldiers keep coming and I stop them with my supernatural power," he thought that he would "eventually die" but not until he had made a transcendent sacrifice. He imagined himself as a "sacrificial stone" for the creation not only of "new human beings" but of "superhumans"—these resplendent creatures taking the form of very young children, two or three years of age. "To create a world for those children, we would fight."

Kuno recalled being struck by Asahara's "desire for destruction" and his constant invocation of Shiva as a "god of destruction." But Kuno accepted the Aum principle that Shiva, and by implication Asahara, destroyed only because "the world is rotten" and that Aum would "afterwards create a new world that is good."

Consciously, Kuno enthusiastically embraced this entire perspective during most of his time in Aum: "I thought it was perfect." But his unconscious turmoil was revealed in a series of bizarre psychological experiences that were to undermine his functional Aum self. The sequence began with an episode of severe amnesia during which he "forgot he was a member of Aum" and could not even remember his name. When referred to Asahara, who declared, "I am guru," Kuno asked, "What is that?" He was then guided through various Aum activities, including the election campaign, during which he put on an Asahara mask and shouted with the others, "Please vote for Asahara." But he soon began to feel uncomfortable and dizzy (from a chemical used on the mask, he thought) and had to be taken back to Aum headquarters. There, he "lost consciousness" and experienced a powerful hallucination that he later described as a near-death experience: he entered a dark tunnel, saw a tiny light shining ahead, and then encountered "a huge goddess about thirty feet high with a three-dimensional quality like a hologram, and her face looked like mine." The goddess demonstrated to Kuno the important events of his childhood and high school years, and declared, "It's you!" Then she struck him hard with a club, causing pain so extreme that he thought that he would die. At that moment, he recovered much of his memory.

He remained confused about the event when he described it to me but stated that "because of my memory loss, I was able to see the entire situation and I came to think Aum was strange." He found himself critical of Aum's claims and activities in general. With the help of outsiders, he managed to extricate himself from the cult well before the Tokyo sarin episode. His amnesia had undoubtedly been related to inner resistance to the absolute compliance to Aum he had been manifesting. His attacking-goddess vision, which might have been induced by LSD or a related drug, though he adamantly denied this, seemed to suggest his uneasy merging with Aum and its guru (whom the goddess undoubtedly represented in part), as well as a perception of violence on the part of the guru, of Aum in general, and indeed of himself. The vision revealed him to be a victim of Aum but also ("her face looked like mine") a participant in its violence. Childhood experiences of victimization and violence probably sensitized Kuno to Aum's abuses and could have thereby contributed to the wisdom of his vision.

Ogata, a restless student with a long-standing interest in reincarnation, trained specifically to become an "Armageddon warrior." He was assigned to an Aum paramilitary unit in a remote area of Japan near the city of Gifu. Like others so assigned, he was informed that the military exercises were for the purpose of making a film, but his rigorous training included the intense practice of various martial arts. "We were told that Armageddon would occur in 1997 and that when the war came, our unit would be fighting in the vanguard, so we had to be serious about our military training." He also understood that "I must brace myself for death." This would be a great war in which formidable enemies "would have to be subdued by Aum's powers."

The survivors of Armageddon, Ogata understood from Asahara, would be those Aum members who achieved the highest spiritual attainment, that of mahāmudrā. They, in turn, would be the founders of the postapocalyptic utopian spiritual community of Shambhala. Then "Japan would be an Aum country." In this way Ogata's paramilitary training was bound up with Aum's bizarre gyrations between visions of ever-expanding killing and of ever more perfect spiritual peace. He remembers being so immersed in and controlled by Aum that "I was in a situation where even thinking about it was futile. There was nothing to do but to obey and do what I was told." Ogata's compliance in potential large-scale violence was bound up with Aum's karma theory: "If bad karma accumulates too greatly [we were taught], then at one point it explodes, so Aum's teachings tell us not to let any more evil accumulate. One must instead do *poa* and make the world at least a tiny bit better. Under this teaching, murders were committed."

Ogata remembers how his Aum self reacted to descriptions of cult violence. "When I heard the story [of the kidnapping of two young people] from the guy who was the driver and brought them back, I said, 'If this is what is necessary to make them *shukke*—if that is what needs to be done—then it has to be done!" Then he added, "I am now afraid of myself, the man who said those words. I mean, before I joined Aum, such acts were unpardonable. But in Aum things I used to believe were wrong were easily accepted. I was in a state devoid of reason. It was mind control." In our interviews, he was concerned and distressed by the way in which his internalization of the Aum ethos had reversed his moral standards and led him to accept, even embrace, visions of both individual and cosmic violence.

Hirota, a young scientist who was also a spiritual seeker, had a chilling encounter that convinced him that the guru did not expect Armageddon "to occur spontaneously" but was actually "trying to make it happen." He was with Asahara at the recording of a radio broadcast in which he and others, on the air, were to provide the guru with information for his prophecies. During a brief interlude when the microphones were turned off, the guru paused and portentously declared, "Now it's war!" From the guru's "facial expression and body language," Hirota was convinced not only that Asahara "was pleased such a war would come—and soon" but that "he was actually trying to pull the trigger" of Armageddon itself.

Since Asahara had been telling followers, "We have to avoid this war," even while preparing and strongly wishing for it, Hirota himself felt "betrayed" by the guru's "great deception." Hirota became frightened by the guru and, although still very much under his influence, began to notice an "evil aura" about him that was to play an important part in his eventual escape from Aum. He described having been "sucked into the depths of his [Asahara's] darkness" and compelled to follow him because "any doubt meant inadequate spiritual practice." Hirota found himself "leading a life of half doubt, half belief." He was confused by the way the guru shifted in his interpretations of salvation, now associating it with the traditional Buddhist principles of compassion and mercy, now with images of Armageddon-centered violence. But he continued to share the pervasive Aum conviction that Asahara was the world's true savior. Because of that belief, "those who did not want to kill people were propelled by faith and, as a result, they killed." Caught up in Asahara's mahāmudrā system, "they could not feel easy until they proved their faith. The guru gave them this opportunity in a very radical way." Disciples became entrapped in the guru's "darkness," which called forth "the darkness in our own minds."

Asahara himself, Hirota came to think, was so fixed on Armageddon that he considered it "all right to destroy himself as long as he destroyed as much of the world as possible." In this life, the guru felt, "he could not do everything," but (as Hirota heard the guru say) "we must do as much as we can." To Hirota, the implication was clearly that in the next life the destruction could be resumed. Hence, the guru "denied the legitimacy of the world itself, of human existence."

Transformation, Aum Style

The guru's closest follower, Yoshihiro Inoue—who reportedly once said, "If Master ordered me to kill my parents, I would"—described how disciples could be shamed into the violence of Asahara's vision. As the guru was "the savior of humankind," any order of his, however likely to jeopardize Aum, was "a mahāmudrā for his disciples," an ordeal that tested their absolute obedience to him; any failure to carry it out successfully was "the result of disciples' bad karma." The only way to overcome the shame of failing the guru was to make a total plunge into his bizarre psychological universe. Take the case in which Asahara ordered the strangling of an Aum member who had attempted to free his friend's mother from drugging and medical mistreatment. When those involved, including Inoue, had some difficulty, mental and physical, completing the act, the guru, who was present, shouted: "If you can't do it, I will do it myself!" The specter of the guru's having to descend from his godly status and kill with his own hands because his disciples had failed to carry out his order was so shaming that, as Inoue said, "I had no choice but to do something." He then helped restrain the victim, who was suffocated. Toward the end, such shame was accompanied by deep fear. Knowing the doctrine all too well and having witnessed the *poa* of others, Inoue spoke of "an actual horror" of being victimized by *poa* himself, nor could Asahara's loyal disciples be critical of the guru for killing them. "This blind dedication to the guru," as Inoue later observed, "caused degeneration in the guru as well as the disciples."

A former Aum disciple made an important point about the shift in Asahara's guruism:

> The guru in 1990 tried to spread botulinus in order to have a connection with contemporary people. . . . [He was seeking a similar connection] in 1993 when he dispersed anthrax, and even with the sarin incident in Tokyo. In this way the guru's salvation changed from salvation by means of enlightenment and liberation in this life to salvation in the future by means of *poa* and making that connection.

Impelled by his megalomania, the guru sought to subsume every human being on earth into his uniquely "authentic" immortality system, the only viable path to immortality now available to humanity. As a concept, *poa* offered that possibility. By killing everyone in the world and viewing it as *poa*, Asahara could generously dispense the immortality that he alone controlled while carrying out his function as a world-ending guru.

This wildly fantastic killing project required intense psychic participation from high disciples. It forced them to create a relatively autonomous Aum self, a "sacred carefree mind" that would enable them to sweep away the doubts of the prior self. They, too, had to become part of the "transformation."

The Aum experience of "transcendence" thus became directly associated with killing, an ardent version of the *Vajrayāna Resolution*, a pamphlet distributed among trusted Aum members and sometimes read aloud:

I will *poa* all wrongdoers.

I will *poa* all wrongdoers.

I will *poa* all wrongdoers.

I will do whatever is required for salvation of the world. . . .

I will practice complete Vajrayāna. . . .

I will not stop this practice even if I die from it. . . .

I will practice Vajrayāna without a care.

Now, as the Bible explains, Armageddon is finally approaching.

I will join the holy army to *poa* all wrongdoers.

I will *poa* one evil, two evils, and more.

Poa is world salvation.

Poa is virtue.

Practicing *poa* will lead me to the highest world.

Asahara liked to kill with verbs: to *poa*, he explained was "to transform a person doing bad things." "Transform," then, was a euphemism for a euphemism: to *poa* was to murder, and murder, of course, ends all possibility of transformation in a victim—but not in the murderer.

Aum's overall mission became the total destruction of "the other." As one astute observer summed it up, "When you meet the guru, clone him! When you meet others, *poa* them!" Or to put it another way, killing everyone outside of an elect circle of disciples promised to render members of that circle exuberantly immortal, exclusive in their claim to purity and life, omnipotent in their dispensing of existence, and the sole mediators of the only "connection" that counted for the polluted others of the world—the connection through which the all-powerful guru would practice altruistic genocide.

4 | Clones of the Guru

Aum violence was made possible by the extremity of its guruism—
an extremity in human relationships that is almost impossible to
imagine. Outsiders are likely to have no equivalent experience to draw
upon. And insiders—Aum members—can only start to recast it in
their minds when they have begun to extricate themselves from its
demands and rewards. The oneness with the guru sought by each disciple can seem to resemble that of an infant with its mother just prior
to birth. But this regressive model has limited application because
we are concerned here with adults who seek a special kind of adult
relationship that, though radically confining, is also experienced as
explosively liberating. Their merger with the guru, moreover, could be
attained in a variety of ways.

The Perfect Man

Short, stocky, and in his early thirties, Isoda was at first edgy and suspicious with me even though he had been introduced by intermediaries

he trusted. A highly articulate man, he soon became intensely involved in our dialogue. By our second meeting he made it clear to me that he viewed my work as potentially useful for understanding what people had experienced in Aum, particularly in the guru-disciple relationship, and for combating future Aums. Over the course of our four meetings, Isoda's extraordinary energy and unsparing self-scrutiny never wavered. He had spent only about seven months in Aum, less time than most former members I interviewed, but the depth of his immersion in the cult was second to none.

He fit well into a general profile I encountered in former disciples, by which I do not mean an ironclad personality type but rather a loosely shared set of tendencies, at the heart of which was a sense of alienation from and antipathy toward mainstream society. As a person with artistic inclinations, he considered himself "useless" for that society and resisted what he saw as its unyielding lockstep requirements and extreme conformity. Like many other former Aum members (and many Japanese generally), he stressed his enormous dependence on a doting mother who, despite his inclinations toward becoming a "reformist" or a "revolutionary," encouraged him to remain childlike even after he had left the family home. Like many others, he gravitated toward Aum at a time of painful confusion in his life—he called it a "deadlock"—concerning his career as an artist and his unappeased spiritual hungers. He looked back on himself as an idealist who "did not fit into society" and "always made trouble."

Impressed by Aum members he encountered at a small public ceremony, he quickly joined the group and plunged wholeheartedly into its religious practices because "my personality is to see things through to the end." He found himself deeply drawn to the group and especially to its guru, who seemed all-knowing and an enormously effective religious teacher. "I had been seeking someone who was much more than myself but had yet to meet such a person. I thought that he could be the one, the person who could be a mentor for me."

Participating in the cult's intense version of meditation, in vigorous sequences of prostration, and in yogic rapid-breathing exercises, he readily achieved "mystical experiences," including visions of white and colored lights, of the Buddha, and of the guru, as well as out-of-body sensations. These came to mean everything to him: "After I joined, I experienced these physical sensations so I started believing in Asahara."

To solidify his attachment to the guru, Isoda, like others, would listen to Asahara's voice for hours through headphones while the guru's words would simultaneously be flashed before him. Disciples under twenty were required to experience these sound and image sequences three hundred times a day; those in their twenties, five hundred times a day; those in their thirties, seven hundred times; those in their forties, a thousand times. The older one was, the more one had been exposed to the world's "polluted data," which was being systematically manipulated by Freemasons and Jews, whose way of maintaining control over the world was to render people stupid. Only Asahara had the special power to "change the data" and replace it with Aum's data of absolute truth. As Asahara himself expressed the principle of such Aum processes, "You repeat five times, ten times, a thousand times, ten thousand times, a hundred thousand times. If you do that, such data becomes central to the core of your heart."

Isoda, now convinced that the guru was (as Asahara himself declared) "the last savior of this century" and feeling a new sense of wholeness, of "life opening up," had his connection to him further cemented by various initiation procedures. Before receiving the LSD for his Christ initiation, Isoda was instructed to put on a diaper, a safeguard against the incontinence some people experienced in the course of the several-hour initiation; disposing of a diaper, moreover, could eliminate evidence of drug use that might otherwise be detected from residual elements of urine on clothing. In any case, the diapering was in keeping with an infantilization that served the disciple-guru connection. Isoda also "signed" with a fingerprint a pledge not to hold Aum responsible for anything that might occur and never to reveal the nature of his secret initiation. He remembered sitting in the lotus position and meditating in anticipation of Asahara's appearance. He described his consciousness as "awfully elevated," so much so that "I began to see lights. I could hardly wait for him to come." The guru appeared surrounded by followers, "like the procession of a *daimyō* [feudal lord]." Isoda acted out the scene before me of Asahara sitting on a chair and chanting in a low voice that he—the guru—and the Lord Shiva were great "victors of truth." Asahara then handed him a wine glass containing the LSD. "What I can remember from that point was that when I touched his finger I was really elated. The touch meant that higher energy flowed from the touch to the lower energy [Isoda's body], and when it happened I was deeply affected." After imbibing the drug, he recalled undergoing only profound disorientation and feeling ashamed—a sense that "this is my fault, not Asahara's"—at his failure to have a further mystical experience. He also felt responsible for a stern look he observed on Asahara's face when the guru handed him the glass.

The initiation intensified Isoda's thralldom to Asahara and Aum. For him, as for others, Asahara was "greater than God, beyond God" and "a perfect man." Isoda thrived for a time on the very extremity of this guru worship. He felt himself drawing enormous energy from Asahara, and the greater his devotion, the greater that sense of energy. He was extremely pleased by the information that he had been "a leading disciple of the guru's in a previous life," and even more so by his swift rise in Aum, because that meant "I was acknowledged by Asahara." He became convinced that "if I followed him my life would become new" and that the bond would be endless: "If you are connected with the guru in this world, then you can stay with him in the next world." As the deity who "controls history," Asahara was seen as more than his "existing body." He could take on other bodies in other dimensions so that he would "always be looking at you and judging you, wherever you might be."

The immortality Asahara bequeathed was cosmic. Death, therefore, was "nothing to be afraid of because you go to a higher world," where you are eternally protected by the guru. Isoda came to feel that his personal existence resided in the guru, that "there is only the guru. He is everything, the only significant person in the universe, so of course you would want to follow him no matter where, even to the next world." By becoming one with Asahara, Isoda shared with other disciples a sense of being part of an ultimate, transcendent force:

He ruled over everything and so he was beyond explaining. You may be around for, say, sixty or eighty years but Shōkō Asahara's life spans past and future. When I was with him I had this real sense of joy at being a member of an elite, a feeling that "I'm different from all the rest of you [outside of Aum]," of being superior and one of a chosen people.

That level of joy and satisfaction rendered Isoda highly responsive to Aum's message of "fusing" with, and becoming a "clone" of, the guru.

The cloning process was rendered more urgent by Asahara's Armageddon preachings. Isoda found much of this prophecy convincing, given his general sense of Japanese decline. "The world," he felt, "was getting worse," pushing itself toward Armageddon with its increasing evil and "sexual corruption," including what Aum called "the three S's—sex, sports, and screen." So Isoda welcomed the suggestion that he join in a special "Armageddon seminar" in which it was fiercely suggested that human beings and their weapons would destroy the world:

Over and over again they showed videotapes of war from all over the world, of the most horrible forms of fighting, of people dying in terrible ways. They showed every disaster, then they talked about Star Wars, nuclear weapons, and plasma weapons that would be used in the next war and would destroy nothing, only kill human beings.

Isoda experienced not just fear but excitement. It all fit in with the coming end of the century and the millennium, the predictions of Nostradamus, and the chance for transforming humankind. Armageddon was a window of opportunity. "If we miss this opportunity, we may not have another one," he told me and then laughed uncomfortably at how absurd the statement now sounded to him. Armageddon was to be a great event, which could only be survived by following Asahara. Like everyone else, he was unsure just how Asahara would save his followers, "but," he added, "I thought he must know how." He was convinced that his personal survival depended upon becoming closer to the guru by means of ever more vigorous and demanding forms of spiritual practice. At this time, Isoda also urged his father, mother, and two brothers to join him in Aum so that they, too, could be saved.

In fact, he began to long for an apocalyptic solution: "There was something within me that was hoping Armageddon would happen because it's faster if we destroy everything first. Then something new would be born." Isoda experienced a "mounting anticipation" in connection with two visionary fantasies he experienced during his time in Aum. In the first, the world has ended:

> The guru is sitting on top of a hill surrounded by people recognized as high disciples, people who are chosen, and among them is me. It was a very heroic feeling. I was very high-spirited in imagining that. Well, I'm going to survive, I felt, survive and rule the world!

The second fantasy was more modest and domestic but no less passionate. He imagined being married to an attractive and talented artist, also a member of Aum, whom he had admired from a distance; together they would share the tranquillity and harmony that would follow Armageddon. The marriage would in fact be "ordered by the guru."

As Isoda's account indicates, for a disciple who could absolutize his merger with the guru—actually perceive himself as the guru's clone—the psychological rewards were equally absolute. With the guru as his instrument of survival, Isoda could anticipate the end of the world "not as terror but as desire." Nevertheless, Isoda experienced ambivalence and doubts. He felt certain exercises to be "silly" and "boring." He questioned the idea that there was a world conspiracy of Freemasons and Jews, especially when told that they were disseminating dangerous "electromagnetic currents." Even concerning Asahara, he sometimes found himself "half believing and half doubting" and wondering whether "all this might be a fake." But as a way of suppressing these doubts he plunged more deeply into the cult's practices and beliefs. For by then his overriding feeling was, "I needed Aum."

Isoda could be considered to have undergone a form of doubling: a division of the self into two relatively autonomous entities with the prior self retaining some of its former standards and harboring doubts, to which the Aum self responded by embracing the cultic experience ever more intensely. This pattern was common in disciples, some of whom, like Isoda, found it extremely difficult to allow themselves to imagine leaving the Aum life. Isoda had completely invested himself in the group, both in the literal sense of having donated to it all his money and property and, more important, in the psychological sense through his "valuable mystical experiences," his embrace of the promise of Armageddon survival, and his participation in the guru's all-consuming goal of salvation.

Having himself experienced many rejections, Isoda sensed that he had been drawn not only to the imagined present perfection of the guru but to the guru's prior experience of constant failure. He mentioned various ways Asahara had been rejected by society: his being sent to a school for the blind, his conflicts with the law, his inability to enter Tokyo University or become a doctor, and even the rumors about his coming from a despised class. In this, Isoda was expressing the guru's special appeal to young people who considered themselves in one way or another failures or outsiders.

Isoda also shared in the megalomania that Asahara had fashioned from his failures. While this was true of other disciples I met, none articulated it as strongly:

> To put it bluntly, I am arrogant. Rather than believing just in Asahara, I believed in myself. I had the belief that I am a great person, so I will survive. . . . I think my personality is like Shōkō Asahara's personality. When I walk down the street, most of the time I'm imagining things, and in Aum when you imagined things in that way, it was about Armageddon. . . . Rather than thinking that Asahara was above me, I felt more like we were equal. That's one reason I left Aum, because there cannot be two leaders.

But that fantasized rivalry was easily subsumed by his identification with the guru's omnipotent system: "I wanted to survive and I wanted to be a hero. This is beyond logic. It was almost like self-hypnosis." Isoda's grandiosity was so intense that he even blamed himself for Aum's difficulties in achieving its nonviolent spiritual utopia: "Because we had been told about how bad karma from our previous lives held us back, and because I joined fairly late, I kept asking myself why I hadn't joined sooner. For a while this became a feeling of guilt, a feeling of 'Damn, because I joined late, the plan for salvation of humanity was delayed!' "

In our interviews, he could mock himself and Asahara for their feelings of omnipotence, Asahara for wishing to be "the king of the earth, of the universe" and for "wanting to construct a robot kingdom with robots as followers." Such attitudes, he insisted, not only derived from Asahara but were "mutually created" by the guru and his disciples. "Asahara was only part of this," he insisted. In the case of the sarin attack, "I don't think that he alone caused the incident." Drawing upon an essay of mine that I had sent him, he went on to speak of Aum as having a "totalistic organization and atmosphere." Such totalism, he believed, was manifested in high disciples who encouraged rather than restrained Asahara's excesses. Although Isoda understood Asahara to have contributed more than anyone else to the creation of the cult's totalistic atmosphere, he believed that the guru himself eventually became caught up, even entrapped, in it.

Yet Isoda was so bound to Asahara that when the sarin attack occurred his psychological state was mainly one of excitement: "I thought, finally Armageddon is here! It has come! People all around me were enjoying it. We are saviors! Finally our turn has come! I didn't ask who did it."

Isoda's final three months in Aum were intense and confusing. Serving as one of several Aum spokesmen, he often had to explain the cult's position to the press—that the United States, the Japanese government, or other enemies of Aum were responsible for the attack. Although still deeply committed to Asahara, he found himself in constant conflict with his immediate superiors in Aum. He came to feel increasingly that there was something "strange" about the group. When others observed his doubts, he was ordered to undergo a month's retraining with particularly intense forms of yoga, meditation, and chanting, after which he experienced "a lot of energy" and a resurgence of enthusiasm for Aum. But that was only temporary. Soon he found himself wavering again. He finally left Aum when a newspaper hired him to work with its reporters on a series of articles about the cult. He was still uncertain as to who had released the gas, but in response to extensive media reports to which he finally had access he became convinced that it was indeed Aum. He also became bitterly critical of Asahara and other Aum leaders not only for the sarin attack but also for their sexual hypocrisy, especially for the guru's "Tantric initiations" of young female disciples while preaching celibacy for everyone else. Characteristically, Isoda also condemned his own sexual hypocrisy, emphasizing the intensity of his sexual desire during his time in the group.

Preoccupied with the question of responsibility and with the hold Asahara had over him, Isoda was troubled by the realization that, had he joined Aum earlier and so risen higher, he might well have played a part in its murderous behavior. "I would be a criminal now. I would have become a terrible person. That is why I feel guilty." All this weighs on him because his Aum experiences made him painfully aware of "very nasty desires inside me," having to do with Asahara-connected impulses toward destroying the world and becoming himself a great leader or king.

But although he came to see Aum's activities as criminal, Isoda, like many other former disciples, had considerable difficulty extricating himself psychologically from Asahara. The difficulty was compounded by his unusual degree of personal identification with the guru, by his sense of himself as like Asahara. In our last interview, which took place two years after the sarin incident, he could still say in a somewhat puzzled tone, "I have for some reason no real hatred for the man. I even have some kind of sympathy. Even after I left," he added, "I felt that perhaps he was a great man."

The Arbiter of Death and Rebirth

Ogata, the "Armageddon warrior," had been preoccupied with death from early childhood. When a number of his relatives died, he asked troubled questions about where dead people went but received no satisfactory answers until told by another boy that "there was something called reincarnation." Ten years later, when Ogata was a university student, that same person, by then a leading figure in Aum, contacted him and began providing him with Aum books and pamphlets about reincarnation, which Ogata read "voraciously." Very much taken as well by an Aum video entitled *Death and Rebirth* and by powerful sermons he heard Asahara deliver on the subject of reincarnation, he decided to join the group. His obsession with death and reincarnation led Ogata into passionate forms of Aum practice: meditation, rapid breathing, the chanting of mantras, and repeated prostration. As he explained, "According to Aum teachings, such ascetic practices are preparations for death—and I thought those teachings were true."

Already deep into the Aum ambience, he was subjected to the accusatory *bardo* initiation, during which his legs were bound to enable him to maintain the lotus position over several hours.

> I appeared before a [hidden] figure who identified himself as Yama, the Lord of Hell. He told me he was facing the Sanzu River, the division between the living and the dead. He said, "I will put you on trial to decide which world you will be born into. If certain things are revealed you will go to heaven; if other things are revealed you can be born a human being, or an animal, or among the monsters in Hell." He talked about six different worlds and afterward declared angrily, "You did *these* things! You did *those* things!" And each time he hit a loud drum—Bong!—and shouted, "Don't lie!" Then I chanted a mantra for about an hour.

Although this *bardo* initiation was followed immediately by a Christ initiation, it was the *bardo* initiation that made the greater impression on him: "It was the most painful. I thought that reincarnation was something like that. Reincarnation was not new to me but the idea gained depth." Now that he was infused with fear, his bond to Asahara as the arbiter of death and reincarnation intensified. "Asahara had created this initiation. I was convinced that the reincarnation he preached was correct. It seemed to me that after death things would turn out exactly that way. That would be the absolute reality."

Both the initiation and the guru's teachings were an "absolute reality" that "came from above us," so much so that "if something was black and Asahara said that it was white, then it was white." His anxious, lifelong dilemma concerning death and rebirth having been solved by Asahara, Ogata could merge with a guru he now invested with omnipotence extending to the world beyond.

The Healer

Yano was a successful businessman in his midthirties when he joined Aum. Like Ogata, he had been overwhelmed by deaths in his family in childhood and adolescence, and such was his general sensitivity that he experienced a traumatic shock at news of the dramatic ritual suicide of the famous writer Yukio Mishima in 1975.

As a married man he underwent the anguish of a young daughter's struggle with a severe neurological condition that doctors did not know how to diagnose or treat. When medicines prescribed for her had little effect, he began to explore "the world of spirituality"—various occult and New Age writings—in search of an alternative approach. One day, while browsing in a bookstore, he began to read Asahara's book *Initiation*. "I felt my body become paralyzed," he said, "but my legs headed for the Aum ashram." He was entranced by Asahara's version of *gedatsu*, or enlightenment, which seemed to promise "emancipation from the death and disease so near to me and from anger toward the world." During a private talk with Asahara (available to anyone at that time for a fee), he brought up his daughter's condition. Without hesitation, the guru suggested a regime of regular yogic postural exercises that Yano or his wife was to do with the little girl. Soon after the regime began, his daughter's symptoms simply disappeared, a result that left him in awe. "The process cured my daughter!" he declared, still with considerable emotion. "I developed confidence in yogic salvation not just for my daughter but for my family and for the world." For as he went further in these and other Aum spiritual practices, he, too, felt healed. "My health had been at its worst. I was playing a lot of mahjong, drinking quite a bit, and smoking heavily, but now I became healthier." He experienced "a surge of energy." As a result, he "could dress more lightly in the winter and had a greater capacity to adapt to nature."

Spurred by these healing experiences, Yano took up Aum's practices with extraordinary devotion and moved steadily up its spiritual and organizational hierarchy. He told me of reaching a stage of awareness in which he was able to know "the Mahāyāna Buddhist truth that one is all and all is one," as well as to achieve esoteric Tibetan Buddhist states resembling Zen enlightenment, or satori. He also had various "*bardo* experiences," states of consciousness somewhere between this world and the afterlife, including "the transition from life to death," though he did not succeed in "going from death to reincarnation" (a step described, he said, by the Dalai Lama). But he claimed to have experienced most of the forms of emptiness and possibly to have been bathed in "clear light" (though he was not certain on this point)—all of which represented highly advanced states much discussed in *The Tibetan Book of the Dead.*

Yano underwent a typical psychological sequence in which his attraction to the guru provided a powerful stimulus for his mystical states that, in turn, deepened his attachment. He could insist with others that "My dedication to Asahara was based on my own experiences." But there was another important pattern, strong in him and probably present in most other former Aum members: a sense of pride or omnipotence in sharing the guru's power, accompanied by an equally strong sense of incompleteness and inadequacy because, whatever one's spiritual progress, there was always an elusive pinnacle one could not reach. That sense of incompleteness in the face of the guru's imagined perfection left Yano vulnerable to endless self-condemnation, to shame and guilt, and to anxiety about death associated with doubts about the quality of his next rebirth.

Spiritually involved to the degree he was, it was inevitable that Yano would become a monk. But for a married man to do so, Aum's rules required that either his wife and children join him in worldly renunciation or he resort to divorce, which Yano did. One may say that he chose guru worship and mystical experiences over his family life, despite his devotion to that family.

Another example of his struggle with incompleteness—that is, his struggle with guruism—occurred during a special seminar when he made a vow to distribute a hundred thousand Aum flyers. After distributing sixty thousand of them he developed "a bad feeling" and was unable to fulfill his vow. At that point, "I felt a strong pressure in my head coming from above." At first he thought this represented the guru's anger, but he came to believe that it was instead the guru's *shaktipat*, or energy empowerment. With his sudden understanding that the guru was personally liberating his energy, "it became very easy for me to complete the vow and to distribute the remaining forty thousand flyers." Only the guru's transmission of "life-power" could overcome Yano's sense of incompletion. He experienced this empowerment as another form of healing, even though such healing invariably proved temporary.

The pattern recurred, for instance, when Yano undertook "extreme practice," in which he and thirteen other disciples engaged in a particularly intensive combination of meditation and "standing worship," or continuous prostration: "We were supposed to stand up and throw ourselves down a hundred thousand times. But I did it just ten thousand times and then I got stuck. I had difficulty completing it." While some people, including his immediate superior, gave him encouragement, Asahara "did the opposite." He said "ambiguous things," such as, "So that's the way it is" and "It can't be helped." He had Yano sent to a small containment cell, where Yano pursued his spiritual practice for two months, with mixed results. "I did go into the light several times, but it was no use, because I would then go back into darkness." He now sees himself as having experienced "thirstlike desire" for his children and his wife, an "attachment" to them that meant "I couldn't help escaping." Feeling his own "defilement," he left the facility and made his way back to his family. When Aum representatives appeared to urge him to return to the group, Yano said he would do so "only if Asahara would come and get me." As Yano had by this time become a leading figure in Aum's business dealings, the guru did send high disciples. They succeeded in convincing Yano that "it was not too late" for him to achieve the spiritual level he yearned for, while also appealing to his responsibility to the guru and to the people who worked under him. The mixed reception his wife gave him played a part in his decision to return to the group.

Yano was undoubtedly even more confused than his account suggests. He was experiencing considerable ambivalence toward the guru, and his insistence that Asahara bring him back can be understood as combining grandiosity, resistance, and a wish to deepen his subservient union with the guru.

Over the course of his involvement with Aum, Yano had taken on increasing administrative responsibility, guiding other disciples and also running several of Aum's many business enterprises. During the period of his maximum involvement, Asahara would call him every other day, asking him informally, "How's it going?" ("*Dō da?*") In describing these calls to me, he imitated the guru's voice in tones that were loud, affectionate, humorous, and a bit mocking—reflecting his many-sided perceptions of Asahara, but especially the deep pleasure and awe he experienced from this regular contact with the voice of a near deity.

Yet in a crucial late encounter with the guru, Yano held back. In early 1995, he was summoned by Asahara, who asked him this question: "Do you know what 'the good' is?" As Yano described it, "I knew what I should have answered, what I was supposed to answer. I was to say that 'the good' is to obey the guru's order. But instead I said, 'I do not know.' " Asahara burst into derisive laughter and said, "Is that so? Maybe you should be the manager of a karaoke bar." Soon afterward Yano was transferred from Tokyo to a provincial city. He is now convinced that the guru was giving him a "loyalty test" before assigning him to "secret work"—that is, illegal activities of some sort.

When I asked him what he might have been assigned to do had he given the right answer, Yano suggested a possible role in the subsequent kidnapping of Kiyoshi Kariya, the notary public who was killed by Aum doctors. The guru, he speculated, "wanted to decide what I should be assigned to do. It was a kind of personnel management decision on his part."

Even at the time, Yano knew—or at least sensed—what the guru's question signified, for it turned out that he had earlier received an order from the guru to take someone into custody—an order, he said, that he regarded as "strange" and that he managed to avoid carrying out. He undoubtedly came upon additional evidence of Aum's violent tendencies, possibly including its weapons stockpiling, all of which he evidently fended off or numbed himself to. He found it remarkable that, given his high status in the cult, he was never ordered to do "secret work." (Probably some of his doubts were detected.) I gained the impression that he had done much psychological work to avoid acknowledging to himself the destructive nature of the secret work that was going on all around him.

Yano's experiences convey the powerful healing component of extreme guruism along with the complexity and depth of the guru-disciple connection. Yano recalled moments of distrust of Asahara, including an early "intuition that something was wrong, that his eyes looked strange." But given the pressures and appeals of the Aum environment, "I interpreted such intuitions as evidence of my defilement." One may speak here of a taboo ambivalence: critical feelings occur and, if not quickly suppressed, are attributed to personal badness or "defilement." In this totalistic pattern of "doctrine over person," the disciple feels impelled to intensify efforts at absolute devotion for reasons of both external display and inner purification. Looking back, Yano could call Asahara "a pathetic being who utilized his disciples to express his revenge against society" and who manipulated them by preaching Armageddon. But having said this, Yano could not quite bring himself to directly condemn Asahara or Aum.

Discussing his continuing Buddhist practice, Yano told me that "in Shin Buddhism there is a paradox. Bad people may be closest to the Pure Land and may have a real moment of salvation. So perhaps we can say that Asahara is the one closest to the Pure Land." Given the range of destructive actions that take place in the world, "Aum was no big deal," he also said, expressing not only his continuing tie to Asahara but his need to diminish any sense of personal culpability for Aum's crimes. Like that of Isoda and a number of others, his identification with Asahara included an embrace of the guru's grandiosity. Thus he derided people who "look at these matters from a common-sense standpoint" and who fail to see "the paradox [that] Buddhist nihilism is the real core of Aum doctrine." While that comment has a kernel of truth, it was part of a cosmic philosophical stance that enabled Yano to speak critically of the guru and yet reassert, at least in part, the guru's claim to higher mystical purposes. In this way, Yano remained under the spell of his "healing" experience.

The Psychotherapist

Nakano had been interested in the occult since childhood and had even practiced a bit of yoga in his teens. At the age of eighteen, he left his home in a small provincial city to attend a university in Kyoto. The loneliness that followed was, for him, an experience of "a new kind of silence." In the home he had come from, there was an active family life and "someone was constantly making noise of one kind or another," but in the house where he lived as a student, "unless I myself did something, there was no sound at all." When he met with a friend from high school who had joined Aum, he was impressed by the intensity and absoluteness of his friend's new convictions and awed by his description of the ability of ascetic spiritual practice to bring meaning into one's life and enable one to acquire "supernatural power." Nakano expressed interest in Aum and agreed to meet with a "realized person," who, unlike Nakano's friend, did not overwhelm him with a set of beliefs but listened to him carefully and encouraged him to ask questions.

Feeling appreciated and understood, Nakano readily agreed to the suggestion that he try Aum for a six-month period (a suggestion frequently made by Aum recruiters). As he became involved with various Aum spiritual practices, he maintained his willingness to "try" whatever was offered. He became passively receptive ("I just did the practices I was told to do. I didn't think about what they meant") and imitative ("I followed what I saw others doing"). His immersion was both rapid and cumulative. At the beginning of a particularly intense sequence (the "one-hundred-hour practice") he thought that repeated listening to the guru singing songs was "kind of silly," but by the end he "was listening without any feelings of resistance."

He experienced a "turning point" when his immersion began to conflict with his university work. He went back to the same spiritual adviser, the "realized person," and described troublesome sexual urges and a continuous appetite for food (both of which one was supposed to overcome through spiritual practice), along with a sense of lethargy and general loss of interest in life. The adviser told him that he had "fallen into his subconscious" and that his "subconscious desire for food and sex was emerging." But the adviser also assured him that he had already made up his mind concerning his conflict: his very symptoms were an indication that he inwardly desired Aum's ascetic practices. "Moved" by these words, Nakano agreed and a few months later become a monk.

This was an example of Aum's application of "therapeutic" skills in its recruitment and general organizational maintenance. The adviser demonstrated these skills in encouraging his "patient" to make (or seem to make) his own choice, but he did so from within Aum's definition of psychological health and only with the goal of binding Nakano ever more strongly to the cult rather than of enhancing his personal strength and autonomy, as a proper therapist would do. In the same fashion, the adviser-therapist "helped" Nakano resolve severe conflicts he was experiencing with his parents, who opposed the cult, by contrasting the painful situation he faced at home with the receptivity and understanding he experienced in Aum.

Until he became a monk, Nakano had looked upon Asahara as a "distant figure who talked to us in one-way traffic." Now, however, the guru became a presence, a powerful figure with whom he felt more directly involved and whose focus on Armageddon seemed to strengthen his hold on Nakano. Nonetheless, Nakano had moments of wavering. At one point he had another talk with his adviser, who urged him to intensify his religious practice because he had "a special spiritual talent." From these words Nakano experienced what he called a "startling illumination."

But Nakano's most powerful "psychotherapy" came from none other than the guru himself. He was experiencing difficulty with a work assignment, a sense of spiritual stagnation, overall confusion about his life in Aum, and feelings of depression and worthlessness. His immediate superior arranged for him and two others with similar problems to meet Asahara. The guru, in the brief remarks he directed at Nakano, said, "Little is gained by doing what you are good at. What is most important is to do something that is difficult for you." For the first time, Ogawa experienced the full realization of being a true Aum *shukke*, along with "sheer pleasure that he met with me personally." He remembers telling others in Aum that he had "gained power" and "energy" from the guru, influenced, as he told me, by the idea that this was what was supposed to happen.

Six months later he had a more profound encounter with Asahara. He was having stronger doubts about Aum and suspected that "something was wrong"—among other things, that the work he was doing with complex machinery could be connected to the production of weaponry. Unable either to work or to meditate, he was also having difficulty suppressing his sexual desire. He was masturbating frequently, thereby violating an Aum rule against ejaculation. One day he fled his work assignment for another Aum facility. He explained that "by escaping I wanted to attract their attention," which he did. Asahara met with him again. This time the guru spoke to him at slightly greater length, indicating that he knew that Nakano was thinking of going back to the university and changing his course of study there. He even referred indirectly to something Nakano had considered a personal secret, that an attraction to a young Aum woman had been a factor in his becoming a monk.

Though Nakano understood that Asahara might have access to some personal information about him, he was nonetheless "surprised" and "shocked" by the guru's knowledge of, and interest in, these personal details. He was awed as well that theirs was close to a real exchange. "We were sort of discussing things, not just my listening to him." Inevitably he credited the guru's omniscience. Asahara, Nakano thought, "guessed what ordinarily could not be guessed and understood everything about my mind." Losing "any will to resist," he wanted "only to bow to him, only to follow him." He also felt affirmed by Asahara's emphasis on the strong karmic connection between them—which for Nakano still exists. "At that time he was looked upon as Buddha, and I thought our connection was one between Buddha and his disciple. Now I feel that he was not Buddha but rather someone I've met often in the cycle of reincarnation. Maybe in a past life we did spiritual practice together."

Yet he soon found himself "melancholic" again. His ambivalence toward Asahara—a common feeling among Aum disciples—came to be dramatized for him in an LSD-induced vision he experienced as part of an initiation procedure:

You may find this very contradictory, but in my hallucination Asahara appeared many times. I sensed much more strongly the karmic connection between him and myself. In that hallucination I felt that I had betrayed him many, many times in past lives. I felt that ours was more than just a pure master-disciple relationship. The hallucination lasted over ten hours. When I woke from it I kept crying, "Master! Master!" It was such an intense experience that when I woke up from it I felt empty.

Ogawa was left with a sense of a negative, or "contrary," tie to the guru and a vision of betrayal that "made me think I might betray him again. In a way, I put that thought into practice." His trusted immediate superior was not available to discuss these matters so "I decided to run away. I often explain to other people that I quit Aum specifically because I liked Asahara." I believe he was saying that he had begun to perceive many things dangerously wrong with Aum and its guru, perceptions that had been muted by Asahara's strong influence over him; perhaps, too, he wanted to leave before his sense of the guru became more tarnished. As the guru's hold was intensified by the "psychotherapy," he felt himself both moved and threatened. The LSD experience enabled him to begin to articulate to himself, in Buddhist terms, the fierceness of the negative side of his ambivalence and something of its self-protective aspect. But by invoking imagery of betrayal, as did a number of other Aum members I spoke to, he was revealing a considerable dimension of self-blame, of guilt over his break with and flight from a guru with whom he felt such profound karmic ties.

The Erotic Guru

There were many dimensions of the erotic in Shōkō Asahara's guruism. Male mergings with the guru could contain a homoerotic component, but the erotic currents in the guru-disciple relationship were more directly experienced and articulated by female disciples. Harada, for instance, brought to Asahara and Aum a hunger for a messiah. Influenced by her reading of Nostradamus, she thought that such a messiah could well be Japanese. "I don't know why, but my heart was telling me to find a messiah and I thought a messiah was coming."

Asahara soon became that messiah, existing in her mind not only as a holy, godlike entity but also, from her early encounters with him, as a wise and caring human guide: "He seemed to understand everything about me, smiling and saying to me that [Aum's ascetic life] must be hard for me. He seemed to understand the meaning of my being reborn into this human world. He said that I had a mission. He was really like a father of the soul. He touched my heart." For her the guru was earthy and "modest" in his attitude. His ideas seemed "simple and powerful," so easily understood that "everything he said made sense to me." When that feeling of personal closeness was no longer possible because of Aum's rapid expansion, Asahara became a more distant figure for her, which made her feel "lonely all the time."

On joining the cult, she had been greatly affected by Aum's "astral music," the guru's composition from "a higher astral world." After becoming a *shukke*, she "graduated from astral music" to trance-like chanting of the guru's mantra, which resounded everywhere about her. In this way the guru's music continued to inhabit her in a more "advanced" manifestation. She had a series of intense mystical experiences that took the form of dazzling white lights, the first after drinking "nectar water" said to have been "energized" by the guru. Subjected to demanding routines of extremely intense breathing, focused meditation, continuous chanting, and holding the lotus position for long periods of time, even while sleeping, she felt herself "deeply immersed in showers of lights." When a high disciple informed her that "Master said you have had special experiences," her awe of the guru deepened. She became convinced that "Master can understand everything, like a god or Buddha." She was also aware of competition from other disciples for signs of the guru's favor and intensified her spiritual pursuits and work efforts with the sense that "Master is always looking over me."

She experienced Aum as a spiritual pyramid, a mind-reading hierarchy, with the guru sitting at the apex ("providing a ladder to a higher world"), and top disciples just below him, with those at each level able to command absolute power over and obedience from those at the next level down. "Master can tell his top disciples directly exactly what they think; they have powers to read the minds of ordinary disciples." In this way, every Aum member "experiences supernatural power."

Asahara's power was transmitted both through Aum's comprehensive teachings, which for Harada "explained and justified everything," and through direct personal experiences of mystical transcendence that confirmed for her the truth of the guru's claims. Both these dimensions of the cult were deepened by her experience of the perfect salvation initiation. In her case she wore the headgear throughout a four-month initiation period. She was convinced that she was experiencing the guru's brain waves, which were "very flat, like a dead person's." Her own mind, she felt, became "flat" and "calm," so that she no longer had disturbing dreams dominated by intense memories of family life and vivid sexual images ("manifestations of all my desires").

Her sexual longings were, in fact, redirected to the guru. "I fell in love with him. I really did. So it was as if I was always waiting for my lover to call on me. It felt like a one-sided love." As she put it, "I was totally attracted to Master—to his character, his speech, his voice, his teaching." This was true, she added, of many of his female disciples, some of whom could become quite jealous of one another. "Oh, she is very close to Master. Why?" Harada quoted them as saying. "Because she's beautiful, that's why." Harada was aware of and could even accept the guru's manipulation of such feelings "because he was using them spiritually to guide people to higher stages." Her understanding of the principle of merging with the guru was highly sexualized. "His teaching says that we must always be conscious of uniting with the guru, and if you are conscious always in that [sexual] way, then you can attain a higher stage more quickly." Sexual images were perceived as integral to Aum's version of Tantric practice: "I would visualize Master and consider myself to be like a consort. And then we would merge. When I did that, my energy would sharply rise. That [energy surge] really happened and that's why it was wonderful. Whenever my energy was a bit down I would do that. My body would tremble and then my body would jump. It was a very happy feeling. That's why we came to believe Master to be really powerful." She could call forth such erotic imagery no matter how far from the guru she might be (as during a trip she made with other Aum members to Europe) and experience the same bodily pleasure.

While in Aum she heard about and approved of the guru's Tantric sexual initiations of young women. "As I believed Master was a Buddha, I thought it was a wonderful initiation to get from Buddha because of its energy." She said that she could actually feel something close to what these initiated women experienced, even if it was "only imagination." Yet she recognized that her experience was "similar to sexual orgasm" and compared it to what she had been taught in Kundalinī yoga about the movement of sexual energy from the pelvis upward in a process of spiritualization or sublimation. She emphasized that "we do not discharge" but rather "raise our energy" so intensely that it feels like "union with a god, like union with the Buddha." She greatly missed this kind of experience in her post-Aum life and sometimes still found herself, more or less against her will, imagining erotic merger with the guru and experiencing bodily tremors.

Guru Magic

Akiya had long been deeply involved in matters occult and mystical and was impressed by Asahara's claim to both enlightenment and supernatural power. He considered the faked photograph showing Asahara levitating to be "proof" of high spiritual achievement. Joining Aum in its earliest days, he had immediate access to the guru and their first encounter was decisive.

Asahara told him that, in terms of the bodily energy centers, or chakra, of Kundalinī yoga, "you are strong at the top of the head but weak at the forehead." Akiya was astounded because he had been aware of such forehead "weakness" in the Taoist meditation he had previously practiced. Soon afterward Asahara performed *shaktipat*, transferring energy to Akiya by touching him on the forehead. "I immediately felt warm," he reported, "saw a bright light, and experienced his energy shooting up my spine like a snake crawling on it or something flowing." After that, he had similar mystical experiences in his own spiritual practice. All this affirmed for him the "reality" of Asahara's special powers and Akiya came to think of him as "a great teacher" who possessed "profound knowledge and experience" in spiritual practices, enabling a disciple like Akiya to deepen and extend his own spiritual awareness.

Akiya now feels that a significant change was taking place in Asahara himself. According to him, Asahara had invited an Indian holy man whom he considered his mentor to come to Japan to take part in Aum practice. The guru had planned to have this holy man demonstrate a type of *samādhi*, an advanced state of consciousness in which mental activity is said to cease. The holy man was to perform "underwater *samādhi*," remaining alive for a week in a closed water tank by suspending his heartbeat and breathing. According to Akiya, though, he was weakened by offering *shaktipat* to members of an Aum seminar and, with his spiritual state deteriorating, became visibly attracted to some of the women in the cult. The underwater *samādhi* had to be canceled.

Because of his mentor's failure, Akiya said, Asahara developed the sense that "I alone can lead my disciples." With disciples offering praise and adulation at every turn,

> he could come to believe: "I am a great person." Since he felt he had achieved final enlightenment, he could not make a mistake. And even if it was a mistake, he could never correct it. He insisted that he was right and the disciples believed him. As a result there could be no criticism of his interpretations and teachings and he began to create a system in which it is always Asahara who is right.

This totalization of guruism, moreover, could be accepted—indeed embraced—because disciples like Akiya seemed to prosper:

> My mind changed greatly. I felt more relaxed and more pure. I experienced a form of self-awareness, of having become better. I became happy and wanted to convey this feeling to others, to let them know about this happiness.

But absolute guruism was accompanied by the increasing urgency associated with Armageddon. Akiya remembered the 1986 sermon in which Asahara declared that "Japan would sink into the ocean, there would be a third great war, and the world would end." It was with what Akiya called the "great prophecy seminar" at Ishigaki Island that the urgency became more pronounced. Akiya remembered it as chaotic, everything hastily arranged. "We must save people quickly" was the message. It was always "Hurry, hurry!" Akiya was deeply impressed with the guru's personal intensity. "You could feel his desire. In order to study Nostradamus, he went to France, searched for the original books, then developed his own interpretation." (In actuality, Asahara sent disciples to France but Akiya's version conveys a sense of the guru's Armageddon-linked passion.)

Akiya ascribed great importance both to the responses of the disciples to Asahara and to the guru's capacity to "move the people who were around him, so that what was originally just a flash of an idea, just an image or a vision, began"—thanks to those responses—"to gain greater reality." In return, Asahara felt bolstered in his vision and "became more assured until finally he himself believed it." The process never ceased, because "people were so eager to believe." The guru's predictions, like the rest of his behavior, depended on the evolving reality of the continuous guru-disciple interaction.

Asahara's style of guruism enabled him to slip past his own inconsistencies. For instance, when asked why he needed to use astrology if his prophetic visions were fully accurate, he answered that astrology could add precision to his basic truths. When the emperor did not die as the guru had predicted, he pointed out that the emperor's brother had and that the two so resembled each other as to be confused in his vision. When disasters occurred that he had not predicted or there were other inaccuracies in his predictions, he would say something like, "There is even more bad karma in the world than I realized." And whatever explanation he offered, his disciples eagerly accepted it, reflecting that acceptance back to him in such a way that his most obvious errors came to have a strange kind of prophetic truth. In that sense, while his followers strived to be his clones, he himself became, in large part, their creation. The more tenuous the interaction, the more extreme the guruism.

"As Asahara's personality became too big a presence," Akiya explained, "whatever this large presence wanted had to be achieved." Even those who had originally come to Aum's yoga classes seeking gentle forms of spiritual improvement now "became trapped in the idea of salvation"—salvation as defined by the attack guruism that emerged from the guru-disciple dynamic. As Akiya observed, "If you claim ultimate truth, anything can be justified, everything can be permitted," especially when "the time span addressed is not, say, a hundred years but tens of thousands, hundreds of millions, thousands of millions of years. So that if a terrible incident takes place in this transitional phase, it can be viewed as something that is right in this larger span of time." The magic of a world-ending guru, that is, can extend into the infinite past and the infinite future.

The power of such guruism is conveyed by a former disciple of the Indian guru Bhagwan Shree Rajneesh (who, preaching sexual liberation in the early 1980s, attracted converts from throughout the world to a ranch commune in Oregon, where some of them eventually became involved in disseminating bacteria that resulted in a local salmonella outbreak). Describing the state of "true bliss and abundant joy" he experienced in Rajneesh's group, the disciple comments, "Those who dismiss 'evil cults' have no idea at all how rapturous this state can be and how no other pleasure can compare with it." The experience of Aum members suggests that it is indeed a state that can become addictive. As the former Rajneesh disciple puts it, "Most people who have spent any time in a religious cult will have tasted this bliss and it is what keeps them coming back for more." It is also what the philosopher William James calls the "joy which may result . . . from absolute self-surrender." He describes the sense of truth that such a religious experience offers as "*super*-lucent, *super*-splendent, *super*-essential, *super*-sublime, *super everything* that can be named." That experience of joyous transcendence must involve both parties in what the social scientist Charles Lindholm terms "the ecstatic merger of leader and follower."

In earlier work I describe this state of experiential transcendence as so intense and all-encompassing that in it time and death disappear. Human beings have always sought such states, whether through religious or secular mysticism, often with the help of cultural rites, drugs, oxygen deficit (through rapid breathing), sleep deprivation, or some other form of imposed ordeal. But they can also be experienced in more familiar activities such as song, dance, battle, sexual love, childbirth, athletic effort, mechanical flight, and artistic or intellectual creation. All these activities are marked by a sense of both extraordinary psychic unity and ineffable illumination and insight. The self feels uniquely alive—connected, active, integrated—and in touch with larger, cosmic forces. All traditional cultures have provided opportunities for, and made space for, the experience of transcendence, but in the postmodern world such opportunities seem diminished or marginalized. The hunger for them, however, remains and becomes bound up with our myriad confusions. Gurus and disciples can draw upon contemporary and ancient cultural elements to create rituals for orchestrated experiences of transcendence, thereby creating a bond that allows for group-sanctioned action, including violence, even murder.

Close study of the Aum experience tells us that guru, disciple, and the bond between them are all more complex than usually described. Shōkō Asahara was simultaneously dignified, ascetic, empathic, supportive, wise, spiritually genuine, innovative, pragmatic, childish, inconsistent, fraudulent, manipulative, gluttonous, promiscuous, exploitative, duplicitous, grandiose, schizoid, paranoid, delusional, megalomanic, and murderous. His disciples were ecstatic, divinely energized, reflective, calm, harmonious with others, self-negating, passionately submissive, ambivalent, self-divided, profoundly anxious (about their standing with the guru and their next rebirth), death-obsessed, antagonistic (not only toward society but toward the guru and one another), intensely competitive (with other disciples for the guru's recognition), desirous of escaping suffocation by the guru, grandiose, and violent. In both guru and disciples, we may encounter forms of doubling, one self bound to totalistic guruism and the other subversive of guruism in some tabooed fashion. The absoluteness of guruism, then, has to be asserted ever more vehemently to suppress these tabooed inclinations—to suppress, that is, the underlying ambivalence inherent in the guru-disciple relationship. Groups like Aum become particularly dangerous when that bond is under stress.

5 | The Ecstatic Science

The Nazis mandated a policy of reconstituting the professions in ways that contributed to their movement. They called this policy *Gleichschaltung*, which means "coordination" or "synchronization" and also connotes the mechanical idea of shifting gears. Whatever Aum's differences from the Nazis, it followed a parallel principle. Its members were required not to give up their professions but rather to reconstitute them in Aum's image. One did not have to cease being a physicist, chemist, engineer, physician, lawyer, architect, musician, designer, artist, scholar, businessman, police investigator, or military man; the point instead was to bring a radical Aum perspective to whatever professional work one did.

For instance, Yano, the businessman who experienced Asahara's healing power, was assigned to corporate and administrative tasks within Aum that utilized his business experience. Kiyohide Hayakawa, who had a background in engineering and architecture, was made minister of construction and put in charge of acquiring land, building cult facilities, and developing Aum's technology, especially its high-tech weapons. A professional designer I talked to, in addition to his other activities in Aum, designed many of its books and pamphlets. An animator worked on Aum's films. There were talented musicians who played at Aum concerts or helped compose the "astral music" attributed to the guru, just as there were scholars and students of religion who helped write and translate the guru's books and pamphlets.

Professionals, intellectuals, and university students could be drawn to Aum's unusual array of concepts and doctrines. What now seems—even to most of them—simplistic and extreme was experienced by many, during the cult's most active days, as admirably systematic, inclusive, visionary, and yet reasonable. They found in Aum not only a spiritual home but an opportunity to use their talents or knowledge within an oppositional subculture.

Asahara held out this opportunity to scientists in particular. In a lecture at a science-oriented university in Tokyo in 1992, he spoke of the advantages of conducting science and technology research in an environment like Aum Shinrikyō, as opposed to universities or private corporations, and boasted of Aum's investment of several million dollars a year in such research. Asahara's quest for scientists was inseparable from his weapons hunger. But he also wanted to affirm his religious absolutes with equally absolute scientific claims. That project required a "sacred science." As evidenced in his attempt to confirm the experiences of the Buddhist saints, "sacred science" blended Asahara's limited knowledge with his customary grandiosity and his con man's urge toward mystification and high-toned mumbo jumbo. In one Aum publication, he wrote in typical style: "With the help of instruments like the Astral Teleporter, which faithfully reproduces the vibration of my mantra through electric signals; a device that awakens Kundalinī through magnetic fields; an FET [Field Effect Transistor], which correctly reads waves sent out by each chakra; an electroencephalograph connected to a computer; and so on, I have finally succeeded in scientifically verifying the teachings of the saints of the past, especially those of Buddha Sakyamuni."

Included were extensive diagrams showing brain waves (electroencephalogram recordings) that culminated in the desired "flat waves" of the guru (ostensibly transmitted to disciples in the perfect salvation initiation). In the book, he claimed to demonstrate scientifically Aum's achievements in consciousness and offered a short course in brain physiology along with discussions of epilepsy and schizophrenia. Interspersed with such material were descriptions of esoteric Buddhist doctrine at a how-to level ("You can become a Buddha"). The whole exercise was guided by the principle that "to gain a good understanding of the astral world we need to see how far contemporary physiology has studied and understood the brain." Some of the information may have been scientifically accurate, as Aum did establish laboratories for scientists working on brain waves, but the work was always subsumed by Aum's spiritual visions and quickly became distorted by them or by dreams of producing fantastic weapons of mass destruction.

Such scientific claims, however, could be deeply persuasive and comforting to disciples. As Harada, who was in Aum for five years, explained when talking about the perfect salvation initiation and other experiences, "They had a scientific approach. We were always told there was scientific proof. We didn't doubt it." Science was invariably invoked in Aum's attempt to accelerate enlightenment and salvation. The weapons Aum science was to produce had the same purpose. In the remaking of humanity, science and technology were to be indispensable.

Science and "Serene Madness"

Hideo Murai, the minister of science and technology, was the exemplary Aum scientist. A bizarre but revelatory figure, Murai was described by one former disciple as "Aum's number-two man, if there was a number-two man," and by another as "Asahara's brain." He was generally seen as totally subservient to the guru, or as yet another former disciple put it, "able to become completely empty and then be filled with the guru's intentions." But others spoke of an opposite flow, of Murai's strong influence on Asahara. What seems to have taken place was a kind of ongoing dialogue between the two men in which the guru would suggest, sometimes on the spur of the moment, a wildly visionary scientific project and Murai would quickly respond with an absolute commitment to carry out that project. A disciple who had considerable contact with Murai explained that "Asahara was very interested in connecting the spiritual world with contemporary science. He would talk about something as it came to his mind. Then Murai would suggest an option or plan that might be possible. Then Asahara would say: 'OK, why don't you try that?' Murai then did his best to create something very close to that proposal." Both men, the observer continued, were bent on "turning outrageous ideas into feasible projects" and using science to make the spiritual "more rational, more modern." As others expressed it, "It was Murai who seriously tried to realize Asahara's casual ideas, which were like delusions" or "Murai tried to materialize everything the master ordered"—and did so with a "serene madness," a fanatical calm even greater than that of the guru.

This "dialogue" reflected at the highest level of the cult the same dynamic that animated the least prominent of Asahara's followers—the mutual reinforcement of guru and disciples. Although Asahara's will held sway, one should not minimize the contributions made by Murai to the guru's project of "scientific spirituality." The situation is reminiscent of dialogues certain Nazi doctors carried on with Heinrich Himmler (who himself represented the Führer's overall vision). Himmler would suggest desirable "scientific" goals (proving Nordic superiority, sterilizing inferior peoples) that the doctors would then try to realize through "research projects" and as the dialogue continued, the doctors themselves would provide original suggestions for projects that Himmler would then take up and sponsor as if they had been his own.

Murai was considered "one of the busiest people in Aum," with a hand in every scientific or technological contribution to personal enlightenment or weapons creation. Under his charge, administrative and intellectual, were such efforts as the study of brain waves, the perfect salvation initiation (said to have been his idea), computer improvements for gaining access to technical information, and the scientific and technological programs for making, stockpiling, and using automatic, chemical, and biological weapons and for exploring the possibility of obtaining nuclear weapons.

Crucial to the Murai-Asahara dialogue was Murai's absolute conversion to Aum. Even by Aum standards, Murai's discipleship was, as one former member put it, "extraordinary, . . . almost scary." No disciple was as self-negating in his devotion to his guru, so much so that Asahara frequently singled him out, publicly praising him for giving himself over so completely to the guru's will. Beyond his scientific duties, Murai paid scrupulous attention to the dyeing process for the special purple silk robes that Asahara wore as his religious uniform, and he labored to create a special round cushion that could float in the air so as "to enable the master to appear as if he had a halo behind his head." Despite his high rank, Murai would demonstrate his asceticism by eating leftovers or choosing the most uncomfortable bunk when he visited a cult facility. Aum members thought him saintly and Asahara once called him "the only disciple who has reached the realm of the gods." He was perhaps the only disciple who, as the young scientist Hirota put it, "knew the entire scheme"—by which he meant the whole constellation of Aum, including its weapons development, its violent acts, and its public deceptions.

The fantasy science that emanated from the Murai-Asahara dialogue owed much to the work of the Croatian-born scientist Nikola Tesla, or at least to Tesla's work as embraced by Aum. A towering figure in the development of electricity who became an American citizen in 1891, Tesla made many brilliant discoveries, especially in his studies of high-voltage phenomena, inventing—among other things—the Tesla coil, still of considerable importance for radio, television, and various forms of wireless communication. He was also an eccentric character, histrionic, visionary, and given to flights of scientific fantasy that sometimes involved the creation of weapons of ultimate destruction. He once referred, for instance, to a discovery that could "destroy anything, men or machines, approaching within a radius of two hundred miles," recommending it as "a wall of power offering an insuperable obstacle against any effective aggression." His attraction, from Aum's viewpoint, is self-evident. Of particular interest to Aum was a statement he made to the effect that one could create voltage of such intensity that it would divide or polarize portions of the earth, resulting in a devastating effect resembling an earthquake. In a similar vein he boasted that he was capable of splitting the earth in two "as a boy would split an apple—and forever end the career of man." His work so fascinated Aum that a delegation was sent to Belgrade to visit the Tesla museum there, and Murai went to great lengths to collect any writings by or about him. Long depicted in Japan as an ingenious mad scientist, Tesla had special appeal for Murai, Hirota speculated, precisely because he himself was one.

The mad scientist responded with alacrity to his guru's most far-fetched demands. At one point Asahara told him that he wanted "a metal lighter than air." It was theoretically possible to create such a substance was Murai's instant reply. "I can make it." Murai even catered to the guru's fantasy of transcending Earth's gravity by somehow tapping the gravitational pull of the sun and the moon in a way that might enhance spiritual emancipation. But the best Murai could do was to invent a revolving bed that ostensibly achieved an advantageous relationship to gravity. The project was discontinued after Murai eventually concluded that the bed "would make one dizzy." Murai could repeatedly violate the most basic aspects of his own scientific training because for him the guru's divine omniscience, which included scientific knowledge, superceded anything he had previously known. Thus when Asahara announced that he had found a fallacy in Einstein's theory of relativity, Murai's comment was, "Master has long surpassed Einstein."

The dark side—and it was extremely dark—of Murai's "serene madness" was his plunge into weapons of mass destruction, as well as his direct involvement in various murders and in the cremation of the victims' bodies. Undoubtedly under the influence of Tesla, he and Asahara also talked about creating a ten-trillion-volt electrical current probably meant for use with imagined laser weapons, which Asahara believed would be more powerful than nuclear devices. As minister of science and technology, Murai oversaw work done by others in producing not only Aum's weapons but illegal drugs like LSD and a barbiturate-based "truth serum," and even an electroshock apparatus meant to erase memory.

While other Aum scientists and doctors played major roles in these projects, Murai was the ultimate scientific authority—which, given the results, suggests that even considerable ability in practical applications of science may coexist with immense doses of fantasy. He was also capable of becoming Asahara-like in his charismatic authority and prophetic desires. "I want the present world, which is so full of pain, to be extinguished," he once said. For him any Aum act, however violent, was profoundly justified because, as one cult member remembers him saying, "Aum occupies holy space while the present world is a garbage dump."

Murai's leadership, like Asahara's, had two faces. Some disciples remembered him as approachable, honest, kind, and considerate. But one man who joined Aum before Murai told me of the contradictions in his behavior: "To me and other senior followers he was always smiling and gentle, a good person. To his subordinates, he gave outrageous orders in order to realize Asahara's outrageous ideas. To them he was out of control and imperious." Another man, who worked under Murai, described him warmly as a thoughtful and caring person but ultimately "beyond my understanding, a mystery." Among some relatively high-ranking Aum members, however, Murai was less a mystery than a pathetic figure, a "clown" who could rarely even come close to succeeding in his many bizarre projects. At times Asahara shared this judgment, despite his own part in creating these projects. The guru, after trying on an "electric hat" that wouldn't stay on his head, laughed loudly and said sarcastically, "Well done. You spend a lot of money but you cannot make practical things." Yet Murai brought a charismatic energy to even the maddest of these projects.

In a sense, Murai, Asahara, and all Aum members, in fact, were involved in a form of perverse play that contained odd and dangerous combinations of fantasy and actuality. There was, for example, the Battle Cry [Otakebi] Cultural Festival it held during the summer of 1994. In one musical drama celebrating Murai's ministry's successful manufacture of "a powerful weapon," soldiers of the Truth [Shinri, as in Aum Shinrikyō] Army, led by Murai, excitedly welded pieces of iron on stage, using actual burners, while large numbers of "enemies" advanced on them. Murai shouted, "We must hurry. We don't have much time left!" as they constructed a huge slingshot with which they shot a ball into the ranks of their enemies, annihilating them. Then Murai himself sang a song entitled "Reborn into a Higher World."

The weapon being celebrated was not identified but the drama took place soon after the Matsumoto sarin attack, and those most responsible for producing the gas were featured in the play. (That same summer Murai was promoted to the highest rank of disciples, and others involved in "secret" and "dangerous" work were also promoted for their "pious act.") At the festival's awards ceremony, Asahara declared: "War is inevitable. We will make survival kits and distribute them to all disciples."

Of course, it is not unusual for movements of all kinds to create dramas celebrating their achievements or their military and spiritual power. But one is struck by the degree to which the entire Aum process was enmeshed in fantasy, so that Murai, the hero, was simultaneously the leading actor in the play, the leading scientific planner of mass murder, and the leading accumulator of virtue. We know that, even in play, Aum was deadly serious. Yet there is a suggestion here of a kind of dual consciousness, an awareness of putting on an imaginative "play" while at the same time acting out an earnest, near-literal depiction of the Aum warrior project. Somewhat similarly, the participants in a Balinese dance ceremony experience horror and fear as they struggle against a powerful monster but know as well that they are engaged in a form of play, serious in itself but distinct from ordinary life. Aum, however, broke down this distinction by eschewing most ritual tradition—and finally by aggressively enacting its fantasies. Murai, like others in Aum, could switch back and forth between playful transcendence and actual intent, or experience them simultaneously in ways that enhanced the cult's hermetic behavior and unfeeling violence. In that sense, all of Aum can be seen as a form of unrestrained play, and the exchange between Murai and Asahara as, in the words of one disciple, "scenes from some kind of comic dialogue."

How does one become a scientist with "serene madness"? What we know of Murai's background hardly provides a complete explanation, but a few factors do stand out. Murai was always a brilliant student, a "genius type" who deeply impressed his teachers and would patiently explain to fellow students the solutions to problems that seemed to them insoluble. He was poor at sports (his mother said that he would tremble with fear when taken to a swimming pool), spent his lunch hours in the library, and was regarded as "serious and gullible," a characterization consistent with his extraordinary compliance with authority: he never missed a day of classes and always wore his school uniform even though it was not required. One person described him as "gentle and timid, not the leader type." A former Aum member I interviewed who had known Murai as a child remembered him similarly, as quiet and studious, but on encountering him in Aum ten years later, observed in his eyes a fierce new intensity. A friend from his university days thought of him as someone who pursued immediate interests single-mindedly, "forgetting to eat or sleep," but who was incapable of sticking with anything for long, always turning instead to his next passion. Once, for instance, he briefly threw all his energies into creating an electronic circuit that would enable him to photograph the moment when a soap bubble burst.

Murai would later write that, from elementary school on, he was preoccupied with the idea of obtaining supernatural powers, a claim that could well have been influenced by his Aum status but was consistent with the recollection of one former Aum member, a childhood acquaintance who remembered Murai's interest in reincarnation. In many ways, Murai fit a more general Aum profile: gentle, serious, alienated from other children, curious about the fundamental questions of life, and having an incipient spiritual perspective. But unlike many other Aum members, Murai made his way through a string of elite educational institutions, earning an undergraduate degree in science, doing graduate work in astrophysics, and landing an excellent job with a leading Japanese corporation, the Kobe Steel Company. It would seem, however, that while he succeeded in a more or less conventional fashion, a side of him was intent on transcending ordinary life experience. When he decided to marry, he arranged for the ceremony to be held in Nepal because he was interested in seeing—and spiritually experiencing, we may assume—the Himalayas.

In 1987, on joining Aum, he told his mother, "I want to be delivered from earthly bondage by doing yoga." His ambition was in keeping with the spirit of a book that had greatly influenced him and that would figure importantly in present-day commentary on Aum. When Murai's parents attempted to dissuade him from becoming a *shukke,* he handed them a Japanese translation of Richard Bach's *Jonathan Livingston Seagull* and declared, "I want you to read this. It reflects my feelings at this moment." The book is a parable about a bird who defies his parents and his flock by seeking perfection in flight in ways that challenge the limits they impose. Cast out from the flock, Jonathan is discovered by highly evolved gulls who instruct him in spiritualized flying. Returning to the flock, he conveys his new wisdom to its most promising members. Much could be said (and has been said in Japan) about Murai's statement to his mother, depending upon one's sense of Bach's book. I would stress the book's repeated theme of transcending the ordinary, of finding "a meaning, a higher purpose for life" that defies the vision of one's more prosaic group or flock—and above all achieving a perfection that overcomes all boundaries. ("I am a perfect, unlimited gull!") In this achievement the body is discovered to be merely an extension of the spirit: "Your whole body, from wingtip to wingtip, is nothing more than your thought itself, in a form you can see." The kitsch mysticism of *Jonathan Livingston Seagull* is very much like Aum's. Both the book and the cult hold out the sentimental promise of transcending the limitations of one's species with superhuman (or supergull) power or perfection, a process rendered in labored and grandiose terms.

When Murai visited a classmate just after helping to murder the Sakamoto family, he kept saying, "Supernatural power really exists. Once you have it you can start seeing the invisible." To a university friend he declared, "The guru can float in space." Asked whether he could do so himself, he said he could not at his present stage, "but when I am delivered from earthly bondage I will be able to do it." Asked by a fellow Aum believer how he managed in the tiny, dark room he had chosen for his living quarters, he replied, "It is too small and dark for those who are at a loss and want to escape, but this room is as broad as the universe for those who wish to meditate."

There is only one recorded example of Murai's resisting or disobeying Asahara. That came toward the end of a special meeting held shortly before the Tokyo sarin attack at a secret Aum weapons factory near Mount Fuji. Just prior to the meeting, Asahara had angrily rebuked Murai for his failure to produce larger amounts of usable sarin gas and in a rage had thrown various objects at his disciple, including a bowl of hot soup and noodles. At the meeting with his own underlings, Murai spoke of his "lack of ability" in carrying out the instructions of the guru; even in issuing "impossible orders," he said, the guru was always trying to test the limits of his disciples' devotion. Murai was leading the group in religious chanting to end the meeting when a disciple came rushing in to announce that there was a call from the master. Although it was unheard of for anyone in Aum, especially Murai, to fail to take such a call, and despite the disciple's insistence that the call was urgent, Murai is said to have first made a very slight move, as if to rise from the lotus position in which he was seated, and then simply to have gone on chanting. While the incident is difficult to evaluate, it is possible that Murai was expressing long-suppressed doubts about and antagonism toward the guru, especially considering the abuse he had just received and his probable perception, however partial, of the dire situation Aum would face following the imminent sarin release.

Such speculation is given credence by subsequent events. After the Tokyo attack, Murai's behavior seems to have grown increasingly unsteady. At a press conference he said two things that undermined Aum's public position: that the group had assets of ten billion yen (one hundred million dollars), which was probably an accurate figure but was far higher than any sum previously admitted to by official spokesmen, and that an Aum plant under police investigation had been producing chemicals for agricultural purposes, a statement that virtually no one believed but that contradicted Aum's previous insistence that it had no such plant at all.

On April 23, 1995, Murai was knifed to death on the steps of Aum's Tokyo headquarters by a hitman for the *yakuza*, the Japanese mafia. The prevailing theory in Japan was that Asahara, who was known to have contacts with the *yakuza*, ordered the murder because Murai was talking too much and endangering everyone, especially Asahara, who was desperately trying to avoid arrest; Murai knew much too much about Aum's murderous activities; and a dead Murai might be made a scapegoat for various plots and crimes of which Aum was then being accused.

Subsequent Aum statements blaming Murai for whatever violence might have emanated from the group lent credence to these theories. Moreover, the dying Murai was initially reported to have uttered the word *yuda*, meaning Judas, implying that he had been betrayed by someone in Aum. Some thought that Judas was an oblique reference to the fact that the entrance to the lower level of Aum's Tokyo office was locked that day, requiring Murai to go to the front door, where he was more vulnerable to an attacker with a knife. There was also speculation that the Judas might have referred to Fumihiro Jōyū, who has remained loyal to Asahara and is considered the likely future leader of the cult. Later Jōyū and others claimed that Murai had said not *yuda* but *yudaya*, meaning Judea or Jews, which would have been consistent with Aum's anti-Semitic doctrine and with Aum's denial of involvement. But another theory has been advanced: that the *yakuza* killed Murai for their own reasons. He was thought to have gone to them for help in selling Aum's illegally produced drugs but to have seemed increasingly dangerous to them because of his loose talk. Whoever was behind the killing, Murai was the only Aum member known to have been murdered by a person or group outside the cult.

What, then, produced this quintessential Aum scientist? There was first of all his tendency toward totalism, manifested in his complete immersion in anything he undertook, including his mystical aspiration to transcend the human condition. Equally important was the way his early brilliance and his serious focus on traditional science yielded to the strong occult and science fiction currents prevalent in Japanese culture. Murai and his confederates in Aum both tapped and caricatured trends in scientific work that could be described as visionary or even (in their extreme inwardness) mystical. The visionary and the mystical can contribute to the scientific imagination when they are balanced by rigorous regard for evidence and a measure of intellectual self-criticism. But any such restraints were collectively dissolved in Aum and in Murai himself by his extreme conversion to Asahara's world-ending guruism—a guruism whose technocratic dimension made a Murai indispensable. Not only did Murai go as far as anyone else in becoming a clone of the guru, but the guru, driven by his scientific-technological ambitions, took steps toward becoming a clone of Murai. The relatively seamless blending in Murai of visionary science and Aum's absolute guruism created the "serene madness"—really a moral madness—that we have encountered. Part of that moral madness was, as one observer put it, the idea of "making plastic models"—that is, of arrogating to oneself the right to employ science and technology to destroy and then remold not only individual human beings but the entire human world.

Like Nazi doctors and Chinese Communist administrators of "thought reform," Aum leaders and scientists saw themselves as advanced practitioners let loose in a vast human laboratory that required of them neither ethical nor intellectual restraints. It would be foolish simply to dismiss Murai as an isolated fanatic. Rather, he reveals in caricature some of the lethal psychological and cultural combinations abroad in our time.

The Occult Scientist

In his late twenties when I conducted a series of interviews with him, Hirota described to me his own bizarre journey through Aum's labyrinth of mystical science. From the beginning he emphasized that his background in science was conducive to Aum's occult mysticism. Inasmuch as he had studied environmental sciences and astronomy as an undergraduate and then as a graduate student at a prestigious university in Osaka, he explained, "my interest in the universe was close to my religious interests." What he studied at the university, however, "was vigorously scientific without any occult element." Once in Aum, he was assigned to help develop "astrology software" and "to program planetary movements," he further recounted. "The idea itself was occult, but the work required scientific knowledge." As it turned out, the work involved astrological predictions, one of which—concerning the devastating earthquake in Kobe in 1995—became a focus of Asahara's march to Armageddon.

Hirota felt the urge to blend science and the occult well before Aum entered his life. A solitary child and young adult, he had long been concerned about the meaning of life, preoccupied with ideas of death and suicide, and subject to periods of depression sometimes severe enough to interrupt his studies. He embarked on an intense spiritual search, reading Western philosophers like Nietzsche, Kierkegaard, and Heidegger, as well as the works of mystical gurus from various parts of the world, including Madame Blavatsky, Gurdjieff, and Krishnamurti. He also investigated a number of Japanese new religions and for a time worshiped at Mormon churches. While these explorations afforded him periodic satisfactions, he was always conscious of what he called his "bottomless abyss of emptiness" and unable to overcome his "endless pessimism."

The apocalyptic strain in Japanese popular culture was particularly attractive to Hirota. He was, for instance, a devotee of the animated TV show *Space Battleship Yamato*, though he saw little irony in the fact that part of his assigned work in Aum was to help construct a version of that show's imaginary antiradiation device, the "cosmo cleaner," for the protection of the guru and his followers. Equally important to Hirota were elements of the New Age occultism and religion imported from America that flooded the culture in the 1970s and 1980s, especially the translated writings of Nostradamus, so compelling to other Aum members as well and to Asahara himself. "The year 1999 was key in Nostradamus's prediction, an ominous prediction widely known through television and the other mass media when I was in elementary school." It contributed, he thought, to his having "more anxiety than hope about the future."

His anxiety was further fed by Cold War threats of nuclear annihilation and by the access he had to scientific information on global environmental pollution, including the possible destruction of the ozone layer. He was also frightened to hear scientists at conferences "secretly say that people should not live in Tokyo, where high-rises and highways would suffer catastrophic collapses in the next major earthquake." The research reports he heard made him "think of the deterioration of the earth in ways that ordinary people would not sense." Earthquakes and nuclear bombs merged into a fearful if amorphous vision of "something terrible happening in Tokyo." From television films he had seen, "an image of a big bomb being dropped on a megalopolis was familiar," and he associated this nuclear threat with his fear of "an urban earthquake." It was something he simply could not shake off. Further complicating his emotions was his antipathy toward his city—"It's funny to say, but though I was born in Tokyo, I hated Tokyo"—suggesting that at least some part of him wished for such destruction.

Aum felt like a perfect fit for Hirota: "Asahara was preaching what I was searching for." Having previously found himself incapable of "drawing upon fundamental life energy of my own," he now found himself—thanks to the guru—suffused with that energy to the point of ecstasy. He was pleased by Aum's strong interest in science and, at the same time, became deeply involved in its ascetic disciplines and his resulting mystical experiences. He responded strongly to Asahara's insistence that in the face of Armageddon disciples engage themselves ever more intensely in Aum. The guru's prophetic visions tapped into Hirota's own apocalyptic imaginings and further "stirred up my sense of crisis" so that "I could do nothing but follow him." Hirota was moved by Asahara's claim to be suffering from "sarin attacks" that might kill him at any time: "I believe that the guru was my guide and savior and that his existence was more important than mine. When told his life was in danger, I felt it was shameful for followers to do nothing."

Hirota was especially drawn to Asahara's "method of cloning," which he described as the disciple's "becoming empty" so as to allow the guru's "will and desire" to be planted within. Aspiring to be a clone, to achieve what he called "100 percent infusion with the guru," Hirota embarked on the Aum project of "overturning values and common sense" and blocking, rejecting, or reversing one's own perceptions, as in "training by heat":

You immersed yourself in hot water, 46 to 50 degrees Centigrade [122 degrees Fahrenheit], and did a meditation that was meant to block out the sense of heat. If you felt hot, then your training was insufficient. It's a way of deceiving yourself. However hot it was, you were not supposed to feel heat.

The procedure, Hirota indicated, was somewhat successful for him. But he also recalled occasions when people died during the heat training. Either their deaths were ignored or Asahara declared that "the level of spiritual training was insufficient and that's why they died," once adding the rhetorical question, "Isn't it a pleasure to die in the middle of spiritual practice!"

The encounter with death was at the heart of Aum practice, regarded as both spiritually and physically curative. Asahara claimed to have cured himself of cancer by means of the hot-water practice, which was viewed as a form of painful but beneficial karma dropping. Hirota was further assured that "Asahara always did these exercises first." Death was to be inseparable from a disciple's immersion in extreme guruism. Some would even declare, "I wish he would *poa* me!"

Hirota told how he came to recast his scientific worldview in order to adjust it to Asahara's higher truths:

> The guru was concerned with ideas about reincarnation and had a broader perspective on time. The term *kalpa* meant ten billion years. He would talk about a spiritual journey over that long period of time. . . . I studied astronomy, which suggested the figure of four billion years for the history of the earth and ten billion years as the age of the universe. In Aum my sense of time expanded even more and I began asking questions like, "Before I was born twenty-nine years ago, where was I?"

The guru, he added, "had a unique perspective on the rise and fall of civilization from the standpoint of reincarnation. He believed that civilization's destruction was part of the process—a necessary part of the process." For Hirota that was "a very deep thought," and the guru "was such a vast personality that it was difficult for me to analyze him. He was too deep a figure for me as a disciple."

Hirota described to me the convoluted sequence by which he ended up "predicting" the Kobe earthquake of January 1995. He had been told that, on becoming a renunciant, he would be entrusted to work on "the study of the creation of the great universe," research that he knew would combine his background in science with his and Aum's spiritual concerns. He was then assigned to an "astrology team" and instructed to create "astrology software." Hirota soon came to realize how important this work was for Aum when Murai took a great interest in it and even the guru discussed it with him. He felt "honored and very happy to be personally selected by him and asked to do it." Although his past scientific experience did not, of course, include astrology, he understood that in Aum a work assignment was considered a sacred task and part of one's spiritual practice. His scientist self, that is, had yielded to the guru's immortalizing power.

During our interviews, Hirota expressed shame and guilt at having strayed so far from the principles of science that he had originally been taught and at having played a key role in a prediction that might have contributed to Asahara's murderous behavior. When I asked him whether the prediction was his or Asahara's, he answered, "I cannot really say which one of us it was." It seems to have emerged, in fact, from a kind of dialogue between them—some of which took place during a weekly Aum radio broadcast—in which the guru was declarative (though softly) and Hirota awed and subservient. For the sake of making a prophecy on a radio broadcast, Hirota explained, "Asahara-san asked me to study the astrology of natural disasters. I told him there was such a thing as earthquake astrology [based on computer software developed in America] and he told me to work on that." Asahara insisted that he be precise about the site of an earthquake so that the guru could make a "true prediction." At some point, Asahara spoke of the likelihood of an earthquake in Hokkaido, the northernmost Japanese island, but Hirota's calculations provided coordinates that suggested a more likely place was Hyōgo Prefecture in central Japan, and "since Kobe was the only place I had visited in Hyōgo Prefecture, the name of Kobe occurred to me first." (Asahara did not know in advance what Hirota's answer would be so that for his on-air prediction he was depending considerably on the work of a disciple.) During the actual broadcast, Hirota responded to the guru's query by saying, "Around Kobe." Nine days later, on January 17, 1995, the devastating earthquake actually occurred.

Immediately after the broadcast, Hirota felt "embarrassed" by his boldness and far from certain about his prediction. When the earthquake in Kobe occurred, he was "very shaken." As reports indicated that five to six thousand people had been killed, he felt somehow implicated in the disaster. He had a sense "that just thinking that this kind of thing might happen could actually invite the outcome." He was particularly upset when, not long after, he was publicly associated with another Asahara prediction (which he had nothing to do with) that something dire would happen on April 15. "The Kobe earthquake occurred [on January 17]; the subway sarin incident occurred [on March 20]; suspicion of Aum was increasing; ominous predictions were made, and one of them happened to come true. Japan was seized by Aum panic."

Now Hirota was "a great success" in Aum and praised by the guru, who told him, "You did a good job." Almost immediately Asahara embarked for Kobe with Aum trucks loaded with supplies to provide aid to victims of the earthquake. The radio broadcast was repeated a number of times and then incorporated in one of Aum's books, which went so far as to pronounce the earthquake not a natural disaster but rather an attack on the part of evil forces—either the Freemasons or the United States—who made use of special "earthquake weapons." This claim angered and further troubled Hirota.

Asahara, however, was jubilant. To him, the earthquake was a harbinger of Armageddon. Hence Hirota's unease and even fear that he had contributed to Asahara's world-ending vision:

> Asahara had this strong feeling about Armageddon and, whatever occurred, he would say that it was what he predicted. In this case, it happened to be what he did predict. So he felt that his vision about Armageddon was directly expressed by the earthquake.

Hirota's feelings were complicated by his inability to reject Asahara's vision: "My sense of crisis about Armageddon did not go away easily, even after I left Aum. Not that I believed in ominous predictions, but I still feel there is no assurance there won't be an ominous event in the future."

Hirota's extreme discomfort about the whole matter made it difficult for him to discuss it. He still cannot free himself from the idea that his astrological prediction was accurate and, by implication, "scientific." When asked directly about the accuracy of the astrological knowledge he applied, he answered: "I think it was luck that my prediction came true. Yet at the same time I felt that astrology—since there was a traditional astrological method—could be right. What shall I say? What was the question? I prefer to avoid answering it. But I came to think that astrology was a scary discipline." Had he been asked at the time whether he thought astrological knowledge was scientifically reliable, he added, "I would have said, 'Yes, I do.' " He now saw that opinion as part of "Aum's character, Asahara-san's character, and my own character also"—that is, as an expression of the guru-disciple relationship and of Aum "science."

Hirota emphasized that in Aum the guru owned everything, which was an accurate observation but also a means of diminishing his sense of guilt:

> Characteristic of the life of a believer is the thought that all things belong to the guru. Disciples belong to the guru. They think, "My deeds are all devoted to you." I happened to be given a particular form of work and I did it. . . . It was natural at the time for me as a follower to think that my deed was for Asahara-san's use. So the prediction of the Kobe earthquake was, after all, his prediction. Yes, I made it, but . . .

It was a sentence he could not quite complete.

His discomfort only increased as he came to understand the nature of Asahara's world-ending project:

> I was very troubled. At first I couldn't grasp Asahara's scheme, his Armageddon. I had a role assigned to me and I just followed instructions. The Kobe earthquake was not brought about by Aum—it was a natural disaster—but I did not feel good about it. I was fearful that I was being used by him. Asahara was scheming to bring about tremendous destruction. He thought that Armageddon would not happen spontaneously, so his idea was to make it happen. His idea is so dangerous that I still can't sleep at night just imagining it.

Hirota's guilty sense of having contributed to Asahara's destructive energies was tied in with shame at having betrayed his own scientific background: "Just a year before I had been a scientist working at the university. I didn't believe in astrology. Now I made a prediction using astrological knowledge."

Another former member of the Aum astrology team described the team's great importance by noting that Murai created much of its astrology software, and that, despite his formidable responsibilities in Aum, he dropped into the team's office every day to check on its progress. At one point, Asahara himself ordered a certain task to be completed within a week and appeared at the office to express his anger when his deadline was not met. But the guru soon gave the group extra funds for books and materials and remained in frequent touch with its members. Indeed, the team was assigned to follow Asahara in his travels, so that it could provide him with instant horoscopes of Aum members or determine the auspiciousness of scheduling Aum activities at particular times or places. The team members were always tense because they never knew when Asahara might appear. Over time, the guru became increasingly obsessed with obtaining astrological readings on all his *shukke* as a way of evaluating their essential faith or disloyalty. He was also preoccupied with his own horoscope, described as "extreme" and known as a "Grand Cross" because in it the positions of Venus, Uranus, Mars, and Neptune formed a large cross. What pleased Asahara was that both Adolf Hitler's and Thomas Edison's horoscopes fell into this category. He also had his horoscope compared with those of Mao Zedong, the Japanese prime minister, and the new emperor, Akihito.

Hirota was able to resist Murai's attempts to get him to change his mind when he left Aum soon after the sarin incident. But on hearing of Murai's murder, he found himself shocked and upset. He had an impulse to rush to the scene to offer his own blood to save the life of his former superior. He prayed for him, recalling his guidance, patience, and kindness. But he also began to devote himself to exploring and exposing Aum's crimes, focusing on Asahara's acts but by no means excluding Murai's.

Aum's version of scared science rendered it a cultic movement of our time. Certainly Aum was not unique among cults in claiming scientific validity for its most extreme expressions of spiritual fantasy.

But where most cultic groups try to add a scientific gloss to their spiritual claims, Aum specifically recruited scientists like Murai and Hirota and then radically subsumed their science into the group's dogma and practice. In this way Murai and Hirota, like other Aum scientists, became proponents of "science fantasy" (visions more absurd than those in the wildest science fiction) and "fantasy science" (imagining and pursuing omnipotent scientific products and achievements). Murai was central to, and the creator of, much of this environment of apocalyptic science, but Hirota readily joined in.

There have been notable efforts to marry science and mysticism but Aum brought to science not so much genuine mysticism as distorting mystification. People like Murai and Hirota became bridges between an absolutized sacred and a plundered profane. Without such sacralized scientists, the guru could not have blended his world-ending fantasy with dangerous material actuality; without their scientific knowledge bent to his will, he would have had neither the imagination nor the means to "force the end." Aum's version of sacred science, applied equally to spirit and weapons, became its path to the killing fields.

6 | Killing to Heal

I s there something about Aum that attracts doctors?" asked a Japanese journalist who investigated the cult. To which I might respond with another question, "Is there something about doctors that enabled them to make special contributions to Aum's deadly project?" The more I studied Aum's medical behavior, the more I was reminded of the experience of Nazi doctors and of the more general potential of doctors to replace healing with killing in the service of a movement or cause.

The Nazis used German physicians to medicalize their killing project, that is, to transform it into something on the order of medical treatment. Nazi killing took place first as "euthanasia" within medically controlled institutions where certain forms of illness or hereditary defect or even undesirable behavior were classified as "life unworthy of life." Some German doctors readily offered their skills for this purpose, while most others either supported the process or in one way or another contributed to it. This medicalized killing project was later extended to death camps like Auschwitz, where doctors performed "selections" at a railroad ramp, sending most arriving Jews immediately to the gas chambers while permitting a small number of the healthiest-looking among them to become slave laborers, only, in most cases, to die later. In addition to participating directly in mass murder, these doctors also came to symbolize the overall Nazi vision of killing in the name of healing, of destroying those who had "infected" the Nordic race in order to "cure" that uniquely gifted race of its temporary "illness."

There are, of course, enormous differences between a national political movement and a small antigovernment religious cult, though the Nazis were cultic in function, drew heavily upon apocalyptic religious symbolism, and wallowed in mystical experience, while Aum became highly politicized and militarized in pursuit of secular as well as spiritual goals. What Aum and the Nazis particularly shared, however, was the frequent tendency of despotic and totalistic groups to seize upon the shamanistic legacy of the physician, a legacy that includes not only the "white magic" of healing but also the "black magic" of killing. For doctors deal regularly with death and can easily be viewed—by despotic regimes and by themselves—as powerful manipulators of life and death, as gatekeepers between this world and the next.

We cannot say whether Aum drew directly on any specific models for its extensive use of medicalized threat, torture, and killing. We know that Asahara admired Hitler and was fascinated by the Nazis. At a minimum, Aum probably absorbed something from the Nazis' use of doctors in the service of a murderous project, but it also might have drawn upon Japan's wartime medical abuses of the 1930s and 1940s, which included grotesque physician-directed experiments and vivisections on Chinese and Allied prisoners of war. There have also been more recent examples of doctors involved in various kinds of abuse: as torturers in Chile, as falsifiers of medical reports on governmental killings in apartheid South Africa, as psychiatric jailers of political heretics in the former Soviet Union, as colluders in mind-manipulation experiments by the Central Intelligence Agency in the United States and Canada, and as facilitators of mass suicide and murder in the Peoples Temple cult in Guyana.

Aum could have turned to many places for models, but in a sense it needed no specific models at all. Totalistic groups seeking forms of absolute control tend to seek out physicians for their death-linked knowledge and power. And physicians themselves can be all too amenable to the feeling of omnipotence that such collaboration affords them. The shamanistic legacy is important here, but so is the physician's own attraction to the totalistic doctrine in question. In the case of the Nazis, physicians were drawn to the ideological promise of personal and national revitalization as well as to self-serving opportunities for privilege and power within the regime. While the intensity of their ideological involvement varied greatly—some could even make fun of the movement's more extreme biological claims—elements of Nazi ideology were crucial to the process by which German doctors were socialized to killing. Aum doctors, by contrast, were all fiercely involved in the cult's theology in ways that rendered them highly amenable to torture and killing. They, too, had misgivings, or what could be called a doubting, non-Aum self, but, like their Nazi counterparts, they were all too able to overcome such misgivings in the service of the "higher cause."

Aum's reversal of healing and killing was probably the most systematic since the Nazis'—on a vastly smaller scale but with *visions* of medicalized killing extensive enough to dwarf even those of the Nazis. Certainly, Aum dramatizes for us a widespread tendency to medicalize large killing projects and to place doctors at their center.

Like the Nazis, Aum put forth a medical ideology that claimed radical ethical advances. Nazi medical organizers told doctors that they needed no longer engage in selfish individual practice but could serve as "physicians to the *Volk*," the people or community, as "biological soldiers" or as "cultivators of the genes." With Aum, the ethical claim was highly spiritualized but no less a medical promise. The following declaration entitled "Toward Future Medicine" was printed in an Aum publication called *Sickness Is Cured*:

Aum Shinrikyō upholds Three Salvations, namely, "liberation from illness," "path to this-worldly happiness," and "path to satori." As for the first, "liberation from illness," a group of Aum Shinrikyō doctors, led by the most holy soul of truth Reverend Shōkō Asahara, is aiming for a new therapeutics; in addition to utilizing techniques culled from the frontiers of Western medicine, they are researching the essence of various practices, such as Oriental medicine (acupuncture, herbs), Tibetan medicine, Ayurveda (ancient Indian medicine), and yoga. We have been placing particular emphasis on preventive care and improvement of one's constitution, which modern medicine has tended to neglect. In combination with the above, methods like astral medicine (derived from the astral world, a higher dimension) and holy empowerment by spiritual achievers (energy transfer) have yielded splendid results in curing fatal and rare diseases, imparting superhealth, and bettering mind and body.

The declaration is a medical version of typical Aum rhetoric, grandiose in its fusion of scientism ("techniques culled from the frontiers of Western medicine"), appropriated Eastern wisdom, and a concretized spiritual world ("astral medicine"). Its reference to "spiritual achievers" and "energy transfer" as curing fatal diseases is consistent with its dark version of *poa*, in which high achievers enhance the reincarnation of low achievers, or bad people, by killing them. The author of a book quoting the declaration comments dryly that "the head of this supposed vanguard of medicine, the holy guru, did not even have a medical license." But the guru did, of course, have what he and Aum considered ultimate license. In Aum he could realize his earlier ambition of becoming a physician, indeed a physician like none other. The declaration, then, can be understood as a medicalized projection of ultimate guruism, a spiritually sanitized version of what was to become medicalized killing.

What Aum Doctors Did

Medicine was completely in the service of the cult's theology and central to its various levels of violence. The three Aum "ministries" headed by doctors—the ministry of healing, the ministry of health and welfare, and the secretariat of the sacred emperor (or household agency)—were closely coordinated with the cult's projects in Nazi-style integration, or *Gleichschaltung*. They were also examples of Orwellian naming: the ministry of healing used the Aum hospital to drug, blackmail, and kill; the ministry of health and welfare produced deadly substances; and the secretariat of the sacred emperor envisioned, planned, and carried out acts of murder.

In-patients were kept at the Astral Hospital Institute in Tokyo, a small unit separate from other Aum facilities. With just nine beds, it nonetheless had a staff of as many as ten doctors in eight departments, an incongruency that reflected its broader role, which was in Aum's criminal projects. Indeed, the "hospital" was a place where physicians from the ministry of healing detained and drugged recalcitrant followers, members of their families, or others designated as enemies of Aum. These same doctors, assisted by Aum nurses, presided over a category of "patients" called "the ordained in custody." As one doctor later explained in court, these were followers who were drugged and kept in the small cells known as "shield rooms," lest they escape.

In a typical case, a sixty-three-year-old nonfollower who suffered a stroke in January 1992 was taken to the Aum facility at the suggestion of a relative who belonged to the cult. The patient was kept in the Aum hospital for fourteen months, during which time doctors and nurses constantly demanded "donations," insisting that his illness would be cured by the act of giving. He was also subjected to "thermal therapy," immersion in extremely hot water to "extract toxic elements" from his body. He ended up donating a valuable piece of land to the cult and later, on release, sued for its return. Other patients were subjected to combinations of thermal therapy and "cleansings" of the stomach with large amounts of hot saltwater. One patient later testified to being struck not just by the low hygienic standards of the hospital but by the "bizarre atmosphere" in which doctors and nurses regularly wore strange headgear said to connect them with the brain waves of their guru. A number of patients never had the chance to tell their stories because they were killed by the procedures of these ostensible healers. Aum medical personnel could be coldly cynical (as they extorted money and property or harmed or killed designated enemies), but they were always motivated by the underlying ethos in which everything was done to serve the cult's higher healing purposes.

Doctors used their knowledge of drugs, for example, for such "healing" as flushing out spies, defectors, or simply wavering believers. They established "S-checks" (S for "spy") in which they administered intravenous infusions of amobarbital and later thiopental as aids to interrogation; periodically in the course of questioning, the semicomatose suspect would be shaken forcefully. They came to use the term *narco* not only for S-check but for the use of drugs in the various initiations. Later, electroshock was added to the treatment package for the purpose of erasing memories in what came to be called the "new narco."

Doctors engaged in various forms of medical deception to conceal the identities of Aum lawbreakers, including operations on the fingers to eliminate fingerprints and, in at least one case, on the face to change a fugitive's appearance. Doctors also made false diagnoses of sarin poisoning on Aum members to prove the guru's claims of gas attacks from the outside. None of these measures worked very well, but they are striking examples of the application of medical knowledge and procedures for purposes of falsifying reality. One could also include under medical deception the use of drugs in kidnapping and incarceration and the application of medical knowledge in the incineration of the bodies of people killed within Aum facilities. Some of these procedures could be quite haphazard, with doctors called upon to improvise.

As the cult's interest in barbiturate and LSD-related preparations increased, doctors used their status to obtain these drugs, and when legitimate pharmaceutical companies would become suspicious of large orders for particular drugs, they would request different but related drugs instead. Aum doctors also played an important part in the cult's manufacture of drugs, many of them illegal. Thus, from early November 1994 through mid-February 1995, Aum illegally manufactured more than seventeen hundred grams of thiopental, its barbiturate of choice. The work, involving endless experiments and modifications, was done mainly by the ministry of health and welfare, which upon request allocated drugs to the ministry of healing.

Inevitably, doctors figured prominently in the manufacture and use of sarin, cyanide, and other gases and of biological agents such as botulinus and anthrax. After Hideo Murai had been given the task of carrying out the Tokyo sarin attack, he met with three people: the minister of healing (a physician), the minister of health and welfare (a veterinarian trained in genetic research who was looked upon as a doctor), and the head of the Secretariat of the Sacred Emperor (a physician). This group was essential in planning the attack. Doctors also were deeply involved in planning some of Aum's most bizarre schemes, such as a proposed occupation of the Diet and the massive sarin release scheduled for November 1995. Beyond these grandiose projections of large-scale murder, the same physicians helped plan, and carry out, individual killings.

Doctors also contributed greatly to Aum's fantasies about medical resources that would help the group survive Armageddon. Thus, a leading Aum physician declared during a radio dialogue with Asahara that, although World War III would destroy the global industrial and medical infrastructure, "Aum Shinrikyō would not have a problem" because it would establish its own industrial infrastructure and preserve its medical knowledge and supplies, rendering it "capable of rebuilding the medical infrastructure itself from the ground up." (Another medical scientist, after discussing ways of combating the dangers of biological warfare, came to a more sober conclusion: "I also recommend that you prepare your mind for death.")

Whatever Aum activities doctors participated in—whether evaluation of disciples' brain waves or "secret work"—thereby gained a certain aura of scientific and therapeutic authority. When Seiichi Endō, the former minister of health and welfare, himself deeply implicated in murderous acts, testified that Aum's pattern of guruism and discipleship created a sense of "extraterritoriality," he meant specifically that Aum's seeming capacity to kill people without police interference led to a sense that Aum could live by its own laws. The deeper psychological meaning of that "extraterritoriality," however, had to do with Aum's sense of uniqueness, omnipotence, and ultimate purity of purpose, so that any action it undertook, from forceful proselytizing to killing, could ultimately be seen as therapeutic for humankind.

Like Nazi doctors, Aum physicians were by no means inherently cruel or evil. In neither group had any of them killed or maimed other human beings prior to becoming part of a murderous ideological project. Much more than their Nazi counterparts, Aum doctors, in their pre-Aum professional lives, tended to have been sensitive and highly conscientious physicians inclined toward spiritual practices. But their impulse to heal, on undergoing Aum distortions, became a fulcrum for killing.

"I Wanted to Help People"

Perhaps the most prominent, certainly the most accomplished, physician in Aum was the cardiac surgeon who became minister of healing, Ikuo Hayashi. As head of the Astral Hospital Institute, Hayashi initiated or oversaw virtually all the abuses perpetrated by the "medical staff" both within the hospital and at other sites. Under his leadership, the deaths in that small, improvised facility—estimated at more than twenty—far outnumbered its beds. Hayashi's "medical" influence extended into every manipulative or lethal area of Aum's function, including all phases of the Tokyo sarin attack.

The son of a prominent physician and himself a graduate of the highly regarded medical school of Keio University in Tokyo, one of Japan's leading private universities (where, in addition to doing well in his studies, he was captain of the tennis team), Hayashi spent a year at the Mount Sinai Hospital in Detroit, where his son was born, before becoming chairman of the department of cardiac surgery at a leading hospital in the Kyoto area. Serious and evidently not naturally gregarious in his youth, he was seen as an unusually conscientious and reliable physician. But in a book he wrote after his trial, he claimed that fear, which he always sought to overcome with "reason," had long been the dominant emotion in his life. He also told of a deep preoccupation with moral questions and of embarking, as a high school student, on a search for a single law that would encompass and solve all human problems, a search that he wished to make his personal "life theme." He became a spiritual seeker and a devout Buddhist. For a period of time he belonged to Agonshū and was exposed there to various components of New Age Buddhism, including versions of Tantrism and Kundalinī yoga, as well as the Armageddon predictions of Nostradamus.

In 1988, he apparently dozed off while driving home after a laborious operation, causing an accident in which a woman and her daughter were seriously injured. The story in the Japanese press emphasized

Hayashi's concern for them, his hospital visits and his gifts to them. Some observers believe that Hayashi's misery and guilt rendered him vulnerable to Aum. It is also possible that some form of already-existing dissociative state or other psychological difficulty contributed to the accident.

When Emperor Hirohito, whom he revered, died on January 7, 1989, Hayashi not only experienced a terrible personal void but associated the death with that of his father a short time earlier. Hayashi chose his forty-second birthday, sixteen days after the emperor's death, to begin practicing yoga as taught in Asahara's writings. He joined Aum and soon began to demonstrate what his hospital colleagues viewed as bizarre behavior. He prescribed various Aum treatments for his cardiac patients, including purgations that involved swallowing large amounts of hot water or even physical objects like strings or bandages. Taken to task by the hospital director and forced to resign, he became an Aum renunciant and helped create the Astral Hospital Institute. He sent notes to former patients describing his "intention to achieve satori as soon as possible in order to serve society with an unbiased spirit."

He explained his attraction to the cult in an article he wrote in an Aum publication entitled "As a Doctor, as an Ascetic." Of the sudden deaths that sometimes occurred during heart surgery, he declared that "strange forces beyond rational analysis were at work." While "the job of the doctor is to save people," he went on, "it cannot compare in level or scale to the great master's efforts to save all souls." Although highly formulaic, the article was an emphatic articulation of Hayashi's abandonment of prior standards of medical reason in favor of Aum theology, Asahara's absolute guruism, and the "large-scale activity of salvation."

Hayashi's immersion in Aum's asceticism was extreme. Like many other renunciants, he generally slept just three hours a night. He went much further, however: upon reading in the Aum magazine *Mahāyāna* that the Buddha once ate canine feces as a technique of self-discipline, he forced himself to eat his own. Though older and more accomplished than most other Aum members, he threw himself into the Aum group process, embracing its "common goal" and "sense of unity."

Later he would claim that Asahara did not like him very much, and was always "distant," perhaps because "he was feeling a sense of inferiority for what I once had—a good family, education, and profession. My presence was something that reminded him of his past frustrations." Similar sentiments were expressed to me by other former Aum members from privileged backgrounds, though they sensed as well that Asahara especially valued such esteemed converts. In any case, nothing in Asahara's attitude diminished Hayashi's uncritical embrace of his absolute guruism.

Hayashi was made to view his past achievements as "harmful social influences" and thus a source of guilt. If Asahara's behavior seemed strange, Hayashi, like others, saw it as the guru's "device" or "gimmick" for drawing out disciples' anger in order to give them access to their deepest spiritual feelings. Similarly, when everything seemed to be going badly, Hayashi thought, "The guru must have some profound plan; he must be creating these inconveniences on purpose" because "our work and practice leave much to be desired." Hayashi's effort was always directed toward achieving a state in which he could enter into and live out the "guru's will." Like others, he attributed to the guru's all-pervasive beneficence his mystical experiences, particularly the feeling of cosmic transcendence when he and several high-ranking cohorts ingested the first Aum-produced LSD. Since all truth emanated from the guru, "it seemed unnecessary for any of us to think on our own." That sense was magnified still further for Hayashi when Asahara began to announce routinely that he might die at any moment. As Hayashi saw it, without the guru there would be no salvation and all training would be "useless."

Hayashi could effectively articulate highly advanced medical principles—what Aum called its "cutting-edge medical technology"—in the service of absurd fantasies of Armageddon survival. The group would survive "comparatively easily" by taking advantage of such medical developments as "external [artificial] circulation, . . . new devices to exchange blood plasma, perform artificial hemodialysis, and absorb toxins with artificial columns, . . . and artificial organs such as livers, joints, and so forth." Moreover, their "chances of retaining all body parts" would be "greater than in previous wars." Hayashi talked of advanced microsurgery for the reconnection of arms and legs; the use of animal skin or one's own previously harvested skin cells for treating burns; stored mixtures of blood and glycerol for bleeding; and a method called ECMO for combining an artificial lung with external circulation techniques. "If we get these things ready," he declared in an Aum radio broadcast, "I believe we can use them in the coming final war." What was originally a finely tuned medical mind descended to an absurdist monologue of medical mystification as Hayashi offered himself completely to Aum's cosmic melodrama.

That does not mean that Hayashi's knowledge was wasted in Aum. Indeed, his skills were made use of in every form of its medicalized criminality: in abductions and incarcerations, in plastic surgery for disguise, and in drug production and use. It was he who originated the hot-water immersion, initially as a form of therapy, and who pioneered the use of drugs in conjunction with various Aum initiations and the S-check. He played a central part in Aum's decision to produce its own thiopental, by providing samples to its chemists and by testing samples on those disciples suspected of being spies. All these policies emerged from his discussions with Asahara, during which, like Murai, he was free to initiate ideas for further draconian policies.

He was the one, for instance, who suggested to Asahara that electric shock be employed to eliminate memories, after which the guru ordered Murai to build the necessary equipment. Delighted with its effects, Asahara used the childish term *dokkan* (an imitation of the sound of an explosion, like "boom!") to describe the procedure until Hayashi suggested that it be called the "new narco." It came to consist of a sequence of thiopental, producing a semicomatose state, then five to seven electric shocks, followed by more thiopental and further interrogation to determine the degree of memory loss. Thiopental was also used in attempts at subliminal indoctrination, a procedure called "learning while asleep," which could be followed by training in "resolve." In all this Hayashi brought to Asahara both genuine medical knowledge and medical fantasy related to his perception of the Aum mission.

The medical fantasy combined facts of human physiology and brain function with popular-culture concepts of total mind control (or "brain control"). Hayashi's ideas about mind control might have been influenced by his reading in early 1994 about the work of D. Ewen Cameron, a Scottish-born psychiatrist who came to head the Allan Memorial Institute in Montreal, where he originated a form of therapy called "depatterning" or "psychic driving," which included extremely intensive use of electric shock treatment, sometimes in combination with barbiturates and other drugs such as LSD. The American Central Intelligence Agency came to sponsor the work because of its own fascination with accounts of the Communist practice of mind control, or "brainwashing." Hayashi claimed to have been repelled by Cameron's work but could well have drawn upon some of its features, such as a form of indoctrination in which a patient had to listen endlessly—sometimes even while asleep—to tape recordings of himself saying words thought to relate to a basic conflict, and similarly to the interpretations of the therapist. (I have a more than passing interest in the matter since I served as an expert witness on behalf of victims of Cameron's "therapy" in a legal procedure.)

It was Hayashi's drug-related functions that made him a leading figure in Aum's kidnappings and incarcerations. In court testimony after his arrest, he described giving orders before the March 1995 police raid that about twenty renunciants in Aum custody who had already been drugged be given additional sleeping pills so that they would not be able to talk to the police. Hayashi was also directly involved in the murder of Kiyoshi Kariya, the notary public who had tried to help his sister escape from the cult. After a team led by a doctor, Tomomasa Nakagawa, picked up Kariya on the street and forcibly carried him back to Aum, Nakagawa and Hayashi applied "narco"—a continuous thiopental intravenous drip—while interrogating their prisoner on the whereabouts of his sister. Failing to extract the desired information, they sought to contact Asahara, but when the guru could not be reached the two doctors continued the thiopental drip, taking turns overseeing Kariya. On the morning of March 1, 1995, during Nakagawa's watch, Kariya died from an overdose. Shortly afterward, Hayashi administered "new narco" to the six Aum members involved in the kidnapping, in order to eliminate their memories of the event. One of them afterward claimed not to remember anything that happened the entire previous week. (Hayashi would later claim to have had qualms about the new narco procedure and even to have eventually, without Asahara's permission, ordered it discontinued, giving as his reason its failure to produce results. He would also insist that in all the actions related to Kariya's kidnapping he and others had the firm conviction that "we were transmitting the Aum idea of 'love.' ") Hayashi extended his interest in drugs to personal experiment. During a trip he made to the United States with his wife in 1994 he tried peyote and was able to see "blue lights." Upon his return he arranged for Aum to produce mescaline, the active ingredient in peyote, and the first successful sample was presented to Asahara as a gift on his fortieth birthday.

In his enthusiasm for Aum, Hayashi brought to the cult not just himself but something of an entourage consisting of his wife, their two young children, and his lover. His wife, Rira Hayashi, also a physician, said later that she had argued vehemently with him about joining Aum and had considered divorce. But she did join along with him, probably came to hold many of his views, and was made one of his three vice-ministers. In that capacity she participated in such activities as administering electric shock and operating on an Aum member to remove fingerprints. On the trip to the United States, she collected technical information relating to sarin manufacture. (There were even more dire arrangements contemplated in connection with that trip: Hayashi later told the Japanese police that there had been discussion of mailing packages of sarin gas to various locations in the United States, to be picked up by him while he was there; there was also talk of smuggling as much as twenty-one tons of sarin into the United States aboard a ship or in ice sculptures. The purpose of all these plans was to mount a sarin attack or a series of attacks there.)

Eiko Murakami, Hayashi's lover, had been a nurse in his hospital unit in the pre-Aum days. At the age of twenty, she had begun a long affair with him, culminating in her joining Aum shortly after him. She would later say bitterly, "I wouldn't have joined the sect or committed any crimes if I had never met Hayashi." But she did commit crimes, participating in the kidnapping of an elderly innkeeper both by driving the car that was used and by injecting him with a tranquilizer. When asked by her lawyer during trial hearings how she perceived her nursing vocation, she recited the nurses' Florence Nightingale Oath, which includes the sentence "I shall shun all poison and neither administer nor dispense harmful drugs knowingly."

Hayashi provided another kind of medical service to Aum by becoming its authority on antidotes to sarin poisoning, a necessity that arose in December 1993, when the minister of home affairs was brought to him suffering from the effects of exposure. The minister had made the mistake of momentarily removing his gas mask while participating in the attempt to murder Daisaku Ikeda, the leader of the rival religious group Sōka Gakkai. Hayashi saved his patient, and his success was one of the reasons he was chosen by the guru himself to be among those who would release sarin in the Tokyo subways. Hayashi had already seen to it that large amounts of the antidotes he used, atropine and a preparation known as *pam*, were kept at the hospital and in the main Aum facility. He took supplies of both with him to the headquarters from which the subway attack was mounted.

He was to need them, as most of those involved returned to the hideout with signs of sarin poisoning. He treated them personally with shots of *pam*. Driving back to the hospital, he himself had visual symptoms and telephoned Eiko Murakami to meet him with atropine at a nearby bookstore. In the car together later, they heard a radio report of the sarin attack. Murakami asked Hayashi if sarin was what was affecting him and, obviously unaware of Aum's responsibility for the attack, expressed her disbelief that anyone would do such a thing to innocent people.

Hayashi would testify that he was a reluctant participant in the sarin release and had even avoided attending a "practice session." He came to feel that he had been required to take part in the action because the guru wished to keep him quiet and to control him by deepening his complicity in Aum's acts. Hayashi believed that his developing ambivalence toward the guru had been noticed by Asahara, who subsequently considered him dangerous and "disposable." He remembered being joyous at hearing that he was to be assigned to important "special work" but, upon learning what he was expected to do, horrified at the thought that he would bequeath to his wife and children "the legacy of a murderer." He recalled Murai's telling him that "if you have qualms, you may refuse." That, he quickly realized, was Asahara's way of saying, "Of course you will have qualms, but you have to do it and you were chosen to do it." Since the task "had been assigned me as my destiny by the all-seeing guru, the matter had been irrevocably decided," Hayashi reasoned, for he still believed that Asahara was a victor of truth, "someone who can see through past, present, and future" and that "his orders were essentially right." He was terrified, in any case, that if he refused, the guru would have him *poa*'d, probably by Dr. Nakagawa, his best friend. Moreover, he felt that "it would be cowardly not to do it." As he further explained, the feeling "I do not want to" did not turn into "I will not." He felt trapped, controlled by the order, imagining before him "a tiny figure, rusty with a pinkish tinge, that of my own self, which could do no more than 'not want to.' "

When he saw women and children on the subway platform, he said, he experienced "internal conflict" but overcame it by reasserting in his mind the justification that Aum was a separate national entity at war with Japanese society: "This is a battle. Too bad if they're women or children. If they are *poa*'d, their souls will be able to remain in the human world and placed on a higher level." After he entered the subway car, however, his uneasiness returned. He dealt with it by focusing on duty and detail: "I'm the one who has to do it. When should I take out the bag of sarin and pierce it?" At the same time he thought, "The woman sitting diagonally across from me will certainly die. I hope she gets off somewhere along the way."

Whatever his inner division, he ended up being involved in virtually every stage of the planning and execution of the sarin attack. Like many Nazi doctors, he was troubled by his part in the killing project but able to overcome his conflict sufficiently to carry out his role. After puncturing the sarin bag with his umbrella and leaving the train, he banged the umbrella repeatedly on the ground, both to get rid of the sarin on the tip and "because I felt agitated and I wanted to release my feelings"—undoubtedly a combination of allegiance to the guru, discomfort and doubts about the action, diffuse anxieties and resentments, and self-condemnation for having such complex emotions. The ambivalence within his compliance was also expressed during a meeting with the guru immediately afterward when Asahara gave him a mantra invoking Shiva to justify the attack. Asahara met with the others who carried out the attack, but Hayashi was the only one who wrote the full mantra on a piece of paper. The guru was angry that Hayashi was unable simply to memorize it; very likely, moreover, he did not want any record made of his responses to the criminal act. He probably also sensed that Hayashi's inappropriate note taking was an inchoate and ineffectual expression of resistance. For his part, Hayashi was disturbed by a comment of Asahara's: "They are saying it was Aum who spread sarin." As Hayashi explained in his court testimony, the purpose of the sarin attack was to deflect society's attention from Aum but its result was to make Aum the focus of attention. "If Asahara had been a genuine victor of truth he would have been able to foresee exactly what would happen." He was reflecting here the partial collapse of his image of an omniscient guru.

Hayashi was arrested a few weeks after the sarin attack and was soon visited in jail by an Aum lawyer who brought him an Aum journal. Although he took this as "a message that I should not confess," he quickly turned against his guru anyway. "I began to think that Asahara was really a miserable person." Defecting from the cult psychologically was painful, as evidenced by his thought that "it would be better to commit suicide while I still believed in Asahara and Aum." Yet he took on the task of exposing everything he could about Aum, though he carefully waited until his wife and two children were safely out of the cult's hands before beginning his public confession. Cooperating completely with the prosecutors, he was the first defendant fully to reveal the details of the sarin release and the first to confront the guru in open court. He spoke of Asahara as his "former master" and the guru's doctrine as "totally in error, so that it cannot be called a religion." Revealing all was a necessity because he realized that "Asahara has the kind of mind that cannot in itself tell the truth." He spoke of his "chagrin and regret," of remorse for the victims and everyone else, "to the point of not knowing with what words to apologize." Telling "all that I know" became "the only thing I can do," and "my duty as a human being." He was tearful during his testimony, which had a powerful impact in the court and, when reported in the media, elsewhere as well.

He now found himself able to see and condemn his reversal of healing and killing. "I am a medical doctor and I wanted to help people one way or another, but in the end I could not carry out that purpose," he said, comparing his "grotesque" behavior as someone "whose real task was to sustain people's lives" with "sublime" actions of the Tokyo subway workers who "used their hands to get rid of the sarin" in order to save others. During one of his last court appearances, he told his lawyer that he was reading for the fourth time a book by the prominent novelist Haruki Murakami filled with searing accounts of those who survived the attack or were relatives of the dead. When his lawyer asked why, he answered, "Who else should read that book if I don't?" In December 1995, while in prison, he made a formal request to the Japanese Ministry of Public Welfare to rescind his medical license because "I caused irredeemable harm to society through acts that made me unfit to be a doctor." The request was granted.

Hayashi was the first participant in the sarin attack to be convicted. When it came time to pass sentence, the judge ruled that, while Hayashi deserved the death penalty because of his murderous deeds, he also deserved the leniency of a life sentence, given his confession, which helped link the cult to the sarin attack; his commitment to "telling the truth in court as his last mission . . . even if [the facts] were against him"; the "passivity" of his role in the gassing (as the crime had been ordered by Asahara); and the desire of the next of kin of two dead subway workers that he not be executed. After the sentencing Hayashi faced the judge and bowed deeply.

When the judge offered Hayashi an opportunity to convey a message to his former underlings, he quietly addressed a doctor who had worked closely with him and was now also in prison: "Ken'ichirō Katahira is someone who thinks for himself. I would like Katahira, who is a psychiatrist, to analyze for his own sake the pathology of Shōkō Asahara and then to atone for his own deeds." Hayashi was explicitly saying that Aum's destructiveness called for psychiatric evaluation but was perhaps also suggesting that the same was true of himself. He had sufficiently extricated himself from the guru and Aum to confront his own behavior, which left him not only horrified but puzzled.

Any explanation must begin with Hayashi's spiritual search, with his fear, and with an urge toward totalism that rendered his search extraordinarily intense. We cannot say how much of a prior tendency toward dissociation he brought to his pre-Aum medical career, but he certainly experienced in Aum a powerful fusing of the all-encompassing answer he sought with a dissociative response—doubling, the formation of two selves that are morally and functionally antithetical although part of the same psyche. Hayashi's doubling is best understood in terms of his medical identity. His pre-Aum self included what he called "vocational truths and morals," in his case those of an idealistic doctor whose medical work was infused with Buddhist compassion. He felt stirrings of that pre-Aum self in January 1995, at the time of the Kobe earthquake, in the form of an urge to drop everything and offer his medical skills to the victims. Even in the killing of Kariya a short time later, Hayashi first swore to himself, "I must absolutely not let him die under narco," just as he inwardly insisted at the time of the sarin attack, "I do not want to." But in each of these cases his prior medical self was overwhelmed by the rewards and pressures of his Aum self. Through that self he could experience not only personal transcendence but a realization of his lifelong vision of purifying the world. So he went ahead with Kariya's overdose as with the sarin attack: because his submission to the guru's will was "inexorable" and defiance of it terrifying but also because his Aum self told him that one must, in the guru's words, "put one's heart in an act of *poa*" and carry it out energetically for the sake of universal salvation.

Like the Auschwitz self of Nazi doctors, Hayashi's Aum self enabled him to cling to the virtue of his medical identity even as he used his medical knowledge to control and kill other human beings. As that medical identity was increasingly incorporated into his Aum self, he could experience Aum's killing as a form of greater healing. Only with his arrest and incarceration could he reassert—now with equal zeal and considerable insight—his humane pre-Aum medical self.

The Medical Warrior

Tomomasa Nakagawa, the other prominent physician in Aum, is an extreme example of how the cult could turn relatively mild spiritual seekers into murderous medical warriors. Nakagawa became more of a "hit man" than Hayashi but also played an important role in planning the guru's most ambitious enterprises. Asahara made him his personal physician as well as the head of the secretariat of the sacred emperor, the so-called Household Agency, a unit closer to the guru than the ministries.

A graduate of a reputable Kyoto medical school, he joined Aum while still a medical student, becoming a *shukke* after his internship and some additional medical work. He was described as a very dedicated student, generally liked and trusted, the kind of young person who always wanted to please others. As he once said, "There is no one I dislike." A former fellow student thought that "his naive and unsuspicious character" might have led him to Aum.

Nakagawa had had mystical tendencies and experienced spiritual confusion before joining Aum. He felt that in exploring the stages of Tibetan Buddhism, he had also come to experience his patients' pain in his own body. Although he took this to be a form of divination or occult correspondence, he feared that he was going crazy. When he encountered Asahara, the guru was able to provide a quick "cure" by absorbing the problem into Aum doctrine and practice. Nakagawa found, after some months as a renunciant, that the difficulty had been transformed. "When I hold the hands of a patient, the pain [of the patient] goes away. Instead, the bad elements go into me, so that I have to drink liters of hot water to purify my body." That Aum process of "purification" later came to be associated with extreme violence.

Even among guru-fixated high disciples, Nakagawa stood out as someone who embraced and sought to anticipate Asahara's every whim and vision. In November 1989, just two months after becoming a *shukke*, Nakagawa took part in the murder of the Sakamoto family, assigned to the team by the guru because of his fanatical devotion as well as his medical background. When the original plan for Nakagawa to administer a lethal injection to Sakamoto failed, it was apparently Asahara who gave orders for Sakamoto's wife and fourteen-month-old son to be killed as well. In a 1996 court procedure, Nakagawa admitted that he had helped strangle the adult Sakamotos and suffocate their child. He also participated in the separate burials of the three bodies (the guru had determined that the fires required for cremating them would draw too much attention). When the group returned they were assured by Asahara that the infant would now have the advantage of not being raised by a father performing evil deeds and would be reborn at a higher spiritual level. The guru also had the group listen to a reading of a portion of the Japanese penal code, apparently to impress them with the fact that each of them faced the death penalty if caught and convicted.

It was Nakagawa whom Asahara had assist in the murder of Kōtarō Ochida, the pharmacist who attempted to rescue an abused patient. It was Nakagawa, too, whom he chose to help kidnap Kiyoshi Kariya and to conduct, with Dr. Hayashi, the interrogation that ended in their administration of a fatal dose of thiopental. Nakagawa's role in Kariya's death was particularly gruesome. Hearing that the interrogation was proving fruitless, Asahara had sent instructions through Hideo Murai that Kariya be strangled by Yoshihiro Ida, another prominent disciple, to enhance Ida's "religious training." But when Nakagawa returned to the room where the prisoner was kept, he found him already dead. He nonetheless made Ida place a belt around Kariya's neck and tighten it, and only then did he declare the prisoner dead. This macabre charade was undoubtedly meant to implicate Ida in the killing in order to make him more amenable to participating in future crimes. Nakagawa, Ida, and other Aum disciples then became involved in the prolonged and clumsy incineration of Kariya's body in the basement of Satyam 2, finally dissolving the remains in nitric acid before dumping them into a nearby lake.

Nakagawa was also part of the team that released sarin in Matsumoto in 1994. He worked with Seiichi Endō, the minister of health and welfare, in producing the sarin used in the Tokyo subway attack and made the attack possible by preserving, through underground burial, sarin that the guru had ordered destroyed because of increasing police suspicion of Aum. In addition to assisting in attempts to release cyanide gas in the Tokyo subway and to use VX gas in assassinations, he helped make a package bomb mailed to the governor of Tokyo in May 1995, at the time of Asahara's arrest, that injured a municipal worker who handled it.

Nakagawa was involved in every level of Aum drug use. He advocated the use of LSD not only for cult initiations but as a chemical weapon. During the last year or so of the cult's active existence, when Asahara was exerting pressure on its top leaders to produce sarin and to detect spies, Nakagawa obtained a polygraph machine for testing the loyalty of all Aum members at the sarin plant. During that period, the secretariat of the sacred emperor became increasingly important, actively collaborating (usually with the ministry of science and technology) in Aum violence and serving as a broad planning group for realizing the guru's increasingly aggressive visions.

Yet Nakagawa was by no means without conflict about what he did. A close Aum observer described Nakagawa to me in terms of contradictions: "He had a reputation for decency within Aum, but he was involved in secret work and he killed. He was a *shukke* and yet he had a girlfriend within Aum. Some of the time he was deeply committed to the discipline and practice and at other times tried to cast everything off." This last observation evidently refers to Nakagawa's having been at one point accused of insufficient faith in the guru and subjected to a severe retraining procedure, accusatory and punitive in tone and spirit. My informant's final comment was, "I wonder how he could keep both faces." He was referring, I believe, to Nakagawa's rather stark form of doubling. Nakagawa's way of resolving his version of the more general Aum inner split was continually to annihilate that part of the self that was doubtful or resistant and reassert his Aum self in ever more extreme and purified form. That meant quick and total mobilization of his medical background—his physician self—on behalf of Aum fantasy and violence. His spiritual search, along with an intense need for acceptance and approval, had brought him to Aum, where previously suppressed violent and sadistic tendencies could be called forth on behalf of total purity.

Yet Nakagawa's attempted resolution of his doubling did not fully work. During much of his time in Aum he was, according to my observer, "struggling with the idea that he killed these people" and especially haunted by his part in murdering an infant. His deep inner division could well have been responsible for a detail in the Sakamoto killings that is often overlooked: it was Nakagawa who dropped an

Aum badge later found by the police in the Sakamoto home. While at the time the police were uncertain of the significance of the badge's being there, there is at least the possibility that Nakagawa was unconsciously leaving a trail that would implicate Aum in general and himself in particular, that he simultaneously murdered and felt guilty, thereby becoming a criminal who at some level wished to be caught and punished. And indeed, during his testimony he said that he regretted not having been arrested much earlier, and, on learning that the police had known the location of Aum's headquarters after the sarin attack, he declared, "Why wasn't I arrested before I blew off a municipal worker's fingers?"

The Veterinarian, the Chemist, and the Psychiatrists

Seiichi Endō, a veterinarian, did graduate work in virology at the Kyoto University medical school before dropping out to become an Aum renunciant. In the cult he seemed to have the status of a physician. He was given the special task of developing biological weapons and provided with a personal laboratory for the production of sarin, other nerve gases, and illegal drugs. His personality and background sound like those of other Aum doctors and scientists—serious, studious, somewhat naive, thought well of by his professors, but puzzling to everyone because of his religious interests. He would disappear for periods of time and at one point took a leave from the university to go to India to train in yoga.

But according to those who observed him in Aum, he distinguished himself as the group's most consistent scientific bungler. He did have some successes, producing a form of mescaline (reputedly before anyone else in Japan) and, despite mistakes and false starts, leading his ministry in the eventual manufacture of considerable amounts of impure but reasonably potent thiopental. When it came to his work on sarin and other nerve gases, however, Endō's efforts were strikingly ineffectual. Casualties would surely have been enormously greater had not the sarin Endō produced been both minimal in quantity and highly impure.

As early as 1990, Asahara assigned Endō to bacteriological research aimed at creating biological weapons. Although he and others managed to produce a certain amount of botulinus toxin and anthrax bacillus, they consistently failed in their efforts to release these toxins effectively into the atmosphere. Endō fully shared the guru's malignant ambitions in this area, including dissemination of Q fever bacteria and even the Ebola virus. But Endō found himself constantly in the position of reassuring an angry, impatient guru that he would soon find a way to overcome some technological impediment that had interfered with the success of a particular biological or chemical substance. To be sure, Endō's failures had to do not only with his own scientific limitations and the general difficulty of releasing biological weapons but with the grandiosity of Asahara's projections and demands. Endō, however, joined in that grandiosity. It was he, for instance, who had Aum order from the United States the most advanced biotechnology equipment, much of which he was unable to adequately utilize because neither he nor his coworkers knew how.

Then, too, Endō had his anxieties and ambivalences, which could well have played a part in undermining his efforts. After being captured in early April 1995, he was very quick to turn against his guru and was the first to disclose in detail Asahara's and Aum's part in the Matsumoto sarin attack. In court he declared, "I would like Aum followers to face the fact that what they took to be 'religious experiences' were merely the result of drug use." He spoke of his need to atone to Aum's victims and their relatives by "clarifying what exactly the Aum teachings were that controlled us." Throughout the course of the court proceedings, he maintained this critical stance toward the cult, although at one point he dismissed his lawyer in response to what he claimed was a "message" from Aum. He was in many ways the prototypical Aum medical scientist: bright but only half-educated, fanatical in his embrace of Aum guruism (partially because of underlying ambivalent feelings), full of self-condemnation in the light of his inability to actualize the cult's extreme fantasies of murderous "healing," but committed nonetheless to contributing fully to medicalized violence.

Far more successful in realizing Aum's scientific goals was Masami Tsuchiya, the person most responsible for whatever success Aum had with sarin. Indeed, those who observed Endō specifically contrasted his deficiencies with Tsuchiya's skills. A graduate student in organic physical chemistry at a leading university and a part-time teacher at a local prep school when he encountered Aum, he became so enthusiastic about it that he attempted to convert some of his students. His alarmed parents forced him to enter a temple that also served as an institution for the mentally ill, but he fled the temple and became an Aum renunciant and eventually its chief chemist, although in both organizational and spiritual categories his rank was lower than Endō's. Actively involved in manufacturing not only sarin and VX gas but thiopental, LSD, heroin, and mescaline, he was engaged in deep meditation during the period preceding the Tokyo attack and took little part in last-minute production of sarin. That he should at that crucial juncture have been so profoundly immersed in spiritual practice suggests considerable psychological dissociation, indeed to the point of immobilization.

In court Tsuchiya, according to one journalist, "behaved as though he were pretending to be dead" and refused to enter a plea. He exercised his right to silence except on one occasion, when he made an assertion of faith that reflected both his continuing fanaticism and his instability. He made clear that he was ready for the death sentence: "My mission is to be a believer in guru Asahara and die." Declaring that Asahara had transmitted "numerous secret rites" to him, he thanked the guru for teaching him the religious techniques of *poa* and enabling him to experience "various high worlds or forms, ranging from the Heaven of Holiness to the Heaven of the Transcendental Child . . . to the perfect and absolute monist world of nirvana." Nothing, he said, could shake his faith in Aum's leader, and he concluded his statement "by praying for the victory of the great, perfect, absolute guru *Sonshi* Asahara."

The only other time Tsuchiya showed any animation was when a police forensics expert described to the court the chemical structure of sarin. At that point, according to a reporter, "Tsuchiya's eyes shone and he took notes furiously." When begged by the members of the court to confront what he had done and to plead guilty, Tsuchiya "made a deep bow to them," which observers took as "an indication of his mental turmoil."

If Tsuchiya's combination of professional brilliance and a spiritual state close to madness made him particularly well-suited to Aum, Ken'ichirō Katahira, the psychiatrist whom Hayashi characterized as "someone who thinks for himself," seemed an unlikely type to succumb to the cult. A graduate of the medical department of Hiroshima University who had practiced both at the university hospital and at a hospital in a nearby city, he was nevertheless one of three doctors arrested during the March 1995 police raid, for having illegally sedated and detained two recalcitrant Aum followers. A member of Aum from its inception, he also helped Hayashi sedate other followers who were under suspicion. Hayashi's characterization of him notwithstanding, his demeanor at his first court hearing in October 1995—his half-closed eyes and air of serenity—suggested continuing Aum-like behavior.

A second Aum psychiatrist's story is still more puzzling. Unnamed, he is described in a newspaper report as having joined the cult in his early sixties, having observed the beneficial effects of yoga in psychiatric treatment. He became devoted to the guru and found numerous ways to serve him. When an Aum lawyer asked him, for example, to testify that the human rights of a female follower had been violated by commitment to a psychiatric hospital, he demurred because he had not examined the woman, but he assured the court that it could rely on the judgment of Asahara. The issue was an important one for Aum as a number of its recruits had been committed to psychiatric hospitals or had at least spent time in them. He and others brought their psychiatric authority to bear in contesting those hospitalizations, which also meant contesting definitions of mental illness while reinforcing and legitimating Aum's claims.

Although he became disenchanted with Aum and left it in 1989, his story would be unremarkable had he not decided in February 1995, at the age of sixty-eight, to return. His explanation? "Several allegations, including those of kidnapping and lynching, have focused on the cult, and my own suspicions about it became stronger. I went back to the cult not to defend it but because I felt that I, too, as someone who once participated in the cult, wanted to be found guilty." While there is no reason to disbelieve his sense of guilt, one may also assume that he experienced a surge of allegiance to Asahara—to whom he had been bound in discipleship and joint omnipotence—and therefore a strong desire to share the guru's and Aum's fate. Apparently he was not arrested and he had probably committed no crimes. But he seems to have undergone at an advanced age something analogous to the youthful confusion and quest more readily observed in Aum's recruits.

Aum Healing: A Case History

Perhaps no series of events more emblematically represent the workings of Aum's doctors and other medical personnel than those that culminated in the death of Kōtarō Ochida. They began in October 1991, when a middle-aged woman identified in a prosecutor's brief as "Patient A" joined Aum at the urging of two Aum members, one of them her son. They persuaded her that at the Astral Hospital Institute she would be cured of the Parkinson's disease for which she had been unsuccessfully treated at various hospitals for four years. Over the course of a six-month stay in the Astral Hospital Institute, she was given a number of types of medicine and subjected to Aum's thermotherapy—the scalding-water treatment—but her condition did not improve. The doctors began to insist that she make a financial contribution to the cult. "Your disease will be cured," they told her, "if you donate money to Aum." Over a period of three and a half years, she contributed a total of 45,000,000 yen (about $450,000). Eventually she was transferred from the hospital to the main Aum facility, where she was put through a variety of Aum spiritual procedures, including the perfect salvation initiation. But there was no report of improvement.

During her hospital stay, A was befriended by Ochida. Initially enormously enthusiastic about Aum's visionary approach to medicine, he had become disillusioned with its treatment methods, and he left in early 1994. By that time, A had been his patient and the two had become close, possibly even sexually intimate. Ochida feared that the Aum treatment would kill her and approached her son Hideaki Yasuda to help him rescue her forcibly from the group. At first Yasuda resisted but apparently he was persuaded by Ochida's insistence that his mother would die if they did not act. While Yasuda's father and brother waited outside in a getaway car, the two men snuck into the Aum facility and found A lying in a small room with electrodes on her head and tubes in her nostrils. Quickly detected by Aum members, however, they were overpowered and brought before Asahara, his wife, and several leading disciples, including Hideo Murai.

Declaring, "There is probably nothing else to do but to *poa*," Asahara turned to the others, who readily agreed. But Asahara made a distinction between his two prisoners, pronouncing Ochida the main perpetrator, who had manipulated Yasuda and was motivated only by his sexual tie to A. Hence his judgment that, "according to the rule of karma, Yasuda should *poa* Ochida." In that way Yasuda could "reduce his bad karma." To spur him on, the guru taunted him with putative details of his mother's sexual exploitation by Ochida and promised that he could go home if he carried out the killing. If he did not, Asahara made clear, he, too, would be *poa*'d. When Yasuda asked Asahara if he would really be permitted to go home, the guru replied, "Have I ever lied before?" Yasuda insisted he could not look at Ochida's eyes while carrying out the act and was given tape to blindfold his victim. As he leaned over Ochida, he said, "I'm sorry," to which the victim replied, "That's all right. I'm ready. I'm sorry to involve you in this."

Handed a rope with which to strangle Ochida, Yasuda struggled at his task and others were enlisted to hold the victim down. Specifically ordered by the guru to help Yasuda, Dr. Nakagawa held Ochida, a friend of his, from behind. Periodically he checked Ochida's pulse, also at the command of Asahara, who insisted that he confirm Ochida's death medically. Later Nakagawa would report that seeing his friend writhe in pain made him think, "Since he has to die anyway, I'll help him out by speeding up the process."

Yasuda was permitted to leave as promised, but with orders that he say nothing to his father and brother and that he come to Aum training once a week. Meanwhile, again at the guru's order, Nakagawa took the first steps to dispose of the body. Murai and the guru agreed that it should be cremated in the cult's basement microwave incinerator, an elaborate three-day process. Yasuda, fearful of Aum, did not reappear as instructed and instead went into hiding in a northern area.

The guru gave such high priority to his capture that the kidnap team sent after him included Nakagawa and Aum's other high-ranking doctor, Ikuo Hayashi, who were prepared to drug him in the usual fashion. Tracked down, Yasuda avoided capture by calling the police, causing the kidnap team to flee.

Eventually Yasuda, Asahara, his wife Tomoko, Nakagawa, and others who were present at Ochida's murder were accused of the killing or of complicity in it. Patient A survived her Aum therapy.

7 | Megalomania

Aum's danger to the world—and its greatest significance—lay in its joining of megalomania to ultimate weapons. That combination found quintessential expression in the guru's reception of his high disciples upon their return from carrying out the subway attack. First the guru invoked his all-encompassing authority to render mass murder altruistic and absorb it into a mantra of spiritual practice. Then, all the accounts agree, Asahara rewarded his returning murderers with praise and juice and cookies and ordered them to repeat one thousand or ten thousand times or more sentences like, "It was good to be given *poa* by the great god Shiva and all the victors of truth" or "It was good to be *poa*'d by the grace of the guru and the great god Shiva and all the victors of truth." The only disputed point is whether Asahara was saying that the act was ultimately sanctioned only by the god Shiva or that he, the guru, shared sufficient status to join Shiva in granting the *poa*. Probably the guru hedged a bit on this point.

At this postsarin ritual, guru and disciples alike displayed a certain unease. Both were involved in the completion of a murderous melodrama staged in concordance with an extravagant world-destroying vision. But even as that vision held sway, the guru and his disciples seemed to retain portions of their selves that doubted its truth or rightness and felt anxiety about the destructive act that could not, notably in Dr. Hayashi's case, be entirely quelled by the declaration of ennobling *poa*. Even Asahara slipped into something close to psychotic denial when he said to Hayashi at a separate meeting, "They claimed it was Aum who spread the sarin." Either he was insisting, even as he gave his *poa* blessing to the disciples who carried out the act, that the incident was an attack on Aum by outside forces or he was expressing surprise and concern that the authorities suspected Aum as its perpetrator. It is likely that he embraced both of these stances. His megalomanic self enabled him to view any event—in fact, all of history—according to his own narrative needs. Thus he could declare in a radio talk three days after the attack that the police were "Lucifer" and that not only the attack but the police raid represented "a step in the expansion of the Aum Shinrikyō plan of salvation."

Functional Megalomania

The guru brought to the amassing of ultimate weapons what I have called a functional megalomania. Within megalomanic function, self becomes world. The megalomanic self lacks limits and boundaries; it resists or denies restraints of any sort. Hence the self envelops the world; the world dissolves into the self. Or put another way, the totalized self replaces the external world.

Contemporary ultimate weapons can hold a special lure for the megalomanic guru because they enable him to feel that he alone—or perhaps with a few disciples—is capable of destroying the world. He can claim a kind of world-controlling as well as world-ending power. Indeed, as the Cold War suggests, megalomanic feelings can be experienced by just about anyone who becomes involved with such weaponry and can play a part in attracting strategists as well as scientists to the weapons in the first place.

As a clinical phenomenon, megalomania is generally encountered in advanced paranoid schizophrenia. In that condition, the patient usually is alone with his delusions and hallucinations, his totalized self condemning him to radical isolation from the external world it replaces. In contrast, a guru like Asahara had disciples who interacted with his megalomanic self in ways that reinforced it, rendering it functional. The arrangement offered seductive rewards—mutual ecstasy and a shared sense of absolute truth—that could sustain it for long periods of time as disciples became more and more immersed in the guru's megalomania, both endorsing it and realizing their own megalomanic potential. The extreme cultic process, in other words, became a version of collective megalomania. The arrangement, however, was inherently unstable, subject to the breakout of suppressed antagonisms between guru and disciples and, more dangerously, apt to result in violent attacks on the external world by guru and disciples whenever they felt their bond with one another, or anything else in the arrangement, to be threatened.

Megalomania contributed greatly to Asahara's attempts to actualize his world-ending visions. The idea of vast destruction in the service of spiritual renewal became something more—and less—than a metaphor or mythic truth. The megalomanic self, in fact, insists upon the breakdown of such distinctions, claiming dominion over myth and metaphor no less than over actual events. The ultimate power of the weapons themselves, their promise of destroying humankind or even the planet, contributes greatly to the breakdown of those distinctions. In our time, the wildest fantasy of total annihilation holds the all too evident possibility of becoming an engine for the literal destruction of the world.

The *Oxford English Dictionary* defines megalomania as "insanity of self-exaltation." As characterized in the *Psychiatric Dictionary*, the megalomanic person considers himself "possessed of greatness" and may "believe himself to be Christ, God, Napoleon" or "everybody and everything." Asahara epitomized this sense of multiform omnipotence in every way. In some of his books, for instance, his biographical description lauded him not only as a guru who had attained final enlightenment and as "one of the greatest holy persons presently existing on this earth" but also as a universal genius: "Master Asahara shows his genius not only in the spiritual domain but in various fields such as science, medicine, music, writing, translation, education, etc." The "etc." is the operative word here—his genius is unlimited. (The list could have been expanded to include his roles as a filmmaker, animator, or, as another of his blurbs had it, "leading television personality.") The genius, like the self, is multiform and world-encompassing.

That genius was extended to his physiology with the claim that he possessed nirvana-like brain waves and uniquely distinctive DNA. When Asahara spoke of himself as a catalyst for "chemical changes that we cannot imagine in the usual sense" but that would lead to "a new form of matter," he was offering further proof of his bodily genius.

The guru's most insistent megalomanic claim was to deity. In addition to declaring himself an avatar of Shiva, he professed to have achieved "the state of a Buddha who has attained mirror-like wisdom" and to be the "divine emperor" of Japan and of the world; the declared Christ, who will "disclose the meaning of Jesus' gospel"; the "last twentieth-century savior"; the "holiest holy man," one "beyond the Bible"; and the being who will inaugurate the Age of Aquarius and preside over a "new era of supreme truth." For disciples transfixed by guruism, he could indeed be all these things.

An external manifestation of the megalomanic self was Aum's organization into "ministries" and "agencies" suggestive of a huge governmental structure. Aum doctrine on past and future lives reflected a similar megalomanic organization. While everything in cult life was ostensibly determined by cause-and-effect karma because "Buddhism is mathematics," the guru controlled the equations. It was he who could threaten the most dreadful realms of rebirth—the "realm of hell" for those who killed, the "animal realm" for the ignorant—or promise "Brahma heaven," with its eight subrealms culminating in nirvana, "the state of ultimate extinction." Much of Aum's spiritual project dealt with preparing for the next life, the transfer of consciousness to a higher dimension—Asahara's "great *poa*." An indication of Asahara's megalomania was his manipulation of *poa* from a concept of ideal spiritual transformation to a euphemism for murder.

Asahara became the judge and repository—not to mention the traffic director—of all the world's bad karma. He claimed to have taken on that totality of badness, carrying it all in his own mind and body as a way of countering and eliminating it. Whether he ordered *poa* or provided his direct *shaktipat* touch, all currents flowed through him, to be held, recast, or guided by him. This karma control also made Asahara the personal storehouse of the world's salvation, which at every point depended upon his bringing about the "dropping of karma." He could embrace a vision of overcoming the laws of gravity because he was the detached arbiter of the world's spiritual gravity.

Asahara was never more megalomanic than in his recitation of his past lives. These included that of an absolutely loyal disciple (who killed at the order of his guru), a guru to many of his Aum followers ("Most of my close disciples were also my disciples in their former lives"), and the king of various upper realms of rebirth. He also claimed to have had previous existences in America, including one as Benjamin Franklin, a charter member of the first American Freemasons' lodge. Reflecting on past lives, he once commented, "It becomes very difficult to tell who is a friend and who is an enemy." And in a sermon he declared that there would eventually be a union of Aum Shinrikyō and the Freemasons in which the latter would come to revere the former: "This is all related to one of my former lives, so I can say that the two are certain to unite."

Asahara's most expansive past-life claim concerned the very origins of civilization. Visiting Egypt and observing its oldest pyramid, he was struck by the realization not only that he had seen it before but that "I designed it myself a long time ago." This was not just an ordinary recollection of a past life but an expression of "a supernatural power called the Divine Knowledge of Past Lives" that he acquired "just before I attained supreme enlightenment." Thus he was able to ascertain that at the time of the pyramids' construction he was "Prime Minister Imhotep," the spiritual adviser to the pharaoh. Because the pharaoh did not want to die, Imhotep/Asahara "built a shrine [where] the king could master the secret techniques of *Poa*." There the pharaoh and his followers could "discard their bodies . . . and go to higher worlds." The pyramids Imhotep/Asahara built remained in such good condition because he "energized [them] with a strong uplifting energy." In keeping with these claims, one Aum commentary is entitled "Master Asahara Solves the Mysteries of Egypt" and another "Pyramids Were Instruments for *Poa*." Asahara thus claims not only architectural authorship of the pyramids, but authorship of

Western civilization itself, including its religious practices. All of this authorship, moreover, is bound up with the organizing principle of *poa*, which comes to signify immortal spiritual continuity.

In his "current" life, Asahara was attracted to such world-destroying figures as Hitler, Stalin, and Mao, both identifying himself with the omnipotence of mass murderers and incorporating them into his megalomanic self. He was, as we know, especially drawn to Nazism, speaking sympathetically of *Mein Kampf* and pronouncing that destiny dictated 1999 as the year that the postwar ban on *Mein Kampf* in Germany would be lifted, at which time not only would "many people . . . sympathize with Nazi ideology" but Armageddon would break out. "I don't think it is absurd to say," he added, "that the Nazis will be revived like a phoenix after Armageddon."

It was essential for Asahara to be distinguished absolutely from all other human beings. He alone was completely free of "defilement," of any need for further spiritual quest, of desire itself. Since he was, of course, free of none of these, the claims can be understood as compensatory, as an extreme psychological reversal of his actual "defilement" (cruelty and murderousness), his radical spiritual insecurity (inner doubts about his exorbitant claims), and his insistent desires (for power over other human beings, sex, and forbidden food). The megalomanic claim to have no desire meant, in practice, the presence of unlimited self-aggrandizing desire.

Breakdown

Toward the end, as Asahara's control over his environment faltered, his megalomania ceased to be functional. Threats from the outside (groups contesting Aum's activities and the developing police investigation of its murders) and from the inside (insufficient numbers of renunciants and strains in guru-disciple relationships) undermined the shared fantasy so necessary to the workings of such megalomania. The guru's intensified paranoia drove him toward external violence as well as toward various forms of self-destruction. He became more extreme and more fragmented.

His sense of embattlement increased precipitously. Now he saw the influence of the Freemasons extending everywhere in Japan, even into the highest reaches of the imperial household. Hidden within the logos of Fuji television, Toyota Motors, and the Japanese currency he found the Freemason sign, proof that the mass media, industry, and the economy were dominated by them. His agitation about spies within Aum grew, as did the use of "truth serum." He presided over an increasing number of murders of Aum members. While he spent endless hours on the telephone reaching out sympathetically to his highest disciples in those final months, he could resemble the coldest mafia boss in ordering that designated enemies be *poa*'d.

In March 1994, after complaining that he and his family were the subject of sarin attacks, he declared that "there is no choice but terrorism from now on." He would explode angrily at disciples who displeased him by not immediately achieving his fantasied goals. In April 1994, he declared to a small group of followers, "You must die!" (borrowing a phrase made famous in a film about the *yakuza*). Increasingly he threatened his leading disciples with *poa* should they try to escape. His con-man tendencies became more bizarre: now he simply assumed that stating a lie rendered it true and that anyone doubting any of his words became an enemy of Aum. All this represented psychological decompensation, the breakdown of his megalomanic system.

Asahara's degeneration was reflected in his everyday behavior. Just as no man is a hero to his valet, no guru is a saint to his driver. In a revealing book, one of Asahara's former drivers, Satoshi Tamura, details the guru's increasing gluttony, hypocrisy, and cruelty. According to Tamura, the guru who crafted his role as the "sacred blind man" and the "blind savior" whose coming is predicted in the Book of Revelation could actually see well enough to catch a baseball or serve a tennis ball. Because he did not wish to be observed violating Buddhist dietary rules, he had Tamura go to his restaurants of choice and order out triple portions of various meat and fish dishes. He instructed Tamura to eat the same food in similar excess. When Tamura raised a question about the guru's eating habits to a superior in Aum, he was told that the guru was giving him a mahāmudrā, a response that made Tamura "ashamed of myself for doubting the Master." Asahara would speak proudly of his "bodhisattva stomach," which enabled him to eat anything. He would even sponsor contests among his disciples to see who could consume the most, sometimes at festivals that featured orgies of eating. Asahara would then claim that his own weight gain resulted from the bad karma he was taking on from disciples, that performing *shaktipat* sent "bad energy" to his stomach. Tamura dates these eating patterns—at least in their most extreme form—to sometime in 1994.

The guru often traveled with an entourage of seven cars, what Tamura called the "*daimyō's* [feudal lord's] procession." While assuring Aum members that poor health prevented his appearing among them, he would indulge in various amusements, including visits to gaming rooms. Once, in a game called Horse Race, he predicted after a bit of meditation that his horse would win. When it didn't, Tamura was left upset and confused: the guru's predictions were never supposed to be wrong. Asahara also enjoyed "karaoke parties" in the private rooms of bars, where he would bring his lovers and other members of his small group and let everyone take turns at the mike. Asahara's favorite song to sing was, appropriately enough, the Japanese version of Frank Sinatra's "My Way." "Once he grabbed the microphone," according to Tamura, "he would never give it back."

Visiting Kobe in the wake of the earthquake of January 1995, the guru declared soon after arriving that absorbing the bad karma of the people killed there was simply too painful; he ordered Tamura to drive to a restaurant outside the city, where he indulged himself in his usual manner. An accompanying truck turned out to have limited space for food for the victims because so much of it was taken up with the possessions of Asahara's children, including bicycles, toys, and soccer equipment. Tamura describes the guru's children as spoiled and full of a sense of power: his teenage daughter carried around large numbers of ten-thousand-yen (one-hundred-dollar) bills, and his twelve-year-old daughter teased and dominated other Aum children with the claim that she alone had dropped off all of her bad karma.

Tamura also recounts guru-disciple encounters replete with sadomasochism. Asked by Murai what to do about a slight injury suffered by a subordinate, the guru disdainfully replied, "If you urinate on it, it will be cured." Murai dutifully carried out the suggestion. Another time a renunciant admitted that he had fallen in love with a young woman and had been told by a high-ranking member that the best way to overcome this "defilement" was to eat her feces. Asahara first ridiculed the idea but later changed his mind and had the renunciant do just that. In 1995, Tamura writes, Asahara arranged a series of large dinners (for as many as five hundred disciples) at the cult's main headquarters; these he scheduled according to his whims, to begin at midnight or even 3:00 A.M. He would then keep the disciples waiting for hours, during which time they would assume the lotus position and chant a mantra like "Master, please appear." At one such dinner scheduled for 1:00 A.M., Asahara did not arrive until 8:00. In most cases he would soon leave, allegedly because he was unwell, and go to a restaurant to gorge himself.

No matter how cruel or contradictory, the guru's behavior could always be interpreted as a mahāmudrā. Or the behavior could be connected in some manner to another religious tradition—for instance, the yogic practice of eating and drinking to great excess to increase the strength of the stomach, and then vomiting everything up as an act of purification. Asahara would begin with something resembling a Buddhist or Hindu principle and either contort it to the point of caricature or find a rationale for avoiding or violating it. In an important sense, his displays of power and entitlement, and of transcending all boundaries and violating every taboo, were all efforts to sustain his functional megalomania. What rendered such efforts especially intense and desperate was the need to fend off a growing sense of external threat and internal disintegration. Such compensatory behavior could include every variety of fraudulence, hypocrisy, and exploitation. For underneath the megalomanic claim to be "everybody and everything" was an overwhelming terror of being nobody and nothing.

During the months prior to the Tokyo sarin attack, Asahara's connection to reality was so muddled that we must suspect him to have been, at least some of the time, psychotic. By now, the totalized self was in pieces, no one of which was capable of keeping things going effectively. His delusions could be understood as efforts, ever more futile, to reassert his megalomanic function as the sole dispenser of world existence. However decompensated, Asahara was sufficiently coherent even after the sarin incident to convey to his disciples the message that his capture was to be avoided at any cost and that continuous terror was to be employed to prevent it. A collective Aum megalomania was still operative in the bizarre assumption that terrorism (letter bombs, additional releases of lethal chemicals, and assassinations) would so divert or intimidate the police that the guru would be left alone.

His actual arrest was in fact delayed by the police until they could be sure that his most prominent followers were in custody and could not attempt violent retaliation. Two months after the sarin attack, the police found Shōkō Asahara in a small hidden cubicle in Aum headquarters dressed in his purple priestly robes, lying in his urine, and surrounded by piles of Japanese currency totaling about ten million yen, or a hundred thousand dollars. The guru's inability to leave the cubicle probably accounted for the urine, though it might also have reflected his psychological deterioration. The money could have been placed there for the guru's use, should he have decided to flee. Whatever the case, the symbolism of useless money and humiliating urine could not have been more apt. A kind of de-guruizing process—and the subversion of whatever functional megalomania remained—began when the police gave him orders that he had to obey and ignored his insistence that "no one is allowed to touch the guru's body." To the last, though, he invoked his con-man self: told he was being arrested for murdering eleven people in the subway attack, he replied, "Could a blind man like me possibly do such a thing?"

During his first months in prison he tried to sustain his guru self by holding to a routine of meditation and fasting. He also sought to maintain control over his disciples, though, given his isolation, he could do so only partially and temporarily. The one continuing disciple I interviewed, a slight woman in her twenties who worked in an Aum bookstore, told me ten months after Asahara's imprisonment that, while on the "phenomenal level" he was of course not with her, "on the astral level we are in close touch with each other. I still feel his presence." When she and other disciples were in the vicinity of the prison, she added, they could "feel his energy, the wonderful vibrations that come out from him." Despite the fact that a few prominent disciples have continued to profess complete faith in their guru and that Aum as an organization has never ceased to exist, in captivity neither Asahara's megalomania nor his guru self could long hold sway.

Legal authorities further negated Asahara's guruhood by denying him the right to appear in court in his priestly robes, stating that these had "religious meaning" and could influence witnesses who had been or were still cult members. Instead he wore a mangy sweatsuit and seemed unkempt beyond the clothes. He continued nonetheless to make weak attempts to hold on as guru. When asked in court to confirm his real name as Chizuo Matsumoto, he replied, "I abandoned that name." Refusing to enter a plea, he launched instead into a brief discourse on the spiritual purposes of Aum Shinrikyō and "the perfect freedom, perfect joy and happiness of those who practice the Supreme Truth." His statement suggested a disinclination to accept any responsibility for Aum's crimes, but it probably also reflected a certain amount of confusion and mental deterioration.

Little of his functional megalomania survived his relegation to the status of a prisoner subject to the will and demands of others. Perhaps the final assault on his megalomanic guru identity, however, was the humiliating defection of former high disciples who not only implicated him in the sarin attacks and various individual murders but, much worse for him psychologically, mocked his spiritual claims. In open court, for instance, Shigerō Sugimoto, a leading member of Aum's inner circle, declared, "I was deceived by the claim that the guru was a person who had achieved final liberation." The idea of Asahara's taking on other people's karma "was complete nonsense"; instead, "he sought to satisfy his own desires." Sugimoto now saw the guru as a "foolish human being" who had nevertheless managed to use him. Dr. Hayashi pointed out contemptuously that the same guru who boasted that he could "foresee everything and stand above society" to the point of choosing the time of his death was now preoccupied with saving his life.

In the fall of 1996, after a series of confrontations in court with angry and accusatory former disciples, the megalomanic, totalized self appeared to break down altogether. The moment of dramatic shift from assertive guru to disintegrating human being seemed to some observers to occur on September 20, 1996, when Yoshihiro Inoue, perhaps his closest disciple, began detailing Asahara's full role in directing the sarin attack. As he testified, making clear his complete rejection of Aum's founder as a "false guru," Asahara muttered, "You'll go to hell" and "Think about death," becoming so agitated that he ignored the judge's instructions to sit down and be quiet. He showed signs of what was described in newspaper reports as "mental instability" and on several occasions had to be removed from the courtroom.

At times, Asahara seemed actually to exhibit sympathy for his former disciple, objecting to the "tormenting" cross-examination to which "a great soul such as Inoue" was being subjected and suggesting that he, the guru, would "take all responsibility." But he more frequently declared himself to be "totally innocent," once insisting that the sarin attacks were "Inoue's plot." As Inoue testified at length about Aum's production of sarin, the guru began to make convulsive movements, "spasms in which his face appeared twisted and his head was shaking up and down." After a brief recess, Asahara, now sitting close to Inoue, abruptly said to him, "Witness Inoue, I may appear to be mentally disturbed, but would you jump [levitate] from where you are?" The question was an attempt, however bizarre, to reclaim Inoue's discipleship.

A former disciple who attended these court sessions regarded Asahara's spasms as "a kind of hysteria" but added that "shaking" was considered a mystical phenomenon in Aum and that his invitation to Inoue to jump was, in effect, an invitation to share that mystical experience with his guru. Asahara seemed to be undergoing a "collapse" of his personality and to be increasingly "confused by his own words." The observer was "shocked" by the transformation of a guru who always appeared to him to have "an air of dignity" and of "total confidence" into the "disturbed" person in the courtroom. He emphasized that, as any criticism of the guru was taboo in Aum, direct denunciation by so close a disciple as Inoue "had to be shocking" to Asahara. He also noted that while Inoue at first spoke "in a faint voice, as if he felt sorry to be testifying, his tone became stronger as the guru's became weaker."

Inoue later told his lawyer that, listening to Asahara, he cried "tears of regret, distress, sorrow, and shame." Both guru and disciple were experiencing the psychological consequences of the breaking of a bond that had defined their Aum selves for so long. Inoue's testimony epitomized the resentful withdrawal from the guru's megalomanic self by those disciples most responsible for having sustained it. Now that self had little possibility but to live in psychosis. Asahara's feeble efforts to reassert his guruhood were made in the language of paranoid schizophrenia. Thus, at one point he said to the judge:

> I'm not the soul to obey you. . . . I want to practice alone. . . . My way of living is different from yours. I want to make that clear. You are causing me, a blind person, to have illusions. You are dispensing ultrasonic waves to make me crazy. You are using the death penalty as a threat. Why are you talking about burning with laser beams? If you want to shoot me to death, then do it, . . . kill me by torturing me, by freezing me and burning me and removing my energy, . . . taking away my life force. . . . You are trying to brainwash me by letting me hear the sounds of the guillotine . . . or of people falling from a building—and making me believe these are real. . . . So take me out of here to the jail and continue the lynching there.

Of the trial he said, "It's completely mad—myself included perhaps."

Asahara's court outbursts frequently concerned his own death. He interrupted the proceedings by asking, "Am I going to be killed?" When an objection he raised was refused, his question was, "If you reject it, does that mean an instant death penalty?" In response to testimony about Aum's production of botulinus virus, he said, "That's ridiculous. If that were the case I'd be killed." At various times he would resort to odd postures—bizarre movements of his lower jaw and shoulders and peculiar motions of washing his face or combing his hair or drinking water—thereby calling observers' attention to himself. Even in his apparently psychotic state, he made bitter references to the defection of his disciples, insisting that "the doctrine of Aum Shinrikyō is based on Buddhism and the reason disciples develop a crazy attitude is their lack of truth." Turning to Ken'ichi Hirose, a former disciple, he declared, "I spoke up because there was no human being there. . . . I am not even sure whether or not this witness is Hirose."

Asahara objected to his hearings and trials as "abnormal," "absurd," "foolish," and "completely crazy." He would demand that the trial be stopped or would yawn loudly or murmur to himself. As the hearings went on, his demeanor became yet more bizarre. A *Japan Times* reporter described Asahara's behavior at a court session in May 1997: "He mumbled continuously in Japanese and English, sometimes moving his head vertically in a violent manner. He was heard once saying 'never kill' in English." Sometimes, switching back and forth between the two languages, he would explain that he was "translating" his English into Japanese. On another occasion, when Asahara mumbled a great deal and seemed to be confused, his lawyer explained that the guru was "talking to the prosecutors, his own lawyers, and his former followers, and playing all the roles himself," adding that he might be "trying to spark his memory by talking to himself" since "his weak eyesight" prevented him from reading the documents. Here and on other occasions, it is quite possible that Asahara was hearing voices.

Asahara was frequently ejected from the courtroom for interrupting the testimony of disciples. At times he would answer questions simultaneously with the witness to whom they were directed or insist that he had "already been found not guilty" in sixteen of the seventeen cases for which he was being tried. Other times he would shout objections in either English or Japanese, stand silently and refuse to sit down, or fall asleep during sessions. He also refused to meet with his own lawyers and was generally uncooperative in his dealings with them.

In short, his megalomanic immortality system was shattered. To some degree, the guru's preoccupation with his death reflected a realistic fear of being given the death penalty, but Asahara was undoubtedly also expressing a sense of the psychological death he was experiencing in becoming flamboyantly psychotic. As he felt himself being annihilated by enemies, his paranoia became bound up with delusions but remained for him the most psychologically manageable interpretation of his situation.

Many—perhaps most—Japanese believed that Asahara was faking, pretending to be insane in order to absolve himself of legal (and perhaps personal) responsibility for his crimes. It is a possibility that cannot be completely dismissed. The visionary-megalomanic guru always existed in company with the con-man manipulator; we can probably say the same of the psychotically fragmented guru. Asahara could indeed still have been consciously playing the role of the crazy man even as he was being overwhelmed by the disintegration of his once-proud guru self. He could well have been deceived by his own role-playing, unaware of the powerfully disintegrative forces that rendered his faking no more than a pathetic set of gestures. His feeble attempts to dismiss the very existence of his disciples turned accusers were surely a psychotic response to the collapse of his world.

That breakdown of the self was inevitable. What was more surprising—and more ominous—was the prior alliance between the functional megalomanic self and weapons that could destroy everything.

8 | Ultimate Weapons, Ultimate Attraction

We can hardly be surprised that a megalomanic fantasist like Shōkō Asahara came to view sarin as something more than a harmful nerve gas, but no one could have anticipated the extent to which it entered into his and Aum's imagination. Aum's embrace of sarin had to do, at first, with the cult's success in producing it as a weapon. Once embraced, however, sarin became an organizing principle for Asahara's megalomania, for Aum's rhetoric of persecution, and ultimately for its Armageddon project.

Aum is known to have embarked seriously on the production of sarin in 1993. In April of that year, Asahara first spoke publicly of the gas, suggesting that the Japanese Self-Defense Forces remedy its state of unpreparedness by producing chemical weapons, especially sarin. About a year later Aum began to make public statements claiming that its members, Asahara included, were being victimized by sarin attacks. (Subsequently, Aum would claim that such attacks had been responsible for illnesses experienced as early as 1989.) From 1993 on, people living in the cult's Mount Fuji facilities did indeed encounter foul odors and notice that the surrounding foliage was dying—almost certainly the result of leakage from Aum's sarin laboratories.

There were also reports of sarin casualties in Aum. I was told of Aum members experiencing aching eyes, bleeding noses, coughing, and blackouts. Some of those so afflicted were convinced the gas was being released from within Aum by "spies" using "a big electric terminal" to disseminate it. Others believed that it was being sprayed from enemy helicopters. In one incident in late January 1995, Ogata, the ardent young Armaggedon warrior, detected a foul odor and witnessed about fifty people becoming ill, many of them passing out. He himself passed out after trying to rescue some of the children and was hospitalized for three weeks, during which he was given daily doses of a sarin antidote. Kuno, who left the cult before the Tokyo attack, is convinced that the entire incident was "self-staged," that Asahara intentionally released the gas himself in order to demonstrate Aum's victimization. Ogata now also suspects that Aum leaders may "ultimately have been willing to go that far" but remains uncertain as to whether the release was accidental or planned. In any case, Aum doctors produced data suggesting sarin symptoms among its members, thereby giving a medical stamp to this bodily claim of persecution. They stressed their use of antidotes, thereby conveying the message that, while others attack, Aum heals.

From his first mention of sarin in 1993, Asahara spoke more and more frequently about the gas, always in a persecutory vein. Aum was being attacked with sarin by a host of enemies: the United States or the CIA, the Japanese government or its CIA, religious groups like Sōka Gakkai, and various "Jewish Japanese," including the emperor, Crown Princess Masako, and prominent political and industrial leaders. Behind all of them, of course, were the evil manipulations of international Jewish and Freemason conspirators. But sarin's real importance for Asahara was at the imaginative center of his world-destroying project. It became the linchpin in the merging of his megalomanic self with ultimate weaponry.

The function of his megalomanic self came to depend upon a combination of extreme fantasy and concrete weapons planning focused on sarin. There was not only his wild vision of a vast November 1995 release of sarin that would initiate World War III but also the purchase in Russia (and delivery to Aum in Japan) of a large MI-17 helicopter capable of carrying and spraying huge amounts of sarin over urban populations. There were Aum's extensive missions to obtain materials involved in the manufacture of sarin. There were the test releases of the gas in a remote area of Australia in 1993 and then in the city of Matsumoto in June 1994. In February 1995, there was the guru's statement to a small group of high disciples in a Tokyo hotel that Aum had no choice but to "disperse seventy tons of sarin in Tokyo." That amount, itself fantasy, could have killed virtually everyone in Tokyo and much of Japan. Denied the time for more elaborate planning by the imminence of police raids, Asahara turned to sarin in ordering the attack in Tokyo. His choice was all but inevitable: in the year before the attack, the nerve gas had become the idiom for almost everything articulated, and acted upon, by Asahara and Aum, evidence of the way in which a megalomanic self can be reconstructed around whatever ultimate weapons it perceives to be available. Such a self, with the help of devoted scientifically trained disciples, can turn bizarre world-ending fantasies into actual arsenals of ultimate weaponry. In the process, the very distinction between the psychology of omnipotence and actual mass killing may cease to exist.

Magic Poison

Press reports immediately following the Tokyo attack spoke of Aum's scientists researching the Nazis' development of poison gas, as it was the Nazis who first produced sarin, though they never used it. Aum also obtained much information about sarin from its extensive contacts in Russia as well as from various manuals and texts available in the United States. Still, one wonders whether Asahara's strong identification with Hitler and Nazi Germany might have been a factor in his intense attraction to the gas. Aum also worked on the manufacture of tabun, another nerve gas originally produced by the Nazis, and of hydrogen cyanide, the poison gas used by the Nazis in Auschwitz.

Although biological weapons are generally considered easier to make than chemical weapons and Aum scientists had been working on them for about three years before they took up sarin, Aum never developed a possessively worshipful attitude toward them. It is possible that Asahara was stirred by thoughts of himself as a spiritually transcendent Hitler, embracing both the Führer's gas and his visionary murderousness. We know that he was attracted to the Iraqi dictator Saddam Hussein as a non-Western, Hitler-like figure who was being martyred by the United States and who had already used chemical weapons, including sarin. (What we do not know is whether Asahara was aware that Iraq's chemical arsenal consisted largely of sarin.)

Asahara seemed fascinated by what he took to be sarin's efficiency. For him, this "poor man's atomic bomb" was also the "energy-saving atomic bomb" because it could kill people without wasting energy on destroying buildings. The guru made its production the center of a remarkable industrial outreach program that included elaborate corporate arrangements for acquiring a wide array of technical equipment, much of it computerized, in Japan, the United States, and Russia. Some of the most sophisticated equipment came from the United States, including what one former disciple called "chemical software." Aum sought to disguise the nature of its American operation by also ordering antiquated computer chip materials, which were meant to suggest that it was engaged in a computer-manufacturing process that would justify the acquisition of chemicals like arsenide, chlorides, and fluorides, used as well for manufacturing sarin and other gases. The necessary chemical formulas were especially available in Russia, whose empire had collapsed and whose often desperate military and industrial scientists were under great economic duress. An Aum manual also refers to an "Uncle Fester," an American source of sarin know-how. Uncle Fester, as it turns out, is a common pseudonym for people who publish information on producing terrorist devices. Much of Aum's information was apparently available on the Internet.

In the entrepreneurial activity of obtaining information and materials, as in the actual making of the gas, Aum mixed incredibly bold, sometimes brilliant outreach and planning with naive, childlike inefficiency and amateurism. Although the primary vision of sarin production and use came from Asahara himself, he was influenced by his dialogues with Aum scientists, doctors, and planners, especially Hideo

Murai. It was finally Masami Tsuchiya, Aum's chief chemist, who, having learned a lot about the gas in Russia, succeeded in producing it in usable form late in 1993. But while Tsuchiya and his helpers made the sarin that was released in the 1994 Matsumoto attack, they frustrated the guru with their inability to expand production radically in a large laboratory and an additional small building at the main Aum facility. As noted, there were extensive sarin leaks, as well as several near fatalities among the sarin makers, including Tsuchiya, who is said to have lost consciousness on several occasions.

Even more troubling to Asahara were the increasingly suspicious media reports of poison emanating from the Aum compound—troubling enough that he had Tsuchiya shut down the large laboratory completely. It was then that the area was remodeled into a hall of worship that could be displayed to visitors. The destroyed laboratory had been enormously ambitious in scale, managing to produce small amounts of tabun, soman (another nerve gas), VX, and mustard gas, as well as sarin. Also destroyed was a van with a specially designed gas-releasing nozzle that had been used in the Matsumoto attack. When, not long afterward, the police were about to close in and Asahara and Murai decided upon a sarin attack on Tokyo, the gas had largely to be made anew. Asahara ordered Seiichi Endō, who had until then been focusing on biological weapons, to apply himself to something close to instant sarin production. With the help of Tomomasa Nakagawa but only limited assistance from Tsuchiya, who was by then in deep meditation, he quickly produced a small amount of sarin whose significant impurities, however, impaired its effectiveness. But for Asahara, as an American commentator put it, "impure sarin was better than no sarin at all." One way or another, the guru would have his "magic" for meeting the emergency.

That emergency was brought about by Aum's abduction and killing of Kiyoshi Kariya, the notary public. To be sure, the police would eventually have found other reasons to raid Aum facilities—the cult had long been suspected of responsibility for the sarin killings at Matsumoto as well as other murders. Inevitably, Asahara's attack guruism and his impulse to force the end would have led to a confrontation that threatened Aum's existence and thereby brought about a radical breakdown of the guru's megalomanic self.

Sarin, then, was simultaneously a "defense" or "deterrent" against alleged evil and a trigger for Armageddon. The immediate evil being "defended" against was the authority of the state, and the Tokyo subway release was a desperate strategic effort, however absurd, to employ a limited amount of the gas to divert the police and confuse the public. The guru was enraged at his disciples for their inability to produce the ultimate sarin "magic" on which he had staked everything. He sensed that failure meant his psychological annihilation. As his agent on a divine world-ending mission, sarin had taken on mystical proportions for him. He had ordered three major releases and imagined an all-important fourth. The first release, while aimed only at sheep in the Australian outback, had nonetheless been a serious experiment in the dispensing of existence. (Tsuchiya is said to have expressed a certain sympathy for the twenty sheep felled, insisting that it was human beings and not animals who deserved to be killed.) The second release, in Matsumoto, though aimed at judges threatening to curb illegal Aum activities—a focused dispensing of existence—had also been an experiment in overcoming barriers to Aum's Armageddon project. The third release, in Tokyo's subways, though a hasty diversion, had been aimed randomly at people who happened to have gathered there, and it would have killed enormous numbers of them had the sarin been purer. As Aum's first attempt at random mass killing, even if on a relatively small scale, it could be viewed by Asahara as an Armageddon thrust. All these releases had immediate tactical goals while being subsumed to an activist Armageddon project. The great release planned for November 1995 was to be the actual harbinger of Armageddon, but it undoubtedly included elements of "defense"—of countering evil forces—as well. A "defensive" strategy of incessant aggressive action ultimately proved inseparable from world salvation once the guru had attached his megalomania to this powerful weapon.

Little Sarii

So central was sarin to Aum's imagination that a December 1994 pamphlet (found by police at cult headquarters) devoted mostly to the chemical principles involved in producing it contained two little songs of tribute:

SONG OF SARIN THE MAGICIAN

It came from Nazi Germany,
A dangerous little chemical weapon,
Sarin, sarin.
If you inhale the mysterious vapor,
You will fall with bloody vomit from your mouth,
Sarin, sarin, sarin,
The chemical weapon.

SONG OF SARIN THE BRAVE

In the peaceful night of Matsumoto City
People can be killed, even with our own hands,
The place is full of dead bodies everywhere.
There! Inhale sarin!
Prepare sarin! Prepare sarin!
Immediately poisonous gas will fill the place.
Spray! Spray!
Sarin, brave sarin.

The songs are bizarre, even by Aum standards, suggesting something on the order of a grade B film featuring a stereotypical mad scientist expressing sadistic joy at the death and suffering of his victims. They turn out to be parodies of two well-known animated television shows and a theme song identified with one of them, many versions of which have been bandied about on the Internet.

Both songs refer to a lovable television cartoon character known as Sarii (for Sally) the Magician, a child of about ten or twelve who moves among ordinary people but has secret supernatural powers that she uses to solve all sorts of problems. Sarii has long been one of the most popular of all *manga* and animation characters and was undoubtedly a prominent figure in the childhoods of leading Aum members. The line "It came from Nazi Germany" is a parody of the show's theme song, which begins, "She's from the land of magic. . . . She spreads dreams and hope throughout the town with her magical power." The term *Sarin the Brave* parodies another TV cartoon,

Raidin the Brave, about a robotlike creature who constantly overcomes enemies.

Some of this kind of parody entered into Aum discourse. According to court testimony, leading Aum figures used the term *mahō* (magic) and even Sarii-chan (little Sarii) as euphemisms for sarin gas, and Aum clearly contributed something to the pamphlet, whether it was written by present or former members or by outsiders inspired by the cult. Certainly the songs suggest the way Aum could mix cynicism, naivete, and a perverse gallows humor in the service of its spiritual mission.

The pamphlet evolved, in any case, from an interaction between Aum and popular culture in which each fed on the other. The ditties blend Japanese popular culture themes of saccharine, childlike goodness and viciously detached sadism, which Aum drew upon as it tapped the barely suppressed rage of the young against their society. All of this the cult then offered back to that society. One can, for instance, identify an Aum-linked rage in an incident that took place at a rock concert in Tokyo on April 30, 1995, five weeks after the Tokyo sarin attack. When a Japanese rock band called (in English) Timers sang a song entitled "Disperse Pudding," the audience screamed, "Disperse *sarin*!" (The Japanese word for pudding, *purin*, is fairly close in pronunciation to *sarin*.) The incident does not mean that most Japanese were not appalled by Aum. It does suggest that many young adults viewed their society as so corrupt and hypocritical that any degree of mockery, if not violence against it, was justified.

Biological Warfare

Less is known of the guru's emotions and attitudes concerning biological weapons than of his feelings about sarin. Certainly, biological weapons had a prominent place in his mind, which is not surprising given their deadliness and the relative ease with which they can be produced, even if their release and control pose great difficulties.

Besides botulinus toxin, Aum succeeded in producing anthrax spores, and it showed interest in such pathogens as cholera bacteria. In 1992 Asahara and his leading scientific and medical disciples embarked on an "African Salvation Tour," ostensibly to provide relief from suffering and illness but in reality to attempt (unsuccessfully, as it turned out) to obtain cultures of the lethal Ebola virus. Both nationally and internationally, Aum also purchased considerable equipment for large-scale production of biological weaponry, though the sums involved never reached the levels of those in the sarin project. Included were air filtration media for "clean rooms," various forms of molecular modeling software, sophisticated computer hardware, laser equipment, and serum bottles. A striking indicator of Aum's biological ambitions was the extaordinary amount of peptone, a substance used to cultivate bacteria, found by the police at the main facility, suggesting that Aum intended to stockpile materials aimed at killing hundreds of thousands or millions of people.

Aum's biological program might have been influenced by extensive Japanese military experimentation with and use of biological weapons during the 1930s and 1940s. The contagious-disease-causing pathogens then employed were anthrax, salmonella, typhoid, and cholera. Botulinus, however, differs from these in producing a toxin that attacks the nervous system, acting like an extraordinarily lethal nerve gas. In any case, botulinus and other biological agents have been stockpiled worldwide and can be made all too readily available by commercial companies—as can widely published information concerning their preparation—if requested under the guise of scientific research.

As early as April 1990, Aum was ready to attempt a botulinus release in Tokyo. Seiichi Endō had cultivated the bacteria from a sample obtained a few months earlier. The plan to release the toxin was apparently coordinated with the Armageddon seminar Asahara was then conducting on Ishigaki Island, the idea being that most Aum members would be contemplating the end of the world at a safe distance. For Aum expected to produce a major urban disaster, possibly destroying much of the national government. It mounted special spraying devices (known to would-be bacteriological warriors elsewhere) on three trucks, which then were driven through central Tokyo. Toxin was released near the Diet building, near American naval installations south of Tokyo at Yokohama and Yokosuka, and at Narita Airport, northeast of Tokyo. It is unclear just why this effort and similar ones failed, but a major factor seems to have been Endō's miscalculations of the toxin's viability. His limitations as a scientist were important here: he had run tests on laboratory animals that had also failed but had somehow convinced him that important technical problems had been solved. It must be added, however, that the effects of botulinus toxin, like those of many other biological weapons, are unpredictable. "Even for pros, some batches kill, others don't," is the way that one authority put it. Still, had Endō been a bit more knowl-edgeable and skillful, there might have been a terrible array of victims in the largest metropolitan area in the world.

Aum's subsequent efforts are equally frightening in retrospect. In June of 1993, after returning from a trip to Russia where he apparently picked up considerable information on germ warfare, Endō presided over another attempt to release botulinus toxin, this time near the imperial palace in Tokyo. Apparently the attack was meant to coincide with the celebration of the wedding of Crown Prince Naruhito to Masako Owada, the accomplished young diplomat whom Aum had designated a "Jewish Japanese" enemy and a secret member of the Freemasons, to boot. Once more nothing happened. This batch of toxin was apparently vulnerable to exposure to the air and harmed no one.

By then, Aum had also produced anthrax spores and, about three weeks later, released these through a specially equipped industrial sprayer from the roof of its Tokyo headquarters. There were some relatively minor effects—people living nearby complained of a foul odor and reported the deaths of small birds and pets—but again the effects would have been much greater had there not been technical problems in the release. On March 15, 1995, imitating a technique that had been experimented with (though without the actual agents) by the U.S. Army and the Central Intelligence Agency, Aum tried to use briefcases containing dispensers to release botulinus toxin at Kasumigaseki, one of Tokyo's largest and most crowded subway sta-tions. Again nothing happened. Whether by error or design (a show of humanity, resistance, or both), the key ingredient—the toxin—had been left out of the briefcases.

As deadly as this attack and the others could have proved, Asahara did not press his scientific disciples as hard to produce biological weapons as to produce sarin. Did Asahara turn so aggressively to sarin only because of Aum's failures with biological weapons, or did biological weapons lack the profound appeal of sarin, with its associations to Hitler? What would have happened had Asahara placed biological weapons at the center of his megalomanic self? What if he had embraced a vision of a biological Armageddon and declared to Murai and Endō, "We have no choice but to disperse seventy tons of botulinus toxin"?

Weapons and Fantasies

Aum's chemical and biological weapons were reflections of Asahara's increasingly militarized mind-set. A relatively peaceful militarization might accompany any cultic group's *expectation* of Armageddon; Aum's militarization, however, was part of its guru's grandiose assumption that his cult could become a great power capable of initiating, controlling, and surviving a world war. Armageddon itself, then, became the ultimate military extension of his megalomania. Aum's militarization was spiritualized—even sacralized—but it was also concrete and material, rendering Aum something close to an extended weapons factory and storage depot. The cult's weapons interests spanned a spectrum from handguns and automatic rifles to imagined nuclear, laser, "plasma," and "artificial earthquake" weapons. On every level, megalomanic fantasy invariably combined with concrete efforts at production, but the greater the potential level of destructiveness the more fantasy dominated.

Aum conducted its weapons explorations globally. In Russia, it sought rifles and automatic weapons, information about and materials for manufacturing sarin and other chemical weapons, helicopter training and helicopters for the dissemination of chemical or biological weapons, rockets for the delivery of nuclear or other ultimate weapons, and even existing nuclear weapons or help in making them. The cult also sent members to Russia for special "shooting tours" in which they were instructed by military contacts in the use of some of the weapons that they had purchased or wished to purchase. In the United States, Aum concentrated more on computers and other advanced technology that lent itself to weapons research and development, but members also obtained helicopter training.

Partly inspired by the Gulf War, Asahara soon began to imagine brilliant new dimensions of destruction, weapons that no search could have found anywhere on earth, weapons that would "make the atomic and hydrogen bombs look like toys." By 1993, his message was that "the main weapons will be plasma and lasers"—compared to which "atomic bombs are not so frightening anymore." Both these new weapons systems entered prominently into Asahara's fantasy. With lasers he apparently took the additional step of giving Murai the formidable order to make these nonexistent weapons available in Aum. In 1994, cult members broke into at least two commercial laser laboratories in Japan. One member was arrested with sketches and maps of the interior layouts of the facilities of six major electronic firms in his possession, as well as lists of Aum members who worked for various electronic and chemical corporations, yet the police seemed incapable of grasping the ambitiousness of Aum's plans and did little to interfere with the cult's activities. (Many Japanese believe that some form of political or police corruption contributed to a rather astonishing failure to interrupt Aum's militarization in the face of increasing evidence of its dangerousness and illegality.) In the United States, the cult tried to pull off a vast commercial deal to purchase a half-million-dollar laser system from a California company. Negotiations ended in failure because of Aum's insistence on the almost immediate delivery, in the weeks just prior to the Tokyo sarin attack, of a system that needed to be custom built and to meet export control requirements.

Kiyohide Hayakawa, Aum's preeminent weapons entrepreneur, sought out prominent Russian scientists for help on the cult's laser research. An Aum group led by Asahara himself met in Moscow with Nikolai Basov, a Nobel Prize winner for his research on laser technology. (In subsequent publications the cult proudly displayed photographs of Asahara with Basov.) From all these efforts Aum was able to acquire or design various "blueprints" of imagined laser weapons, and Murai's attempts to achieve what the guru ordered led to some kind of laser test in October 1994. Local residents of Kamikuishiki, where Aum had its main facility, described a broad red beam emanating from the Aum compound. But the test, like the rest of the laser enterprise, had more to do with the guru's fascination with the image of a "death ray" than with anything approaching an actual weapon.

"Plasma weapons" took Asahara even deeper into fantasy. For him the term seemed to suggest the use of microwaves as weapons, or as he put it on one occasion, "weapons that use light and electric waves [and] do not need an army." Asahara connected both laser and plasma weapons with Ronald Reagan's proposed Strategic Defense Initiative (SDI), popularly called Star Wars, and moved further toward delusion in suggesting that, although this space-age weaponry under development "seemed to have vanished" after the SDI program collapsed, it had surreptitiously been brought to "advanced" levels. As unreal as plasma weapons may have been, scientifically speaking, they were real enough to Asahara, and he spoke of them either as if they had already been tested and used or they were on the immediate horizon. They had, he claimed, a major advantage over nuclear weapons because while "a one-megaton bomb can completely destroy a one-hundred-square-kilometer area . . . the affected area is useless because of the radioactivity"; however, "with plasma weapons, the area remains intact." (Asahara was fascinated by the idea of "juicing people"—as the nuclear strategists called it—while preserving property, a feature of the neutron bomb.) In the same spirit, he spoke of the existence of "a 50-kilowatt plasma weapon which can be carried in a car and can instantly kill any living thing within two hundred to four hundred meters." He contended that only a small number of the bodies of the hundred thousand Iraqis killed in the Gulf War were recovered because most had been vaporized by plasma weapons. The reason Japan would be devastated in World War III, he insisted, was that it would lack the infinitely advanced weapons that the United States secretly possessed.

"Not only will [laser and plasma] weapons appear," he claimed, "but there is also a possibility that there will be better weapons. I believe this includes an extremely large laser. This weapon changes the whole space between the weapon and the target into plasma, making it look like a solid-white belt, a 'sword.' This is the very sword written about in the Book of Revelation. The sword will exterminate almost all living beings." This confluence of ultimate weapons with Revelation narrative starkly expressed the purpose of Aum's militarization and, indeed, of Aum itself.

Aum's more conventional weaponry had its own importance. The cult had acquired an AK-74 machine gun in Russia and smuggled it into Japan, undoubtedly by breaking it into its component parts, and was attempting at its factory near Mount Fuji to produce a thousand of them. It also had materials or blueprints for rocket launchers and various other forms of military equipment. In addition, Asahara seemed to have a special liking for personal handguns and was pleased when Hayakawa arranged for two Tokarev pistols to be brought to him from Russia by an intermediary.

It is believed that two hundred Aum renunciants were put through military training in groups of fifty each, led mostly by members of the Japanese Self-Defense Forces who were also members of Aum. At least fifty AK-74s (presumably produced by Aum) were used in this training process.

The manufacture of the AK-74s was, in typical fashion, haphazard and beset by psychological problems. Consider again the experience of Nakano, who had required "psychotherapy" from the guru partly because of his troubled sense that the work he was doing with complex machinery might be connected with weaponry. His suspicion had been fed by the secrecy surrounding the unit to which he was assigned, identified as a "metal factory" and headed by Murai as a section of the science and technology ministry. It was in a secret location, so that after being driven there he "didn't know exactly where it was." Those working in the factory were isolated not only from the outside world but also from other Aum members. Nakano was troubled by the strangeness of it all, by "their not telling me clearly what they were doing"; he had doubts, moreover, that the metal products being produced were "religiously meaningful." Despite having those doubts temporarily assuaged by being shown that at least one of the products was a small religious object related to Aum practice, he could not overcome his uneasy feelings about the whole enterprise and his sense of being increasingly alienated from his spiritual goals:

> The key word for me was *salvation*, saving myself and saving others as well. My image of salvation and of the things that I would do as a renunciant was of performing spiritual practices, guiding others, translating sacred texts. But I was in an isolated location, operating

this machine. The word *salvation* . . . did not fit the work of manufacturing things.

While Nakano's two psychotherapeutic meetings with the guru restored his intense discipleship, his misgivings persisted: "Even though I had seen what Aum did from the inside, I didn't know anything definite about it. Everything was maybe: maybe Aum was illegally making rifles." That is, despite encountering evidence of weapons making, he was psychologically unready to accept the implications of it. He began to resolve his conflicts through the LSD-induced vision that led to his running away. Much like a dream, it offered feelings and insights he was not yet able to experience in ordinary waking life that suggested a new form of action.

Nakano left Aum before the subway attack and, although at first uncertain about who was responsible for it, was soon able to recognize Aum's culpability. He went to the police and told them about his work in the "metal factory," suggesting that "maybe I was involved in making rifles." As he explained, "I wanted to make things clear, and to me the most criminal matter, the closest thing to me, was the suspicion about making rifles. So in offering information, I thought that this suspicion could be confirmed within myself. That is, the suspicion would cease to be a suspicion but become a fact." And that is what happened, as the rifle parts the police had confiscated and now showed to him had "the same shape as a design I had been given."

While Nakano was undoubtedly seeking to protect himself legally, it was clearly of great importance to him to resolve his confusion and ambivalence. But that does not mean he was completely free of the guru. He could step back from his discipleship but could not let go entirely. After all, the guru's weapons-encompassing megalomania had held sufficient sway over Nakano for him to have worked for the better part of a year on the illegal manufacture of automatic rifles.

A Guru's Nuclearism

Asahara was hardly alone in his bizarre and contradictory struggles with nuclear weapons. From the unfortunate moment they appeared in the world, they have penetrated the human psyche in odd and dangerous ways. Both individually and collectively, many people everywhere have run a sequence from fearful awe to radical embrace, from terror to the "power surge" of nuclear omnipotence. In following that sequence, Asahara could be said to have expressed a classic form of what I call "nuclearism," a profound attraction to and identification with the weapons and their power. Asahara viewed them as near deities, possessing a capacity not only for unlimited destruction but also for godlike creation. He did not, however, stop there. In filtering his nuclearism through his megalomanic self, he merged with and sought to act upon the weapons' capacity to destroy the world. He did this as a citizen—a highly alienated one, to be sure, but a citizen nonetheless—of the only nation that had experienced nuclear annihilation.

There is much evidence that the guru's early sense of nuclear weapons became a touchstone for all his actions and imaginings with respect to ultimate weapons, whether the "poor man's" and the "energy-saving" atomic bombs or fantasy laser and plasma weapons. Asahara had no hesitation about offering the Japanese military—limited though it was by an American-imposed "peace constitution" and by public antinuclear sentiment—the sort of nuclearistic advice on preparing for World War III that only an all-seeing, all-knowing, life-and-death dispensing guru might have access to. He declared that the country "has no chance unless it develops an advanced weapon capable of striking military satellites, . . . no chance unless it has ICBMs with high-tech electronics, the RAM jet which Russia is developing, and atomic warheads." But he also insisted that Japan was doomed, predicting that American "nuclear warheads loaded with atomic or hydrogen bombs may strike Japan in 1996."

Like many nuclearists, he embraced the illusion of civil defense, in his case a claim that it was possible to protect Aum members from the inevitable nuclear holocaust. At various times he spoke of the problem of reliable shelters and broadcast and published "symposia"—consisting mainly of statements by Aum scientists—on surviving nuclear attack and World War III. These elaborate discussions involved the usual combination of relatively accurate information with bizarre pedantry and unbridled fantasy. Held out as models for shelters were an underground facility in the Kremlin capable of withstanding "a direct nuclear explosion in the twenty-megaton range" and one in the United States supposedly "equivalent to or better than the Kremlin's." There was talk of such matters as the need for airtight seals on future shelters, the problem of "panic from being shut up in a closed and cramped space," and the oxygen requirements of the population to be saved. Sometimes the scenarios of surviving a twenty-megaton nuclear bomb sounded like caricatures of Cold War–era statements issued by the U.S. Federal Emergency Management Agency, which tended to be laughed out of court. There were boasts that Aum was capable of devising a "perfect plan" for survival. There were references to Kasumigaseki, one of the largest and deepest of the country's subway stations, as the only nuclear shelter that could be relied on in all of Japan. That same station would later be one of the five targeted for the release of sarin gas.

In the end, though, the emphasis was inevitably on spiritual practice as the truest means of survival. Asahara frequently invoked a "superhuman" spiritual state that could be achieved in Aum. On a radio broadcast Murai offered a pseudoscientific gloss on the benefits of such a spiritual state for surviving a nuclear attack: "When a living body containing little or no oxygen is exposed to radioactivity, it suffers little or no damage. Therefore, if we can reduce the oxygen intake by spiritual practice, or if we can create what is called a state of no oxygen consumption by stopping respiration through *samādhi*, we might be able to avoid severe damage to our bodies, even if we are bathed in radioactivity." The guru, though hardly known for his sense of measure, felt an immediate need to modify this claim, stating that it would be "hard to prove" because "an experiment would be very dangerous." He concluded affirmatively nonetheless: "We can only say that there is a probability of not getting harmed by practicing the truth."

Included in Asahara's nuclearism was his obsession with Hiroshima. He referred to it frequently, had visions relating to it, and spoke repeatedly to his disciples about expecting "many Hiroshimas" in the near future. Hiroshima's centrality to his imagination was revealed in an early vision—or "meditation," as he called it—he described in the occult magazine *Twilight Zone* in 1988. His "astral body," he wrote, separated from his physical body, floating through the air and coming to rest on earth in "a desolate wasteland" where he saw a single house and encountered a schoolgirl in its garden: "Her face and hands looked red and swollen. . . . A woman who seemed to be the girl's mother soon appeared. . . . The woman's face and hands looked no less red than her daughter's. 'Hello! Where are we?' I asked. With a look of suspicion, she replied, 'Hiroshima.' 'Hiroshima! Then what year is this?' I asked. 'It is 2006.' Then I asked her what I wanted to know about most. 'Did World War III occur?' Suddenly, the people standing there looked surprised and suspicious. 'Yes, it did.' " Asahara rendered his "meditation" a guru's reading of the future, a demonstration that "World War III will have occurred by 2006." Once more Hiroshima becomes bound up with world destruction, which he, the guru, survives.

He was again a survivor in a 1992 vision. "Four days ago while I was in the astral world," he reported, "I had a vision of being hit by radiation. I think it was about the nuclear war which will occur between 1997 and 2001. From outside, my body appeared to be unchanged, but I had apparently been exposed to radiation. There were several disciples around me and some of them had sores on their bodies. I'm sure that the war, called the final war, will occur between 1997 and 2001." Here he suggested fear of his own susceptibility to the "invisible contamination"—delayed radiation effects in people who had seemed untouched by the blast itself—that so terrified Hiroshima survivors, a suggestion consistent with his own persistent claim of martyrdom. But the passage can also be read as the guru's megalomanic claim that he alone could transcend the effects of radiation, unlike his disciples, who had "sores on their bodies."

In such visions Asahara drew equally on biblical imagery and on the imagery of man's annihilation of the planet so pervasive in popular culture in the half century since the nuclear destruction of Hiroshima and Nagasaki. He invoked the story of Noah, whom he identified with because "nobody heeded his warning," and in biblical language spoke of "great floods, . . . pestilence, famine, and destruction brought about by war." One could begin to understand what was to come, he said, only by imagining the suffering that occurred in World War II and multiplying it many times over. The end result would of course be Armageddon, brought about by an unprecedented mix of futuristic weapons.

The exact sequence of events, weapons, and dates varied in Asahara's warnings and predictions, but there was little variation in the outcome. He would sometimes imagine a series of earthquakes and floods so vast that no one would be able "to find a place to live in peace." Then World War III would break out. In 1988, he offered a precise date for that event: "The great catastrophe brought about by nuclear war will happen between October 30 and November 29, 2003. The peak will occur on November 25." Asahara did not yet understand that prophets are best advised to be vague on the subject of dates.

Asahara's reading of Nostradamus revealed "frightening events beyond description that will regularly occur from now until 2000." Japan, in particular, would be devastated by attacks by the United States and become a "nuclear wasteland." The guru also pictured Tokyo sinking as "the surface of the sea surrounding Japan suddenly rises and engulfs the land," a scene that probably owed much to a 1973 best-selling disaster novel called *Japan Sinks*. That novel, in turn, apparently took its central image from a prophecy of Edgar Cayce, the American mystic, that a major part of Japan would sink, leaving only a series of subtropical islands behind.

Japan's specific annihilation would be a direct consequence of its having ill-treated the guru himself: "The Jews persecuted Jesus Christ two thousand years ago and were expelled from their country fifty years later. This was their karma. Japan has persecuted me and other great attainers. Therefore, Japan will have to suffer severe karmic 'cleansing' in the near future, including an economic decline. . . . According to karmic law, phenomena rebound as surely as spit falls back down when shot in the air." Japan's ultimate karmic cleansing would, of course, be a nuclear one.

Even as Asahara became preoccupied with sarin, he never abandoned imagery of nuclear holocaust. During his last months as Aum guru, he complained about being "sprayed from helicopters or planes wherever I go," then added, "The hour of my death has been foretold. The gas phenomenon has already happened. Next time it might be an atomic bomb."

However total the destruction the guru imagined and tried to bring about, it was to be followed by the most beautiful and perfect renewal (as it was in most of the animated postapocalyptic films and TV shows that so influenced Asahara and his disciples). In Asahara's sermons, all-encompassing death would create all-encompassing virtue. To achieve that absolute virtue, Aum spiritualized its duty to survive. According to certain Buddhist precepts, the devout must "take refuge in the mountains" and "eat the roots of trees." Asahara interpreted those precepts sufficiently broadly to connect them with a coming nuclear holocaust: by the expression *roots of trees*, he said, Buddha meant that "the survivors will eat food free from radioactive contamination." Asahara then converted absurd survivalist declarations into a kind of religious litany: "When gases are sprayed on us, we have to make cleaners to eliminate them. If microwaves are pointed at us, we have to make protective wire netting. If lasers are used, we have to make protective equipment against them." The goal was to "secure a better future life," for which it was necessary to survive as long as possible, for "no matter how sure we are that we can go to heaven, it will not be definite if we do not live long." To which he added: "We must also develop this into a struggle for widening the circle of salvation and finally save all the living beings on earth."

Asahara talked of something like a survivalist Shambhala, a city in the mountains or under the sea or underground, both a shelter from the weapons of World War III and a perfect spiritual community. Another time he declared, "I am preparing to survive with my disciples gathered here today and all the rest of my disciples who practice the laws of the truth." He again drew upon Buddhist scriptures, emphasizing that much time was needed to "transfer our souls to . . . heaven" but combining his spiritual utopia with his version of a scientific one. If the survivors managed to "control epinephrine" by means of spiritual exercises, they would be "stronger against exogenous stress," he said. "Then it would not be impossible to live to the age of two hundred, three hundred, or one thousand." Armageddon would make everything perfect: "After the Third World War, I imagine that this world will be filled with love. Every person will overcome his or her suffering and work for the good of others." He himself could only welcome the total destruction: *"I am glad the third world war is going to happen because Buddhist scriptures and the Bible say so."*

Disciples were deeply affected by these totalistic images of destruction and their guru's urges for it. Former members I interviewed returned repeatedly to his visions. Kuno, who had imagined himself fending off tanks during a nuclear Armageddon, remembered that in Asahara's developing sequence of world-ending events, "nuclear war was, at first, equal to Armageddon." Later, "the story changed and Armageddon became a larger frame of which nuclear war was a part or a trigger. It triggered the final good-versus-evil war involving the entire earth. . . . The Middle East, China, Soviet Russia, America, Japan, and Europe's Economic Community—these would be thrown together and would fight in a nuclear war." Kuno had the impression that Asahara was directly influenced by popular animated films that depicted nuclear wars in which "foolish humans caused Armageddon." Kuno remembered Asahara's "using cartoon terms or images in his sermons, drawing a parallel between them and his own visions." (Aum was also to make its own animated films incorporating some of this imagery.) In addition to apocalyptic animations, Asahara was also influenced by the depiction of nuclear war in the 1983 American television film *The Day After*, about a Soviet-American confrontation. According to Kuno, the film, which uses considerable Hiroshima footage, was shown often in Aum.

Kuno himself expected to survive a nuclear holocaust, but for him that was not the crucial issue. Death, after all, was "a good chance to move upward and be born at a higher place." What frightened him, with Armageddon so close, was his feeling that he had not progressed sufficiently in his consciousness. In other words, for Kuno (and for many others in Aum), *nuclear war was much more acceptable than inadequate spiritual attainment.* Although Aum members undoubtedly also experienced some of the universal fear of nuclear war, they could suppress it, displace it onto continuous anxiety about their spiritual pollution and bad karma, or even transform it into a sense of opportunity for a better rebirth.

While his ordinary disciples grappled with Asahara's fantasies about nuclear annihilation and spiritual rebirth, the guru went about attempting to acquire the necessary weapons. In the same diary in which Kiyohide Hayakawa mused about the price of a nuclear warhead, he listed several possibilities and reputedly made many other references to nuclear weapons. A "case study" on Aum, the result of U.S. Senate hearings on "global proliferation of weapons of mass destruction," notes carefully and dryly, "It is unclear whether the references are reflections of actual discussions or negotiations." What is known is that some Russian cult members worked at their country's leading nuclear research center, the Kurchatav Institute in Moscow. One Senate investigator thought that Aum sought not so much to build or acquire a nuclear warhead as to obtain highly radioactive material for developing an extremely crude "dirty" weapon that could have rendered large portions of Tokyo virtually uninhabitable.

Asahara's scientists sought sophisticated equipment from the United States: an industrial laser system and a "vibration isolation table," both of which could readily have been modified to provide the accurate measurements of plutonium necessary for the development of nuclear weapons. While the transactions were never completed because the American company became suspicious, the Senate report expresses alarm at "the ease with which the cult accessed the vast international supermarket of weapons and weapons technology." Aum's forays extended to Australia, whose uranium deposits, among the most plentiful in the world, were an important reason for the cult's purchase of a large tract of land there. Hayakawa traveled around the country in search of deposits, praising the quality of Australian ore in his diary. An Aum team succeeded in extracting very small amounts of uranium from Australian rock and set up a laboratory on the group's ranch, but the project had to be abandoned and the property sold because Australian authorities, too, became suspicious and began to deny Aum members visas for entry or reentry. I was also told of cult representatives attempting to purchase land on a small Japanese island thought to contain uranium, only to discover that none was there.

All these efforts indicate the extent to which Asahara's weapons-related passions and fantasies were transmitted both to immediate high disciples and to worshipful followers, even those scientifically trained. For this nuclear-age guru, the literal existence of ultimate weapons as physical entities capable of world destruction served as an anchor for his megalomanic self. But as we have seen in so many ways, vast confusions arose in his mind between the end of the world and the end of the self. Weapons-centered destruction of the defiled world had to be achieved for the survival of that self. Asahara experienced a personal sense of "the end of the world" only when his world-ending project was blocked—when he was separated from his stockpile of actual weapons and his fantasies of weapons to come, when he was deguruized as a prisoner and murderer by both his enemies and his friends.

The pattern closely resembles that of a paranoid schizophrenic described by Freud in a celebrated study. Daniel Paul Schreber was a prominent judge who recorded in a memoir extensive details of his psychotic breakdown. (Freud attributed that breakdown to repressed homosexuality, but more recent commentators, myself included, have stressed issues relating to death symbolism, a sense of annihilation, and the loss of larger human connectedness.) Like Asahara, Schreber envisioned himself as the "sole survivor to renew mankind." He had become for God, he said, "the only human being, or simply the human being on whom everything turns"—"everything" meaning the destruction of the world and its re-creation. Like Asahara, Schreber sought to be "the Savior of the World and the Ruler of the World [in] one and the same person" and to control "the Order of the World." The megalomanic paranoia of both Schreber and Asahara required world-ending catastrophe for a sense of transcendent survival, but there are two crucial differences between them. In Schreber's era, there were no nuclear or other ultimate weapons to enter his imagination; nor was he a guru who could attract and maintain disciples. Putting the matter simply, Asahara was a Schreber with disciples and ultimate weapons. By incorporating both into his megalomanic self, he could remain sufficiently functional to kill and to take steps toward an imagined world destruction. The weapons exerted an irresistible attraction for the guru as they alone could offer him control over the death and rebirth of the world.

9 | Crossing the Threshold

Throughout this book I have been trying to describe the behavior and motivations of Aum Shinrikyō's members in their bizarre foray into world-ending violence. Now I want to identify the central characteristics that contributed to its collective dynamic as lived out by the guru and his disciples. Exploring them may put us in a better position to answer the question posed at the beginning of this study: How did Aum cross the threshold from anticipating to forcing Armageddon?

The Features of a World-Destroying Cult

None of the seven characteristics I cite is unique to Aum, but Aum distinguished itself from similar groups in the way it combined them and in the degree of totalism it brought to this extremely dangerous mix. Other groups elsewhere may in the future be all too capable of doing what Aum did, and more. Whatever group might next embark on world destruction is likely to possess versions of most or all of these characteristics.

The first characteristic of Aum was *totalized guruism*, which became *paranoid guruism* and *megalomanic guruism*. Instead of awakening the potential of his disciples, Shōkō Asahara himself became his cult's only source of "energy" or infinite life-power and its only source of the new self that each Aum disciple was expected to acquire (as epitomized by the religious name every disciple took as a renunciant). For disciples there was no deity beyond the guru, no ethical code beyond his demands and imposed ordeals, or mahāmudrās. When the guru invoked a higher deity it was only in order to incorporate the god's omnipotence into his own. Guru and disciples were both energized and entrapped by their claim to ultimate existential truth and virtue.

This megalomanic guruism, the claim to possess and control immediate and distant reality, was not only wild fantasy but a form of desymbolization—a loss, that is, of the symbolizing function that characterizes the healthy human mind. The guru took on a stance beyond metaphor. He could no longer, in the words of Martin Buber, "imagine the real." The Hindu scholar Wendy Doniger points out that most mythology consists of concrete narration in the service of metaphor, of descriptions of behavior meant to suggest, rather than express, primal human emotions and dilemmas. In reading mythological stories, we seek to reconnect their concrete details to the symbolized, metaphorical world in which we exist psychologically. A megalomanic guru like Asahara does the reverse: he embraces the very concreteness of mythic narratives so as to circumvent the metaphor and symbolization so crucial to the functioning human imagination.

This desymbolization became bound up with a second Aum characteristic: *a vision of an apocalyptic event or series of events that would destroy the world in the service of renewal*. All great religions contain variations of that vision, ordinarily causing followers to struggle largely with symbolic meanings. Asahara did not engage in this struggle about such matters as Shiva's dancing the world out of existence so that it might be renewed. That "dance," as one commentator puts it, "is only an allusion," a way to represent powerful human forces, in this case a grandiose version of the great universal myth of death and rebirth, of world destruction and re-creation. Even the early Hindu storytellers, in shaping the myth, warned that much of the detail was meant to be suggestive and timeless rather than literal and prescriptive. But the megalomanic guru absorbed the myth totally into his world-encompassing self so that he could claim to act for and *as* Shiva in embarking on a concrete contemporary project of world destruction and renewal.

A third Aum characteristic was its *ideology of killing to heal, of altruistic murder and altruistic world destruction*. Such a stance readily evoked an "attack guruism" and an "action prophecy" directed toward forcing the end. The concept of *poa*, as manipulated by Asahara, epitomized this stance, encouraging as it did the killing of a spiritually inferior person by a spiritually superior one for the sake of improving the prospects of immortality for both. Similar ideologies (or theologies) have been embraced by others. At the hangings of convicted criminals in the American colonies and elsewhere, for instance, Christian ritual called for a statement of conviction that a confession of guilt by the criminal, together with the hanging, would better prepare him to "meet his maker." Some Christians held much the same conviction with respect to the killing of Jews at the time of the Inquisition or during the Middle Ages. The Thugs of India, a Hindu sect that killed and robbed in a ritual fashion from the thirteenth to the nineteenth century, viewed their victims as sacrifices to the goddess Kali, who was associated with disease, death, and destruction; the victims' reward was entrance to paradise. In Aum, however, the principle of killing to heal went much further. It extended into a vision of altruistic omnicide.

Altruistic mass murder depended, in turn, on a fourth characteristic: *the relentless impulse toward world-rejecting purification*. Here Aum drew upon its version of karma as ubiquitous defilement. Asahara was once quoted as saying that "the essence of the devil is matter," suggesting that what Aum had to "purify" was physical existence itself. Such an unrealizable purification goal kept Aum disciples on a spiritual treadmill in the service of the guru and of a process that was envisioned as transhistorical. Asahara sought, or claimed to seek, a level of eternal perfection that defied the petty external standards of any particular era; yet he didn't hesitate to apply his standards of purification to the most immediate social and political behavior. Disciples were strongly drawn to his compelling rendition of the many corruptions of contemporary society, already vivid in their experience and observations. Aum's radical rejection of the world as impure and evil spoke persuasively to powerful feelings of alienation in young potential cult members—just as the cult's radical eschatology spoke directly to the broader apocalyptic mood of a society that within living memory had received a taste of what a world-ending event might actually be like.

For Asahara, the people of this world were so hopelessly defiled that their inevitable fate was the lowest of reincarnations, the closest to Buddhist hell and therefore dominated by death and suffering. That sense of defilement encompassed just about any personal or social experience outside of the guru's teaching and the world of Aum—to the point where one could say that reality itself was a defilement. With both matter and reality, indeed all of human life, so defiled, the process of purification could be achieved by nothing short of killing on a planetary scale.

A fifth characteristic of Aum was *the lure of ultimate weapons.* If Asahara's consciousness of nuclear weapons was initially related to Hiroshima and Nagasaki, ultimate weapons in general became bound up with his action prophecy in pressing toward Armageddon. For Asahara it was an easy and natural path from nuclearism to dreams of mass killing via chemical and biological devices. Crucial to his pursuit of mass murder was the fact that he was a "floating guru," unencumbered by a restraining god, by a restraining code of traditional values, or even, as a state might be, by the interests of an entrenched bureaucracy. As they did for the United States and the Soviet Union during the Cold War, weapons of mass death increasingly took their place at the center of Aum's structure and function. Aum was the first nongovernmental religious or political cult to achieve this kind of weapons involvement, but it is unlikely to be the last. For such weapons have come to affect human consciousness everywhere and are bound to remain a powerful lure to totalistically inclined, paranoid, and megalomanic gurus.

Essential to success in Aum's killing project was a sixth characteristic: *a shared state of aggressive numbing.* That mental state began with a disciple's merger with the guru, with the ideal of becoming his clone and of thinking and feeling as he did. Vajrayāna, the Sanskrit term meaning "Diamond Vehicle," was interpreted to signify, among other things, pursuit of a "diamond mind" that could be calm, stable, and detached from worldly concerns. Achieving such a "diamond mind," or what Aum called a "sacred carefree mind," could involve fierce dedication to forms of "spiritual practice" that included extreme asceticism, cruelty, and murder. Such dedication was a form of numbing, which one enhanced by an absolute focus on the violent attack immediately at hand, on one's efficacy in carrying it out; a focus that could sweep away past scruples as well as any empathy for potential victims. The principle of viewing the guru's most outrageous demands as an appropriate form of personal ordeal or "test" reinforced the numbing process and resulted in a mental state similar to that cultivated among Japanese soldiers during World War II. In serving the emperor—in essence a distant but highly venerated guru—the soldier was to steel his mind against all compunctions or feelings of compassion, to achieve, that is, a version of the "diamond mind" that could contribute both to fanatical fighting and to grotesque acts of atrocity.

The Nazis cultivated a similar mind-set. Heinrich Himmler, who presided over much of the Nazi program of mass murder, once even said that it was part of the "karma" of "the Germanic world as a whole," for which "a man has to sacrifice himself even though it is often very hard for him; he oughtn't to think of himself." In other words, one should achieve the necessary aggressive numbing for the personal ordeal of having to kill. This was the gist of his famous remarks to SS leaders, chiding members of his audience for misguided compassion in seeking to save "one decent Jew." He referred to the ordeal of seeing "a hundred corpses . . . side by side, or five hundred, or a thousand," and the heroism involved in carrying out the killing. "To have stuck this out and—excepting in cases of human weakness— to have kept our integrity, this is what has made us hard. In our history, this will be an unwritten and never-to-be-written page of glory." Like the Japanese and Nazi killers in World War II, Asahara and his disciples moved in and out of a state of total ideological conviction: from immersion in an ideological vision of *poa*, to cynical killing of ostensible enemies with a rationalizing invocation of *poa*, to various in-between states in which both stances were present.

A seventh characteristic of Aum was its *extreme technocratic manipulation*, coupled with its *claim to absolute scientific truth*. Aum held to a computer theory of the mind: the principles of replacing "bad data" from the culture with "good data" from the guru. The cult's entire effort at spiritual self-transformation was, in fact, reduced to systematic techniques, whether in the form of breathing exercises, drug-centered initiations, or endless repetitions of the guru's words or his assigned mantras. Practitioners were given specific technical functions to perform—running businesses, doing translations, making publishing arrangements, creating artwork, composing or playing music, working in Aum "factories," preparing chemical or biological weapons, drawing up legal contracts—always as cogs in a larger machine of "salvation." Spiritual experiences were ultimately relegated to their compartmentalized function within that Aum machine. Guru and cult constantly pressed for the technological means of achieving faster salvation, whether better drugs for disciples' visions or more effective ultimate weapons for inducing Armageddon. In these and other ways, Aum followed the tendency of totalistic cults to create a "sacred science" and thereby bring two ultimate claims to truth together in a single omnipotent package.

Aum also demonstrated the bizarre consequences of the fanatical conversion of scientists to totalistic guruism, of what might be called megalomanic science. Despite its scientific and technological bungling, one cannot ignore the extent of Aum's success with its weaponry or the deadly consequences of turning scientific energies to the service of religious fanaticism. In merging the two, Aum made a grotesque pioneering foray into the most dangerous of all contemporary imaginative combinations.

The Aum Dynamic

Aum's trajectory toward mass killing stemmed from the characteristics just described. But such killing does not suddenly materialize. It is part of a process with its own momentum. I have long studied that kind of momentum in the acts of governments and nation-states that have per-petrated mass killing and genocide. Aum suggests an even more threat-ening possibility: that of murder on a genocidal scale performed not by powerful, weapons-centered states but by small, weapons-haunted anti-states. Yet the dynamic of groups such as Aum can mimic that of larger, more "traditional" genocidal powers.

The model I derived from work on the trajectory of Nazi genocide included, first, a perception of social or historical "illness" or "sick-ness unto death"; a vision of ideological cure (in the Nazis' case, a racial or "biomedical" one); in that cure, a powerful promise of revi-talization together with experiences of transcendence (continuous "high states"); the further ideological vision of specific forms of killing as a means of purification and healing; the focused utilization of pre-vailing technologies; the evolution of professional killers and killing professionals, both groups constantly interacting with a fanatical leader; and finally, a momentum toward genocide (which may include an impulse toward Götterdämmerung or world destruction) that car-ries one across a threshold beyond which there is no turning back.

All of this was present in Aum. The "illness" was that of universal "defilement." A revitalizing and purifying ideology was held out as a "cure" not only for practitioner-perpetrators but for those they killed as well; the cure delivered on its promise, moreover, with energizing mystical experiences so intense as to make absolute claim to the bodies and minds of disciples. The embrace of technology and science was equally great, if dominated by fantasy; killing professionals and pro-fessional killers (though perhaps less distinguishable from one another than they were among the Nazis) emerged from the constant interac-tion between leader and followers. Aum's particular momentum toward genocide (or omnicide) occurred within the context of contem-porary Japanese society. Though partially sequestered from that soci-ety, Aum had no choice but to act and react within it. No historical outcome—and indeed no single act in an individual life—can be said to be absolutely inevitable. There are always interactions that could have taken other shapes and directions. But the evidence is over-whelming that Aum pressed very hard toward a denouement of mass violence, that while always highly sensitive to how society was treating it (for instance, in its desperate quest for official religious status), Aum acted largely from its own energies and created its own dynamic.

Although in its early years, Aum maintained a relatively benign focus on yoga and Mahāyāna Buddhism, Shōkō Asahara's visions were apocalyptic from the beginning. The first Aum murder took place in February 1989, and later that year Asahara ordered the murder of the three members of the Sakamoto family, preached and published fierce Armageddon prophecies, and actively taught radical forms of Tantra Vajrayāna, including the principle of *poa*. In other words, Aum's internal dynamic, centering on an embrace of Armageddon, was present from the group's onset but radically accelerated in 1989 and came to be associated with a weapons-focused impulse to initiate an apocalyptic event.

The acceleration was closely linked to a growing sense that Aum's existence was threatened, that the cult had to act to prevent its demise. Its continual difficulties acquiring and retaining members, particularly renunciants, and increasing suspicion and legal pressure from the outside world fed that fear. But underneath everything was its own megalomanic and paranoid dynamic, which drove it toward provocation and confrontation, even as it created profound problems for its disciples. Aum experienced a form of collective death anxiety that emanated first from its guru and led to ever more desperate actions.

There was no single moment of threshold crossing. An all-encompassing guruism, a world-ending theology, and a megalomanic obsession with weapons took hold early and propelled Aum into increasingly uncontrolled behavior until its explosion of violence in 1995. Yet there were two especially significant periods in the cult's brief history. The first was in 1989, when the guru resorted to murder to cover up an "accidental" death. He and his leading disciples then required still more killings not only to conceal the earlier ones but to justify them psychologically. By taking on a "habit of killing," the guru retrospectively rendered them more legitimate. The principle here is that atrocity begets atrocity. A second threshold period, this time for larger-scale violence, occurred in 1993 with the cult's manufacture and stockpiling of sarin. In fits and starts, despite frequent failures, Aum evolved a technological momentum that brought new energy and a sense of actual possibility to the guru's already-existing vision of destroying the world to save it.

The threatened police raid, though a crucial immediate stimulus to the Tokyo sarin attack, was not the most influential factor in the cult's crossing of its apocalyptic threshold. Aum had already killed with sarin at Matsumoto the year before and had attempted to release biological weapons as well. Its threshold had long been crossed as it staggered toward its November deadline for releasing sufficiently large amounts of sarin to initiate World War III. Whether or not that larger sarin attack could have been carried out, Aum would undoubtedly have engaged in some significant killing project. By then, the Aum dynamic, intensified by societal resistance, had long reached its point of no return. Destroying the world became the only means of staving off a sense of death and extinction.

The Ownership of Death

Death is the heart of the matter. At issue are the connections between individual death and the death of everything, between death and killing, between death and eternal survival.

The guru took on what could be called the ownership of death. He became the ultimate arbiter of every level of death from that of an individual to that of the entire world. Disciples both legitimated and shared in his ownership. All death everywhere was absorbed and orchestrated within his being. This is a pattern that can be found in visionary prophets and paranoid schizophrenics, who may come to equate a sense of inner death, of extreme numbing or disintegration, with the death of the world. Although prophets and gurus differ from schizophrenics in being supported and confirmed by their disciples, they may similarly require the promise of the death of everything in order to maintain the life of the self. They may come to feel that only the world's death can enable them to overcome their own inner deadness.

But end-of-the-world images have never been limited to gurus and schizophrenics. In becoming human and taking on the knowledge that we die, we also become susceptible to equating our individual deaths with the death of everything. We ordinarily transcend this equation through a sense of belonging to a larger human continuity that extends beyond our finite individual lives (whether through our descendants, our works, our religious convictions, or eternal nature). But during times of confusion and upheaval, that sense of human continuity is threatened by the breakdown of the belief systems that traditionally maintain it. A sense of radical discontinuity can come to predominate, accompanied by unsettling ideas and images that exacerbate anxieties about individual death. Troubled by the meaninglessness of their own lives and deaths, ordinary people can become susceptible to world-ending visions. Aum's members grew up in a country that had experienced more than a hundred years of such confusion and upheaval, including the imperial megalomania of the World War II era and a subsequent half century of precarious national achievement and equally precarious individual coherence. It was hardly surprising that the young people attracted to Aum had already experienced a profound sense of dislocation—including confusions between personal and global death—before they ever encountered the guru.

The threatening existence of nuclear weapons (two of which destroyed Japanese cities) has radically disrupted all efforts to balance individual death with a sense of human continuity. Such ultimate weaponry has imposed on everyone disturbing images of our capacity to destroy our world and extinguish our species with our own technology, by our own hand, and to no purpose. Small wonder we have encountered during the last half of the twentieth century not only intensified end-of-the-world visions but a troubling sense of these visions as closer to actuality. Fear becomes tinged with guilt: what could be more sinful, after all, than destroying the world with our own weaponry? And if that is a genuine possibility—as it must be—how can we continue to believe in human continuity? Our ultimate weapons, along with our capacity to destroy our environment in other ways, undermine what is symbolically regenerative in our mythology of death and rebirth. Our imaginations become impaired. There is a tendency to equate nuclear holocaust with Armageddon—here Aum is far from alone—and we are likely to extend the actuality of nuclear holocaust to any world-ending story from whatever religious or mythological narrative. When we do, talented megalomanic gurus like Asahara can manipulate this already concretized world-ending story and claim ownership of that narrative as part of their general ownership of death.

The act of killing has always been a means of experiencing vitality and a sense of transcendence. In violent criminals, it has been observed, depression and inner deadness can be followed by a violent act that replaces those feelings with a sense of new energy and life-power that is followed in turn by a reversion to depression and numbing. A parallel process took place within Shōkō Asahara, though on a more grandiose scale. We recall the guru's exultation in declaring, "Now it's war!" (meaning "Now it's Armageddon!") He seemed to feel most alive when imagining, and acting to bring about, the destruction of the world. Spiritualizing killing via the concept of *poa* helped him and others in Aum to overcome restraint and even to claim that they were bringing a new dimension of vitality and immortality to their victims. For just as one can kill a person in order to conquer death in oneself, so can one seek to "kill the world" from a similar motivation. The death that one is conquering—or "murdering"—could be one's own or that of one's sacred group. "Altruistic killing," applied individually and globally, further eliminates the idea of death. One is enhancing the ostensible life-continuity and symbolic immortality of one's victim, or of the world at large, which by definition is the opposite of killing. But to sustain such a conviction one has to keep on murdering.

In its own fashion, Aum was very much about survival. The world renewal that was the entire purpose of its world-destroying project was to be brought about by a specific band of completely pure Aum survivors. But since those survivors were (at least ideally) to be clones of Asahara, one can say that only the guru was meant to survive. In that way Asahara and his clones took on a specific psychological pattern of killing to survive.

Most survivors of extreme death encounters, such as those who experienced the Nazi camps or the atomic bombings of Hiroshima and Nagasaki, struggle with an indelible death imprint and with a quest for life-affirming meaning or inner form. But there are others who become despotic leaders and spend their lives seeking such encounters, who become addicted to survival and, in the writer Elias Canetti's words, "need corpses." Such people are likely to have undergone extreme ordeals of their own early in life, which they construe as magical survivals. They come to need experiences of survival in order to feel alive. They lose the distinction between "the other" and "the enemy." Their lives take on a terrible personal momentum aimed at becoming the ultimate and only survivor. Canetti characterizes the paranoid survivor as one whose "deepest urge" is "to be the last man to remain alive": "Such a man sends others to their death; he diverts death on to them in order to be spared it himself. Not only is he totally indifferent to their deaths, but everything within him urges him to bring them about. He is especially likely to resort to this radical expedient of mass death when his dominion over the living is challenged. Once he feels himself threatened his passionate desire to see *everyone* lying dead before him can scarcely be mastered by his reason."

Canetti surely had someone like Asahara in mind. Embedded in that guru's megalomania, moreover, was the strong feeling that he could best survive his own Armageddon. Then he could, like Judge Schreber, become the "sole survivor to renew mankind." Transcendent survival, that is, requires ultimate catastrophe. Rather than be only part of a "survivor remnant" to serve God (as the Book of Revelation describes), Asahara imagined himself as both the survivor remnant (with his clones) *and* God. It was he who would bring about the biblical/nuclear cleansing that he alone would survive. Only he possessed the superhuman power needed (in Schreber's words) to "outlast death" and achieve eternal survival.

10 | Surviving Aum

The people I interviewed were survivors of an Armageddon that never took place. Having nonetheless been through an ordeal with life-and-death consequences, they experienced many of the survivor patterns I have observed elsewhere: indelible images of actual or symbolic death, struggles with an overwhelming flood or a complete lack of emotion (that is, with feeling and not feeling) and with various kinds of self-condemnation that take the form of guilt or shame, suspicion of the counterfeit in encounters with others, and a continuous effort to grasp the nature of their experience, to give it meaning and form, and thereby enable themselves to move beyond it.

These former Aum members were, however, tainted survivors, both in their own minds and in those of most other Japanese, because the group they had been part of, and whose actions they had survived, turned out to be malign and murderous. They had extremely uneasy feelings about themselves in relation not only to the Aum world they had left but to the society to which they had returned. Their struggles around the meaning of their Aum experience included painful questions of personal culpability and responsibility, questions that were always psychological and moral but sometimes legal as well. Like many Germans after World War II, they had difficulty coming to grips with the evil they had been part of.

Their ordeal was bound up with a guru who was all-encompassing, paranoid, megalomanic, and occasionally psychotic but also, in their experience, extraordinarily compelling. Whatever their rational thoughts or retrospective condemnations of him and Aum, they experienced a form of separation that often felt more like a rupture and carried with it a sense of deprivation. In their interviews, a number said things like "disciples are also victims" and spoke about being "thrown out into life." They could not resolve their contradictory feelings—of having known a privileged existence in Aum that seemed to transcend ordinary life and of having been betrayed and abandoned by a guru they revered. A sense of loss, sometimes so strong that it threatened to shatter self and world, dominated their survivor emotions.

They frequently experienced guilt toward the guru and other Aum members for having left the cult—in some cases specifically toward those on trial because, as one put it, "I'm better off than they are." They also experienced related feelings of shame over having in some way "failed" their guru. Many felt diminished by what they had been through. A former student with ambitious pre-Aum intellectual plans now told me sadly, "My goals died with Aum." There is much to be learned about Aum's significance by looking further at the ways in which individual members survived it.

Evidence of Corpses

We can begin with a question: Why did people leave Aum? No one among those I interviewed did so directly because of the Tokyo sarin attack. At the time of the attack, in fact, they generally felt great uncertainty about who was responsible. Given their extreme immersion in Asahara's guruism, they were unable to face what many suspected in their preconscious minds, namely that Aum had done the killing. Too much was psychologically at stake for them to come to such a conclusion.

Isoda, the "passionate disciple" who imagined himself like Asahara, for instance, told me that for a considerable period of time he "did not believe that Aum was criminal." His sense that there was something "strange" about Aum emerged only gradually, but as his misgivings became more consistent, he developed what he called an "impulse" to leave. He actually left, as we know, when given an opportunity for employment on the outside, but he told me that his basic reason for leaving was simply because he was unsatisfied with Aum. "It was no longer useful for me to stay" was the somewhat cryptic way he put it. The extreme gratification of his early mystical experiences was now undermined by doubt and discomfort. He suppressed that doubt during the months immediately after the subway attack by carrying out his Aum assignment to explain to the world why the group was not responsible for it, but in the end his suspicions and his conflicts with superiors, along with his contacts with journalists, all contributed to an inner transformation and a repudiation of the cult.

Hirota, the occult scientist, experienced similar confusion about the sarin attack. Although he found it a "shocking event," rather than blame Aum, he retained a sense of "half doubt and half belief." He described his main source of anxiety about the cult as coming from a growing recognition of the guru's destructiveness. "I sensed his dangerous idea of bringing on Armageddon." That "dangerous idea" was accompanied by his detection of what he called "an evil atmosphere" in the group. With Hirota, as with others, such retrospective description, though containing its own confusions, tended surely to imply a greater clarity than existed at the time. Like others, Hirota left because of an amorphous combination of feelings that included fear, confusion, doubt, and disapproval, adding up to deep discomfort with the group.

With Yano, who had felt the healing touch of the guru, the failure to pass a "loyalty test" and prove his absolute obedience to the guru revealed a rent in the guru-disciple connection but did not immediately result in a conscious desire to leave. That came a bit later, spurred by two incidents. One was the police's discovery of the bodies of the Sakamoto family about six months after the Tokyo sarin attack through information given by former Aum members. As he put it,

"Until then I had wanted to believe that these things [including the sarin attack] were not done by Aum, but there was no way I could believe that now." At the same time, Yano had a meeting with Fumihiro Jōyū, Aum's minister of foreign affairs and chief public spokesman, in which Jōyū strongly objected to Yano's voicing of pessimism about the group's future. Since Jōyū was one of the most powerful people in Aum and the likely successor to the imprisoned guru, Yano began to feel that it was dangerous for him to remain in the cult. The unacceptable attitude he expressed to Jōyū probably reflected inchoate feelings of antagonism toward the guru.

Iwai, the defender of *poa*, was, as we recall, "shocked" at Aum members who acknowledged to her their active participation in the cult's weapons program. What shocked her and caused her to leave was not, however, their involvement with weapons but their behavior. "If they had been living like genuine spiritual practitioners and I learned that we killed people with sarin, I might not have quit. Even if I had known that Aum did the sarin, I might have stayed." Aum's corpses became real for her only when she encountered what she viewed to be extreme spiritual degeneration in those who had done the killings.

If none of these former disciples' explanations was complete, each represented the culmination of months of confused inner struggle— and each was an indication of the difficulty these members had overcoming resistance to the truth of Aum's criminality. Another indication of the power Aum held over these youthful members was that many of them left only after the guru and his top disciples had been imprisoned, after the guru-disciple connection had in effect been broken by the state.

All this suggests a troubling capacity to find the psychological means to live with mass murder. Selective psychic numbing, enhanced by Aum's extreme compartmentalization and its closed, totalistic milieu, did much to make that possible. Moreover, the linking of precious ecstatic experiences to ultimate virtue, as well as disciples' embrace of Aum's sense of being attacked from without, left no psychic space for their imagining Aum, the guru, or themselves as part of a project of mass murder. For some the evidence of corpses could open up such psychic space, but there were those for whom even that was not enough. The corpses could be blamed on others—or not seen as corpses at all.

In listening to members' accounts of their struggles with Aum's behavior and their own, I was reminded once more of former Nazis I interviewed for my book on Nazi doctors. In both groups people had enormous difficulty dealing with their own connection to evil, all the more so because they had so loved their charismatic leader and thrived in his movement. The Aum members, like their German counterparts, sought to separate themselves from that evil by claiming ignorance of the guru's murderous project. They would often deny or minimize whatever evidence of wrongdoing they had encountered though they would also acknowledge (to a greater extent than did Nazi doctors) that they had been avoiding or suppressing such evidence. Of course, the two groups were very different: the Germans were old men when I met them in the late 1970s, more than thirty years removed from their experience; the Aum members were young and fresh from their involvement. With the Nazis, there had been a nationwide pattern of amorphous numbing and denial. Aum was relatively small and intensely turned in on itself, though it too encouraged, even demanded, numbing and denial. And the doctors played a more direct and heinous role in the Nazi killing project than the mostly lower-level disciples I interviewed in Aum. Yet there seemed to be a psychological common denominator in the ways the two groups had extricated themselves from a relationship to evil. Hirota, for instance, came to recognize the "evil atmosphere" but had clearly long repressed that recognition. Isoda came to view Aum as a "terrorist group" but insisted that, had he joined Aum earlier, he himself could well have taken part. And Harada haltingly came to a partial recognition of how the loss of "human consciousness" and "divine compassion" led Aum to kill.

By the time I spoke to them, most of these former disciples had been strongly influenced by the incriminating testimony of prominent Aum members—in particular, of Kiyohide Hayakawa, the weapons procurer; Ikuo Hayashi, the minister of healing; and Yoshihiro Inoue, the minister of intelligence. Only after reading the transcripts, for instance, could Ogata be convinced that Aum had indeed released the sarin in the subways, planned another attack in the vicinity of the Diet building, "wanted to take over the country," and was focused on triggering an actual Armageddon event.

Divided Selves

Most striking to me was the extreme inner division that former disciples displayed—one part of their minds angrily condemning Aum and its guru, another still feeling profoundly connected to him and to the group. This existence of two relatively separate, even warring selves within the same psyche was a version of the doubling that was part of cult life. There was now the self of the bitter survivor and opponent of Asahara, Aum, and guruism in general and the self of the disciple still merged with the guru and still experiencing, through memory, guru-dispensed ecstasy. The Aum self, retaining ties to Asahara in this life and others, was painfully at odds with the post-Aum self struggling to confront the guru's violence and extricate itself from him and cult life. The greatest difficulty the former members I interviewed faced was leaving behind the perceptions of transcendent experience that the Aum self retained (even as the post-Aum self was experiencing extreme loss, bewilderment, or a sense of disintegration, of falling apart). Although the two selves, of course, were never completely autonomous, it proved a daunting task for any former disciple to integrate them into what was, after all, a single psyche.

In the case of Harada, the erotically charged Aum self remained strong, perhaps even dominant, more than a year after her departure from the cult, while her post-Aum self (on which her existence now depended) registered anger, betrayal, and deep confusion. Though decrying Aum's transgressions, she still engaged in its meditation practices and often expressed the fear that since leaving the group she had been "deteriorating." Describing herself as restless and without motivation, she longed for the "feelings of high energy" she had known in Aum. She could recapture that valued state if she imagined an erotic merging with the guru, but when she did so she experienced considerable internal conflict. As a result, she often found herself yearning for the "simple Aum life" of her romanticized memories. Her dreams reflected her divided state: in them, close Aum friends would appear, repeating a refrain of "Why did you quit?"—after which she would join them in the cult's meditation practices. She saw such dreams as expressing the Aum principle that separating oneself from the guru was itself defilement.

She called Aum's violence "childish" but went on to contrast that characterization with her sense of the guru as "dignified," "understanding," and "highly intelligent," sadly noting the "gap" between the two. In this, she was giving expression to residual confusion about Aum reality in general. Like many others, she was deeply puzzled as to how a group of "very nice people, enthusiastic and pure," could be part of "an organization with such craziness and killing." She asked herself why things had to turn out as they did and for an answer imagined contacting Shiva directly. Over time her post-Aum self was becoming increasingly functional, but she was never free from conflict and confusion generated by her still assertive Aum self, sustained as it continued to be by a sense of karmic connection with the guru.

One former disciple actually embarked on a trip to India with a small group of others to seek out the Dalai Lama and ask him whether he had really said that Asahara possessed "the mind of a Buddha," as the guru claimed he had. The group did not succeed in meeting the Dalai Lama but a close associate of his denied to them that such a thing could have been said. Telling me the story, the former disciple added with a wry smile, "Of course I did not have to go to India to find that out."

All those I interviewed struggled with the extremity of Asahara's guruism. Some made an effort to demystify and thereby diminish it. Harada, for instance, spoke quizzically and slightly mockingly of the many Aum writings in which "it is said again and again, 'Master is great! Master is great!'" Hirota related Aum's criminality to the absurd guruism that rendered Asahara "a divine being who could not be criticized." He emphasized the need to "study more about the shadow Aum cast through Asahara's charisma." He was concerned with the general phenomenon of guruistic charisma but even more with his personal submission to Asahara's charismatic shadow. (Albert

Speer, the Nazi architect and member of Hitler's inner circle, expressed to me a similar need to understand more about how he could have been so mesmerized by a person like Hitler. He, too, stressed the importance of exploring more generally the nature of Hitler's charisma.) Hirota related Asahara's charisma to the human capacity for "darkness," by which he meant not only "the darkness in our minds, each of us, darkness we don't really look at" but also "the mental structure of the Japanese as a whole, since our faith in guru-ism was quite similar to Japanese feelings about the emperor system." Here Hirota went further than most of the disciples I interviewed in exploring his psychological and moral involvement in guru-centered evil.

Thoughtful disciples could also criticize Asahara and Aum for their distortions of reality and for their psychological aberrations. Kuno, whose inner resistance caused an attack of amnesia, spoke, for instance, of Asahara's early religious vision as "a hallucination of someone coming out with the words 'I am a god. I am Shiva.' This kind of person was never actually a god. A true god or Buddha doesn't have to appear in this way. Such a claim can only be made by someone who is insane." Similar psychological aberrations could be associated with more general Aum fantasy. Isoda angrily compared the group's life to "the world of an animated cartoon." When, having left the group, he returned to an Aum facility to conduct interviews for a television program, he noticed that Aum members were carefully scrutinizing airplanes flying overhead to determine whether they were American warplanes: "Here were grown men in their twenties, adults doing it with a straight face, and with this straight face talking to me about the incredible power of Freemasons who could even control the weather. They simply had no knowledge at all about the outside world." When I asked him why he felt so angry about this unreality, he replied, "It's my own former self. It's like watching myself, so it's really painful."

To achieve critical perspective on Aum and spiritual resolution, many former disciples sought to embrace various forms of Buddhism. Yano found solace in early Buddhist texts, where he could encounter the compassion and trust of the "live, immediate Buddha." In contrast he now saw Asahara as "a pitiful being who exploited his believers in order to express his revenge against society." He came to view his former guru as a Devadatta, as a cousin of the Buddha who became a disciple and a respected member of the Buddhist community but later tried to have the Buddha murdered in order to replace him. As Yano explained, "I needed an example like that in order to make Asahara's actions—his very being—meaningful to me." But it was Yano's new understanding of Buddhism that led him to conclude that, if "bad people may be closest to the Pure Land," perhaps it could be said that his former guru was "the one closest to the Pure Land." He stressed as well the importance of "Buddhist nihilism" to Aum doctrine. While his meaning was not entirely clear, perhaps even to him, I had the impression that he was attempting to bring a broader religious and historical perspective to Aum in a way that was critical yet defensive.

When present Aum members defended Aum more directly, speaking of the guru's violent actions as "beyond the understanding of ordinary beings," part of a higher purpose, unknowable to others, they too were struggling with their confusion while suppressing their moral and psychological conflicts.

But former members who, like Hirota, were intent upon separating themselves from Aum, interpreted the guru's collapse in the courtroom as a form of ultimate judgment. Stunned by the guru's sudden fall from seemingly untouchable omniscience into mumbling incoherence, Hirota found himself wondering "if he has a sense of shame." For him, the guru had become "a naked king"—that is, the emperor had no clothes.

Troubled Reentry

Former Aum members have had an extremely uneasy relationship with the society they have reentered. They have been met mostly with anger and rejection, but also with curiosity, occasional sympathy, and even a certain amount of lionization, at least when the media have sought them out for further dramatic revelations about the cult. Their own attitudes about reentry were convoluted. They frequently expressed to me their sense of the extreme corruption of Japanese society, a perception that many of them originally brought to Aum. Yet they spoke as well of their "obligation to society," where "society" seemed to mean not so much the specific institutions around them as a larger human community in which truth, reason, restraint, and decency matter. Their obligation to it was usually understood as a duty to convey what they knew about Aum but sometimes also as the need to make amends for what Aum did. A number of them cooperated with the police, responding in varying degrees to legal pressure and their own consciences.

They were particularly suspicious of the media, and many continued to doubt even the most accurate reporting on Aum's misdeeds. Former members tended to decry much of the trial coverage as soap opera but at the same time valued, and were greatly influenced by, media revelations concerning Aum and its leaders. Yano's reference to the "fascism of the mass media" was a far stronger comment than most I heard, but few former members would have disagreed with Harada, who said that it was very hard for her to believe what the media said. That skepticism could contain more than a hint of Aum's equation of the media with defilement. But the media themselves did much to justify such suspicion. While they sometimes helped people leave Aum by providing them with new information or offering them money for television appearances, they tended to sensationalize already dramatic stories and, at their worst, engaged in immoral, self-serving acts of their own.

Former Aum members have had a harder time reconnecting with society than members of other Japanese cults. Their difficulties have included finding work—and finding an overall means of functioning in the world outside Aum. A number have gravitated to Buddhist groups or looked to Buddhist teachers, while a few have become involved with Christian organizations. Some have begun to work with Buddhist or Christian counselors or with secular psychologists and psychiatrists; even a few American counselors have come to Japan to offer advice. Sometimes counselors and therapists have had their own agendas, whether religious or psychological, and former Aum members (apt to be suspicious in any case) have complained on occasion of being exploited by them. They have also complained of being subjected too quickly to interpretations and judgments without adequate consideration of the complexities of their experiences.

Inevitably, there have been dubious claims and a few scandals. In early 1997, for example, a Japanese counselor who described himself as a neurolinguist, a student of artificial intelligence, and a deprogrammer interviewed and hypnotized a prominent former member, then broadcast some of the sessions on television, and finally announced that he was going to marry one of the members he had deprogrammed. The incident embodied not only professional misbehavior but more general cultural confusions in coping with new problems. It also revealed the speed with which would-be gurus can spring from within the counseling subculture.

Most former Aum members I interviewed had made efforts to repair family divisions, but intense generational struggles often remained. While parents were loyal providers of support of many kinds, they were at the same time sources of psychological conflict and representatives of the society from which former members still felt alienated. Indeed, they frequently blamed the entire Aum phenomenon on society's profound corruption and hypocrisy. They also drew parallels between Aum and various social and cultural institutions and forms of behavior, whether the wartime emperor system and its tradition of worshipful obedience, the excesses of left-wing violence in the 1960s and 1970s, or contemporary corporate practices, especially the intense group exercises meant to promote loyalty and enthusiasm. Occasionally former members connected Aum to cults in the United States or Europe or to a Western political movement like Nazism, but their associations more often had to do with the Japanese setting.

Many also expressed opinions about the kinds of people drawn to Aum, starting with themselves. Isoda, for instance, emphasized a quality of softness and dependency in himself and other Aum members that he saw as stemming from their having been indulged and overprotected by their parents, which made it difficult for them to separate themselves from their families and act independently. He also mentioned being "obsessed with ideals" in ways that were ungrounded and unreal.

Iwai said something similar: "My weak sense of self led me to identify with others and to always seek their approval and affection." She felt that "Japan's problem surfaced through me, the weak being."

The problem, in her view, involved a conflict between a superficial claim to individualism and "the baggage of old [Japanese cultural] expectations"—"the longing for the ideal father and ideal mother, the preference for fragile women with long hair and strong men who can lead them." All this, she claimed, followed upon the previous generation's unsuccessful struggle to change society in the 1960s. "We became subjugated to Aum influence and methods that were in ways like the Nazis'. It was not," she added, "a question of being brainwashed but of becoming involved with Aum because of my needs."

Hirota expanded on his ideas about "darkness," stressing that it was in everyone and thereby suggesting that Aum was merely a crucible for evil. "Usually we do not look into that darkness. It is unknown to us and we are afraid of it." Aum, he was saying, could evoke anyone's potential for violent or murderous behavior. A former high-ranking Aum member observed similarly that "there is violence in all of us," and that "religion always has a violent side." Both sets of comments reflected some of the difficulty experienced by former members (especially those of high rank) in confronting their connection to Aum's specific form of evil.

Isoda spoke of utilizing his Aum experience to come to a "healthy" recognition of his own "badness." Others, he said, looked upon him as a "kind, obedient gentleman," but "honestly speaking, I was not that kind of man." Rather, he came to recognize in himself "the desire to cause deep trouble for other people, long-lasting trouble." He perceived, too, a continuous struggle between his "good side and a bad side" that he had expressed in his enthusiasm about destroying the world.

Isoda, we recall, spoke of an awareness of ways in which his own sense of grandiosity resembled Asahara's. Yano, too, expressed a guru-like grandiosity in declaiming religious and moral truths. But Isoda brought the subject up in a self-probing, even self-mocking spirit that enabled him to puncture that tendency and gain a certain critical perspective on it. Yano, in contrast, continued to require it to cope with his post-Aum life. He was a defender rather than a critic of such grandiosity, without insight into the psychological state he was defending.

Even in the absence of such overt grandiosity, former Aum members sometimes still considered themselves part of an elite group. One way of negotiating the treacherous terrain of post-Aum existence was to take a certain pride in the fact that they alone had experienced Aum's unique mystical pleasures and were the ultimate authorities on a dangerous cult that had become an object of extraordinary social, psychological, and legal fascination.

Aum members used the word *gekō*, or "going down," for leaving the cult, the same word used for traveling from the capital to a province, suggesting the idea of diminished status or abasement. In Aum usage the word could also have the quality of a curse, of designated bad fortune or suffering—of being consigned to hell—as punishment for the unforgivable act of leaving. Even those who have become quite critical of Aum could experience this curse to some degree. Many former Aum members, according to an observer who worked closely with them, seemed to lose their center, to experience amorphous fear of some unnamed punishment, and to suffer from an array of psychosomatic and physical symptoms. In their post-Aum efforts to hold their own spiritually and psychologically—to cope with conflicts concerning loss, collusion in evil, and cultural reentry—most showed some movement toward partial resolution of those conflicts while still being haunted by their unending struggle with that troubling image of "going down."

Prison Reflections

Aum leaders reflected on their experiences in their court testimony, though in ways often limited by the need to claim legal nonresponsibility. They nonetheless brought considerable insight to the behavior of the guru and his high disciples. Yoshihiro Inoue told of the opportunity imprisonment gave him for "looking at my own face" and finding "one who had been deceiving himself [by avoiding] his own sense that something was lacking in himself." He now realized, he claimed, the wrongness of Asahara's teaching that "only disciples exercising the guru's will, however unreasonable that might be, can be united with the guru and guided to liberation." In fact, "liberation through carrying out the guru's will was nothing but self-deception." The truth, he added, was that "all sentient beings have a Buddha nature and that Buddha nature can be awakened in each of us to bring about liberation." He spoke of the guru's violation of the Mahāyāna principles of "compassion and sympathy" and of Aum's causing "others and their families nothing but totally irrational suffering." Hence Aum's salvation teachings were "fundamentally wrong." He pledged to continue to "nurture my *bodhichitta*" (Buddha-mind seeking enlightenment).

At the same time, Inoue was critical of Japanese society, emphasizing the "bottomless anxiety" of young people, who perceive that "information is manipulated without our knowing it and that sane thinking is undermined." This was what drove them to "gather around the guru seeking their own awakening and the people's salvation." In that sense, he went on to say, there could be "some meaning in the existence of Aum Shinrikyō."

Inoue's way of assuming personal responsibility for those who worked under him in the ministry of intelligence was to insist upon their overall *non*responsibility: "You are not responsible for the crimes you have committed because all disciples were under the guru's control." He believed they had a future, but it might "take time to realize," he said, implying that some of them might have to spend time in jail. "You should look at reality, not be desperate, and clear away your past for a new life," he advised. Although slippery on the question of responsibility, Inoue was firm in declaring to these disciples that they "must never again be either victims or criminals," two identities that many came to feel Aum had imposed upon them.

Shigerō Sugimoto, a member of the inner circle who had been involved in more than one murder, told in detail of his subservience to the guru's will and of his overwhelming fear of anything approaching disobedience, his "feeling that this crazy guru can do anything to me." He condemned himself as having been "ignorant and a fool and blind," insisting that "my belief that the guru's power was connected with total salvation was a complete failure of my own." Pronouncing Asahara "a foolish human being," he went on to declare, "I can no longer believe that Asahara is a guru and have no devotion to him." He described himself as having been "deceived by the claim that the guru was the ultimately liberated person" and as now knowing that the guru's claim to be taking on other people's bad karma "was complete nonsense." In his mind, "the guru fell from being an eminent practitioner to an ordinary man by whom I was used."

An important commentary was offered by Hisako Ishii, Aum's leading administrator. If Murai was the quintessential Aum scientist, Ishii was the quintessential Aum woman—attractive, efficient to the point of ruthlessness in pursuit of financial gain for the cult, ultraloyal to her guru, whose disciple she had been from the very beginnings of Aum. Imprisoned for her role in helping perpetrators escape following the sarin attack, she made a much-awaited public statement in May 1997. She was cautious and by no means fully contrite, but she acknowledged a shift from having "revered" Asahara as "an absolute leader" to realizing that "he was not a 100 percent guru but rather a human being with weaknesses—not the embodiment of perfection that I had wanted." The result, she said, was that "now I feel that the person I followed was wrong and did wrong." She, too, immersed herself in more genuine Buddhist teachings with the "wish to train myself, one so full of human weaknesses, to reject the evil feelings and base desires that exist in my heart, and to bring myself closer to the good as long as I am alive," for "I surrendered myself to a kind of solidarity which in hindsight was fake."

All these former leaders faced long jail sentences, if not capital punishment, and the content of their confessions was affected by their legal situations. What is clearly authentic in their testimony is their sense of personal deficiency in having been susceptible to Asahara's influence and their judgment of him as a false guru. This disenchantment on the part of those who went furthest in following the guru, along with their detailed descriptions of Aum crimes, had enormous impact on the former disciples I interviewed, none of whom were as criminally implicated. In many cases the testimony helped them begin to take in truths they had long resisted.

"A New Aum?"

There is a widespread belief in Japan that Fumihiro Jōyū had the ambition, and is being groomed, to become the new guru of Aum. It is assumed that Asahara will eventually be put to death, while Jōyū, unconnected to any direct killing, will complete a three-year prison sentence in 1999 for fraudulent financial activities. Though to many outside of Aum Jōyū has been a consummate public liar, he has had a certain charismatic appeal to remaining cult members and especially (because of his striking good looks) to female teenagers and young women. In contrast to most other high disciples, he has publicly and repeatedly expressed absolute loyalty to his guru and to Aum. What kind of Aum he might come to head is another question. There are undoubtedly factions among the present Aum remnant, but it is mainly Jōyū who is mentioned in connection with "a new Aum," with "new people taking over."

There have been reports of an Aum revival, supported by police documents released to the media claiming that Aum expanded from six to sixteen branches during 1997 and to twenty branches in 1998. The cult's continuing recruitment and training activities have understandably alarmed many. It is hard to evaluate these reports, but at the time of this writing it is generally estimated that there are two thousand Aum members in Japan, five hundred of whom are renunciants. Moreover, some who have left Aum remain believers and still offer it financial support. Others retain personal ties. One middle-level former Aum member, for instance, showed me a picture of a disciple serving a long prison sentence for attempted murder and said cheerfully, "Oh, he was a good fellow, a good friend of mine. We trained together to learn to shoot." The remark was casual, but it reflects a post-Aum subculture whose boundaries are not always sharply distinguished.

Among former members, there were what could be called class conflicts, having to do with where in the Aum hierarchy one once stood. Those who were relatively prominent sometimes expressed resentment toward those who were lower in the hierarchy, claiming that they had no right to speak publicly about things they could not have witnessed. Former leaders were especially sensitive about all aspects of Aum. Having built the cult, they found it difficult to accept the murderous truth of what it was that they created in following the guru. According to a close observer, they had "secrets" that they would not tell, secrets that had to do with Aum violence, with the absurdity of that violence, and with their own relationship to it. Such secrets are guarded by survivors of various kinds, especially those who have been perpetrators as well as victims, and here signify the largely unresolved struggles of Aum members in general.

Those struggles could take the form of declarations of faith in Asahara and Aum. Prosecutorial documents assembled not long after the sarin attack quote members and former members of varying standing:

> I think the time will come when people will say that the great master was a great savior, not an ordinary man.

> Aum Shinrikyō is facing a great crisis of destruction by the power of the state and the brainwashing of the mass media. However, even if Aum Shinrikyō vanishes as an organization, so long as individual disciples exist, the religion of Aum Shinrikyō will absolutely survive. And I'm sure that many people will realize that the doctrine of Aum Shinrikyō is the one and only truth.

> On the occasion of the great Hanshin earthquake of last year (1995) and the sarin incident in the Tokyo subways last March, many Japanese came to face death sincerely. Because Aum Shinrikyō was in the mass media almost every day, Japanese people came to turn to Aum Shinrikyō, which revealed the nature of death. Now they have a basic understanding that the great master's teaching is the only truth.

> If the sarin incident in the Tokyo subways was really caused by Aum Shinrikyō, I think it was the great master's mahāmudrā for Japan as a whole to awaken it to the supreme truth.

> If the great master is to be put to death, I wish to be chosen in his place. If that could be done, there would be no greater joy for me.

> Even after these incidents, the great master unalterably remains the spiritual leader of Aum. And I think that followers will believe what he has said to be absolute and will follow him.

> Because I become filled with power in my body when I think of the great master during my meditation, he is to me absolutely necessary even now.

Just after I became an ex-member, wrong data entered me from watching TV for many hours and I had a delusion that it was the great master's failure that made him cause a series of events like the sarin incident in the Tokyo subways. But then I came to realize that these things were inevitable for salvation in the way of Vajrayāna. Even if victims of these events were my own family members, I can now recognize that such people were sent by *poa* to a higher realm.

I believe that the followers who spread sarin, disregarding the danger to their own lives, are not criminals but martyrs to the supreme vocation.

These statements came from Aum loyalists, a distinct minority among the previous membership but the potential core of any continuing organization. True believers argue that reports of Asahara's strange behavior in prison and on trial are mass media distortions in a conspiracy either to make the guru crazy or to make him look crazy. "It is hard for them to find any craziness in Asahara" is the way an observer put it. If Asahara were really crazy, that is, those who remain disciples would have to question the sanity of their involvement with him.

Aum survivors were left with contradictory fragments. These they could reconstitute into sacred Aum doctrine, as did the loyalists quoted above. Others, including most of the people I interviewed, felt compelled to confront these contradictions critically.

11 | A Japanese Phenomenon?

A few months after the Tokyo sarin attack, a talented young television producer—a man in his late twenties—startled me by saying, "I understand those Aum people very well. I feel myself to be very much like them," a sentiment he voiced repeatedly over the course of an hour's conversation. He was in no way endorsing the cult's violence or its collective madness. Rather, he was telling me that Asahara and Aum touched a Japanese nerve, that he found himself drawn to the cult's fervent critique of and hostility toward contemporary society and to its insistent spiritual explorations, however extreme, of questions of personal meaning. While his attitude was hardly typical of Japanese in general, it was by no means rare among younger people, many of whom recognized what they shared with Aum even as they condemned it. This was one expression of a society's troubled fascination with a cult that made everyone ask: Why in our country? Why here?

Once Aum was identified as the perpetrator of the subway attack, Japanese became preoccupied with the cult and especially with its guru. Every day shocking new details of guru-initiated behavior emerged—stories of gruesome murders and corpse disposals, the production and use of lethal gases, the culturing and release of deadly toxins and spores, and ingenious forms of terror, blackmail, and extortion. Widespread fears about further gas attacks were heightened by a spate of reports of odors from noxious substances—evidently largely copycat acts, but a few possibly of Aum's doing—and a plane hijacking in which the hijacker demanded the release of Aum's leaders from jail.

The trials of leading Aum disciples began toward the end of 1995, Asahara's in early 1996. In the Japanese legal system, with its endless hearings, such trials can go on for a number of years; the guru's could last a decade or more. At first the public lined up for seats in record numbers and Asahara's case became "the trial of the century," compared frequently in Japan to the O. J. Simpson trial. Over the years, though, public interest in the trials has diminished considerably. Most of the trials continue at this writing. But two significant figures have been convicted of murder: Dr. Hayashi, who was given a life sentence, and Kazuaki Okazaki, a powerful figure in Aum during its early stages, who was sentenced to death for his part in the Sakamoto murders. The government also belatedly acted to outlaw the production of sarin gas and withdrew from Aum official recognition as a religion. There was much heated discussion about reinstating a long-dormant antisubversion law. Under it, Aum members could have been prohibited from meeting and all former and present members placed under close scrutiny. That effort was eventually abandoned because of fears, raised mostly by liberal intellectuals, of creating an oppressive society while simply driving the remaining cult members underground. Applying the law, it was also recognized, would have greatly impaired the reintegration of former Aum members into society.

On March 20, 1996, the first anniversary of the Tokyo sarin attack, there was an outpouring of media attention, a painful national remembrance of the chaos, the heroic attempts of transit employees to remove the containers of gas, several at the cost of their lives, and the terrible suffering of the victims and their families. Then and during subsequent anniversaries, the Japanese were commemorating the moment when they felt a sense of social safety give way to sudden vulnerability to violence and grotesque forms of mass death.

Many early responses to Asahara and Aum tended to separate the guru and his cult from the rest of society by treating him as less than human—pure evil or part monster. Victims of the subway attack or members of their families were reported as saying things like "I don't consider him a person." A journalist gave voice to a typical sentiment when he spoke of Asahara as "a ferocious animal with an excessively cruel mind." So much a symbol of evil was the guru that a primary school teacher who referred to a student with long hair as "Asahara" was officially reprimanded and subjected to a temporary salary reduction. With absolutized evil, there was no room for humor, or even metaphor.

Yet many commentators and ordinary citizens also wondered what was wrong with Japanese society that it could produce a group like Aum Shinrikyō and a guru like Shōkō Asahara. Stressing the alienation of young people from the larger society and the absence of meaning in their lives, many commentators blamed these phenomena on the legacy of the emperor system, on the lockstep demands of the educational system, or on Japanese corporate practices that suppressed personal autonomy by mobilizing energies for intense collective projects. In the process, a measure of sympathy was often extended to former Aum members for having been betrayed not just by the cult but by society itself.

Japanese institutions were also much criticized for their responses to Aum. The media, in particular, were attacked for their aggressive competitiveness, their questionable reportorial practices, and their generally sensationalized coverage of the cult. Indeed the media's criticism of itself, all too frequently earned, became part of the spectacle of the moment. In the aftermath of the Tokyo sarin attack, one of the worst examples of media corruption was revealed. In October 1989, the Tokyo Broadcasting System, a prominent television station, had taped an interview with Tsutsumi Sakamoto in which he told of Aum's illegal activities. Under pressure from the cult, the company had screened the tape for a few Aum members, intensifying the cult's, and especially the guru's, anger at Sakamoto. Aum's vociferous complaints, followed by the mysterious disappearance of the Sakamoto family, had led TBS to cancel its planned broadcast of the tape. TBS officials had failed, moreover, to report their dealings with Sakamoto and the cult to police authorities. Despite media charges and an in-house investigation, the company had baldly denied having shown the tape to Aum. When the truth was finally revealed, TBS was repri-manded by Japanese officials and threatened with loss of its broad-casting license. In late April 1996, Hirozō Isozaki, the company's president, admitted that the film had been shown to Aum members and, in Japanese fashion, resigned from the company as an expression of his responsiblity for the wrongdoing.

Questions were also raised about the astonishing failure of the police to take action in the face of accumulating evidence of Aum's stockpiling and use of its weaponry. While reluctance to be seen as infringing on religious freedom was a factor here, many Japanese sus-pected bribery in high places or other forms of political corruption. An organizer of an anti-Aum parents group told me how he had been tracked down by cult members and almost killed with VX gas, only to have the police insist that he had been attempting suicide. In another incident, the police falsely accused a victim of the Matsumoto sarin attack of having been a perpetrator of the attack and were very slow to withdraw the charge.

The trial process was criticized for dragging on interminably and for the undignified bickering that went on between Asahara and the judge. Universities came in for rebuke because a few professors of reli-gious studies seemed receptive to much of Aum's behavior and one or two seemed to have been taken in by Asahara. One scholar was forced to resign from his university, and others became cautious about mak-ing public statements concerning Aum.

Japan was profoundly shaken and confused by the Aum debacle. Whatever else was said about the cult in an endless stream of articles, books, and media probes, Japanese could not avoid the realization that Aum had emerged from their society, that it in some way repre-sented them. People spoke of "Aum shocks" and "Aum after-shocks"—as if the cult's activities had been the social equivalent of the Kobe earthquake—and sometimes of an "Aum syndrome" of general malaise and fear. Intellectuals expressed concern that social agitation over the cult might intensify Japanese nationalism or lead to the imple-mentation of draconian social controls, as in the past. There was also a new suspiciousness of introspection, so that a person who raised ethical and spiritual questions of any kind might quickly be told, "Don't be so *Aum*!"

We should not be surprised that Aum, so immersed in global conspiracy theories, provoked a wave of them as it collapsed. In one typical instance, it was claimed that the cult was part of a sustained program to "destabilize Japan" run by a British "Occult Bureau" working through "its agent, the Dalai Lama, who met with Aum leader Shōkō Asahara, in India." While such wild theories appeared mostly at the fringes of society or on obscure Web pages, they were at times published in widely circulated magazines.

Historians have spoken of the "free security" two great oceans have provided the United States and of Americans' nuclear-age anxiety over losing their sense of that safety. Japan's "free security," only decades old, lay in its perception of itself as a well-ordered and therefore safe country. Aum destroyed that. A diffuse Aum-related anxiety now became part of a larger constellation of fears about earthquakes, economic recession or depression, weakening family ties, and increasing domestic and social violence. Certainly, there is now a feeling in Japan of its deteriorating as a nation and a society while its leaders stand by helplessly, leaving ordinary people unprotected.

Psychohistorical Dislocation

Aum is in many ways a product of Japanese history and of a society that may have experienced in the last century and a half more wrenching historical and psychological upheaval than any other on earth. In Japan's extraordinarily rapid journey from a feudal to a modern (and then postmodern) culture, the two overwhelming events were the Meiji Restoration that began in 1868 and the annihilating defeat of World War II. Out of feudal society the Meiji-era leaders created the beginnings of a powerful, modern, emperor-centered state that expanded into a vast Asian empire, only to be crushed in war. By September 1945, Japan was in ruins, its people starving and rudderless.

When exposed to such extremes of social, political, and cultural transformation and collapse in such a short period of time, people experience what I call psychohistorical dislocation, a breakdown of the social and institutional arrangements that ordinarily anchor human lives. What are impaired are the symbol systems having to do with family, religion, social and political authority, sexuality, birth and death, and the overall ordering of the life cycle. Symbols and rituals by no means disappear but, because less effectively internalized, come to feel less natural and more coercive. People experience a profound gap between what they feel themselves to be and what a society or a culture expects them to be.

One Japanese observer has referred to the Meiji Restoration period, with its stunning array of Western-modeled reforms in every area of society, as a time of "thunderboltism." As the historian Carol Gluck points out, the elaborate construction of emperor worship—an ideology melding religion, myth, nationalism, and political need—was, to a significant degree, an effort to contain that thunderboltism, to manage the intense conflicts and confusions accompanying what many experienced as the "disturbing demands of social change." But the new emperor-centered system turned out to have its own thunderboltism. Created artificially but attributed to an ancient past, it had a tenuous claim on national unity that all too often required large-scale social suppression and escalating levels of violence abroad. Psychohistorical dislocation, a "surfeit of change," can give rise to proteanism, a pattern characterized by psychological experiment, individual and collective shape-shifting, and a struggle to retain a sense of continuity in the midst of that change. But such dislocation can also lead people into forms of "restorationism," or what we now call fundamentalism. The Japanese political genius of the Meiji era was to combine the proteanism of a social revolution with a fundamentalist-like plunge into a sacred imperial restoration.

There was, however, a psychological price to be paid: Japan's formidable modern accomplishments have coexisted with an unusual degree of psychological turmoil. In the grip of such turmoil, some people may seek extreme remedies.

The novelist Kenzaburō Ōe, in his 1994 Nobel Prize acceptance speech, described Japan as "split between two opposite poles of ambiguity." He pointed to a long-standing psychological division between Western-inspired modernization and traditional cultural influences, emphasizing as well the painful sense of ambiguous identity that exists on both sides of this inner dividing line. "The modernization of Japan," he explained, "was oriented toward learning from and imitating the West, yet the country is situated in Asia and has firmly retained its traditional culture. The ambiguous orientation of Japan drove the country into the position of an invader in Asia, and resulted in its isolation from other Asian countries not only politically but also socially and culturally. The Second World War came right out of the middle of the process of modernization, a war that was brought about by the very aberration of that process itself." Ōe was telling us that such ambiguity can be lethal and that it pervades both national behavior and the individual Japanese psyche as "a kind of chronic disease that has been prevalent throughout the modern age," one that he himself as a writer experiences as "a deep-felt scar." In his use of the term *ambiguity*, he evoked Japan's particularly troubled version of psychohistorical dislocation and suggested that it could lead either to violent behavior or toward the country's becoming "invisible," without any clear ethical presence among other peoples. Such ethical "invisibility" within Japanese society was undoubtedly a factor in the Aum phenomenon.

The Medieval Link

The kinds of dislocation experienced in Japan readily lend themselves everywhere on earth to expressions of totalism. For within totalism, there is an absolute (and comforting) polarization of the moral universe—no "polar ambiguities" for the successful guru and his disciples. Always there is a claim of "higher purpose" for which one may deceive, harm, or kill. There is, as well, a collective assumption of omnipotence, creating what Albert Camus speaks of as an "imperialism of justice" that, paradoxically, "has no other means but injustice." Such totalism propels a group like Aum toward the dispensing of existence, an impulse that has always been dangerous but takes on new menace in our world.

It turns out that Aum was not alone in its fervor to force the end, to try to bathe the world in its own blood for its own good. For the most striking historical examples of forcing the end, it is necessary to turn back nearly a millennium and not to Asia but to medieval Europe.

The connecting text spanning continents and centuries is the Book of Revelation.

Spiritual imaginings of the end figure prominently not only in Jewish and Christian thought, in Islam, and in a more gradual and cyclic form in Buddhism and Hinduism but in the early Babylonian, Iranian, and Greek religious traditions. Most such imaginings have been nonviolent. Christianity itself, in its origins, has been described as an extension of Jewish apocalypticism, requiring as it does the return and bodily resurrection of a messiah. At the end of Christian Europe's first millennium, however, the more restrained forms of what the historian of religion Bernard McGinn calls "apocalyptic spirituality," with their metaphorical stress on meaningful history and hope for the future, gave way to violent behavior meant to bring the apocalypse directly to earth and based, as has been true all too often since, on a literal reading of Revelation.

Particularly relevant to Aum are groups that took shape in the "millennial undertow" of Western Europe from the eleventh through the sixteenth centuries and often made Jews their designated victims. These millennial movements flourished among what the historian Norman Cohn calls the "rootless poor," who were joined and sometimes led by men of higher social and intellectual standing. "It often happened," Cohn explains, "that certain segments of the poor were captured by some millenarian prophet. Then the usual desire of the poor to improve the material conditions of their lives became transfused with fantasies of a world reborn into innocence through a final, apocalyptic massacre. The evil ones—variously identified with the Jews, the clergy or the rich—were to be exterminated—after which the Saints—i.e. the poor in question—would set up their kingdom, a realm without suffering or sin."

One medieval movement of this sort was the Free Spirit Brethren, a kind of umbrella for many millenarian sects. It emerged in German areas in the thirteenth century, spread throughout much of Europe, and remained influential for several hundred years. Fiercely rebellious, the Brethern espoused, according to Cohn, "a quasi-mystical anarchism—an affirmation of freedom so reckless and unqualified that it amounted to a total denial of every kind of restraint and limitation."

Like Asahara and his high disciples, the adepts of the Free Spirit understood themselves as repudiating moral norms in order to create "the perfect man." They combined a form of gnostic mysticism— "each one," says Cohn, "was Christ and Holy Spirit"—with a policy of "promiscuity on principle," of committing "rapes and adulteries and other acts that gave pleasure to the body." Their mystical sexuality, part of their strong millenarial imagery, was promoted as a return to a state of innocence before the Fall. One Free Spirit guru claimed to have rediscovered the way of performing sexual intercourse originally practiced by Adam and Eve. At the same time he declared himself the savior who would herald the world's third and final age, that of the Holy Spirit. "Cheating, theft, robbery with violence were all justified," according to Cohn, since the being truly united with God was incapable of sin. Living communally and renouncing all individual ownership, the Brethern resembled Aum in seeking to become what Cohn calls "an elite of amoral supermen." Free Spirit visions included "messianic woes in which the majority of mankind would perish by war, famine, or fire, leaving a saving remnant—usually one's own group but sometimes including favored royalty, which would then experience an eternal divinity." The Brethren did not, however, engage in large-scale coordinated violence aimed at bringing about an end to the world.

If the Free Spirit sects did not themselves force the end, they influenced groups that did. One such group was the Taborites, who emerged in Bohemia in the early part of the fifteenth century. Named after the mountain where Christ foretold his Second Coming, the Taborites drew their members mainly from the lower echelons of society and from the ranks of radical priests and former priests who preached the abolition of all evil in preparation for the millennium. To the Taborites, the Church of Rome was the Whore of Babylon and the Pope the Antichrist, both of which would perish in the final struggle. Originally pacificists, the Taborites, preaching apostolic poverty and combating injustice, took on the self-designated mission of purifying the earth. In the process they became violent in the extreme, one of their tracts described as "fuller of blood than a pond is of water." As Cohn explains, "the inescapable duty of the Elect [was] to kill in the name of the Lord," for "beyond the extermination of all evils lay the

Millennium." Indeed, as priests and itinerant warriors, the Taborites were to impose everywhere what they called "plagues of vengeance," engaging in what Cohn terms "the great purification" that would permit Christ to return and rule over a group of surviving saints who "would live together in a community of love and peace" that would re-create "the egalitarian State of Nature." Murdering in the service of the millennium, the Taborites resembled Aum, but they lasted longer (about three decades), reached many more people, and did much more killing.

The Adamites, a radical group originally formed within the Taborites, went even further in forcing the end. Seeking to bring on the millennium according to Revelation, they initiated a "holy war" in which they set villages on fire, murdering all the occupants. Promiscuous like the Free Spirit Brethren, they scorned the chaste. Their leader, known as both Adam and Moses, resembled Asahara in a number of ways, including taking as his prerogative the control of sexual behavior, in his case the giving of consent for any act of sexual intercourse among his disciples. When helpless before a Taborite army, he declared that he had nothing to fear because his people were invulnerable and the enemy general would be stricken with blindness. His followers believed him and were annihilated.

The Taborites were a formidable revolutionary movement, sufficiently successful militarily to defy many of Europe's political authorities. Everywhere they went they created their own large-scale communities, which unlike those of Aum became central to the larger society—until the Taborites were eventually subdued. Where the Taborites' technology was limited to swords and their imagery to biblical disasters and hellfire, however, Aum had the means to imagine a much more concrete and realizable version of world destruction. Even so, one is struck by a certain commonality of mind-set in the megalomanic impulse to destroy the world in order to save it. For as the historian of religion Elaine Pagels points out, it was early Jewish and Christian apocalyptic thinking that gave rise to the idea of a cosmic struggle between good and evil for the fate of the world, of a "split cosmology with the 'sons of light' allied with the angels and 'sons of darkness' in league with the power of evil." Asahara's reliance on imagery from the Hebrew and Christian Bibles, especially the Book of Revelation, is therefore hardly surprising. That polarization, that "split cosmology," tapped fundamental, death-linked, often amorphous existential fears, which could be readily manipulated by promises of collective spiritual perfection and immortality.

Japanese Roots

Asahara's spiritual—and violent—urges were nonetheless largely shaped within his own society and culture. The eminent sociologist of religion Susumu Shimazono calls Aum the "potential nightmare" of Japanese religious experience, and, however unpalatable the idea, Aum was indeed its creature. My interviewees bear this out. They found in Aum religious meaning and extreme answers to commonplace Japanese spiritual hungers and contradictions.

The question of Japanese religiosity is a confusing one to outsiders, and often to the Japanese themselves. They are frequently described as a highly secular people, focused on the pragmatic details of everyday life, and there is much truth in this description. But it is no less true that they have deep-seated spiritual inclinations with respect to the infinitely powerful forces of nature and to the question of individual fate, or karma. Perhaps the confusion lies in failing to see that Japanese can be secular *and* religious, that they can bring to religious rituals highly pragmatic purposes (visiting a Shinto shrine, for instance, to ask for success in a business venture), and to everyday life a rather casual religiosity (keeping a small Buddhist family altar in the home in order to stay connected with dead parents). There is a saying to the effect that Japanese are born as Shintoists, marry as Christians, die as Buddhists—and in between believe in new religions. In fact, their cultural tendency toward a multifaceted religious life fits quite well with the contemporary development of the many-sided, protean self.

Religious pluralism began early in Japan: Shinto and Buddhism have coexisted there for almost two thousand years with much overlapping of religious practice—including Shinto-style shrines in Buddhist temples and Buddhist-style altars in Shinto shrines. Generally speaking, Buddhism has been concerned with family and ancestors,

Shinto with village and community. Shinto has no founder and emerged from animistic connections to the natural world, while Buddhism came from the mind and life of a revered founder and his human-centered spiritual beliefs and practices. As different as they were and are, they blended functionally in the Japanese mind, as did often-hidden religious elements of Confucianism and Taoism. In recent centuries, that religious combination has tended toward a focus on this-worldly experience, but a powerful earlier tradition of other-worldly spirituality, carried out by world-renouncing Buddhist monks, also exists. There have been periodic impulses to reassert an intense other-worldly spirituality, as evidenced by a number of present-day new religions, including Aum Shinrikyō.

Shimazono questions the common assumption that Buddhism and Shinto always promoted harmony in society and between each other. He emphasizes the amount of suppressed violence and aggression in the Japanese religious tradition and notes the many violent religious rebellions that have taken place over the course of Japanese history. Other scholars stress the significance of the influential Tendai Buddhist sect of "warrior monks" who fought against reigning feudal leaders during the eleventh and twelfth centuries. They also point to Tachikawa Ryū, a heretical, cultlike fringe group of Shingon sect Buddhists strongly influenced by Chinese Taoism. The sect, which existed in the fifteenth and sixteenth centuries and emphasized the union of the two great Taoist principles, the yin and the yang, through various sexual practices, became known mainly for its belief in killing as a means of achieving enlightenment. One ritual of transcendence was to murder a kneeling disciple by thrusting a long spear through his anus.

Shimazono also connects violence of the sort Asahara practiced to the general Buddhist principle of nonattachment, which can be experienced as an absence of moral restraint in killing. The scholar Manabu Watanabe highlights a potentially sinister paradox in Buddhism: the prohibition against the killing of any living creature can lead to a sense that killing human beings is in no way different from killing insects. Here I would add two additional psychological possibilities. Recognizing the impossibility of living up to the ideal of killing no creature whatsoever, some Buddhists might more readily accept the idea of killing a human creature. Others, overwhelmed by guilt and shame for that inability, might justify explosive acts of murder as assertions of "sincerity" or of moral consistency.

According to the philosopher Yūjirō Nakamura, the Japanization of Confucianism also led to an extreme version of "sincerity." The concept became associated with an elusive mystical goal of "not deceiving oneself," the pursuit of which sometimes seemed to practitioners to require such absolutized moral consistency that one could not only lie but even kill. (In this sense Asahara was "sincere" because forcing the end was consistent with his convictions. So, too, Hitler was "sincere" in carrying out the mass murder of Jews.) Nakamura chastises those who look only to traditions like the Vajrayāna of Tibetan Buddhism for "outside" sources of Aum's evil. Vajrayāna principles that justify killing, he tells us, "were historically not so distant [from] Japanese culture." The advocacy of violence and killing as a demonstration of dedication to one's guru, and perhaps even as a means of enlightenment, had long since found receptive cultural and religious soil in Japan. Nakamura invokes the great thirteenth-century Buddhist monk Shinran, who established the prominent Shin Pure Land sect. Shinran described a "state of soul [that] took precedence over ordinary good and evil" and declared, as Nakamura puts it, that "if we can do everything by our own will (meaning, if we can render feeling and act consistent) we can perhaps kill thousands of persons without hesitation." Shinran was expressing, perhaps partly as a warning, an extreme version of "sincerity," and Nakamura sees in it a "thesis of murder" that Japanese tended to view as "an exaggerated metaphor"—until Aum Shinrikyō came along and acted literally upon it.

For its guru-centered example, Aum had in some sense to look no further than state-manipulated Shinto. Until the Meiji Restoration an amorphous, village-based, nature-oriented religion, Shinto was consciously and somewhat artificially converted into a systematic state religion by the new regime. Drawing on Western imperial models, Meiji leaders rendered the emperor divine and placed him at the center of that state religion. The concept of the emperor as a god, as a descendent of the ancestor goddess Amaterasu, had long existed but mostly in connection with ritual acts surrounding an essentially marginal figure. Now this idea of divinity was strongly emphasized and embedded in an elaborate national ideology. The emperor became both symbol and actor in a mystical *kokutai*, or national polity, providing the Japanese with a sense of national identity in a sacralized state. Distinctions between Shinto and Buddhism were newly insisted upon. Buddhism was controlled or suppressed (temples and texts were destroyed and celibate priests pressured to marry in order to weaken the Buddhist tradition) until it, too, allied itself with the new emperor cult. Even local Shinto shrines were destroyed or closed: to maintain close control over its new emperor-centered state religion, the regime wanted only a single shrine in each village.

The Shadow of World War II

However striking these various antecedents and influences, none is as powerful in accounting for Aum as Japan's annihilation in World War II and its aftermath. The more I studied Aum, in fact, the more I became convinced that it could be understood only in relation to the impact of that war on Japan.

Some of that impact was impressed upon me by an experience I had in Tokyo in late 1995. I had just finished eating lunch with a close friend, a distinguished scholar whom I first met in the 1950s. As always, our conversation had roamed widely, but had taken in recent events that had shaken Japan, including the Kobe earthquake and the revelations of Aum Shinrikyō's violent acts. We spoke also of our countries' troubles in coming to grips with issues of remembering and forgetting in that fiftieth commemorative year of the war's end. As we left the restaurant, my friend suddenly said that there was a place he wanted to show me just a few minutes' walk from where we were. It was raining slightly and I knew that he had not been in the best of health, so I hesitated, but he would not be swayed. We finally arrived at a small memorial park for the Japanese dead of World War II. Unlike Yasukuni, the national shrine for the dead of all Japan's wars, which retains a right-wing flavor of military nostalgia, here there were simply the names of some of the dead (reminding one of the Vietnam wall in Washington) and a few concrete benches facing a small pond. We sat down together and my friend commented that more than half his university classmates had been killed and that he still wondered why it had been his good fortune to be assigned to a post in Japan, why it was that he had survived. We had often talked about Japan's wartime atrocities and the country's difficulty confronting them, but now he wanted to convey to me a sense of Japanese suffering and loss that was personal and visceral. I understood what he meant. Upon first arriving in Japan in 1952, I commonly encountered families who had only recently experienced such loss, university students whose fathers or older brothers had been killed in the war and who had themselves experienced hunger or witnessed deaths from the fire bombings of Japan's cities.

What could not be faced then or since, however, was the criminal nature of what the soldiers and civilian officials of that sacralized, emperor-worshiping state did in East and Southeast Asia. There were the policies that we might now call "ethnic cleansing"—the creating of "people-free zones" in China; there was the Nanking massacre in which hundreds of thousands of Chinese civilians were murdered in gruesome fashion and tens of thousands of women raped. There was the enslaving of three million people, mostly Chinese and Korean, for labor projects. In addition to the large-scale efforts to carry out biological warfare, there were the grotesque experiments on Asian and Western prisoners, using typhus, tetanus, anthrax, smallpox, and salmonella materials. There was the seizure of 100,000 to 200,000 "comfort women," mostly from Korea but also from other parts of Asia, forced to serve as prostitutes for the military and civilian personnel of Japan's new imperium. There was the systematic bombing of civilians in China's cities from 1931 on, a forerunner of the massive Allied "strategic bombing" campaign against German and Japanese cities.

During the early occupation years, these atrocities were exposed in war-crimes trials. Many Japanese were shocked, but the trials had only limited impact. For one thing, the prosecution of accused war criminals proceeded erratically, and some of them, released from custody, were quickly rehabilitated. For another, there was a high-level American decision against prosecuting the emperor in whose name the crimes had been committed. Most Japanese, moreover, were preoccupied with their own survival. Both authorities and ordinary people, sometimes with American encouragement, colluded in creating what the historian Gavin McCormack calls a "milieu of willful forgetting." But that does not mean that these mass atrocities did not permeate the Japanese psychological experience. They did so in ways that were powerful, lasting, and yet seldom publicly acknowledged. A few postwar novelists, including Kenzaburō Ōe, addressed the issue bravely and directly as, for instance, did the historian Saburō Ienaga, who tenaciously pursued a decades-long campaign through the courts to correct sanitized accounts of wartime behavior in officially approved textbooks. But the subject was largely suppressed, and when it did begin to reappear in popular culture it often took the form of *manga* renditions of exciting battles, Japanese heroism, and ultimate Japanese victory in the war.

Yet the lack of public discussion of the subject after the American occupation ended neither erased it from consciousness nor eliminated the need of members of the wartime generation to find a way to address the acts they had committed and the war they had prosecuted for their emperor. In order to deal with that war and undergo a process of mourning, thereby acquiring a measure of survivor meaning from a terrible defeat, many assumed a stance of simple victimization. They emphasized not the suffering of other Asians at Japanese hands but Japanese suffering in the atomic bombings of Hiroshima and Nagasaki and the strategic bombing of Japanese cities, as well as at the hands of the Russian armies during the war's last days. That suffering was real, but by embracing a victim role they avoided a sense of responsibility or of guilt, an avoidance that also became part of the structure of the postwar self. "Victim consciousness" influenced, and was reinforced by, representations of wartime history that further encouraged numbing and forgetting.

The distinguished German psychoanalysts Alexander and Margarete Mitscherlich describe a similar phenomenon in the lives of many Germans of the Nazi generation. Psychologically unable to confront the evil they had been part of or the degree to which they had loved their Führer, they would fall back on a sense of themselves as victims, which rendered them unable to experience genuine mourning and so unable individually or collectively to "live again." In Japan, there was far less confrontation with wartime evil than in Germany. Important here was the American decision to grant immunity to the emperor, the result of which, as McCormack points out, was a "devolution of responsibility downward onto the lower ranks ... which led, in due course, to denial of responsibility altogether." To which I would add that the imperial system lent itself to such denial because the only responsibility of every Japanese was to serve the emperor, who, as a deity, could not be held to so profane a concept as responsibility, even when he participated in policies associated with atrocities. Instead, under the protection of Japan's occupiers, the wartime deity was rendered a postwar symbol of peace and democracy. While there has been much critical acknowledgment in Japan of the extremity of wartime emperor worship and of the love felt for his symbolic person (in some ways he was the psychological equivalent of the Führer), the process of individual psychological separation from him was for many extremely difficult until his death in 1989. Since the emperor system provided, as McCormack observes, "the kernel of Japanese identity in the modern era," confronting the emperor's culpability in the war threatened the sense of individual psychological integration of many Japanese.

As a result, there was an even greater tendency than in Germany to gloss over wartime crimes and excesses. By the mid-1950s, initial economic successes were already encouraging people to look forward toward a brighter future, not back at the painful horrors of a lost war. Conservative politicians, some of whom were themselves war criminals, did much to prevent serious discussion of the war, often distorting or falsifying wartime events. All this heightened cultural tendencies to avoid confrontations with the past, to compartmentalize psychological experience, and to adapt to whatever group arrangements presented themselves. But such cultural predilections are far from absolute and such a situation far from purely Japanese. The United States, for instance, has faced a similar dilemma in examining its conduct of its own lost war in Vietnam. Without an emperor to restrain them, at least a minority of Vietnam veterans, if not the public at large, have insisted on confronting unpleasant truths about the atrocities American troops committed, truths that have became necessary to their own integration of suffering and loss, while importantly influencing the country's overall historical understanding of that war.

No nation ever fully confronts its own behavior, especially when that behavior is widely perceived as destructive or evil. But in Japan the failure of any such confrontation to occur—the degree of unfinished psychological business in connection with World War II—has been unusually stark. Avoidance and denial have not only angered former victims throughout Asia but prevented significant transmission of disturbing wartime truths across the generations. (When, as late as the mid-1990s, the novelist Haruki Murakami published a series of three volumes depicting the profound absurdity of emperor-centered military obedience, much of what he wrote was new information for a great many of his readers; and even then his emphasis was more on the suffering of Japanese soldiers than on the atrocities they committed.) Efforts at confrontation, admirable in themselves, have been sporadic and much resisted, leaving people with unhealthy mechanisms for staving off old feelings of humiliation and defeat and with reservoirs of guilt and shame associated with inexpressible truths. Transmitted over generations, that psychological combination could render extremely attractive a movement with apocalyptic claims to resolving all conflict and restoring collective glory, claims of a purification that would wash away all evil.

Clones of the Emperor

Aum, of course, was precisely such a movement. It did not arise solely from the troubled postwar social climate, but it did re-create much of the psychology with which Japan pursued its imperial war. That entire military project, after all, had taken the form of a religious war fought on behalf of a deified emperor and his—and Japan's—eternal divinity. The emperor was a godly guru, not to be directly viewed or heard by ordinary citizens. One fought and killed not for oneself but for the emperor; if one happened to kill women or children, one was serving a divinity and so had done no wrong. Each soldier was both a *shinka*, or vassal, and a *sekishi*, or baby of the emperor: a servant *and* a biological extension. Though expressed in the language of its time, that combination was the psychological equivalent of the Aum principle of a clone. If not a biological duplicate, each soldier was to be a spiritual manifestation of the emperor and of all Japanese existence.

Although the emperor religion had been crafted by Meiji leaders in the service of state Shinto, it was Buddhism, especially Zen Buddhism, that provided much of the psychological discipline and motivation for Japanese war making. This kind of Zen involvement dates back to the Sino-Japanese war of 1894–95 and to the insistence of a young Buddhist scholar named D. T. Suzuki (who would later introduce a gentle form of Zen to the West) that religion must serve the state in its struggle against "unruly heathens" and that doing so on the battlefield is an act "religious in nature." Suzuki's teacher Sōen Shaku was a Buddhist chaplain in the Sino-Japanese conflict and sounded a bit like Shōkō Asahara when he urged on his soldiers the belief that they were fighting an evil and that death on the battlefield meant "rebirth of the soul." More than that, such sacrifice would inevitably lead to enlightenment. Another Buddhist writer of the time went further in declaring that the highest form of bodhisattva practice—seeking Buddhahood by saving others—was "the compassionate taking of life." The principle of killing as a form of compassion, which was to reverberate throughout World War II, came close to Aum's *poa* doctrine.

In the 1930s, during Japan's war on China, a Zen writer declared the emperor a "Golden Wheel-Turning Sacred King" on the model of an ideal Buddhist monarch, so that the use of force on his behalf became a means of combating injustice and lawlessness or, in his case, "Chinese defilements." "To wage compassionate wars," he wrote, was to "give life to both oneself and one's enemy." This principle was part of the frequent Japanese refrain that the war was "for the benefit of China"—one was saving Chinese by killing them.

Increasingly, Zen became a vehicle of the state and was actively deployed in teaching the Japanese warrior code. Much as it would in Aum, killing became not killing. As Kōdō Sawaki, one of Japan's best-known modern Zen masters, put it in a 1942 article: "All things, including friend and foe, are my children. . . . Given this, it is just to punish those who disturb the public order. Whether one kills or does not kill, the [Buddhist] precept forbidding killing [is preserved]. It is the precept forbidding killing that wields the sword. It is this precept that throws the bomb."

Brian Victoria, a contemporary Zen priest and a critic of Zen's military role, interprets this passage to mean that killing or bomb throwing, as part of a higher purpose, took place independently of a person's will. But I believe there is a further implication that compassionate killing of those who "disturb the public order" is consistent with the Buddhist precept *against* killing, indeed that one *must* carry out the compassionate killing of any such disturber anywhere ("friend or foe") if one is to best live out that precept. This brings us still closer to *poa*.

There developed a category of "imperial-state Zen"—or more simply, "soldier Zen"—whose most perfect practitioner was said to be Gorō Sugimoto, a major killed in battle in China in 1937. What he advocated in a posthumous volume called *Great Duty* would surely hold for an Aum disciple, if Asahara were substituted for the emperor: "Because of the non-existence of the self, everything in the universe is a manifestation of the emperor. . . . In front of the emperor the . . . self is empty. . . . Seeking nothing at all, you should simply completely discard both body and mind, and unite with the emperor. . . . It is the greatest way in the universe, the true reality of the emperor, the highest righteousness and the purest purity. . . . The wars of the empire are sacred wars . . . holy wars. They are the [Buddhist] practice of great compassion. Therefore the imperial military must consist of holy officers and holy soldiers." Sugimoto was lyrical in announcing his emperor-bound immortality: "If you wish to see me, live in reverence for the emperor! Where there is the spirit of reverence for the emperor, there will I always be." Sugimoto came to be revered as a "god of war," celebrated by Zen writers no less than by military nationalists. His book was read avidly by schoolchildren throughout Japan and used late in World War II in the recruiting of suicidal youth units— boys in their teens. "These rosy-cheeked teenagers," as Saburō Ienaga bitterly comments, "were put in special attack units and blew themselves up crashing into enemy ships."

Japanese Zen masters and scholars of the time could rival Asahara in the self-serving spiritual moralism with which they endowed their advocacy of extreme violence. One of them, addressing Japan's actions in China (where Japanese atrocities were the rule), declared, "Wherever the imperial military advances there is only charity and love. They could never act in the barbarous and cruel way in which the Chinese soldiers act . . . [because] officers and men of the imperial military . . . have been schooled in the spirit of Buddhism." Such moralism was sometimes supported by a principle of annihilating the senses, so that any experience of dying, killing, or mutilating could be viewed as illusory. One could kill randomly and without feeling. Armed with an immortalizing vision of emperor-linked purity, one could fight with extraordinary intensity, subject oneself to extreme asceticism (including intense physical discomfort, very little sleep, and a near-starvation diet), and participate in uninhibited killing. Chinese reports of the actions of Japanese soldiers often spoke of their demonic, seemingly superhuman energy and cruelty. Such a mental state undoubtedly contributed to the notorious Nanking massacre, replicated in a scaled-down way throughout China, East and Southeast Asia, and the Pacific.

Another Buddhist-linked psychological current in the war years was the principle that spirit could overcome material force. That principle—partly believed, partly an expression of desperation—reached such extremes that in the last days of the war Japanese civilians armed with spears were being trained to defeat heavily armed American invaders. Here we may speak of what I call "psychism": the attempt to achieve control over one's external environment through internal or psychological manipulations, through behavior determined by intrapsychic needs no longer in touch with the actualities of the world one seeks to influence. I have in the past applied this term to many of the actions of Mao Zedong and to his fervent followers, who came to attribute to his "thought" near-magical power to alter reality, whether in the production of steel or in the assertion of the limited destructiveness of nuclear weapons. In their version of psychism Japan's leaders and soldiers were also expressing a traditional East Asian faith in the predominance of spirit over matter, a principle incorporated into such disciplines as judo, kendo (Japanese fencing or swordsmanship), and martial arts like karate. Extreme forms of psychism can readily lead to fantasy-driven violence, as occurred in much

Japanese planning and behavior during World War II. Aum's psychism, no less extreme, was exemplified in its guru's claim that spiritual achievement could protect one from radiation in a nuclear war or enable one to survive Armageddon.

There was also in wartime Japan a rigidly hierarchical system of absolute obedience that ran from the lowest-ranking soldier or mobilized civilian right up to the emperor. In the military it meant obedience to one's immediate superior, whose orders, after all, represented the emperor's. The principle became so extreme that at war's end some Japanese soldiers refused to accept the emperor's surrender speech because they had not received orders from their immediate superiors to stop fighting. In Aum, too, orders from immediate superiors represented the omniscient will of the guru and were therefore sacrosanct. Both systems promoted the ideal of absolute purity—as represented by emperor or guru—and the inability to realize that ideal became a matter of personal and group failure. In both, a totalized ideal of purification infused everything and, because it was unachievable, created a constant anxiety stemming from an ever-present sense of defilement. As these belief systems broke down, enormous conflicts arose, occasioned by doubts about the infallibility of immediate superiors and, ultimately, about the divinity of the emperor or the guru. Final outbursts of violence reflected the dissolution of each system and its need to reassert its death-power.

The Japanese military struggle against the United States had its own aspect of "forcing the end." That impulse was expressed even in the attack on Pearl Harbor in December 1941, which initiated a war likely to result in Japan's destruction. Certainly from 1943 on, defeat was inevitable and yet political and military leaders, including the emperor, were unable decisively to sue for peace even as their country was systematically reduced to rubble. Emperor-worshiping fanatics spoke of resistance to the last man and lent their energies to an earthly Armageddon that consisted of the annihilation of Japan through American saturation and atomic bombings. At the same time, the one condition Japan asked in surrendering, that the imperial throne be preserved, suggests that the destruction brought about was part of a vision, at whatever level of consciousness, of emperor-based renewal.

Aum, I believe, was a caricature of a caricature. Asahara's megalomania rendered him a caricature not of the attenuated postwar "peace" emperor but of the deified prewar version that so inspired Sugimoto's Zen obeisance. Asahara contrasted his own mission as "the Christ" with that of the emperor he saw himself as replacing: "There is no doubt that I must be at the center of the world and that soon I must take the leading role. . . . When they drop nuclear weapons on Japan or use nerve gas or bacteriological weapons it is the end for Japan. So what happens to the Emperor, who is at the center of the war criminals?" In the last part of this statement, Asahara resembled outspoken Japanese and Western critics of the emperor who have recently provided impressive evidence of Hirohito's active collusion in the war and its atrocities. But the caricature lay in the way the guru outdid Hirohito, both in his manifold claims of godhead (emperor, Christ, Buddha, Shiva) and in the reach of his annihilative ambition. (Hirohito and imperial nationalists, grandiose as they were, still sought to destroy no more than their Asian rivals, the Western presence in Asia, and possibly, as just suggested, Japan itself.)

The emperor system itself had elements of caricature. Especially toward the end of World War II, its claims of divinity and manifestations of psychism had reached a kind of limit. Its ideology, as Carol Gluck puts it, "had overreached itself" so that "imperial orthodoxy became strikingly incongruent with social and national realities [and] . . . had rigidified to the point that it appeared to defy common sense." Initially influenced by Western visions of kingship and emperorhood, the system had been synthetically constructed as a vehicle for Japan's emergence as a modern state. As a result, it always had elements of artificiality and excess—and always was a more fragile construct than anyone realized, compensating for its vulnerability with totalistic claims and visions. If an ideology at the end of its tether is dangerous in its compensatory actions and assertions, how much more true this must be of a later one that seizes upon that dying fantasy and seeks to outdo it.

After Hiroshima

In Hiroshima and Nagasaki, the war had never ended; or, more accurately, something took place that, although part of the war, carried a separate and terrifying new message of world destruction. One survivor of the atomic bombing of Hiroshima told me of being temporarily blinded by falling debris: "My body seemed all black, everything seemed dark, dark all over. . . . Then I thought, 'The world is ending.' " As another survivor, the writer Yōko Ōta, recalled, "I just could not understand why our surroundings had changed so greatly in one instant. . . . I thought it might have been something which had nothing to do with the war, the collapse of the earth, which it was said would take place at the end of the world and which I had read about as a child." A Protestant minister described the moment of atomic devastation to me in apocalyptic Christian terms: "The feeling I had was that everyone was dead. The whole city was destroyed. . . . I thought all of my family must be dead—it doesn't matter if I die. . . . I thought this was the end of Hiroshima—of Japan—of humankind. . . . This was God's judgment on man." Such imagery of world destruction was to gain a prominent place in postwar Japanese culture.

American occupation forces at first suppressed Japanese responses to the atomic bombings, but when these did begin to appear, some were widely disseminated throughout Japan and later the world. Many of them have gained prominent and lasting places in Japanese culture: personal accounts by survivors such as Yōko Ōta's searing *Town of Corpses*, Michihiko Hachiya's powerfully understated *Hiroshima Diary*, and Takashi Nagai's reflective and disturbing *The Bells of Nagasaki*; poetry by the Hiroshima survivor and hero Sakichi Tōge ("Give me back my father . . . Give me back myself . . . Give me back mankind"); novels like the panoramic classic *Black Rain* by Masuji Ibuse (not a survivor but a native of Hiroshima Prefecture); art like the vast, disquieting murals of Iri and Toshi Maruki (who entered Hiroshima soon after the bombing); documentary films recording the near-total destruction of Hiroshima and Nagasaki and the great director Akira Kurosawa's Hiroshima-inspired *Record of a Living Being* and Nagasaki film, *Rhapsody in August*; and essays like Kenzaburō Ōe's *Hiroshima Notes*.

But it was in popular culture that survivor memories and related apocalyptic impulses and fears penetrated most thoroughly. In 1973, for instance, Keiji Nakazawa, a Hiroshima survivor, published the first of seven volumes of *Barefoot Gen*, a memoir in that most popular of all Japanese forms, the *manga*. This small masterpiece, told from the point of view of a six-year-old boy (Nakazawa's age at the time of the bombing), records in a simple, straightforward manner the experiences of a Hiroshima family, especially the helpless anguish of his mother and himself in the face of the deaths of his father, sister, and brother. Grim as it is, the narrative conveys a sense of hope as Gen manages to find food and aid his mother under extreme duress, even at moments singing and playing in the rubble like the little boy he is. Heroic efforts like his to turn back the forces of ultimate destruction would go on to become central features of most Japanese apocalyptic fiction. The little boy's struggles would be rendered in four feature films (one animated) and an opera, and Gen would become an icon of Japanese memory. (He would also inspire the American cartoonist Art Spiegelman to use the same genre to tell of his parents' experiences in Auschwitz in his graphic novel *Maus*.)

In terms of Aum and its world-ending sensibility, the way in which Japan's nuclear legacy came to saturate the futuristic realm of popular culture was crucially important. Here the apocalyptic tone was set by a single monster film. In 1954, Godzilla (Gojira in Japanese), an irradiated, dinosaur-like reptilian creature of immense size awakened from the depths of the Pacific Ocean by American nuclear tests at Bikini Atoll, stormed into Japanese (and then American) movie theaters stomping Tokyo to radioactive bits. Born of director Tomoyuki Tanaka's "desire to express the horror and fear that enveloped Japan after the American atomic bombings of Hiroshima and Nagasaki," the film also reflected a national outcry over the fate of Japanese fishermen on a boat named *Lucky Dragon* who were exposed to fallout from American atomic tests at the Bikini Atoll and suffered radiation effects, resulting in one death. It was flying over Bikini on his way home to Japan from Indonesia that Tanaka, a skillful mainstream filmmaker, came up with his story; for the name of his monster he and his team combined the English word *gorilla* (with a nod to the famous

American film monster King Kong) and the Japanese word *kujira*, meaning whale. An awesome force of nature, the malign Godzilla, who devastates urban Japan on screen, replicated much of what the American air force had done in the recent war. He is finally destroyed by a heroic Japanese scientist who sacrifices himself in the process. The film gave rise over the years to twenty-two sequels (in which, battling other evil monsters, Godzilla becomes a force for good), not to mention mountains of video games, puzzles, comics, dolls, and toys of every sort. Godzilla could be endlessly exploited commercially because he so effectively helped transmute nuclear fear into entertainment. He took that fear into imaginative realms where a melodrama of world destruction and re-creation could be played out. Whether nasty or beneficent, whether crushing everything in sight or fighting to preserve the earth, Godzilla always reflected his atomic origins. He was also surely a ubiquitous childhood character for Asahara and members of the Aum generation.

The nuclear anxiety of *Godzilla* would soon enough find a counterpart in the realms of outer space. Again an American film genre was the influence, this time as visitors from other planets invaded Japan. Some of these alien beings manifest heartfelt concern about the nuclear tests being conducted on earth, as in the 1954 film *Spacemen Appear in Tokyo*, while others—physically or mentally deranged by radiation, like the nuclear-charged robot in *Electric Man* or the nuclear being H-Man—express only hostility toward humanity. Once more, the courage and advanced knowledge of Japanese scientists enable the worst of these creatures to be defeated and the universe to be saved.

In both these genres, terror combined with exaggerated, partly mocking fantasy. Whatever the combination in any one of the films, together they constituted a particularly Japanese cinematic effusion, a transmuting of the country's unique experience of victimization into stories with box-office appeal. They were also an expression, however odd, of a survivor mission—even, in a way, the popular culture's equivalent to works of witness. They simultaneously reflected and blunted Japanese fears of atomic victimization; their portrayal of world-saving Japanese heroism and scientific knowledge—knowledge possessed only by the enemy in World War II—offered attractive fantasy to counter recent real-world humiliations.

As the Aum generation grew up, such science fiction scenarios gained an increasing foothold in the world of television cartoons, elaborating ever more fantastic cosmic rescues in ever more elaborate and threatened future universes, often portrayed with considerable aesthetic brilliance. These shows, enormously popular among the young, tended to depict postapocalyptic situations—that is, a world or universe after nuclear war—in which the heroes struggle mightily to sustain life and rebuild planet Earth. As one former Aum member wrote, older Japanese "might laugh if they heard that Armageddon was coming," but for his generation, because of those depictions of "world catastrophe," "it was not a question of who believed in Armageddon or who did not."

The American science fiction writer Thomas Disch sees Aum Shinrikyō as the "apotheosis" of an unhealthy interaction between a "malignant . . . millennialist, quasi-religious" version of the genre and an audience that wishes to see in it ultimate spiritual truths, so that "outside of science fiction there is no salvation." "The children of Godzilla," as Disch calls Aum's disciples, graduated from shows like *Space Battleship Yamato*, "in which half-human cyborgs wreak awe-inspiring devastation on whole cities," to *gekiga*, "book-length comics featuring gung-ho tales of rape and murder against Blade Runner-esque backdrops." (Here Disch points as well to a sadistic component prominent in Japanese popular culture.) Also important to Aum was Isaac Asimov's widely read science fiction classic *The Foundation Trilogy*. Hideo Murai even cited it as a model for Aum, depicting as it does an elite group of spiritually evolved scientists forced to go underground during an age of barbarism so as to prepare themselves for the moment, calculated with mathematical precision, when they will emerge to rebuild civilization.

The philosopher Yūjirō Nakamura similarly notes the importance of science fiction for Aum's development but stresses its more general role as well. "Though Aum," he writes, "was, in one sense, vulgar and cartoonish, it captured the broad unconscious of the people, and it nearly conquered the intelligentsia." What was that "broad unconscious"? I would claim that it bore an indelible Hiroshima imprint, a collective image of Japanese annihilation later extended to the entire world. At issue here is the compelling power for many contemporary Japanese of the idea of world destruction and the elaborate, high-tech futuristic imagery that popular culture has spun around it. This has been so central to Japanese—not to speak of global—consciousness that those acting upon it can be viewed as possessing a certain cosmic wisdom. We have seen how combining apocalyptic visions with the experience of "high states" could obscure moral judgment. An out-pouring of apocalyptic fantasy also undoubtedly did much to facilitate Aum's "mystical" states, and the heroic allure of popularly performed apocalypse drew many young people to Aum.

New New Religions

Aum members were the cultural inheritors of every form of spiritual confusion, including the dislocations caused by Western influences, the dramatic, almost world-ending collapse of imperial megalomania, and the painful contradictions and corruptions of a deeply flawed postwar democracy and a decade-long economic boom. No wonder that young people could be attracted to a syncretic religion that seemed to com-bine ancient truths with the latest spiritual trends in Japan, the United States, and elsewhere. New religions like Aum, moreover, had a sub-stantial prewar Japanese tradition to build on.

Japanese new religions, which have flourished in times of social upheaval, have typically been founded by men or women from the lower echelons of society, who have experienced a transcendent vision but have tended to focus on the alleviation of this-world suffering. They have frequently combined seemingly divergent religious elements from Buddhism and Shinto, and sometimes from Christianity, with innovative rituals and communal practices. Some of the new religions that sprang to life in the late nineteenth and early twentieth centuries stressed various forms of "spiritism," in which the souls of the dead were thought to enter the bodies of the living. Many post-1970 "new new religions" (as they are called by Shimazono), Aum among them, are considered inheritors of this spiritism in their focus on altered states of consciousness and experiences of transcendence.

For Shōkō Asahara the most important of the prewar new religions was Ōmoto (or "Great Foundation"), which in many ways resembled Western spiritualism. It was started in 1892 by a woman who had been "visited" by a neglected deity returning to this world to bring about world renewal after eons of an exile enforced by lesser deities. Ōmoto employed exorcistic techniques for dispelling evil influences and had a transcendent vision of paradise but also put sufficient stress on the reconstruction of society to be seen as subversive. As it was highly popular and rejected the practice of worshiping the emperor, Ōmoto became a target for the increasingly authoritarian regimes of the 1930s. In 1935, a year when many new religions were suppressed (particularly if they had no place in them for the emperor), Ōmoto's buildings were torn down. Asahara, who might have been influenced by Ōmoto's focus on world renewal, identified strongly (however inappropriately) with Ōmoto's experience of persecution and was able to enlist a few religious scholars to affirm his claimed affinity with that sect.

In the wake of the war, many Japanese found their spiritual state to be as much in rubble as their cities. With the emperor's radio speech of surrender on August 14, 1945 (shocking not only in its message but also in permitting the divine voice to be heard by ordinary ears), and an American-inspired Imperial Rescript of January 1, 1946, which officially denied his divinity, the ideology of state Shinto collapsed. In the confusion of occupied Japan, there was what was called a "rush hour of the gods," as literally thousands of new religions emerged. That explosion of spirituality continued throughout the postwar era, spurred by the country's radical urbanization, which caused large numbers of its citizens to lose contact with their local gods and communities. New religions could respond to such dislocations by offering improvised sets of borrowings, flexible ways of worshiping gods from a distance, and active grassroots leadership and involvement. Their founders were generally parental and nurturing and could project a certain comforting androgyny as well, as when a female founder claimed to have merged with a male god.

The spiritual and mythological sources they have drawn upon are virtually unlimited. Certain groups have believed, for instance, that a lost tribe of Israel made its way to Japan, that Jesus Christ was buried in Japan, or that the original tablet with the Ten Commandments was brought from Israel to Japan, where it became a hidden treasure of the Japanese imperial family. New religions could be nationalistic or critical of emperor and nation, could combine spirituality with material achievement, but invariably emphasized the importance of a reborn spiritual community.

Accompanying the wave of "new new religions" in the 1970s was, in the philosopher Michael Grosso's words, that "potpourri of pursuits and effects, ranging from the flaky to the intellectually provocative," known as New Age thought. Exploding initially in the United States, it stressed individual transformation and renewal. It variously offered thoughtful (and not so thoughtful) assessments of scientism and materialism and an advocacy of environmentalism and holistic or alternative medicine, as well as bodily and spiritual mysticism. It could also include the far reaches of UFO and science fiction fantasy, "the god-making rhetoric of the channelers, . . . the wisdom of runes, crystals, *I Ching*, Tarot cards," and other garish extensions of American commercial and spiritual exuberance.

New Age America has been as eclectic in its blendings and borrowings as have any Japanese new religions. It has embraced the ancient and esoteric along with the technological and electronic. And it has filtered through modern Western sensibilities various premodern spiritual disciplines (notably Native American) as well as Eastern religions such as Zen and Tibetan Buddhism. New Age apocalypticism has on the whole been relatively gentle, emphasizing the kindly aspects of rebirth and renewal, but its embrace of the prophecies of Nostradamus suggests a considerable attraction to world destruction. The very amorphousness and malleability of New Age precepts have rendered them serviceable to those who have sought more violent transformations in or beyond the world.

In this way, a number of versions of Buddhism returned to Japan with New Age trappings. These were accompanied by related imports of every sort from all areas of American-influenced popular culture, which in turn influenced Japanese television cartoons depicting post-apocalyptic scenarios of collapse and rebirth. Also embraced were New Age environmentalist biology ("spaceship Earth" and "Gaia"), physics (*The Tao of Physics*), and psychology ("self-realization" and Jungian mystical synchronicity); corporations looked to Zen and related spiritual disciplines for the creation of workforces of "industrial warriors." The Japanese became perhaps the world's most ardent New Age consumers.

This may have been so because New Age ideas made direct psychological contact with long-standing cultural emphases on nonrational, holistic experience—even with nature-centered remnants of premodern animism. As a Japanese scholar put it to me, "The American counterculture was the Japanese culture." In popular culture, Japanized New Age currents flowed freely and young people undergoing confusing generational changes often experienced these currents as liberating and energizing.

The same was true of the recycling (via America and Europe) of Japanese religious experience. Purists bemoaned the embrace of New Age Buddhism, but for many Japanese, especially the young, it provided a sense of freshness and vitality lacking in deadened, institutionalized versions while still satisfying old Japanese hungers. In the same period there emerged what one commentator calls a Japanese version of "psychological man." Where once there had existed only communal requirements, questions of individual identity and personal meaning were pondered, so much so that observers began to speak of "the age of the psyche." New religions combined community and individual quest, and the attraction of young people to them was furthered by their parents' tendency to deny their own spiritual urges. But as various religions focused more on spirituality, mysticism, and the individual psyche, young Japanese seekers also became increasingly vulnerable to a cultic emphasis on mind manipulation and practices reminiscent of thought reform, as well as to extreme expressions of "sincerity" and hermetic forms of militant psychism.

These changes occurred in a climate of ever-expanding new-style religiosity so that, at the moment of the Tokyo sarin attack, Japanese society was said to embrace a staggering 23,000 religious groups with a total membership of 200 million people (70 million more than the overall population—which says much about the Japanese proclivity for multiple affiliations). There has, then, been a significant religious underside to Japanese secular culture. Earlier religious suppression has contributed to a resurgence of odd and unruly religious impulses and to new opportunities for religious commercialism, all in a landscape of innovative synchronism, notable confusion, and considerable energy. Much of that synchronism, confusion, and energy has been directed toward apocalyptic outcomes and visions of the end of the world. In other words, there has been a psychohistorical climate that could readily bring into being that "nightmare of Japanese religion," Aum.

Totalizing the Fragments

We have seen how most potential Aum recruits shared a New Age subculture with the guru even before they met him and how the cult dipped deeply into that subculture for one of its central occult projects, "scientific" computer programs for studying astrological charts. Asahara also drew upon the experience of other New Age gurus, like Bhagwan Shree Rajneesh, who had attracted large followings first in Poona, India, and then in Oregon. New Age influences contributed greatly to the guru's protean mode, to his global reach in accumulating a wide variety of spiritual and psychological components. He epitomized the modern Japanese capacity to look simultaneously eastward and westward in this cultural acquisition, a capacity already given much expression in Japanese new-religion tradition.

Consider one of the multiple dimensions effectively put to use in Aum's New Age Buddhism. In traditional Japanese Buddhism, people ordained as monks or priests may take on a Buddhist name. In Aum, this was called a "holy name," but in most Buddhist practice it simply represented a commitment to rules and forms of practice. Only great Buddhist figures like Nichiren, Shinran, and Saigyō took on special honorific names, and these were derived only from Buddhist tradition. Asahara's approach was as flamboyant as it was self-serving. He awarded each renunciant an exotic holy name taken from Sanskrit, Tibetan, or Pali. For late-twentieth-century Japanese, such holy names have a New Age aura, and, indeed, many think that Asahara derived his practice directly from Rajneesh, who also gave Sanskrit and Pali names to his disciples. In any case, these holy names had profound meaning in Aum, conveying to each renunciant a sense of radical transformation and the acquisition of a new and powerful Aum self that was sacralized, preciously elite, and totally cut off from his or her previously profane life. This self could be experienced as combining cutting-edge spirituality with ancient wisdom. The names were markers of immortality and provided Asahara, who awarded them and could also take them away, with what might be called immortality control. Aum's "floating" character and its absence of ties with any Japanese institution or religion enabled it to open itself to and recast these and other New Age influences to fit its needs.

In combining New Age currents and post-Hiroshima apocalypticism with a wide variety of Japanese and world religious traditions, Asahara shaped a cult that was both protean and totalistic. He brought to bear on every aspect of the cult's function two seemingly contradictory qualities: the openness of a rash innovator in a tradition-damaged world and the closed mentality of a dictatorial fundamentalist. Aum also brought both proteanism and totalism to bear on a very Japanese preoccupation with technicism and technology and with profit-centered corporate power. Aum's claim to technical and scientific precision enabled it to anchor fantastic other-worldly visions in highly active this-worldly concerns. Even its exalted spiritual mission was described as providing "good data" for remaking human beings, computerese that echoed the intense technical and technological focus of much of Japanese society. Casting itself in these terms also made business sense for Aum, a group as intent on making big money as any corporation, and it exploited the privileges of corporate power, including the use of "contributions," or bribes, to pursue its expensive projects. At the same time it maintained an extraordinarily intense focus on the media, which it viewed as a valuable outlet for its message and its versions of reality. Ultimately no amount of manipulation could sustain its falsehoods or hide its murderous violence, but its guru went far as "a leading television personality" in using the media to his advantage, including the broadcast of his siren song to the young.

Young Rebels

It was from young adults in rebellion against their society that Aum took much of its energy. These are the people who in any society bring a special passion to articulating, and acting upon, the kinds of dislocation I have been discussing. I have been talking to young Japanese for more than four decades, and in our many dialogues they have conveyed their complex struggles with extraordinarily disparate belief systems pertaining to family, society, religion, and career. Often they have exhibited rapid shifts in convictions, attitudes, and ideals. Whatever their ambivalences and confusions, though, I have invariably been impressed with the way many of them integrate such disparate elements, generally by making use of the various groups so important in Japanese life.

At the same time I have encountered among them a strong potential for totalism, for all-or-nothing belief systems and moral precepts that can be expressed through absolutized forms of group behavior. A version of this was exemplified by Marxist student leaders. One of them told me, for example, that "to change the present society . . . we must somehow destroy its foundation. This is our task now, and the society which will be created in the future—well, I do not think that we ourselves will be able to see it in its magnificence." There is more than a suggestion here of Aum's brand of mysticism—especially when one learns that the same activist's dreams and associations revealed a deep nostalgia for an idealized past as well as a yearning for a visionary, blissful future. Also striking were similar yearnings among the far smaller numbers of students who expressed an urge to return to some form of emperor-centered totalism. One such student spoke to me in 1961 of ancient prophecies of an Armageddon-like "time of purification [before] a birth pain, which is the coming of the Third World War," after which the whole world would exist as one family headed by the emperor.

In the spring of 1960 university students were leading actors in an extraordinary political theater of mass demonstrations against Prime Minister Nobusuke Kishi and the Japanese-American Security Treaty. But their demonstrations, mostly nonviolent and highly colorful (featuring elegant banners and a celebrated zigzag dance), came to symbolize much more: a struggle on the part of young Japanese to extricate themselves from an evil past (Kishi had been a war criminal) and from fifteen years of overwhelming dependency on the United States, a relationship replete with ambivalence and conflict. As the decade proceeded with little social change, however, a totalizing effect seemed to take hold. Rising acts of violence by students and the creation of cultlike political factions seeking absolute "purity" and "sincerity" seemed to establish a Japanese claim, as I wrote at the time, to "the most militant of all youth rebellions and to the most polarized and troubled of all national university scenes." I also spoke then of "a convergence between premodern, non-Western patterns and postmodern tendencies." That convergence, of course, was to become more vivid with the subsequent wave of New Age influence.

Some of the small terrorist groups that emerged during the early 1970s from the remains of the student movement manifested two powerful themes in Japanese psychology that would prefigure the Aum experience: struggles with *totalized group involvement* and with what can be called *death-centered macho*. The most extreme of these small fringe groups, Rengō Sekigun, or the United Red Army, beat, stabbed, and tortured twelve of its own members to death. Contributing ultimately to its violence was a paramilitary training exercise meant to ritualize the merger of two far-left student groups, each of which had individually engaged in airplane hijackings, bank robberies, and armed attacks of various kinds. But soon struggles—including fierce conflicts over feminist and sexual issues—and extreme isolation in a remote mountain cabin, along with fears of capture or death, set the scene for the group process leading to the killings. It was known as "communist transformation," a vague, highly manipulable blend of revolutionary criticism and self-criticism, Maoist thought reform, feminist consciousness raising, and the Japanese discipline of kendo, which Tsuneo Mori, the creator and leader of the process, practiced. Increasingly severe measures were taken against those considered to be making insufficient progress in overcoming "bourgeois attitudes." The first death occurred after one member was forced to engage in a boxing match with a much stronger opponent, was beaten intermittently while tied to a doorpost, then beaten still more severely because he thanked Mori for beating him, which was viewed as an attempt at *amae*, or "seeking comfort through dependency."

When the victim was found dead, Mori, known for his skill (much like Asahara's) in improvising ideology to cover various situations, declared him to have experienced *haibokushi*, or "death by defeatism." As the sociologist Patricia Steinhoff describes it, Mori declared "that the man had died of shock . . . not from [the others'] actions, but from his own failures. He had *chosen* defeat and death because he had not been strong enough to achieve the state of communist transformation, despite their help." The others had felt compelled to participate in the beating to demonstrate their more advanced state of transformation. All undoubtedly experienced guilt over a sense of insufficient transformation (as in Aum) and, as deaths mounted, considerable fear of becoming the next to undergo death by defeatism. In the midst of the killings, according to Steinhoff, Mori invoked "the traditional Zen-based samurai ethic of overcoming all physical limitations through a higher union of spirit and body," which she compares to the attitude of the Japanese military during World War II. "True revolutionaries could overcome all conceivable levels of torture without succumbing to death."

Again as in Aum, the first death was unintended and in that sense "accidental," but it, too, was brought about by the never-ending purification practices of a totalized group. This was not altruistic murder in the Aum sense; there was no theological claim of immortalizing benefit to the victim. But the rendering of the death as the victim's own doing paralleled Aum's blaming the victim for insufficient progress in spiritual training. "Death by defeatism" resembled *poa* in the crucial psychological function of divesting the killers of moral responsibility for killing.

In the late 1970s and the early 1980s, Japanese youth became politically far more quiescent, but inner rebelliousness and dissatisfaction with society did not disappear. Rather they were rerouted to such outlets as new religions, cultic groups, personal expressions of taste in music and literature, or forms of hostile demeanor and confrontational styles. This generation—sometimes called the Aum generation—is usually seen as having been preceded by an immediate postwar generation that embraced democracy and worked extremely hard to rebuild Japan, a radically rebellious generation of the sixties, characterized by idealism and commitment (if later giving way to violence), and a "withdrawn generation" that passively accepted Japan's stunning new affluence. The Aum generation gave indications of a deep uneasiness with Japan's materialism (or "economism"), a hunger for meaning, and disillusionment with American legacies: a democracy seen as corrupt and a "peace constitution" that had not prevented Japan from building a vast military "defense" force. More than that, many young Japanese shared in a broadly cultural, in fact worldwide, disillusionment with modernity—with the ostensible benefits of science, technology, and rational thought—an attitude inseparable from ambivalence toward Western cultural influences. While any statement about a generation must overgeneralize, many in the Aum generation seemed to experience a malaise that covered over potentially explosive impulses, a listlessness, and a longing for the kind of energy promised and largely delivered by Shōkō Asahara and Aum.

Jumping off Kiyomizu

Aum, then, drew directly upon the contemporary Japanese self and its legacy of cultural psychology. By that I do not mean fixed or unique behavior patterns but rather certain emphases, combinations, and expressions of thought and behavior, all within a context of human commonality. The same two overriding features of the Japanese self so evident in the United Red Army—struggles with totalized group involvement and with death-centered macho—had special importance for the creation and function of Asahara and Aum.

The intensity of Japanese group formation has been remarked on by most observers, myself included. In earlier work with young people, I stressed the psychological power of groups, which attracted them but also triggered resentments and an urge for greater individual autonomy. I often found that they attempted to resolve such conflict by seeking realization of the self via the group. But when it became too severe, it tended to contribute to hermetic group formation, that is, to groups' sealing themselves off from much of the outside world in order to further their own principles and interests. Young people's efforts to break out of groups perceived as suffocating (family, school, company), moreover, sometimes led to their joining new groups more closed and totalistic than those they had left. Group totalism, as in the example of Aum, can radically impair perceptions of realities within as well as outside the group and help spur both hostility toward outside forces and feelings of persecution by them. Resentments toward one's own group, on the other hand, must be suppressed, blamed either on oneself or on the outside world. For what one most fears is expulsion or ostracism, a threat that can be equated psychologically with death.

Death-centered macho—the calling forth when confronting death of extreme energies that in themselves can be bound up with killing—has a long history in Japan. The literature of Bushidō, the traditional code of the warrior (influenced originally by Buddhism), is essentially a meditation on death: "The essence of Bushidō lies in the act of dying." "Every morning make up thy mind to die. Every evening freshen thy mind in the thought of death." The "great man" must be willing to "sacrifice body for the sake of spirit . . . [so that] his spirit will be alive eternally even if his body perishes." Dying, then, is equated with the experience of transcendence and with the achievement of immortality. A noble failure in battle can be even more immortalizing than success, so long as one achieves a heroic death. The model of the samurai contemplating and achieving his heroic death was extended to Japanese soldiers in World War II and especially to kamikaze pilots late in the war. Many of the latter (but not all, as some were fearful and felt coerced) were said to undergo a temporary "rebirth" *prior* to their deaths, becoming calm, proud, and exemplary in behavior as if having already become (in the language of the time) "gods without earthly desires."

Major military decisions not infrequently hinge on death-centered macho. Just before ordering the attack on Pearl Harbor and initiating war with the United States, a country the Japanese had no possibility of defeating, Admiral Hideki Tōjō, the prime minister, observed to one of his leading advisers that there are times when a man must close his eyes and jump from the veranda of Kiyomizu-dera, a famous temple outside of Kyoto, into the ravine below. "Jumping off Kiyomizu" is, in fact, an old saying that suggests taking a desperate plunge, embarking on an overwhelming task even if there is little prospect of success, because it is the right or necessary or "sincere" thing to do. As in the case of the samurai seeking his death, there could have been a suicidal dimension in Tōjō's use of the phrase: the idea, in some part of his mind, that he was leading Japan to glorious destruction.

Aum's destructive expression of group totalism and death-centered macho may have lacked the cultural structuring and conscious ideological awareness that characterize samurai and kamikaze actions, but the Kiyomizu that Asahara jumped from was a high mountain and below it was not a ravine but an abyss, for he was initiating a war not against a stronger nation but against all humankind.

Contemporary Japanese commentators are quite right, then, in recognizing their own selves in Aum. But that recognition only tells us that apocalyptic violence must take the form of the particular culture in which it occurs. Destructive expressions of the Japanese apocalyptic turn out to have much in common with versions of our own.

12 | Forcing the End, American Style

Having explored some of the important Japanese sources of Aum, one is tempted to look at it as an arcane, even exotic aberration that took place in an alien cultural setting. There is a related temptation to view the problem as solved; with the murderous guru and his culpable disciples brought to Japanese justice, the book on Aum can be closed.

Both temptations should be resisted. Although Aum was Japanese, there was hardly a religious tradition or geographical region—from Russia to Australia, India to the United States—that Asahara did not ransack for the components of his spirituality, his weapons systems, and his rationale for mass murder. Conversely, there are impulses closely related to Asahara's found in each of these regions and their spiritual traditions. And given the expanding availability of ultimate weapons, no national boundaries can contain those who are bent on forcing the end. In fact, the capability of doing so is likely to descend to ever smaller, more driven, and more technologically sophisticated groups.

We have only begun to grasp how, from 1945 on, the specter of global extinction has affected human consciousness and collective behavior. But for a half century at least, the human hands in which the possibility of extinction resided were those of the leaders of two super-powers, the Soviet Union and the United States. In recent years, with the collapse of one of the superpowers, the fear has developed that reckless leaders of "rogue states" could acquire sufficient weaponry to initiate world-threatening destruction. Now, Aum Shinrikyō has demonstrated, in however bungling a manner, that such a project can be mounted by a small cult combining zealotry and weaponry.

For all these reasons Aum should be seen not as an end point but as a threatening beginning, an expression of a new dimension of global danger. There is no lack of hunger in groups throughout the world for absolute moral clarity—not just for a leader but for a guru or savior—and of a sense that only the most extreme measures can bring about a yearned-for transformation of existence. Nor does there seem to be any lack of prospective gurus or saviors ready to emerge from such social climates. They, in turn, require disciples in order to cope with their own profound vulnerabilities. Everywhere there are potential gurus and potential disciples longing to be, in William James's phrase, "melted into unity." Their hungers are sustained by the imagery of annihilation, whether involving weaponry or the destruction of the human habitat, what we misleadingly call "our environment."

In every society a subterranean "apocalypse culture" can be discov-ered, sometimes in odd places. The religious scholar Malcolm Bull, for instance, implicates contemporary American intellectual life when he speaks of "postmodern theories of posthistory" as having "surpris-ingly close parallels . . . [with] fundamentalist millenarianism." Our terminology in general suggests endings rather than new beginnings—or even, as Jacques Derrida has it, "an apocalypse without vision" or "an end without an end." So we speak of living in an age that is not only postmodern but also post-Freudian, post-Marxist, post-Communist, postideological, postrevolutionary, postcolonial, postwar (whatever the war), post–Cold War, posthistoric, postnarrative (in terms of literature), and postfigurative (in terms of art). Within the realm of the postmodern there is talk of what could be called the "postauthor" and the "postself." Although these "post"s are often meant to serve as springboards for renewals of one sort or another, the terminology nonetheless leaves us in a kind of nothingness, in a more or less permanent postmortem. The world is frequently experienced as already dead, requiring only the clearing of debris. That lifeless world and its terminology of deadness can become associated with mythic visions of destruction and renewal, with apocalyptic promises of radical transformation.

We have seen the potential dangers involved in rendering that mythic principle a basis for action, especially in a world containing so much ultimate weaponry. The report on the U.S. Senate's hearings on Aum Shinrikyō speaks of the cult as having crossed a threshold that rendered "the specter of terrorist groups using weapons of mass destruction" an actuality. In that report, Bruce Hoffman, a British authority on political violence, is quoted as referring to "the nightmare scenario that people have quietly talked about for years coming true," and "the cutting edge of high-tech terrorism for the year 2000 and beyond." Aum, in other words, may have been a kind of bellwether, an indicator of future trends.

In the worldwide "counterculture" of potential perpetrators of apocalyptic violence, the contours are so confusing that, as one commentator notes, "die-hard redneck bigots now look like the long-haired biker hippies killed by die-hard redneck bigots in movies like *Easy Rider*." And an approaching millennium is a time, in any case, when human beings tend to experience both a sense of decline and death—of "old gods failing"—and a special yearning for regeneration. In our contemporary drama of death and rebirth we encounter an intense version of what another observer calls the apocalyptic "juxtaposition of terror and bliss," one bound up with supernatural prophecy, annihilative technology, and the urge for survival.

It is highly unlikely that the Aum Shinrikyō experience will simply repeat itself in Japan or elsewhere—but quite likely that Aum-like traits will coalesce in groups as yet unknown to us. We do well to reconsider, with Asahara and Aum in mind, the American cultic landscape and its global interactions. To be sure, there is no certainty at all that the next urge to force the end will take threatening form in the

United States as opposed to, say, post-Communist Russia, the Middle East, or the Indian subcontinent. But the United States has been a particularly fertile environment for cults. Examining a few American cults of recent times through the prism of Shōkō Asahara can deepen our understanding of cultic phenomena and our thinking about possible futures as well. Certainly, several of our most sensational cults—the Charles Manson Family, Jim Jones's Peoples Temple, and Marshall Herff Applewhite's Heaven's Gate—take on a different aspect in the wake of Aum. The same is true of the cultic milieu of the present-day extreme right, where fantasies of using weapons of mass destruction to transform and purify the world are powerfully present.

Charles Manson's Armageddon

Charles Manson and his "Family" are usually thought of more as a criminal gang than as an apocalyptic community. In fact, they were both. Manson's group committed at least ten murders and probably many more as part of a project that was meant to destroy the "bourgeois world," initiate a race war, and bring about Armageddon. The known murders took place in 1969, nine of them in two Los Angeles mansions: that of the film director Roman Polanski, where his wife, the film actress Sharon Tate, and six others were murdered, and that of a wealthy businessman named Leno LaBianca and his wife, Rosemarie LaBianca, both of whom were killed. If Aum can be understood as the dark side of Japanese postwar culture, the Manson family was the dark side of the late 1960s American counterculture.

Like Asahara, Manson came from a deprived background. Illegitimacy, poverty, abuse, and family chaos caused him to be shunted from one foster home to the next. His legal transgressions came earlier and in greater number than Asahara's, and he was incarcerated for most of his life: first as a child runaway, then for burglary, forgery, car theft, and pimping. Like Asahara, he experienced powerful feelings of rejection by society, declaring himself "an outlaw from birth." He recreated himself as a guru in his midthirties, in the all-accepting hippie subcultures of San Francisco's Bay Area and then southern California, making use of a small musical talent (he played the guitar and sang sixties ballads, some of which he wrote). He attracted his first "disciples" through a series of sexual conquests, mostly of teenage girls, which he later transformed into a philosophy of absolute love and a form of earthly perfection (resembling that of the medieval Free Spirit and Taborite sects).

Like Asahara and other gurus, Manson had early revelations of divinity. At about the age of twelve he had "a vision of Jesus" looking in at him through a window and later, in prison, he had another, which he experienced as a call to divinity: "The Infinite One just came into my cell and opened up my head. He showed me the truth, but I didn't want it. I cried and yelled at him, 'No. No. Not me.' But he showed me the truth." While Manson was even more of a con man than Asahara, in at least a portion of his mind he was sufficiently convinced of his divine specialness—something his early experiences with LSD reinforced—to function as a guru who could attract followers.

His guruism rivaled Asahara's in its extremity. Together with his expanding group (never more than about thirty-five people) he engaged in mystical experiences that combined sexual and Christ-centered transcendence—hence his defiant declaration, "I am the God of fuck." Like Asahara, Manson underwent a mysterious transformation from ignorant nonentity to all-knowing guru. He spoke of himself as having been "a half-assed nothing who hardly knew how to read or write, . . . didn't know anything except jails." More than Asahara or most other gurus, he emphasized his disciples' influence on what he became, to the point of describing himself specifically as their creature: "I am only what you made me. I am only a reflection of you. . . . What you think in your mind as you look at me is how you're judging yourself and the world." But there was no doubt of the magnetic power he could exert. Disciples spoke of his eyes as "hypnotic" and saw him as one possessed of divine powers, as a healer who knew their innermost thoughts and offered them a new dimension of freedom and happiness. They came to feel that he was "love, pure love, their father, their leader, their love." Susan Atkins, a disciple involved in the Tate murders, conveyed the pathological blurring that resulted: "The whole world is like one big intercourse—everything is in and out—smoking, eating, stabbing"—a communal merging of the sexual, oral, mystical, and murderous.

Manson and his followers thought of themselves as Christ and his disciples. One follower described him as "both Christ and the devil," a duality Manson seemed to encourage proudly. Like Asahara, Manson became the vehicle for everyone's divinity. "We were tuned into God—at least Charlie was, and the rest of us through him," was the way one of his followers put it. As with Asahara, the fusion of guru and disciple was a near-absolute one: "I became Charlie. Everything I was, was Charlie. There was nothing left of me anymore. And all of the people in the Family, there's nothing left of them anymore, they're all Charlie too."

Manson brought to his guruism an ideological mix that was highly eclectic even for the 1960s, drawing on such sources as Scientology and especially one of its offshoots, the Process Church of the Final Judgment, a satanist group that revered Hitler, preached a fierce, imminent millennialism, and imagined a highly activist role for itself as a chosen people in forcing the end through murder, violence, and chaos. Manson also drew on hypnosis and various forms of popular psychotherapy, including the psychiatrist Eric Berne's concept of "transactional analysis"; Robert Heinlein's science fiction novel *Stranger in a Strange Land* (Manson named his first child Valentine after the novel's hero, a telepathic, sexually active Martian who attracts fanatical followers); Nazism (he spoke admiringly of Hitler and, after his conviction for murder, carved on his forehead an inverted swastika similar to the one the Process used as its logo); various countercultural practices, including unlimited sexual experimentation, the extensive use of LSD, and the glorification of the dropout; and on vague Eastern spiritual influences. Manson repeatedly referred to karma and offered his disciples a *poa*-like view of death as "only a change." "The Soul or Spirit can't die," he said; it would appear again in some form. He invoked what the British scholar of religion R. C. Yaehner calls "the left-handed Tantra" of Hinduism, in which there is no distinction between the killer and the killed because "there is no good, there is no evil."

For Manson as a guru, there was complete blurring of the boundaries not only between life and death but between anything and anything else. While Asahara's multiplicity was notable, Manson was, quite literally, proteanism gone mad: "I'm a guitar, a cup of coffee, a snake, a pocket full of names and faces. I see myself in the desert as a rattlesnake, as a bird, as anything. You guys are stuck play-acting as humans. I don't need to be human." With a mocking clinical edge, he said, "I've got a thousand faces, so that makes me five hundred schizophrenics." (He had once been diagnosed as schizophrenic, though over the course of his criminal career psychiatrists generally put more emphasis on his antisocial behavior and paranoia.) One psychiatrist, after examining a disciple involved in the Tate murders, suggested "a condition of *folie à famille*, a kind of shared madness within a group situation." Still, at the height of his function, Manson could more or less make his manipulative proteanism work for him. A former disciple told how he constantly changed his hair and beard, "and with each change he could be born anew—Hollywood slicker, jail tough, rock star, guru, child, tramp, angel, devil, son of God." Over time, however, being worshiped by others and having to sustain himself as Jesus, God, or Satan took its toll, as it seems to with most gurus, and his paranoia and megalomania intensified. As with Asahara, violence became the prime means of staving off further psychological fragmentation.

Manson's Armageddon lacked Asahara's high-tech visions. The weaponry of his murderous thoughts and actions was confined to knives and guns. But he did imagine his Family initiating a process that would force the end through a brutal race war. What he envisioned was igniting a vast revolution in which members of militant groups like the Black Muslims or Black Panthers "would come out of the ghettos and do an atrocious murder with stabbing, killing, cutting bodies to pieces, smearing blood on the walls," until most whites had been annihilated. Like Asahara, he preferred having his disciples perform the violent acts he conjured up. The purpose of the Tate killings was to show blacks how to go about their murders. By instructing the murderers to write in blood on the walls of the Polanski mansion "black" words like "Pigs" and "Death to Pigs," Manson intended to create the impression that blacks had been the killers. He was convinced that whites would then retaliate and the race war would begin. This reasoning bears a certain resemblance to Asahara's near-psychotic plan to initiate Armageddon by deceiving the world into thinking that the sarin gas in the Tokyo attack had been released by one or more of his enemies. As Manson imagined it, the blacks would triumph but would be too weary, and in any case would lack the ability, to govern and so would call upon him as a savior to take over. The Family would then greatly expand and become, as a post-Armageddon expression of renewal, "a pure, white master race," with surviving blacks confined to menial labor. "It would be our world then. There would be no one else except for us and the black servants," is the way that one disciple explained it. Manson, of course, would rule.

Manson gave the name "Helter Skelter" (a phrase taken from a Beatles song) to the chaotic process of race war and world destruction of which he dreamed, and he brought to his vision of Armageddon a hatred of the world not unlike Asahara's. His rage, however, was less masked by regularized cultic practices, closer to the surface, and more directly expressive of paranoid deprivation: "One by one this fucked-up society is stripping my loves from me. I'll show them! They made animals out of us—I'll unleash these animals—I'll give them so much fucking fear that people will be afraid to come out of their houses."

Like Asahara, Manson invoked the Book of Revelation and incorporated its details into his paranoid-megalomanic reading of history and the future. Where Asahara blended its prophecy with his version of Hinduism and Buddhism, Manson connected it to messages he believed he had found hidden in the words and music of the Beatles, particularly in their *White Album*, released in December 1968. Manson associated one of the songs on that album, "Revolution 9," with "Reve*lation* 9" (that is, chapter 9 of the Book of Revelation) and took the song's wide variety of noises, shouts, screams, and gunfire, the repetition of the refrain "Number 9, number 9, number 9," and finally the lullaby "Good Night" to represent Armageddon. To him the Beatles were prophets who were seeking Jesus—in other words, Manson himself. He recognized them in the reference to creatures with "faces of men" but "the hair of women" in Revelation 9. They were, he was convinced, the "four angels" mentioned there as responsible for killing "the third part of men" (which to Manson meant the massacre of the white race). Most important, the "king over them," the angel given the key that opens "the bottomless pit" from which arise the forces of destruction, was, at least for members of the Family, unambiguously Manson. Another song in the *White Album*, "Blackbird," includes the line, "You are only waiting for the moment to arise," which (according to a disciple) Manson understood to mean that "the Beatles were programming the black people to get it up, get it on, start doing it." The album, in short, was the prophetic signal to start the revolution that would bring about Armageddon. In "Revolution 9" there was even a background voice pronouncing three times the word "rise," which Manson's murderers would print in blood on a wall of the LaBianca residence. As Manson said to his group, "Are you hip to what the Beatles are saying? Helter Skelter is coming down. The Beatles are telling it like it is."

Like Aum after them, the Manson Family crossed the threshold into killing when their guru came to fear the demise of the cult—because of severe internal difficulties (problems with money and tensions between him and his followers) and external pressure (police investigations due to the group's clumsy criminality). Manson responded to threats of the imminent collapse of his unstable world with increasing rage, paranoia, and vehemence toward "the cops, the niggers, the establishment," as well as with psychological fragmentation and more sustained psychosis. "When things stop working out, it all seemed to fall right back in my lap. Then the head starts reeling, pressure mounts, tension increases, frustration starts and there ain't no rhyme or reason to a fucking thing" was the way he put the process.

As would be true with Asahara, Manson directed his rage and violence in part at members of his group, while demanding from them ever-greater intimacy and loyalty. He had an urge to flee and abandon his disciples (part of a lifelong pattern, perhaps present in some measure in most gurus) but realized that "something inside me needed them, more than they thought they needed me." In his evening talks he began to refer regularly to violence, killing, and torture. He and his followers started to carry weapons—he a "magic sword" that he periodically brandished, they knives honed to an extreme sharpness. Close followers were sent on what amounted to murder rehearsals, "creepy crawls," during which they were to be thinking about killing while simply breaking into houses and rearranging furniture. As would happen in Aum, followers received their guru's abuse and his plans for the murder of outsiders as tests of their absolute loyalty and unconditional love. While the planning and carrying out of specific murders like those at the Polanski mansion represented the crossing of a behavioral threshold, the murder rehearsals and atmosphere of violence represented the prior crossing of a psychological one.

Whether in the case of the medieval sects, Aum Shinrikyō, or the Manson Family, the impulse to destroy the world draws upon available cultural and historical materials. In the Middle Ages these had to do with papal power, feudal structures, handheld weapons, and interpretations of the Book of Revelation. In the latter half of the twentieth century, groups have drawn upon a global stock of materials, including post-Freudian psychological techniques, New Age occultism, the more belligerent writings of many religions, and the Hitler legacy, as well as aspects of nuclearism (articulated strongly by Asahara and in the background landscape for the Family). Yet, significantly, from medieval times to our own, the Book of Revelation has consistently been a powerful organizing text for apocalyptic dreaming and for the efforts of all varieties of violent cults to "murder death."

The designated victims of a guru (Jews or Freemasons, whites or blacks, or most of the people in the world) are seen as carrying a death taint, which makes them dangerous and threatening. They are as if contagious, and their deadly contagion divests a disciple of any onus in killing them since they are, so to speak, already dead. Murder of this type becomes necessary to guru and cult as a means to reassert their power over death. But people like Manson and Asahara are haunted by a death taint of their own, having to do with their death anxiety, their incompletely suppressed sense of their evil, and their ever-present tendency toward inner fragmentation and a feeling of psychological death. No wonder Manson could say (sounding more like Asahara than Asahara), "The only way anyone can live on earth is *one world under the last person.* I am the last and bottom line: you will all do what I say or there will be *nothing.*" Becoming the last survivor, at least in fantasy, is the ultimate form of "murdering death," and so the guru must imagine himself as the ultimate survivor, whether strictly in his own person or through his followers, in whom he dominantly resides.

Manson's Family was, of course, a tiny, irregular cult run by a highly unsystematic guru—a private cult, one might say—but it was aimed nonetheless at forcing the end. Although Manson lacked any thought of combining end weapons with that goal, it is important to note that by the late 1960s many of the other factors that would contribute to an Aum-like entity—from a global mix of spiritual practices to a form of killing that was part of a sacred world-ending purification—were already in place on the American cultic landscape, as was the urge to overcome the threat of cultic death by murdering others.

Revolutionary Suicide—and Murder as Well

During the latter part of November 1978, news began to emerge of mass deaths in a jungle clearing of Guyana, a small nation located on the northeastern coast of South America. Only the fall and winter before, Jim Jones, the charismatic guru of an American cult called the Peoples Temple, had moved most of his members from California to a plot of land there, renamed it Jonestown, and soon declared it to be "the best heaven you could build on earth." Jones's guruism had emerged from existing religious structures. He had originally founded his group as a Pentecostal church in 1956 in his home state of Indiana, but he soon transcended ordinary Pentecostalism and its healing practices to become a prophet for and supporter of the oppressed. He moved his church to Ukiah in the Redwood Valley of northern California in 1965, largely because the area had been designated as "the safest place in the United States" in the event of the nuclear war he was certain would soon occur. Subsequently he expanded the church to San Francisco and Los Angeles, where he preached racial harmony and turned his group into a cultlike movement for social justice. He deified socialism and identified his own claim to be God with it, thereby replacing the oppression of the traditional "sky god" with worship of himself. Feeling under attack in the media and by former cult members, he began in 1975 to resettle his contingent in Guyana, which he imagined as a utopian community, while also espousing what he called "revolutionary suicide."

During the Indiana phase, the group attracted mainly working-class whites; in Ukiah, well-educated white students and professionals; in San Francisco and Los Angeles, mostly urban blacks. The group came to be numerically dominated by blacks, many of them elderly and female, but its leaders were principally from the better-educated white contingent. At its height in California, the Temple claimed between three thousand and five thousand members, and for a time Jones himself received considerable public recognition—as chairman of the San Francisco Housing Authority, as recipient of the 1977 Martin Luther King Humanitarian of the Year award in San Francisco, and as a political acquaintance of Rosalynn Carter.

Now Jonestown was a graveyard. Aum Shinrikyō did not yet exist. The Manson murders had occurred almost a decade earlier.

It took quite awhile for the dead to be counted but they came to number 913 in Jonestown itself, 4 in the nearby city of Georgetown, and 5 in the party of Leo Ryan (including Ryan himself), a congressman who had come to investigate complaints against the cult and whose group had been attacked at the Jonestown airstrip by cult gunmen. The great majority at Jonestown had died from a prepared potassium cyanide poison, swallowed in a mixture with grape Flavor-Aid (KoolAid–like drink) or injected. Three people at Jonestown, including Jones himself, had been shot, while in Georgetown a cult member had slit the throats of her three young children before doing the same to herself (with the aid of a friend). Even to observers of totalistic behavior, the numbers were staggering.

I was traveling in Germany interviewing former Nazi doctors at the time, and the poisonous mixture brought to mind both the counterculture (the KoolAid–like drink) and Auschwitz, though at that death camp the cyanide used to kill the Jews was administered in gas form. According to the first reporter to view the carnage at Jonestown, "many had died with their arms around each other, men and women, white and black, young and old." This suggests another dimension to Jonestown: its dream of perfect racial harmony in a utopian community. There was, however, a more sinister finding: the dead at Jonestown were by no means all suicides. We will never know exactly how many people were murdered there, but they may have added up to between a third and a half (or even more) of the total dead. For one thing, 260 small children died there, and at least 70 adults died of cyanide injections, which suggests they resisted drinking the poison mix. One survivor estimated that 30 to 40 adults "objected" and another 100 or so were "reluctant." In fact, distinctions at Jonestown between suicide and murder have proved difficult to make.

Shocking as it was then, Jonestown becomes even more shocking through the lens provided by Aum Shinrikyō. For despite its suicidal denouement, the Peoples Temple resembles Aum Shinrikyō in the nature and extent of its violence, and in other ways as well. A closer look at the Peoples Temple offers us a better understanding of what happened in Aum and what could happen elsewhere.

Jim Jones's guruism closely resembled that of Asahara. Like him, Jones combined compelling spiritual talent with a profound urge toward destructiveness. Like his Japanese counterpart (and Manson), Jones came from the impoverished margins of society, in his case from rural Indiana. He, too, felt deeply neglected as a child, recalling the absence of "any love, any understanding" at home and the discomfort of school functions where "everybody's fucking parent was there but mine." The result, as Jones told it, was that "I was ready to kill by the end of the third grade." Like Asahara's, his rage was to be expressed in early episodes of violence, including a couple of incidents in which he shot real bullets at other children. He also showed early talent for manipulating others.

Far more than Asahara, he demonstrated precocious signs of being a brilliant public performer, immersing himself in the primal gyrations of Pentecostalism, preaching animatedly to other children, performing special rites for dead pigeons and other animals, and as a teenager wrapping himself in sheets and preaching on street corners. He emerged as a talented preacher and healer who, like Asahara (and other Pentecostal healers), did not hesitate to resort to fraudulent methods to display his incipient guruhood—using animal intestines, for instance, as the "cancer" being excreted by a person he was "curing." When he acquired disciples, he could—again like Asahara—treat them with great dedication, respond to their personal problems, and convey to them a sense of meaning and hope, but he could also be sadistic in testing their loyalty.

Jones thus shared with Asahara an early and sustained combination of talent as a religious teacher, leader, and con man, as well as swings of mood and behavior that could take him quickly from saintliness to cruelty. Nothing that either man did was free of a diffuse rage toward society at large. Jones differed from Asahara in being an American populist-preacher-guru who mingled freely with his followers and applied his ecstatic religion to a progressive social cause—that of combating racism and creating a fully integrated spiritual community.

Like Asahara, Jones was visionary and grandiose from the beginning of his spiritual career. As one observer puts it, he "claimed the platform that Jesus occupied almost two millennia earlier." Jones insisted later in his career that "I have come in the very person . . . of Christ the Revolution!" and "I am the only God you've ever seen." In his sermons he shouted his disdain for the traditional deity—"If there is a God in the sky, I say, FUCK YOU"—while his disciples embraced him as the kind of God he wanted to be. Twelve weeks after the Jonestown disaster, a survivor who had participated in the murders of the Ryan party declared, "He was the God I could touch." One could also say that he resembled Asahara in becoming both God and anti-God, Christ and anti-Christ.

Jones's psychological difficulties were evident early and only intensified over time. Like Asahara, he experienced a severe personal crisis at about age thirty, five years after founding the Peoples Temple. Others observed in him widespread fears and persistent anxiety. Like Asahara, he came to imagine enemies everywhere. While he could be courageous in combating actual incidents of racial harassment, he would at times stage such incidents himself (as later in Jonestown he would stage "sniper attacks," a six-day siege, and even a "kidnapping" of his beloved adopted son). Once he shattered a window from the inside and accused enemies of throwing a rock at him. On a number of occasions he suddenly "discovered" glass in his food (which he apparently put there himself). In these and other ways, his tendency toward paranoia increased—as did a pattern, when he felt pressured, of sudden collapse and brief blackout. He even claimed at one point to hear the voices of extraterrestrials.

Like Asahara (and many others who show paranoid tendencies), he became more grandiose the greater his anxiety and inner conflict. He also resembled Asahara in his increasing tendency toward megalomania and in episodes that were close to or actually psychotic. As with gurus in general, a pattern of decompensation and breakdown was greatly accentuated by faltering control over his disciples. Jones and Asahara, to fend off threats to their guruism, escalated their demands on their disciples, ultimately insisting that they be ready to die for their guru—in Jones's case, through acceptance of a doctrine of revolutionary suicide as an ultimate expression of loyalty.

Like Charles Manson, Jones prophesied chaos and race war in the United States but, unlike him, declared himself on the side of blacks and of racial justice; nor did Jones see race war as a way to Armageddon and purification of the world. He looked to nuclear weapons for that.

Nuclear End, Socialist Beginning

The sociologist John R. Hall has spoken of Jones and his followers as "an apocalyptic 'warring sect,' fighting a decisive Manichean struggle with the forces of evil," a description equally apt for Aum Shinrikyō. In both cases, fierce apocalyptic visions gave rise to extraordinary spiritual intensity and to violence. Jones himself warned of the "great desolation, or the apocalypse, or the Armageddon that will spring forth at nuclear hell." His millennial visions combined Pentecostal doomsday imagery with this-worldly political and military catastrophes, including "bombs, earthquakes, fascist revolutions." Indeed, nuclear holocaust became a consuming preoccupation of the Peoples Temple, so much so that Jones decided on the various relocations of his cult largely on the basis of an assumed safety in a nuclear war. (Guyana, for instance, was chosen in part because it was a place where there would be "no radiation coming our way.") One must recall that in 1956, when the Peoples Temple was formed, Americans were struggling with nuclear threat and with the illusion that backyard shelters could protect families from a nuclear holocaust.

Sustained nuclear fear—that is, fear of extinction—fed Jones's constant feeling of being under attack from many enemies in a hostile world. In this sense Jones could be said to represent a distorted end point of American society's overall struggles with nuclear fear.

There are, however, two important ways in which his relation to nuclear weapons differed from Asahara's. The American guru imagined himself as a potential victim of a nuclear holocaust, never as a possessor or wielder of weapons of ultimate destruction (though, like Asahara, he imagined certain survival benefits for his cult from a nuclear war). Moreover, within the context of anticipated nuclear annihilation, Jones prepared an alternative mini-apocalypse, that of collective suicide. His activist impulse to force the end rivaled Asahara's but was aimed only at the separate world he had created. His mini-apocalypse by his own hand was a way of both living out and pre-empting the larger one he feared.

Yet Jones's hatred for the larger world was sufficiently extreme to resemble Asahara's. Capitalist America was absolute evil: "America's system is representative of the mark of the Beast and America is the Antichrist." Nuclear holocaust, he believed, would bring about a cataclysmic purification that would result in "total annihilation of all life in America." (Asahara would imagine a similar fate for Japan.) Jones's anticipation of that holocaust could be joyous, as the bomb "will have blown away the Nixons, and the Kissingers, and the Rockefellers, and the DuPonts," so that "I'd be glad to be blown away too, just to see them blown away." As Jones further explained, "If you're born in capitalist America, racist America, fascist America, then you're born in sin"—not the case if you are "born in Socialism."

Jones's millennial renewal, his immortalizing principle, took the form of revolutionary socialism. Jones was hardly alone in this. Medieval millennial movements were frequently revolutionary, and modern socialist and communist revolutions have given expression to powerful millennial impulses, however politically transformed. What Jones called "Apostolic Socialism" could have been termed "Pentecostal Maoism." For Jones it was a matter of nuclear world destruction in the service of socialist renewal, "nuclear redemption for divine socialism." Survivors of the nuclear apocalypse, he felt at times when despair for the future did not overcome him, would be confined to members of the Peoples Temple and citizens of socialist states. "After the bombs have fallen, China is going to dig out of their lovely caves a year later," Jones declared.

Like Asahara, Jones constructed a highly eclectic theology blending Pentecostalism with additional Christian influences and inspiration from such varied sources as Karl Marx, Father Divine, Stalin, Hitler, Gandhi, Martin Luther King, Jr., and Fidel Castro. He drew, too, from encounter groups and possibly from psychological studies having to do with mind manipulation, as well as from Brazilian religious sects such as Macumba, with its West African elements. His focus on racial equality and social justice evoked enormous loyalty from the black members of the Peoples Temple despite the absence of black leadership, and, as in Aum, women (both white and black) tended to have greater power than they had experienced in the outside world. The Temple carried through its socialist doctrine by providing various support systems, including health care and housing for the elderly, while maintaining a strong work ethic. Like Aum, the Peoples Temple thrust itself into the political process, but more as a group seeking allies than as one imagining the overthrow of governments. Though the group generally supported progressive causes, Jones was sufficiently opportunistic to make contacts all over the political spectrum, even at one time befriending a leader of the John Birch Society, then prominent on the paranoid right.

Like Manson (and more so than Asahara), Jones used sex as a focal point for his guruism. For all three, sex was inseparable from the guru's mystique and deification. Like the other two gurus, Jones was sexually active with followers, mostly women (with whom he had lasting relationships that helped solidify loyalties), but with a few men as well. He could also give mesmerizing sermons on sexual matters, combining street talk, Christian images, and a principle of "revolutionary sex": "You should present your whole body as a living sacrifice, wholly and acceptable to your god. . . . If it would save you, or promote a revolutionary cause or this movement, you should give your vagina, your penis, your asshole, if it's called for, and if you can't, then you're not a dedicated Communist." Jones's sexual rules for the Temple fluctuated greatly. At times he advocated members' sharing their sexuality with many others, while at other times he instituted puritanical rules that bound members only to their own spouses or even to complete celibacy.

As Jones became more erratic and brutal, he began to bully members publicly about their sexual inadequacies and would sometimes declare himself the only true heterosexual among them. He also engaged in homosexual encounters in which he humiliated his partners, taking pleasure in revealing to them their homosexual inclinations. Such was the "therapeutic" atmosphere that one of these male partners declared, "Your fucking me in the ass was, as I see it now, necessary to get me to deal with my deep-seated repression against my homosexuality. . . . I know beyond doubt that you are the very best sexual partner in the world and I don't think I've ever thought I really could compete with you."

The Collapse of the Guru

Like every other cultic group, the Peoples Temple offered its members powerful feelings of transcendence. These high states, instead of taking the form of individual mystical experiences as in Aum, were essentially communal. Among Temple members there were a great many families—couples with children, women with children, adults with one or both parents. Jones—or "Dad"—would hold forth at large meetings and people could thrill to the visions he held out to them, visions that carried them to "the Promised Land." There could be utopian moments of communal love and shared purpose in overcoming the destructive, racist currents of American society. Jones tried to live up to his bold interracial principles in his own family, which included his wife, their biological son, and a number of adopted boys and girls of different races. But his instability led to many forms of family conflict, and over the years the efforts of his wife, Marceline, to protect him and legitimate his actions (despite her resentment of his sexual activities) were ever threatened by his bizarre behavior.

And bizarre he became—increasingly paranoid, grandiose, and despotic. Typically, in September 1988 he wrote a long, floridly paranoid letter to President Jimmy Carter marked "URGENT URGENT URGENT" and including details of how he and the Peoples Temple were being destroyed by dangerous enemies who were also planning to blow up bridges and poison the water supply in Washington, DC. He became more abusive at public meetings. What had previously resembled group psychotherapy (the term used was "catharsis") now became punitive public displays. Jones ridiculed those he felt offended by, accused them of being "elite" or "insensitive intellectuals," condemned their work and sexual habits, and subjected them to public humiliation. There was also more physical violence: extensive spankings and then beatings of children, teenagers, and adults. A small paddle named the "Board of Education" was increasingly used. Children, and later adults, were made to take part in boxing matches in which they had to face bigger, stronger opponents (contests strangely similar both to Asahara's staged wrestling competitions at his school for the blind and to practices in the United Red Army). These spectacles had begun in California but in Guyana became increasingly violent and sadistic. In Jonestown, a pseudomedical "extended care unit" was also established, where potential defectors or those who broke rules were taken and drugged in order to be "reintegrated back into the community"—and here the similarity to Aum increases.

Jones began to express his greatest vitriol toward a group called Concerned Relatives, which, inspired by defectors, had itself become militant in custody cases and in efforts to expose the practices of Jones and his cult, calling them "drug addicts," "sexual perverts," and "terrorists." On Jonestown radio, the guru encouraged fantasies of torturing and killing these relatives. "I'd like to string up my father by the nuts and shove a hot poker up his ass and make him realize what he's doing," was the typical testimony of one disciple whose parent had publicly criticized the cult.

Jones had been taking large amounts of painkillers, tranquilizers, and amphetamines since the early 1970s. Some of the women surrounding him, much concerned about his comfort, made repeated trips to Mexico and South America to obtain the drugs he claimed to need. Now Jones's addictions worsened, his speech became slurred, and he greatly deteriorated both mentally and physically. On one occasion in Guyana he dashed into the bush with a weapon, thinking himself a prisoner during the Russian Revolution, and had to be rescued and calmed down by his son Stephan. At other times father and son would have violent shouting matches. The boy's rage was so manifest that when Marceline had to leave Jonestown on trips she would tell Stephan, "Don't kill him. Something will work out." Jones would often be "too sick" to preside over meetings or broadcasts. To be sure, he was still worshiped by many loyal followers who understood their lives to have been changed and enriched by their guru. But there was a growing sense that this was becoming a worship of madness. His hold over his followers weakened, and his addictions distanced him from them.

The deified guru tends in any case to retreat psychologically, often through paranoia or madness, from the community he has created. But in another sense the guru, as a deity, has always been "outside" his own community. God, after all, belongs to no group—and the lonely isolation of the guru contributes both to his spiritual gifts and to his destructive megalomania.

Jones's hatred for the world was inseparable from his long-standing struggle with despair. Though he thought the mind would survive the death of the body, the effort of life often seemed hardly worth it to him because "I don't believe in anything loving in the universe." He could convince himself and his flock of the nature of the American Babylon they inhabited, but he and they seemed less certain of the Promised Land he offered. One disciple quoted Jones on the matter succinctly: "Dad's been saying it for a long time: Life is shit."

Such despair could be countered by the communal functioning of the guru's alternative world. But each defection, for Jones as for Asahara, profoundly threatened the shaky well-being of that world. Defectors are a central vulnerability of totalistic groups. Not only do they expose excesses of guruist authority to the antagonistic outside world but the defections themselves undermine the group's truth claims and the power of its authority. Jones associated all defections with the Peoples Temple's own apocalyptic demise. The group experienced its first major defections in 1973, when four young interracial couples fled Ukiah, accusing Jones and his leadership of racism (there were no blacks in high positions) and sexual hypocrisy. Significantly, Jones responded to this eight-person defection by initiating, within his inner circle, the group's first exploration of the idea of collective suicide. (Jones had in fact been thinking about suicide since childhood.) The guru's functional paranoia was undermined by even this early loss of full control over his community. His megalomania caused him to experience each defection as a disintegration of his own self, so that each defector immediately became for him not only a traitor and betrayer but an attacking enemy.

The process was exacerbated in the cult's last years by defections of people in leadership positions, who were more important than ordinary members to Jones's psychological function and particularly dangerous to him because of their knowledge of the group's inner workings. When Debra Layton Blakey, who had dealt with the group's finances, left in May 1978, she deposited a statement at the American embassy in Georgetown declaring her fear that if the court responded to Concerned Relatives' efforts to force Jones to return John Stoen, a four-year-old whom he considered his son and toward whom he was fiercely possessive, to the child's mother, Jones would "carry out his threat to force all members of the organization in Guyana to commit suicide." She added, "I know that plans have been made to carry out this mass suicide by poison that is presently at Jonestown. I also know that plans are made to kill members who are unwilling to voluntarily commit suicide."

As such exchanges and lawsuits mounted, Jones not only claimed fatherhood (which remained uncertain) but became obsessed with the child and seemed to anticipate Asahara's guruism in seeking to make the little boy a clone. His hair was groomed liked Jones's, he could already spout socialist rhetoric, and he was even encouraged to swear the way Jones had as a child. For Jones, the child became a kind of sacred child, a crucial megalomanic component embodying Jones's and the Temple's existence in the present as well as the future.

Like Asahara, Jones responded to public criticism with aggressive attacks on his detractors. But in his case the underlying fear was more evident. He feared the Treasury Department, the FBI, the news media, defectors, families of cult members and, above all, disloyalty from within. Jones's anxiety was suffused with images of annihilation. In one only semicoherent Jonestown rant, he spoke angrily to a follower who had annoyed him: "You people just tear me apart. . . . You're killing your leader [which even] the CIA hasn't been able to do." When Congressman Ryan arrived in Jonestown and insisted that sixteen people who wanted to defect be permitted to accompany him back to the

United States, Jones became distraught, declaring, "I have failed" and "All is lost." His lawyers tried to tell him that he should let the small number of defectors go without further incident, that most of his community of nearly a thousand would still remain intact. But Jones experienced the defections as the death of the Temple and of the self. He reacted with violence. The airport killings, carried out by his most trusted security men, the "Red Brigade," were initiated either by his order or at least with his approval.

Like Asahara's, Jones's war with the external world was accompanied by increasingly destructive demands on his own group as the guru followed the treacherous path from hero to despot. Like Asahara, Jones had always been inclined toward dictatorial rule, but in a way that included a measure of effectiveness in the outside world and of communal nurturing and enhancement. Now his rule became tyrannical and hermetic, increasingly dissociated from both the outer world and the faltering community itself. This kind of process has been called "the end of charisma," which in our terms would mean a loss of the guru's capacity to inspire in his disciples intense life-power and an exuberant sense of immortality. Jones did retain some of that capacity, but in a very confused and diminished form, which is why the "revolutionary suicide" required an eerie combination of persuasion, coercion, and medicalized murder.

"The Greatest Decision in History"

Revolutionary suicide became, for Jones, the only means of asserting life-power. He took the term from Huey Newton, the Black Panther leader, who meant by it a form of revolutionary martyrdom, of constant struggle on behalf of the revolution even in the knowledge of one's doom. Jones literalized the concept by equating actual collective suicide with glorious revolutionary resistance. In that way he brought to both the concept and the act the three elements generally present in suicide of any kind: a sense of entrapment and despair, a "suicide construct," or long-standing image of the possibility of killing oneself, and a quest for an unbound or immortalizing "future."

On New Year's Day 1976, seventeen months before he left the United States, Jones staged his first "rehearsal" by serving his "planning commission" wine on what seemed to be a festive occasion, then announcing that it contained a poison that would kill them within forty-five minutes and that by their deaths they would be protesting the world's inhumanity. After a few of Jones's "plants" dramatically keeled over, Jones revealed the hoax as a test of loyalty and an opportunity for reflection on the issue. From Newton's writings and through exchanges like this, Jones fashioned a suicide ideology in which communal self-annihilation would be both resistance to persecution and a claim to immortality.

In Jonestown such suicide rehearsals became part of what Jones called "White Nights," ritualized expressions of crisis during which he would hold forth at length on the threat posed by the Temple's enemies and the liberating possibilities of collective suicide. Then a liquid said to contain poison would be distributed for disciples to drink. As a religious scholar, David Chidester, writes, White Nights "immediately escalated every crisis to the point of death." Since these were called suicide rehearsals, many must have realized that there was no actual poison in the liquid. But for Jones, the sequence of crisis and rehearsal served the function of further instilling and regularizing suicide theology.

"Ever since as a child I saw a dog die, I wanted to commit suicide," Jones is quoted as saying. The combination of an early suicide construct and youthful violent thoughts and acts meant that for him the image of killing himself was never very far from one of harming or killing others. Because he had been so long preoccupied with death and dying, he could later disagree with Paul's biblical view of death as God's enemy and declare, "Death is a blessed friend to me." Indeed, his personal myth was that he remained alive only for altruistic purposes, only because he was needed by others. ("Little animals I stayed alive for . . . later my mom needed me . . . then always blacks.") While his nurturing capacity might actually have helped him stave off suicide, Jones's suicide construct was from its beginnings infused with pain, anger, and violence—and so could readily combine with his evolving paranoia and megalomania. Jones revealed the unbounded grandiosity of his decision for collective suicide when he replied condescendingly to his wife's request that he hold back: "My good wife, if you don't get control of your emotions, you can destroy the greatest decision in history." At various times he equated his suicide plan for his cult with that of the thousand Jewish zealots who killed themselves when besieged at Masada in A.D. 73, with the resistance of the Jews in the Warsaw ghetto, and with the martyrdom of heroes of the Russian and Chinese Revolutions and the American civil rights movement. He had only stayed alive this long, he told his followers in Jonestown, "to save you from jails, torture, concentration camps, [and] a nuclear war [in] which your skin will roll off your backs, your eyeballs will be burned out."

One senses in the chaos of Jonestown profound similarities between Jones and Asahara. Although their large-scale violence went in opposite directions (self-destruction versus world destruction), each mobilized megalomanic energies in a way that fueled and sacralized the killing process. Each offered a theology—revolutionary suicide or poa—that turned killing into something other than self-murder or murder, that made killing an act of healing and redemption. Revolutionary suicide promised Jones's disciples what I have called "revolutionary immortality," a state in this case achievable only through death, whether by one's own hand or someone else's.

Jones united guru and followers in a status that was both underclass and elite. White and black, they all became "niggers" because cruelly persecuted. His mass suicide was to be an egalitarian event: "When we die around here, we're all going to get the same treatment." At the same time, his followers were incorporated into his megalomania, rendered a "chosen people, the avant garde, the front line, the first ranks of the revolution" and "a people upon whom the ends of the world have come." Their mission was more sacred than Jesus', the occasion of their deaths "a greater day than the day of Nazareth." Jones had so incorporated the members of the community into his personal apocalyptic vision that their collective suicide would itself be the desired world-ending event, a prelude to universal spiritual and political bliss. His manipulations during the White Nights could be understood as efforts to motivate his followers to merge with him in this solipsistic drama.

In the meantime, Jones proceeded with the detailed planning necessary to force his particular Armageddon. He and high-ranking followers not only stockpiled the cyanide compound, tranquilizers, and sedatives to be used—receiving a final delivery of the cyanide a little more than a week before the suicide-murder took place—but engaged in the extensive organization needed to carry his plan out. The Peoples Temple in Jonestown had a medical doctor, Larry Schacht, and a number of nurses among its members. Schacht was apparently responsible for creating the formula and overseeing the mixing of the poison, which was administered by mouth or injection by nurses and others considered part of the "medical staff," who undoubtedly had to undergo some preparation for their part in what was to be an elaborate event. Since white members of the cult had more of the requisite medical skills, killing in Jonestown meant whites killing blacks (or at least guiding their self-murder), with black guards equipped with guns and crossbows providing "armed security" and making it clear to all that no one was permitted to leave or to opt for life. As in Aum, the plunge into violence was further energized by the active involvement of the leadership around the guru—in Jones's case mostly women—whether through their ideological enthusiasm and loyalty to Jones or their despair about their leader and the cult or because, as Stephan Jones, who survived by being away from Jonestown, put it, they "drove his madness" by their "acquiescence to his bullshit."

The Final White Night

On September 10, 1978, sobbing as he spoke by radio from Jonestown to supporters in San Francisco, Jones pleaded, "For God's sake, find some country that will give us asylum. . . . For God's sake, we're tired. . . . We're tired. We're tired." There is no reason to doubt the despair behind the words—his and his group's energy, the central feature of any guruist community, was fading.

Jones's physical state was very much part of the equation. At various times, he had complained of heart attacks, diabetes, and lung cancer, among other diseases, and, like Asahara, often declared himself close to death. His autopsy revealed none of these conditions. Jones resembled Asahara in manipulating his followers by claiming nonexistent illnesses, but largely because of his addictions, he was physically sicker than the Japanese guru. He had persistent respiratory symptoms, phases of extreme weight gain and loss, along with slurred speech, fatigue, insomnia, fugue states, possible delusions, and the worsening paranoia and megalomania already noted. Certainly his own fear of illness, decline, and death—of the demise of his self as well as that of the cult that was so much an extension of his self—helped trigger the final killing frenzy. As early as May 1978, during one of his White Nights—many of which were recorded and thus provide an extraordinary body of evidence on the violent collapse of a cult—partly drunk, he stated that all of Jonestown could "step out of life easily," and he spoke despairingly of "the last white, goddam miserable, motherfucking, son of a bitchin' night." He was saying, in effect, that he felt so inwardly dead, so psychically numbed that he had ceased to be capable of imagining further life. He would later say that he died on that night, that while his body painfully lived on, his will and capacity to convey his goodness to his people had ceased to live.

Such unyielding expressions of despair, John Hall tells us, indicated that his suicidal project "emerged as a proposed collective penance for . . . failure"—that is, "failure of the group to succeed with its members and . . . to endure within the wider society." This kind of penance would suggest Jones's susceptibility to a sense of guilt toward those he led or deceived. Guilt and despair were also present in his declaration that "it is much easier to die for [your people] than to live for them." Several times, in fact, Jones went so far as to make death his transcendent sexual object. In February 1976, he declared, "The last orgasm I'd like to have is death, if I could take you all with me." During a White Night two years later, he said, "The only fuck I want right now is the orgasm of the great fuck in the grave." (In this mobilization of sexual energy on behalf of an immortalizing suicide, Jones resembled not so much Asahara as another Japanese lover of death, the writer Yukio Mishima.)

In a rambling monologue on the last White Night, the one that turned out not to be a rehearsal, Jones made clear that the killing project was to encompass everyone in the community. It was a troubled pep-talk for joining the project but also a confused apologia for carrying it out. Jones emphasized the painlessness of the "medical" arrangements, demanded speed and efficiency, and repeatedly made uncomfortable references to the children's being killed.

In his first few recorded sentences, he says mournfully, "I don't think it is what we want to do with our babies—I don't think that's what we had in mind to do with our babies." But soon he is affirming the need to kill them: "We had better not have any of our children left when it's over because they'll parachute in here on us." The children, he warns, will be "butchered" if that happens. He assures the group that he will treat his "child god," John Stoen, no differently from the rest: "Do you think I'd put John's life above others?" Later, probably reacting to parents' unwillingness to be separated from their children (who are to be killed first), he concedes that anyone "has a right to go with their child. I think it's humane." But Jones becomes upset, apparently because many of the young victims are frightened and some are crying: "Can't some people assure these children of the relaxation of stepping over to the next plane?" At some psychological level Jones and a number of others seem to sense that killing children who care little about "revolutionary suicide" threatens to morally undermine the project.

Although cyanide is hardly a therapeutic medication, the killing process was almost entirely medicalized. The directions of a woman leader serving as a nurse reveal a dramatic shift from exhortation to lethal action: "You have to move and the people that are standing there in the aisles, go stand in the radio room yard. . . . There's nothing to worry about. Everybody keep calm and try to keep your children calm. And all those children that need help, let the little children in and reassure them. They're not crying from pain. It's just a little bitter-tasting."

At various points Jones, in less focused terms, urges quicker distribution of the poison: "Please get us some medication. It's simple. . . . There's no convulsions with it. . . . Just, please get it. Before it's too late." He demands again and again that everyone speed up the process: "Get movin', get movin'. . . . Let's be done with it." He could be overseeing, with particular concern about allaying children's fears, an urgent mass inoculation for the prevention or cure of disease. In that sense, the process resembled the Nazi reversal of healing and killing and presaged Aum's similar reversal.

The transcript makes clear that there was resistance to the

orchestrated dying and killing. A sixty-year-old black woman named Christine Miller, having raised objections to collective suicide on previous White Nights, can be heard arguing that the group should not die but seek sanctuary in Russia. When Jones declares that this is no longer possible and that his is the only way, she courageously insists, "Well, I don't see it like that. I mean I feel like . . . as long as there's life there's hope." Jones then calls forth his omnipotent guruism: "I'm going to tell you, Christine, without me, life has no meaning. I'm the best thing you'll ever have," and reaffirms the revolutionary nature of their act. Still, Miller will not be deterred. "I said I'm not ready to die," she replies and invokes the children: "I look about at the babies and I think they deserve to live—you know?" In further exchanges she asserts her right to speak and everyone's "right to our own destiny as individuals." An influential black cult member, Jim McElvane, intervenes, baldly reiterating the ultimate guruistic principle: followers must dissolve their sense of self into that of the guru. "Christine," he says, "you're only standing here because he was here in the first place. So I don't know what you're talking about, having an individual life." When Miller speaks up once more, Jones again responds, initially with an annoyed expression of guruism—"How can you tell the leader what to do if you live?"—then with an assertion of loving concern for her existence: "Your life is precious to me. It's as precious as John's . . . and I've weighed it against all evidence." She replies, "That's all I've got to say," and is not heard from again on the tape. Her body was found with the rest.

Another woman seems incredulous: "Are we gonna die? . . . You mean you want us to die?" Others continue to invoke the children. The resistance might have gone further without the emotionally powerful testimony of a male loyalist, delivered with tears: "We're all ready to go. If you tell us we have to give our lives now, we're ready— all the rest of the sisters and brothers are with me." But neither he nor Jones can stop the protest of parents and children. Jones feels the need a number of times to address both directly: "Look, children, it's just something to put you to rest." And "Oh God. Mother, mother, mother, mother, mother, please. Mother, please, please, please. . . . Don't do this. Lay down your life with your child. But don't do this." And "Keep—keep your emotions down. . . . Children, it will not hurt . . . if you'll be quiet." He insists that parents deceive their children: "If you quit telling them they're dying, if you adults would stop some of this nonsense. Adults, adults, adults. . . . I call on you to quit exciting your children when all they're doing is going to a quiet rest." Jones is clearly troubled, but then plays a communal trump card: "Are we black, proud, and socialist or what are we?" Yet he still at one point has to clap his hands for attention and admonish the children and probably the adults, too: "Stop this, stop this, stop this. Stop this crying all of you."

To overcome the resistance and maintain his control, Jones asserts his guruist authority, relying on compelling personal statements by loyalists reinforcing that omnipotent authority and on efficient work by the medical and security personnel overseeing the dying and the killing. Even as Jones blames the mass suicide on the "betrayal" of defectors, notably Timothy Stoen, John's father, he acknowledges his own prior impulse toward it: "He has done the thing we wanted to. Have us destroyed." And he expresses paranoid rage along with vengeful joy on learning that Congressman Ryan had been "murdered" (his word): "What a legacy! . . . Red Brigade showed them justice."

Jones brings forth his despair and spiritual fatigue as active components in the self-destructive dynamic. He repeatedly seeks to make contact with such feelings in his followers with statements like, "Death is not a fearful thing. It's living that's cursed" and "Death is a million times preferable to ten more days of life." He paraphrases Saint Paul: "I've been born out of due season, just like we all are—and the best testimony we can make is to leave this goddamn world." He asserts a basic view of death as dominating all life: "It's far, far harder to have to walk through every day, die slowly—and from the time you're a child 'til the time you get gray, you're dying." He also speaks in more immediate terms, groaning and slurring his words: "I tried so very, very hard." He finds some responses of the kind he wants, including that of a woman who calls upon people to be "happy about this," adding, "I was just thinking about Jim Jones. He just has suffered and suffered. . . . I wish you would not cry. . . . I had a beautiful life."

Jones's grandiosity expresses itself in Christ-like claims: "I've laid down my life, practically. I've practically died every day to give you peace." One man replies in kind. "And I'd just like to thank Dad for giving us life, and also death," he says, ending his statement with a somewhat confused and ambiguous comment: "So I would like to thank Dad for the opportunity for letting Jonestown be not what it could be but what Jonestown is."

The term *revolutionary suicide* comes up only infrequently, four times in the entire transcript. While it was central to Jones's vision, he seems to sense that his followers require more direct language about his and their feelings if his suicide project is to succeed. And he himself is clearly struggling with the event and the scene before him—people taking poison and dying within minutes, people being injected with poison, people resisting the poison and resisting their deaths, children sensing what was happening and crying bitterly—all of which leads him to use emotion-drenched words. But he does declare early, "We're not committing suicide. It's a revolutionary act." Later he reemphasizes the point, insisting, "This is not a self-destructive suicide." Yet one has to wonder whether he and at least some of his followers feared that it was. Certainly, his last recorded sentence has a defensive, even plaintive tone: "We didn't commit suicide, we committed an act of revolutionary suicide protesting the conditions of an inhumane world."

Suicide, Genocide, and Omnicide

Even the most megalomanic mind is constrained by what exists and has existed in the world. Medicalized killing was the method most available to Jim Jones as he imagined forcing his kind of Armageddon. His impulse was a world-ending one, and he succeeded in obliterating his world, if not the world, for he and his Temple leadership were acting on a genocidal impulse. They wanted every human being in Jonestown killed.

To be sure, a considerable number of his followers cooperated by embracing his suicide theology, his version of *poa*, and by expressing in the most total way possible, through their own self-obliteration, their willingness to merge with the guru in death as in life. But those driving the event, notably Jones, wanted no one left alive, willing or not. They could perceive themselves as immortalizing their community in death only in its totality.

The term *genocide* applies because a whole, even if small, group, as defined by its religious and political beliefs, was to be destroyed. The fact that the killing was carried out by the group's own leadership suggests the term *self-genocide*. Whichever it is called, the act lacked omnicidal ambition only because Jones's imagination could not encompass the thought that the world-ending weapons in the possession of the United States and the Soviet Union in 1978 might also fall into his hands. It tells us a great deal about the swift course of our history since Jonestown—and about the equally swift expansion, as well as descent, of the murderous imagination—that such a thought, too far-fetched even to be a fantasy for Jones, is now alive and operative in our world.

In the face of what was perceived as a threat to the existence of the Peoples Temple, its act of dying and killing was also its effort at survival. By a sacrificial offering to the god of revolution, Jones sought to have his and the group's name live forever, but even this claim to revolutionary immortality was mired in confusion. Jones's paranoia and megalomania, as well as his long-standing suicide construct, caused him to prod and coerce those followers who, despite having largely merged with the guru, resisted his vision of dying to survive. The genocidal dimension of the act—the insistence that everyone had to die or be killed—was meant to erase all confusion and despair, and thereby, paradoxically, to ensure revolutionary survival.

Aum differed most obviously in seeking its survival through the violent purification of the world. Its theology, along with Asahara's version of paranoia and megalomania, drove it to unlimited—that is, totalized—external violence. Aum's requirements for its survival were omnicidal. But since a part of Asahara undoubtedly sensed that the violence unleashed would destroy Aum as well, we may say that Aum, too, was in some degree collectively suicidal. What determines whether a group seeks to destroy itself or to destroy the world has to do with its basic ideological impulse and the psychology of the guru in relation to that impulse. But once a group becomes committed to forcing the end, its violence can become external or suicidal or, more likely, some combination of both. Whatever their differences, there is a chilling similarity between Jim Jones and his cult and Shōkō Asahara and his. A reconsideration of Jones through a post-Aum prism leaves us with a sense that there has already been an Asahara-like figure on our American landscape. It leaves us, too, with a question: What would Jim Jones have done in millennial America had his totalizing mind had access to omnicidal possibilities?

13 | Inward Aum?

In March 1997, Americans were shocked to learn of the discovery of thirty-nine bodies in a mansion in Rancho Sante Fe, outside San Diego, the result of the group suicide of a cult known as Heaven's Gate, the largest mass suicide ever to occur in the United States. Just ten days earlier I had returned from Japan, where I had been interviewing former members of Aum Shinrikyō. The San Diego mass suicide and Aum's mass murder reverberated together in my mind.

In a number of ways the two groups could not have been more different. Heaven's Gate had been a gentle group from the time of its formation in the mid-1970s. Instead of inhabiting fixed facilities for coercive mystical practices and worldly weapons making, Heaven's Gate had been a wandering cult known mostly for its claim that its members would someday be picked up by UFOs and transported to heavenly realms. Far from aggressively attacking the world, it had preached and practiced an amiable form of nonviolence.

Indeed, so gentle, meticulous, and mutually cooperative had the group been in its last act that its collective suicide could almost have been considered a work of art. All the dead had short haircuts, were dressed in similar black tunics, slacks, and Nike running shoes, and wore arm patches bearing the words *Heaven's Gate* and *Away Team*. Each had been provided with a small carrying bag, a five-dollar bill, and a roll of quarters. Those who wore eyeglasses had placed them neatly at their sides. All but two were draped in purple shrouds. The two not so draped represented the last of four orchestrated shifts; the first shift consumed phenobarbital in a dessert of pudding or applesauce, as well as vodka, then put plastic bags over their heads; the second shift cleaned up their mess, placed shrouds over them, then consumed their own phenobarbital and vodka and were in turn cleaned up and shrouded by a third shift. The fourth and final shift of two had no one to place shrouds over them. The whole process of collective dying seemed so calm, good-natured, and purposeful that one might not associate it with violence, or even with death. Indeed the group itself claimed that its members were not dying at all, merely transitioning to the "Next Level." There was no hint of resistance as there had been at Jonestown or of the mayhem of the Tokyo sarin killings.

Killing oneself is very different from killing others, and there is an enormous moral gap between Aum's efforts to destroy the world and Heaven's Gate's hermetic self-immolation. Yet however strongly one may uphold a person's right to take his or her own life, one must recognize the violence of that act and the force of the impulses that bring it about. Suicide can have many different meanings, but it always involves, as the eminent American psychiatrist Karl Menninger put it, "acute, generalized, total self-destruction." The "cide" in suicide is associated with killing and murder (homicide, regicide, genocide, insecticide), and we should not be surprised to discover that, as in Jim Jones, suicidal and homicidal impulses often coexist. In the collective suicides of Peoples Temple and of another cultic group, the Solar Temple, in Switzerland and Canada in the 1990s, there were clear-cut murders as well.

Had the members of Heaven's Gate put revolvers to their heads and blown their brains out, few would have questioned the violence of their act. But I would contend that true violence lies in the killing, in the self-murder, whatever the method. There is a parallel here to efforts to render execution by the state more gentle, more "humane." Yet whether accomplished by guillotine, firing squad, hanging, electric chair, gas chamber, lethal injection, or some as yet undiscovered method, it remains a violent act, a form of killing.

What made Heaven's Gate so deceptive a phenomenon was the way it combined a soft external patina with an intense expression of the violent urges of our historical moment. Once more we are faced with a totalistic impulse to collude in the world's annihilation. As we shall see, the self-directed nature of the destructiveness and the willingness of its perpetrator-victims to die did much to blur awareness of the violence not only of the immediate act but also of the apocalyptic, world-ending vision that lay behind it.

Heaven's Gate shared with Aum an impulse toward martyrdom but preferred to achieve that state by provoking violence in others. As early as 1975, Marshall Herff Applewhite, its guru, was said to have asked his disciples whether they would be "willing to bear arms for this cause," explaining that instead of killing others, "we mean to incite people to kill us." At the time, Applewhite saw himself and Bonnie Lu Nettles (with whom he founded the cult) as the "two witnesses" described in that now-familiar source the Book of Revelation, who are destined to be killed and then resurrected. Not long before the mass suicide, the cult did purchase a few rifles and handguns, but its members were so uncomfortable with the weapons that they were left in storage.

In the castrations of eight men belonging to the group, including Applewhite, Heaven's Gate initiated its own violence toward itself. These were both physical assaults on the body and metaphorical murders of sexuality or life-power. Some commentators have minimized the significance of these castrations, pointing to the act's place in the Christian tradition (usually mentioning Origen, a third-century ascetic who castrated himself in his zeal for purity). But even in the distant past, castration was considered an extreme act. Its violence seems still greater in the context of twentieth-century America, so much so that the cult members seeking it had great difficulty finding surgeons who would perform the operation.

Gurusim—Gentle but Total

Marshall Applewhite's gurusim was considerably softer than Shōkō Asahara's yet equally controlling, his paranoia and megalomania gentler but ever present. Applewhite engaged in what could be called tandem gurusim, and before that was himself something of a disciple. Bonnie Lu Nettles, his guru partner from their meeting in 1972 until her death at the age of fifty-eight in 1985, was a nurse and a born-again Baptist deeply involved in astrology, metaphysics, and other forms of the occult. Five years older than Applewhite, bright and self-assured, she was his and the evolving cult's source of spiritual wisdom, with Applewhite serving as a charismatic articulator of their combined formulations. Quite likely, her maternal support and spiritual guidance enabled Applewhite to remain psychologically functional, for he had previously experienced a psychological breakdown related to deep sexual confusion. He had led a double life as a married heterosexual and a homosexual who had affairs with students at the universities where he taught music and theater. His emotional problems forced him to leave his university job in 1970; he was described as odd in his behavior and almost incoherent at the time, suggesting that he may have been at the edge of psychosis. In this he resembled Asahara, but he differed from the Japanese guru in his prior successes as a singer, actor, teacher of music, and musical director at various universities and cultural institutions. The son of a minister, Applewhite had also spent several years in seminar training.

By the time of his break, following the death of his father a year earlier, Applewhite had begun to immerse himself in the teachings of mystics, as well as in the science fiction writings of Robert Heinlein and Arthur Clarke, and was coming to believe that UFOs represented what people had once thought of as angels. Hospitalized for a heart condition, he had also had, according to his sister, a near-death experience. As with Asahara (and many other gurus), his decisive religious vision came at a moment when he felt himself to be falling apart. He experienced a "presence" that brought him "all the knowledge of where the human race had come from and where it was going." That vision, as told to Nettles, enabled her to identify him as the special spiritual being fortune-tellers had predicted she would encounter.

His psychological breakdown, near-death experience, and a possible psychiatric hospitalization all suggest a survivor-like state in which Applewhite felt himself to have touched death and remained alive. People in that state often take on a "survivor mission" through which they find meaning in their death encounter and seek to influence others in the direction of that meaning. Nettles played a central role in this process, insisting God had kept him alive for the purpose of leading others. For thirteen years Applewhite and Nettles were inseparable, living chastely and sharing visions and fantasies, their psyches so merged that Applewhite could see himself as a character in a novel Nettles had written about a man who dies and makes his way to heaven. Their individual grandiosity merged into a joint sense of prophetic mission and special destiny as the two witnesses in Revelation.

Like Asahara, Applewhite ran into trouble with the law, in his case conviction and imprisonment for car theft. He had simply driven off with a rental car, justifying his behavior by claiming God's authorization and quoting a passage in Revelation, "The Lord will be as a thief in the night." Time in jail gave him an opportunity to write his first manifesto, in which he suggested the idea that "The Two" (he and Nettles) represented a contemporary Jesus and, after being killed, would be taken off in a UFO—their "cloud of light"—for their resurrection. This doctrine was then preached by Applewhite—he was always the main speaker—at meetings in different parts of the country that he and Nettles began to organize, meetings that yielded them their first disciples. Their trademark became their claim of a special connection to UFOs and the related idea of heaven as a physical place to which a UFO could take one.

Applewhite and Nettles were drawn to occult phenomena and attracted disciples similarly inclined. Robert Balch, a sociologist who studied the cult in its early days, recounts that most who joined were spiritual seekers "who shared a worldview where reincarnation, lost continents, flying saucers, and psychic phenomena were taken for granted." In such interests, Heaven's Gate overlapped considerably with Aum, as it did in its affinity for Eastern karma-related thought and the wisdom of *Jonathan Livingston Seagull*. As with Asahara, the apocalyptic ideas of Applewhite and Nettles reinforced their incipient paranoia, in their case further fed by the "assassination" they both feared and sought. Unlike Aum, however, the cult chose to "withdraw into the wilderness." For periods of time the two gurus would even disappear, leaving the other members to split into small groups heading in various directions to spread their message. What the cult's official history refers to as a seventeen-year spiritual seclusion was actually a restless, intense, often confused, peripatetic spiritual journey on the part of gurus and disciples.

Being American, Heaven's Gate spoke of standards of mental health: Nettles once defended the group by declaring that, were he then alive, Jesus "would be branded a fanatic and nut." As Applewhite acknowledged to their disciples, "By social, psychiatric, medical, and religious standards we and you have long since lost our sanity." An early follower remembered telling Applewhite, "I know you're not con artists. That means, either you're who you say you are or you're absolutely mad," to which Applewhite responded, "That's right, Dick. Which do you think we are?" The exchange is reminiscent of Asahara's double sense of himself as a guru and, to a degree, a con man. We may assume that Applewhite also had an alternate sense of himself as a madman or imposter, which he covered over with his functional gurusim.

The orchestrating of disciples' lives was just as great in Heaven's Gate as in Aum, although Heaven's Gate engaged in more of a systematic group process (without Aum's extreme focus on guru-dispensed individual mystical experience) and stressed self-examination, confession, and "reeducation" in a way that more closely resembled Chinese thought reform. As in Aum, disciples could never quite rid themselves of designated personal deficiencies, which in Heaven's Gate were called "addictions." These included the need for affection, "egotism," sloppiness, and above all sexual desire. There were elaborate rules and listed "procedures" for dealing with "major" and "minor" offenses.

In relation to these rules and to the gurus, there was a seeming informality (one member who left the cult spoke of Applewhite and Nettles as "like parental figures or that cool high school teacher that's not quite your buddy but someone you can talk to"), but their psychological hold on their disciples was no less absolute for that. As another former member put it, "Your punishment was him denying you his approval," which was devastating because disciples had given over their lives to the guru, striving to meet his standard of becoming "a pure vessel." Rejection meant shame and fear, even a sense of nothingness. The more friendly, approachable, voluntary atmosphere of the cult (unlike in Aum, disciples were free to leave) could be said to be an Americanized version of a totalistic community. That style of gurusim, along with its promise of a yearned-for trip to the "Next Level" on a spaceship, held the small community together for fifteen years through all its struggles and losses. False alarms about an arriving spaceship did not diminish but actually increased visionary expectation. In 1975, for instance, Nettles declared that a ship would appear at a certain time and place, and the whole group went out to meet it; when it did not appear, she apologetically spoke of having egg on her face and everyone carried on as usual.

Heaven's Gate functioned during most of its life as more of an outlaw group than did Aum, partly because of its assumption that its noble goals entitled it to skip motel payments or steal cars, but also because of Applewhite's paranoia. Group members used fake names in the outside world, falsifying addresses and job references as well.

Heaven's Gate did not have Aum's obsession with extorting large sums of money from its wealthier disciples; people joining it were expected to leave their possessions behind but were not required to turn over their financial assets (though one member's $300,000 trust fund had a lot to do with the group's survival). In general, Heaven's Gate applied less external pressure to its members. Applewhite seemed focused on the quality rather than quantity of his disciples. He was ready to release people in order to concentrate on those who could most powerfully internalize his message and thereby enable him to carry out his mission. That internalization was methodical and sustained, which is why the group could function for so long and include, among its suicides, people who had been with Applewhite for as long as ten or fifteen years. In comparison, internalization of Asahara's message in Aum was more immediate and coercive, far more likely to be accompanied by violence and danger, and ultimately less sustainable.

One is struck by Heaven's Gate's combination of levity and deadliness. Former members spoke of "a lot of joy" in the group, so that anyone walking in "might find us all laughing." They associated this capacity for fun with Applewhite's "great enthusiasm," "childlike innocence," and "laid-back" quality—all of a very different order from Asahara's usual stance of stern, humorless dignity. But this laughing guru could convey his message of self-killing with sufficient power to take with him such unlikely people as a forty-one-year-old rancher and businessman who left behind a wife and six children, and a grandmother of seventy-two who had been with the group for some years. (As her shocked son-in-law put it, "Grandmothers don't run away.") Applewhite could be so compelling because others' needs and expectations were so great. "I think everyone in this class," a disciple said, using one of the group's terms for itself, "wanted something more than this human world had to offer."

In one sense, at least, the gurusim in Heaven's Gate was also more personal: the new names members were given all derived from the original cult names of Applewhite and Nettles, "Do" and "Ti" (notes on the musical scale), but members had a say in choosing their names (as they did not in Aum). Each member's name had a two- or three-letter prefix followed by either "doti" or "ody." (One disciple, for instance, was called "Neody," the "neo" because he "felt new.") The naming process could include an element of punning humor certainly not found in Aum. Beneath the punning, however, Applewhite's pronouncements made clear his control over life and death in the group: "The only way an individual can grow in the Next Level is to learn to be dependent on his Older Member [Applewhite] as that source of unlimited growth and knowledge. So any younger member in good standing forever remains totally dependent upon (and looks to) his Older Member for all things."

Applewhite's megalomania extended to the principle of disciples' not only "bonding" with the guru but being "grafted" to him. The term suggested that there was something in the disciple useful to the guru when joined with and absorbed by him, as opposed to Aum's image of cloning, which rendered the disciple useful only if he made himself into an identical copy of the guru. But the grafting metaphor also suggested that, once joined to the guru, the disciple ceased to exist as an individual entity, while the cloning metaphor implied the possibility of becoming the guru. Yet both were equally expressions of guruistic megalomania, and there were other such expressions Applewhite and Asahara shared. Each, for instance, declared himself to be a version of Jesus and therefore the arbiter of end time, and both envisioned overcoming gravity, Applewhite by means of space travel, which would take one to a point beyond gravity that "seems to be Nirvana."

Like other megalomanic gurus, Applewhite had a somewhat cagey approach to the question of whether he himself was God: "Any time any member of the Next Level is assigned a task to relate to humans directly, since he is of the Kingdom of God, he is rightfully 'God' to them." Here and elsewhere he used quotation marks to highlight his most outlandish claims or to indicate translations of his meanings into more familiar discourse. But those quotation marks also suggested the existence of unspoken doubts, of an unconscious sense of the absurdity or unlikeliness of what he was claiming. Applewhite used a kind of schizoid humor that mocked, probably with only partial intent, his own grandiosity. As with Asahara's very different expressions of megalomania, one gains the impression that there was a significant element of performance on the part of both men, that each was consciously working on a convincing self-presentation as a megalomanic guru.

Like Asahara's (and Jim Jones's), Applewhite's physical and emotional state played an important part in his decision on the apocalyptic event. Just as Asahara told his disciples he was physically ill and likely to die soon, Applewhite told his that his body was "deteriorating." Like Jim Jones, he claimed he had cancer, though an autopsy showed no evidence of it. The only significant finding was coronary arteriosclerosis, a condition consistent with feelings of diminished vitality and a vague sense of ill health. Whether that condition caused Applewhite's fear of death to intensify or whether he feigned ill health to create a greater sense of urgency in his followers remains uncertain. At the very least, he seemed to be experiencing a sense of deep spiritual fatigue after more than two decades of stressful existence: constant travel, evasion of authorities, the loss of his close partner and personal guru, the endless manipulation of needy, sometimes antagonistic followers, constant rejection and ridicule by society, and despair over how little he had accomplished. Like Asahara and Jones (as well as the Mao Zedong of the Cultural Revolution) Applewhite wanted to bring about a transcendent, revitalizing event before (or as) he died.

Whether seen as a clone or a graft, the disciple was under intensifying pressure to merge fully with the guru as the denouement seemed to approach. While Aum spoke of obedience and loyalty, in Heaven's Gate the word was *trust*. As one member wrote in a diary, "Rescue team approaches. Species advancement shedding human bodies requires trust. This is a big item. Do is like a guide. We want to be with Ti and Do only." And in another entry, "For us to shed our vehicles is totally opposite of somebody committing suicide. It's a final act of trust for us. For us, the trust has proven itself." Totalized trust, like Aum's totalized loyalty, meant offering oneself to the guru for *anything*, including collective violence, whether externally or self-directed.

The Next Level

In return for their totalized trust, disciples were given a promise of something beyond present earthly existence. The Peoples Temple offered revolutionary immortality; Aum's vision for its members was that of becoming "new beings" or "new human beings"; Heaven's Gate seemed to go further, envisioning "the shedding of . . . human [or "mammalian"] creature characteristics" as preparation for the "Next Level" (or the "level above human"), which was both spiritual (the "Kingdom of God") and biological (the "next evolutionary Kingdom")—"a literal and physical Heaven," reachable by spaceship for those properly prepared.

Applewhite's religious mythology entailed two-thousand-year-old "soul deposits" from the Kingdom of Heaven that linked him with Jesus and his followers with Jesus' disciples. Convoluted as this spiritual narrative may seem (cultic narratives invariably require elaborate mystification), it was simpler than Asahara's and Aum's narratives of past lives, complex future reincarnations, and multifarious heavenly realms, all ultimately subsumed within a *poa* principle. The gurus were similarly firm, however, in insisting on being the only pathway to, indeed the keeper of, higher levels, and each led his followers into an orchestrated act of violence as the only entry to that more-than-human state.

According to Applewhite's cosmic evolutionary scheme, the two-thousand-year interval between Jesus and himself represented the amount of time it takes for a civilization such as Earth's to decay. The soul, residing in the body, a "temporary container," itself serves only as "the housing or container of the new creature or Next Level fetus which must gradually displace the human element residing in the container" and bring about "an abortion of the human mind." But to get into the Next Level requires a "final act of metamorphosis," a "disconnect," or "separation from the human kingdom . . . [and] from the human physical container or body." Applewhite recognized the difficulty people have in taking such steps because "we are here and most humans are thoroughly 'hooked' to humanity." Invoking his Christianity, Applewhite identified "propagators of sustained faithfulness to mammalian humanism" as the "anti-Christ," while acknowledging that to them "we are, and will be seen as, their anti-Christ."

Applewhite's style of thought here resembles Asahara's in the way it combines dexterity and intelligence with paranoid delusion. Applewhite could, however, bring a certain playfulness to his grandiosity, often reflecting a schizoid silliness (as when he and Nettles spoke of themselves as "Guinea and Pig" because "God has sent us here as an experiment").

Where Aum chose spiritual doctrines that justified killing, Heaven's Gate Next Level theology invoked a Christian prohibition against external violence: "Humans were, from the beginning, given a 'prime directive' NOT TO KILL OTHER HUMANS." Applewhite specifically condemned weaponry: "Weapons designed for killing humans are inexcusable. There are numerous methods of controlling a violent person without the necessity of murder." Yet in doing so, he also expressed an idea resembling *poa*: "The irony is, each killer sends its victims to exactly where they want to go (to their chosen heaven)." The contradiction is only apparent, for while Applewhite was rejecting externally directed violence, he was embracing martyrdom—embracing equally, that is, the principle that "Thou shalt not kill" and "Thou shalt be killed." Where Aum sought the immortality of post-Armageddon perfection by murdering others, Heaven's Gate sought its Next Level immortality by *being* murdered, whether by others or by themselves.

Like Aum, Heaven's Gate hated the present world, viewing it as in its final stage of devolution. One could say that both Aum and Heaven's Gate lived off the anticipated death of everyone but themselves. But where Aum saw the world's defiled occupants as polluted and corrupt, Heaven's Gate's image was that of pernicious or dead foliage: "The weeds have taken over the garden and disturbed its usefulness beyond repair." All was "decay and destruction." Ordinary people who lacked soul deposits from the Next Level were simply "plants" bound to die along with the rest of the foliage as the earth itself was "spaded under." That apocalyptic ecology could also embrace the Book of Revelation, as when Applewhite equated this "Harvest Time" with the "Last Days" and the "Second Coming," declaring, "Those are finally here!" He connected existing violence in the world to the "spading under" of human plants: "Weeds are now getting rid of weeds—from gangwars to nations involved in ethnic cleansing. This is simply a part of the natural recycling process which precedes a restoration of the planet in preparation for another civilization's beginning."

As Aum had its Freemasons and Jews, Heaven's Gate, too, had its source of ultimate evil, the "Luciferians." Sometimes described as members of an evil race of "space aliens," sometimes as "technically advanced humans," the Luciferians were "one-time 'students' of the Kingdom of Heaven—'angels' in the making—who 'flunked out' of the classroom." Like most devil figures, the Luciferians "made deals" with human governments—in their case, to permit them to engage in biological experimentation in return for secret information about space travel and telepathic communication. (Here Applewhite exploited UFO abduction stories as part of his world-ending vision.) Just as for Aum the evil Freemasons were to join defiled humanity in bringing about Armageddon, so the evil Luciferians were to interact with decaying human "plants" at the age's end to "destroy each other."

The raison d'être of Heaven's Gate was its determined search for what it came to call a "Last Exit." In 1994, the original hope for a designated spaceship having faded, Applewhite began to suggest the possibility of a different route: "It may be necessary to take things in our own hands." Astronomers made that task easier in July 1995 when they spotted a comet that came to be named Hale-Bopp. It quickly entered the group's psychological constellation. First, there was an Internet rumor that a photograph showed Hale-Bopp's small trailing shower of light to be none other than a spaceship traveling behind the comet. Second, the comet itself could be viewed as a powerful sign of Earth's imminent destruction, since comets have long been associated with disaster, celestial magic, and messages from a deity. In any event, the time of the cult's collective suicide was made to coincide with the comet's closest approach to Earth in March 1997. Undoubtedly, though, if Hale-Bopp had never appeared the cult would have found another sign, as its continuous struggles and those of its guru were propelling it toward an exit of some kind.

Applewhite evidently encouraged one member to leave the group just prior to its collective suicide because he worked at an entertainment company and wished to tell the group's story on film, a project Applewhite approved of. In other words, however close to dead the planet was, it was apparently viable enough to provide a place for Heaven's Gate's narrative to reverberate. Apart from the would-be filmmaker, the group promoted such reverberations by making a series of presuicide videotapes. In one of them, a young woman conveys the extent to which the guru and his followers shared an overwhelming rejection of life on this earth: "They had a formula of how to get the human kingdom to a level above humans. And I said to myself, 'That's what I want. That's what I've been looking for.' . . . I've been on this planet for thirty-one years, and there's nothing here for me." As relaxed as the people on film seem, the very existence of the videos suggests the possibility that, as at Jonestown, the collective dying was accompanied by a lurking sense of failure to transcend the reality of death as death, along with an urge to live on, still arguing about the world to come.

Dying and Not Dying

For members of Heaven's Gate, suicide did not—could not—mean death. Above all, it could not mean suicide. Rather, it meant privileged survival. As a former member put it, "Suicide isn't the proper term for what they did. . . . It was like . . . going to bed and knowing that they would wake up still alive, but not in that body." Their collective suicide was a means of achieving a place among the immortals. With an Orwellian reversal of meanings, the group had entitled one of its Internet communications, "Our Position against Suicide," suggesting that "the true meaning of 'suicide' is to turn against the Next Level when it is being offered." In other words, the cult members who took barbiturates and vodka were not the suicidal ones—the rest of us were.

The meticulous collective act of suicide and the suicide notes left behind tell us much about the shared mind-set of Heaven's Gate's members. The uniforms, carrying bags, and modest amounts of money on their persons suggest a kind of field trip by a very proper, well-behaved, deindividualized group. All died from a combination of drug suppression and suffocation from the plastic bags. The scene was all the more grotesque for its apparent peacefulness. When a former member was asked about their dress he called it "just a fun kind of uniform, . . . something kind of representative of moving into the New Level, being fresh and clean." One gets a sense of an odd innocence about death—also in its way Orwellian—an ordered pragmatism that took into clear account the mess the dying would nevertheless create, and a certain fastidiousness in the idea of cleaning up after one another, of trying to avoid soiling the "fun kind of uniform" and to remain "fresh" for the arrival. As with the videotapes, one also gets a strong sense of a visual message being left behind.

The video statements were not, as one observer put it, so much suicide notes as part of "suicide press kits" that also included letters, computer discs, and a large number of Internet essays and commentaries. Many individual videotapes express joy at the prospect of entering the Next Level ("We couldn't be happier about what we're about to do"), though not without glimmers of quickly covered-over self-questioning or doubt ("People in the world who thought I'd completely lost my marbles—they're not right. I couldn't have made a better choice"). They also express a sense of the culmination of a spiritual journey. For the group's entire vagabond existence could be seen as a wandering search for the time and place of its self-destruction. Prior to the decision for suicide its members' anticipation of self-destruction had been accompanied by anxiety and confusion. As a former member said, "We didn't know if we were going to be caught by the FBI, or if there was going to be another Waco, or if somebody was going to shoot everybody, or if everybody was going to have to do it themselves."

Once the decision had been made to "leave their vehicles," there was a general sense of relief and the group embarked on excursions for "fun" to *Star Wars* films, UFO events, wild-animal parks, restaurants, and ice-cream parlors. A kind of happy feeling can occur in people who commit suicide for individual rather than cultic reasons: the decision has been made, there is no more need for struggle. For Heaven's Gate, as for Jim Jones and Peoples Temple, a feeling of entrapment and inner death, a long-existing suicide construct, and a quest for an immortalizing future all acted to create mounting psychic pressure. When these three elements combine and reinforce one another, suicide can be pursued fiercely, with much energy directed toward finding the right stage, and once the choice is made, the pressure removed, the last moments of life can seem suddenly filled with vitality and self-assertion.

Members who died in the mass suicide point out on the videotape that the group had, in effect, died to the world. "We all committed suicide when we destroyed our old lives," one observed. Another notes that their bodies have already been deadened, sexually and otherwise: "After twenty or so years of denying your body every sense . . . the body isn't that valuable to you. . . . It becomes just a suit of clothes like they talk about, like a container." Still another views his castration, which he values ("I can't tell you how free that has made me feel"), as a helpful prelude to the mass suicide: "I can't see that this next step that I'm prepared to take, and I'm looking forward to taking, is anything more than a clinical operation."

There was, of course, a clinical aspect to the suicide. Aum and the

Nazis engaged in the medicalized killing of others, Peoples Temple of others and themselves. Heaven's Gate engaged only in the medicalized killing of themselves—that is, in a medicalized form of suicide. Just as Aum and the Nazis, invoking medical principles, viewed those they destroyed as "life unworthy of life," so the members of Heaven's Gate viewed their own lives, or at least their *human* lives.

Like Asahara, Applewhite made a plea for others to follow his salvational plan. Heaven's Gate's use of an elaborately designed Web site reflects its up-to-dateness while the words themselves suggest the concreteness of its final delusion: "During a brief window of time, some may wish to follow us. . . . If you should chose to do this, logically it is preferred that you make this exit somewhere in the area of the West or Southwest of the United States. . . . You must call on the name of Ti and Do to assist you. . . . We suggest that anyone serious about considering this go into their most quiet place and ask, scream with all their being." Here, then, was the cult's call for others to participate in "revolutionary suicide," in its version of *poa*. That message of immortality via suicide—an "extinction transmission," as one writer calls it—was disseminated via the Internet throughout the world.

Cultic groups interested in suicide tend, like Jim Jones, to invoke Masada. Applewhite invoked the event—"a devout Jewish sect" faced with possible murder, rape, and torture deciding "to evacuate their bodies by a more dignified, less agonizing method"—as an example of "*non*suicide" and therefore a model for which his group, also bent on nonsuicide, needed to be "mentally prepared." It is easy to point out that there were no enemy troops surrounding Heaven's Gate, threatening them with death or torture, but psychologically speaking, Applewhite and his disciples felt as though there were. Their particular Masada was the imagined death of the planet.

We have seen that Aum, the Peoples Temple, and Heaven's Gate all acted from elements of despair and a profound sense of threat to the group, that all had a long-standing construct of violence, and that all were embarked on a quest to overcome death literally and achieve immortality. If Aum's construct, from its beginnings, was related to external violence, Heaven's Gate's had a very different emphasis on escaping earthly life, which increasingly meant escaping one's decaying earthly body by destroying it. Each attempted to force the end in a manner consistent with its ideology, its way of interpreting the world, its basis for meaning.

Technofantasy

Polar as the two meaning structures of Aum and Heaven's Gate may look, they were closely related in their reliance on technofantasy and New Age visions for the project of overcoming (or "murdering") death. Heaven's Gate created an elaborately imagined world of UFOs and spaceships. As Asahara embraced science and science fiction to concretize his claims of spiritual transcendence, so Heaven's Gate embraced UFOs. The pattern was there from the start, as Heaven's Gate's first poster made evident in 1975:

UFO'S

Why they are here.

Who they have come for.

When they will leave.

Not a discussion of UFO sightings or phenomena

Two individuals say they were sent from the Level Above Human, and are about to leave the Human Level and literally (physically) return to that next evolutionary level in a spacecraft (UFO) within months!

"The Two" will discuss how the transition from the human level to the next level is accomplished, and when this may be done.

This is not a religious or philosophical organization recruiting membership. However, the information has already prompted many individuals to devote their total energy to the transitional process. If you have ever entertained the idea that there may be a real, PHYSICAL level beyond the Earth's confines, you will want to attend this meeting.

Heaven's Gate appeared on the public scene as one of numerous "UFO cults"—and as part of a more general cultic explosion—in the mid-1970s. As early as 1972, when Applewhite met Nettles, she already felt she was communicating as a psychic with "space broth-ers." UFO-spaceship theology enabled Heaven's Gate to blend the highly technocratic with the loosely spiritual: Jesus' "cloud of light" could be figured as a UFO, "soul deposits" arrived for earthly bodies by means of "staged spacecraft crashes."

Members of Heaven's Gate often spoke of their surroundings using science fiction terminology, much of it derived from old television episodes of *Star Trek* or from the *Star Wars* films. In early encamp-ments, as Robert Balch observes, the parking area was the "docking zone"; there was a "decontamination zone" where one retreated if affected by bad spirits; camps became "star clusters"; and people spoke of a "mothership," "vehicles," "holodecks," "crew members," "boarding passes," "space aliens," and "beaming up." The longing for spaceships to appear spilled over into an imagined spaceship world. When disasters occurred anywhere on earth, disciples would wonder, "Is this the signal? Are they gonna come for us now?" Nei-ther the longing nor the watch ever disappeared. This is why the group organized its day into twelve-minute segments, the idea being that twelve minutes were required for running from wherever one was to a nearby field to board an arriving spaceship. The concepts of space and spaceship enabled members to feel " 'lifted out' of this world—literally."

This transcendent spaceship imagery provided cult members with a sense of moral uniqueness much like that provided to members of Aum by their mystical experiences. Applewhite would sometimes per-mit himself to imagine that this moral uniqueness would translate into vast power over human destiny—thousands of people gathering to join him on the space journey or a UFO landing on the White House lawn, its occupants ordering the president to cooperate with them. These were certainly rather gentle fantasies—especially when com-pared with Aum's violent fantasies of taking over the Diet building or releasing enough sarin to start World War III—but they reveal some-thing of the reach of Applewhite's grandiosity.

That grandiosity and claim of moral uniqueness depended upon a particular kind of involvement with science fiction that, in its psycho-logical sequence, resembled that of Asahara and Aum. There was, first, a deep attraction to its visions of transcending earthly constraints; then, considerable confusion about what was science (and what was technologically possible) and what was fiction; and, finally, the dismissal of any such distinction and the subsuming of a version of science fiction to cultic theology in ways that could reassert the immortalizing, godly claim of that theology.

This radical confusion of realms culminated in the poignant and absurd "Away Team" arm patches Heaven's Gate members were wearing when they killed themselves. Right up until the act, members would earnestly discuss with outsiders details of *Star Trek* and *Star Wars*. A reporter who interviewed some of them remembered conversations about *Star Trek* as "the only time they really brightened up and came alive. They just lit up." Enhancing that fascination and the confusion of realms was the fact that one member who joined in the suicide was the brother of Nichelle Nichols, the actress who played Lieutenant Uhura in the original *Star Trek* series. After the group returned from one of its final film excursions, Applewhite commented, "It's funny how we were talking about space and how we're from space, and only tonight when we went out to the movies to see *Star Wars*, we saw his [Nichols's] vehicle in a book, pictured with—guess who—someone [his sister] from *Star Trek*." In Applewhite's thought system—delusional but relatively stable—his Next Level elders were using *Star Trek* and *Star Wars* to influence special human beings like himself. He could thus tell his disciples that Luke Skywalker, the brave and constantly tested hero of *Star Wars*, represented Do in his struggles against the Luciferians.

Such reality-blurring convolutions became part of a shared delusion, as expressed vividly in the farewell tape of one male member of the cult: "We watch a lot of *Star Trek* and *Star Wars*. . . . To us, it's just like going on a holodeck [the *Star Trek* term for a virtual entertainment area that renders wished-for scenes as reality]. We've been training on a holodeck. . . . Now . . . the game's over. It's time to put into practice what we've learned. We take off the virtual-reality helmet, . . . go back out of the holodeck to reality to be with, you know, the other members on the craft in the heavens." He makes the sequence sound like taking the step from training for military combat to actual combat, where the stakes are ultimate and "the game's over." What he was actually saying was that instead of imitating the *Star Trek* world, he and the others were about to enter and become that world—which, as they understood in part of their minds, required that they kill themselves. The determination expressed undoubtedly served to cover over inner doubts (the "you know" perhaps suggests such doubts) about these reality manipulations. Aum members similarly needed to suppress their misgivings as they proceeded from Armageddon theory to violence.

What drew Heaven's Gate so powerfully to *Star Trek* and *Star Wars*? The *Star Trek* prologue, almost a mantra, declares that the spaceship *Enterprise* and its crew "boldly go where no man has gone before," that they "seek out new life and new civilizations." *Star Trek* thus promises to extend the human experience beyond itself, utilizing a particular mode of late-twentieth-century fantasy transcendence—an unprecedented journey that spans all barriers of time, distance, and strangeness. Both in the TV series and in the *Star Wars* films, we encounter humans from the distant past or future, human and nonhuman societies in crisis, planets threatened by robot weapons or doomsday machines. In both there are strong apocalyptic elements: ever-recurring struggles between absolute good and absolute evil, near-total destruction of societies or worlds, followed by renewal and the continuation of a mission. If the protagonists of *Star Trek* and *Star Wars* have families somewhere, they are generally free of them on our screens, functioning as elite teams that themselves constitute self-created, technologically transcendent families.

The prominence of *Star Trek* and *Star Wars* for Heaven's Gate, like the prominence of Japanese animated space sagas for Aum, suggests the way in which narratives of popular culture not only influence but provide *mentorship* for certain cultic groups. Applewhite and his followers found in them models for their special mode of existence. But the guru mentored by science fiction, like all other gurus, requires followers themselves drawn to the unbounded visions of that genre, so that its boldest imaginings can feel familiar and natural. That happened with both Heaven's Gate and Aum. The fantastic, romanticized narratives of science fiction could mobilize cultic energies for their strangely literal apocalyptic forays.

"Science" and Metamorphosis

Like Aum, Heaven's Gate understood its perspective to be scientific and therapeutic. Members could become eligible to board a spaceship only when they completed their "metamorphosis." They spoke of a "metamorphic classroom" in which they were to learn to overcome human traits and "change . . . over their consciousness and behavior to match that of the distant culture [the Next Level] from whence they had come." As a former member put it, "One of the prime things that they were trying to instill was to relinquish all previous ways of thinking about everything and take on a whole new way of thinking about everything. . . . You can call that brainwashing, but every student was enjoying it." Another former member added, "We wanted our brains washed"—and illustrated his point by his own Heaven's Gate–style suicide two weeks after the collective event.

Although Applewhite and Nettles were gentle, they were demanding and made clear that the process was "not frivolous." Like Asahara, they referred to "reprogramming," which for them included breaking all ties with family, friends, and prior activities and surmounting all human "offenses," especially sexuality. Ridding oneself of this scourge was a central task of one's metamorphosis and was known as "getting control of the vehicle," suggesting a therapeutic goal of a robotlike creature devoid of unruly passion. This vehement attack on sexuality was reminiscent of Aum Shinrikyō's, with the important distinction that Applewhite and Nettles themselves were celibate. But only Heaven's Gate resorted to literal, that is, surgical castration.

Any cultic reeducation process is likely to focus on sexual behavior in order to take hold of its powerful energies—whether to control, suppress, or liberate them. In both Aum and Heaven's Gate, sexual purification was seen as central to achieving a more-than-human state. In both, purification in general constituted much of the therapeutic process. At one point Heaven's Gate members regularly drank a "master cleanser," a mixture of lemonade, cayenne pepper, and maple syrup, to clean out their "vehicles," while Aum patients and disciples swallowed bandages and other items meant to cause vomiting.

Heaven's Gate, like Aum, was fond of computer technology. But as an American cult functioning for two years after Aum's Tokyo sarin attack, it made far more use of the Internet—so much so that some called it an "Internet death cult." It was certainly a pioneer in Web site suicide notes, or, as it preferred to call them, "exit statements." In addition to maintaining its own Web site, it sent out multiple e-mails, including, in September 1996, a message that was unusually revealing of their plans for death and unusually violent in its apocalypticism: "Time to die for God! Whether we like it or not, the Armageddon—the Mother of Holy Wars—has begun, and it will not cease until the plowing under is completed." Heaven's Gate made postings aimed at news groups, undertook recruitment "chats" with prospective members, and explored the Internet in search of UFO sightings. It also created a company for designing Web pages (appropriately called Higher Source Contract Enterprises) to bring in money necessary to the group's function. In its self-promotion, it declared (with unintended irony but with some truth as well) that "Higher Source is very much in tune with the current pulse and future direction of technology."

Also like Aum, Heaven's Gate used technology for its theological purposes. Although those who participated in the collective suicide were probably just beginning to grasp the full reach of the Internet, they amply demonstrated its capacity to provide instantaneous worldwide dissemination of the most amorphous or bizarre ideas. More, that Internet connection may actually have contributed to the suicide decision by enhancing their sense of performing an immortalizing act.

The cult exposed its deepest response to science, however, in its reaction to the reported "spaceship" following in the wake of Hale-Bopp. Having rented a telescope in order to view the spaceship themselves, members returned it rather quickly, complaining that it was useless because "we found the comet, but we can't see anything following it." For them, science (or observation) was acceptable only when it confirmed their theology. For both Aum and Heaven's Gate, science itself became a fantasy to which further fantasy could be attached, a means of bringing fantasy to fantasy on behalf of lethal projects.

Heaven's Gate members were described by some who knew them as "such happy people" and referred to in the media as the "cult next door," while their soft-spoken guru could seem benign and likable, if a bit odd. Some have defended the group's final action on the basis of the individual's right to take his or her own life. Certainly the act is of a different moral order from Aum's brutal killings of designated or random outsiders.

Yet as we have seen, the two cults and their gurus had much in common. After twenty years in the "wilderness," the "benign" Applewhite made his own decision to force the end—of his own journey, of his megalomanic self, and of the small cult of "grafted" followers that had come to constitute his entire world. In destroying that world, he was destroying everything. His verbal violence toward the earth and its human occupants was comparable to Asahara's. But he differed from the Japanese guru in assuming that the earth was destroying itself, so that he needed only to annihilate his tiny group to accomplish his apocalyptic aims—to create a survivor remnant from a planet in the process of self-annihilation. In doing so, moreover, he probably believed that he was enhancing that process. However "small" the act, it was meant to be all-encompassing; however "gentle" the deaths, they were an expression of contemporary world-ending violence.

Heaven's Gate, though technologically visionary, produced its deaths by low-tech means, in this way resembling the Manson Family and Jim Jones's followers rather than Aum. But the three American cults make abundantly clear that over the last thirty years the American landscape has been studded with groups with apocalyptic aims, the urge to force the end, and other aspects we associate with the Aum experience. We have to turn elsewhere in the American landscape, however, for evidence of Aum's dreams of technodestruction through advanced, even world-ending weaponry.

14 | American Apocalypse

What has been described as "the most destructive terrorist act ever committed on American soil" occurred on April 19, 1995. That morning, Timothy McVeigh, with the help of a friend, Terry Nichols, detonated a bomb near the Alfred P. Murrah Federal Building in Oklahoma City that killed 168 people. As far as we know, Timothy McVeigh belonged to no cult, had no particular guru, and followed no specific religion. While his rage and his urge to destroy were clearly extreme, he would otherwise seem to have little to do with Aum Shinrikyō.

Yet he had since his teens been deeply drawn to the elaborate martyrology of what the political scientist Michael Barkun calls "the fringe apocalypticism of the racist right," an American milieu where survivalists, paramilitarists, neo-Nazis, white racist millenarians, and a variety of conspiracy theorists mix. Groups associated with a religion known as Christian Identity, none of which he joined, had provided him with a belligerently antigovernment millenarian subculture. But above all else, he had become enamored not with a single guru or a group but with a single text, *The Turner Diaries,* an apocalyptic neo-Nazi novel that dramatically depicts a white revolution in America that leads to a global nuclear holocaust in which all Jews and non-whites are annihilated. McVeigh so admired the book that he avidly recommended it to his army buddies, sold it at gun shows and other gatherings, and was said to have slept with it under his pillow. With the *Diaries* he had no need for either a cult or a guru in the flesh. The book provided this American with entrée to the equivalent of a radical cultic experience.

"Do We Have to Shed Blood?"

Born in 1968 in upstate New York, Timothy McVeigh grew up in a small-town working-class family. He embraced ideological elements of the far right at a young age. According to a neighbor, he was a survivalist by the time he was fourteen years old, seeking to stockpile food and equipment in preparation for a nuclear attack. By the age of twenty he and a friend had purchased ten acres of land southwest of Buffalo, which he said he planned to make into a survivalist bunker. McVeigh also had long-standing inclinations toward what might be called the "gunism" of American culture and toward a privatized national warrior ethos that had spread, post-Vietnam, in the fertile soil of defeat.

Historically, the gun has had an extraordinary hold on the American psyche. The historian Richard Hofstadter once told me that after a lifetime studying American history what he found most deeply troubling was our country's inability to come to terms with the gun and its connection to the warrior subculture treated in his classic essay "The Paranoid Style in American Politics." In becoming close to a religious object, the gun, I believe, has filled some of the psychological vacuum of America's absent traditional culture. Indeed, the resurgence of paramilitary groups in recent years has been associated with and in reaction to political efforts to impose the mildest kinds of gun control. Today when God appears in a paramilitary setting, he is gun-centered. The manuals of private militias emphasize that "Jesus Christ was not a pacifist," that governments which "abuse citizens or . . . perpetuate evil," not armed citizens who resist such behavior, are engaged in rebellion against God and Jesus, and that "Our God is not a wimp. He's the God of righteousness and wrath."

Not only was McVeigh an early survivalist, but at least from high school graduation on he was obsessed with guns and spent long hours at a firing range. One of his first jobs was with an armored-car company, where he was described as "looking like Rambo" when he came to work. In 1989 he joined the army, loved soldiering more than most, and was good at it. In 1990 his unit was sent to fight in the Persian Gulf, where as part of a tank crew he was involved in a grotesque cleanup operation after the hundred-hour ground war. Huge snow-plows were attached to American tanks to remove Iraqi bodies by burying them, alive or dead, in the enemy's own trenches; McVeigh's task was to shoot any Iraqis running from those trenches. He once boasted of blowing off an Iraqi soldier's head with his cannon at 1,100 meters. Such experiences can lead to intense survivor conflicts in which self-condemnation is staved off by psychic numbing and aggressive defense of the act of killing. McVeigh's death immersion during the Gulf War undoubtedly was brutalizing and numbing, yet it also seems to have created a hunger for meaning and transcendence. He felt, as the historian Charles Strozier suggests, like a survivor in search of ennobling experience.

McVeigh was considered an excellent soldier but was observed to be unusually racist and increasingly obsessed with nuclear disaster, Communist attack, and his ever-growing collection of guns, which were "all ready to go all the time." When, after the Gulf War, he tried to enter what could be called the paramilitary within the military—the Special Forces or Green Berets—he lasted just two days in the preliminary qualification program. He may have been rejected because of the results of psychological testing, possibly because of his racism. He claimed it was just a matter of bad blisters from new boots. We have to assume that his failure was an enormous blow to him. He was described as depressed when he returned to his unit and, contrary to his earlier intent, did not reenlist. He surely experienced the failure as a negation of his manhood, which in turn could have caused him to compensate by greatly intensifying his already strong paramilitary inclinations. An unstable person with paranoid tendencies is particularly prone to use violence and killing in response to blows to masculine pride, which can be experienced as death anxiety.

Certainly, he gave evidence of a fiercely antigovernment stance in letters he wrote to a newspaper in early 1992 bemoaning America's sense of decline and closing angrily: "Do we have to shed blood to reform the current system? I hope it doesn't come to that! But it might." He also attended a number of militia meetings; at the same time he was more and more influenced by *The Turner Diaries*. In the end, he found the militias he visited too tame and plunged instead into "small cell" violence of a sort increasingly legitimated by far-right doctrine. By then McVeigh had in his own mind become a revolutionary, "a warrior on the move," probably seeing himself as the hero of his own version of *The Turner Diaries* and a potential movement martyr. His blowing up of a government building, he undoubtedly believed, would initiate a violent process whose "end result," in Strozier's words, "would be rebirth, redemption, hope, freedom, indeed a New Age."

Martyrology reverberates powerfully through the extreme right. Martyrs have been drawn from movement people who died for the cause (however defined), people outside the movement killed by representatives of the American government, and members of historically significant groups whose dates of death form the developing martyr calendar of the far right. Such martyrs now include Robert Mathews, a fellow admirer of *The Turner Diaries* who formed an anti-Semitic, white racist group called the Order, committed robberies, and killed people before himself being gunned down by the FBI; Gordon Kahl, a Christian Identity member who killed two federal marshals in North Dakota before he was killed by local authorities in Arkansas; the family of Randy Weaver, an Identity member whose wife and fourteen-year-old son were shot and killed by federal marshals during a siege of their home in Ruby Ridge, Idaho, in 1992; and the Branch Davidians, an armed but not violent small apocalyptic religious sect led by a guru, David Koresh, many of whom were killed by FBI and BATF (Bureau of Alcohol, Tobacco, and Firearms) agents in a tragically ill-advised assault after a long siege in Waco, Texas, in 1993. The far right also created an anniversary-centered confluence of martyrs. The date of the Oklahoma City bombing, April 19, for instance, was already considered a sacred martyr's date. On that day two years earlier, the BATF had stormed the Mount Carmel compound of the Branch Davidians. On the very same day as the Oklahoma City bombing, Richard Snell, a leading figure in a number of far-right groups, was to be executed for the killing of a black state trooper during a routine traffic stop and of a pawnbroker he mistakenly thought to be Jewish. Various historical occurrences have been imaginatively added to that sacred date: on April 19, 1775, the minutemen (or "militiamen") rallied at Lexington to stop British troops sent to disarm the colonists; on April 21, 1836, the Battle of San Jacinto took place (the twenty-first is considered close enough); on April 19, 1943, "Warsaw burned," that is, the Nazis destroyed the Warsaw ghetto; and on April 19, 1992, federal marshals attempted to raid the Randy Weaver home (though the killings occurred two months later).

The specific April 19 event that galvanized the far right and was pivotal for McVeigh was the assault on the Branch Davidians, in which seventy-four were killed. McVeigh made a pilgrimage to Mount Carmel and clearly timed the Oklahoma bombing to commemorate its second anniversary. He even had the date of the attack as the issue date on the forged driver's license in his possession when he was arrested.

Revolutionary movements are prone to invoke martyrology out of strong conviction and out of an awareness of its manipulative value for the cause. Both motivations were present in the Nazis' embrace of "the fallen" of World War I as martyrs to nation and race, as they were in Asahara and Aum's claim that the guru, like Christ, was being persecuted and that attacks by his enemies had brought him close to death. Martyrdom can become contagious: survivors of martyrs may seek their own form of martyrdom as a means of transcending their death-centered survivor conflicts and achieving "authenticity" and ultimate meaning. Within the far right such contagion and identification with martyrs could result in violent missions in which the probability was high that the perpetrators themselves would be killed, injured, or captured. Timothy McVeigh clearly made himself into a survivor of Waco and Ruby Ridge (which he may also have visited), probably seeing his bombing as revenge for them and part of an ennobling survivor mission in which he would be immortalized by joining the ranks of revolutionary heroes and martyrs. He briefly continued to play that role following his arrest by declaring himself a "prisoner of war" but evidently lacked the strength or dedication to sustain it, preferring to work with his lawyers, however unsuccessfully, to contest the murder charge and avoid the death penalty.

No one knows for certain why McVeigh chose the Federal Building in Oklahoma City for the bombing, but it turns out that the building had been discussed as a possible target in a Christian Identity group twelve years earlier. Whether or not McVeigh knew about this, Oklahoma City was also considered by some far-right theorists one of the centers of a "New World Order plot," an imagined conspiracy involving a diabolical organization of wealthy men (often identified as Jews and sometimes seen collectively as the anti-Christ) who were employing foreign troops through the United Nations to place American "patriots" in concentration camps built by an "occupied" and alien American government, which was using unmarked black helicopters for transport and surveillance. In such conspiracy thinking of the early 1990s, Oklahoma City was identified as a key transfer terminal and processing center for patriot prisoners and as the site of a feared concentration camp with a crematorium capable of incinerating three thousand corpses a day. McVeigh could well have believed in that plot; there is one report of his having thought himself the victim of conspirators who had secretly placed a microchip in his buttock for identification.

Where Timothy McVeigh, an enraged avenger who belonged to nothing more than a vague gun-centered subculture, intersects with Aum Shinrikyō is in his urge to use, if not weapons of mass destruction, then the most massively destructive weapon he could imagine creating, to spark a massive incident that might initiate the struggle to end a corrupt world and usher in a pure and revolutionary new one. For in the American landscape it is the extreme right that expands its gunism into dreams of privately wielding ultimate weapons. McVeigh constructed his bomb from materials at hand, following a description he found in *The Turner Diaries* of a bomb made mainly from fertilizer and exploded at FBI headquarters in Washington, DC, from a parked truck. Because of its lavish detailing of terrorism techniques and weaponry of all sorts, the novel has come to be regarded by many as a terrorist manual. But more important, *The Turner Diaries* presents itself as a sacred text recounting how "struggle and sacrifice saved our race in its time of greatest peril and brought about the New Era." McVeigh's passionate involvement in movement martyrology was bound up with this millenarian "holy terrorism," so much so that the text itself was his guru. Once he had embraced *The Turner Diaries*, McVeigh was no longer alone.

The Text as Guru

The author of the *Diaries* is Andrew MacDonald, the pseudonym of William Pierce, a former assistant professor at Oregon State University with a doctorate in physics. The head of a Nazi youth faction he renamed the National Alliance, Pierce published his novel in serial form in that group's journal, *Attack!* He clearly meant it to be a compelling vision of movement martyrdom that would inspire violent revolutionary action.

In the absence so far of an Asahara on the American far right, *The Turner Diaries* provides an Aum-like vision of a highly spiritualized world-destroying project. Written in the form of futuristic utopian fiction (a form also favored by Asahara), *The Turner Diaries* resembles Hitler's *Mein Kampf* in its virulent mixture of murderous racism and mystical millenarianism, but it is also a very American expression of the apocalypse as a racial holocaust. In Pierce's malevolent imagination, a revolution is ignited when a corrupt government passes a Jewish-inspired law, "the Cohen Act," requiring white citizens to surrender their guns, while exempting black neighborhoods. The result: the rise of a white revolutionary group, "the Organization," with an elite core called "the Order."

The book centers on the sustained heroics of a thirty-five-year-old electrical engineer by the name of Earl Turner who is drawn to the Organization and chosen for the Order. He makes mistakes but rectifies them gloriously in a suicidal mission in which he drops a small nuclear bomb on the Pentagon to ensure the success of the white

American revolution. The book elaborates, proudly and affectionately, on the technical knowledge and steadfast racial totalism needed to carry out a project approaching global omnicide. First there is a vast "cleansing" of America's blacks, Jews, and white "race traitors" through a variety of massacres culminating in nuclear attacks on American inner cities. (The Organization cleverly provokes the Soviet Union into these multiple nuclear strikes.) Then the cleansing is extended to all the globe's nonwhite populations, until finally a white racial utopia is ushered in. Though only about 25 percent of the American white population survives, that is a much larger saving remnant than Shōkō Asahara imagined in his Aum-controlled utopian future, and it too is spiritually purified, in this case on the basis of race.

Pierce's sanguinary impulse, as expressed by the Organization's leadership, includes a megalomanic urge (reminiscent of Asahara's) to transform reality itself—initially through fantastic world-ending visions and later through murderous actions to render them concrete. The Organization's rage toward white "betrayers" believed to be endangering the survival of their own race recalls Asahara's (and Jones's) violent rage toward cult defectors. Like Asahara, moreover, Pierce equates absolute purification with world salvation, sacralizes mass murder, and immortalizes those who carry it out.

For both Pierce and Asahara, mass murder becomes a matter of reverence, not just a prelude to a perfect world but an enterprise that is holy and transformative. It ceases to be murder at all because those being killed are too defiled (in Aum's terms) or carry a racial death taint (in Pierce's terms), are too much like "foliage" or "weeds" (in Heaven's Gate's terms), and therefore are "life unworthy of life" (in Nazi terms). Above all, Pierce forces the end—even if only novelistically— calling forth a version of action prophecy on behalf of an Armageddon that is political and secular yet no less mystical than Aum's.

Pierce also resembles Asahara in being drawn to versions of techno-fantasy and romantic scientism. His hero, Turner, is a kind of American Hideo Murai, devoting himself completely to the scientific and technological requirements of his movement, however far-fetched. As a character in a novel, however, Turner has all the advantages over

Murai. While Murai could frequently be a scientific buffoon, Turner is a practical electrical engineer whose skills range from setting up complex communications equipment to planning elaborate escape tunnels to handling nuclear weapons. Where Murai was a mad scientist, Turner is an American-style creative tinkerer who can miraculously produce the necessary technology for whatever deadly work is at hand.

The technofantasy of the *Diaries*, like Asahara's, extends to absolute control of the human mind. "We are scientific," Turner proudly declares, "whereas the System [the corrupt government and society] is merely brutal." Pierce has his elite group, the Order, create a "loyalty check" that uses the supposedly foolproof methods of clinical psychology, which include monitoring and testing responses via "electrodes attached to various parts of the body" and a "bright pulsing light"—all of which are reminiscent of Aum's "S-checks." Once more, the book is able to hold to a fictional claim to perfection; Aum made the same claim but inevitably experienced real-life fallibility. As in Aum, failing the Order's test can result in death.

Pierce's claim of a sacred science is given its most extreme expression in a grandiose pseudoscientific theory he calls "cosmotheism," which he has written about elsewhere. Although not directly mentioned in *The Turner Diaries*, it underlies the entire volume. Cosmotheism purports to be an evolutionary theory but is really an embellished expression of racial mysticism. It describes a predetermined evolutionary process in which the white race it genetically destined to achieve godhood. While making a scientific claim, Pierce's cosmotheism actually leans heavily on Gnosticism (as did the Nazis, Aum, Heaven's Gate, and even to a degree Jim Jones and Charles Manson), especially its concepts of special "knowledge" that provides individuals with godly potential and of radical division between the "enlightened" and the "unknowing." In Pierce's cosmotheism those gnostic principles infuse a mystical racist vision, for which he, of course, claims scientific inevitability.

Pierce and Asahara both developed profound emotional ties to the weapons that were to force the end. In Pierce's case, it was a matter of deep attraction to weaponry as such, with virtually any object constituting a potential weapon. Hence his fictional fondling of weapons of every variety—American gunism writ large. If for Asahara weapons were an acquired taste, for Pierce they were a lifelong love affair. Yet the two visionaries share both a nuclearism inseparable from their world-ending fantasies and a related embrace of any kind of ultimate weapon capable of serving the required transformative purpose.

In the *Diaries*, Turner and others in the Organization employ pistols, rifles, shotguns, and hanging ropes for "dispatching" individual Jews and blacks but also whites who offend or get in the way. They also make innovative use of anything else at hand, from knives and hatchets to soap bars and pickle jars. Their greater fascination, however, lies with larger, more destructive weapons like improvised bombs and mortars, while their apocalyptic imagination finds its inevitable expression in ultimate weaponry. There is an ecstatic moment when Turner is admitted to an enormous secret warehouse containing "immense heaps of every sort of military weaponry imaginable: automatic rifles, machine guns, flame throwers, mortars, and literally thousands of cases of ammunition, grenades, explosives, detonators, boosters, and spare parts." Awed, he "gasp[s] in surprise," and "wonder[s] how the floor support[s] it all."

Turner and his friends initially decide to make bombs from ammonia nitrate fertilizer because more efficient explosives are unavailable to them. One suspects that Timothy McVeigh was affected by Turner's detailed and loving descriptions of how to make and best employ such weapons (how, for instance, to assemble a bomb, place it, and time the fuse to permit escape) and by his creative use of whatever materials can be obtained. One is reminded of the devoted attention American male adolescents can give to tinkering with the engines of old cars or to putting together machine parts of any sort. Crucial to this innovative spirit as Pierce portrays it in Turner, and as McVeigh may have actually experienced it, is a transcendent commitment to the cause (the kind of commitment that also drove Aum's weapons making). Turner uses his engineering background to expand his expertise into every dimension of bombing, conducting an intensive "seminar series" for selected Organization activists that culminates in the destruction of an urban telephone exchange. In such scenes the reader can sense the power surge experienced when precisely controlled technical work leads to vast physical and societal damage.

Turner enters a new weapons world when instructed by the Organization to "hit" a vast nuclear power complex. His full plunge into the world of nuclear weapons—and Pierce's into apocalyptic nuclear fantasy—occurs, however, when guerilla warfare in California enables the Organization to occupy Vandenberg Air Force Base, where Turner spends four days learning how nuclear warheads work. The Organization threatens the System with nuclear retaliation should it attempt a first strike against the "hardened" (protected by earth or concrete) nuclear silos at Vandenberg. The Organization then takes the initiative by detonating nuclear weapons in Miami and Charleston, so that Turner realizes that they are "in the middle of a nuclear civil war." He witnesses the annihilation of Baltimore, dazzled by the mushroom cloud and thrilled by the vast destruction.

Threatened with annihilation by the System (because of the influence of its "Jewish faction"), the Organization develops a brilliantly successful strategy: it fires most of its missiles at Israel and the Soviet Union, requiring the Pentagon to launch an immediate nuclear attack on the Soviet Union to destroy its retaliatory potential. By instigating an American-Soviet nuclear war, Turner boasts, the Organization disrupts the System and American life in general far more gravely than if it had dropped most of its bombs on American cities. Here the fantasy of nuclear manipulativeness and control strikingly parallels Asahara's vision of deceptively using sarin gas to initiate a nuclear war that will destroy the world and lead to Armageddon. Both nuclear fantasies derive importantly from—and could be considered caricatures of—the nuclear fantasies of the Cold War–era United States and Soviet Union.

Finally, both Asahara and Pierce are fervent admirers of Hitler. Pierce, in fact, is more than that. In a epilogue to the *Diaries*, Pierce writes that the "dream of a White world finally became a certainty" in 1999, "just 110 years after the birth of the Great One." Adolf Hitler was born in 1889, so on the next-to-the-last page of the novel we learn that the cosmic achievement of global racial cleansing has actually been guided by a guru in the wings after all. If, then, for the American far right, the closest thing to a guru is Pierce's text, the text's own guru turns out to be the dead Führer. Ghostlike but still the omnipotent guide, Hitler makes his way into the extremities of our own times.

The Phantom Guru

At least one right-wing activist took *The Turner Diaries* to be a literal as well as spiritual guide to revolution. In 1983 Robert Mathews, a disciple of Pierce's with roots in the tax protest movement (groups who considered federal taxes illegitimate and refused to pay them) and in neo-Nazi organizations, formed a group called the Order whose oath was fully in the spirit of the *Diaries*: "I, as a free Aryan man, hereby swear an unrelenting oath upon the green graves of our sires . . . that I have a sacred duty to do whatever is necessary to deliver our people from the Jew and bring total victory to the Aryan race. I, as an Aryan warrior, . . . bear witness to you, my brothers, that should an enemy agent hurt you, I will chase him to the ends of the earth and remove his head from his body and furthermore, let me witness to you, my brothers, that if I break this oath, let me forever be cursed upon the lips of our people."

Mathews and thirty to forty followers engaged in counterfeiting and in armed robbery to obtain funds for their revolution and murdered Alan Berg, a combative Jewish radio talk-show host in Denver, before Mathews himself was killed in a gunfight with the FBI in 1984. Mathews's small group represented a literal transposition of *The Turner Diaries* onto the American landscape. Mathews was doing what his guru-text advocated, even though Pierce would soon insist that his novel was a fictional vision of violent insurrection not yet feasible in the United States. Mathews's Order was a potential Aum-like vanguard group but lacked Asahara's powerful guruism as well as his talent for organization and for fusing extreme fantasies with technology.

Mathews's group was important in another way. It included a number of believers in Christian Identity, the odd but influential religion that has permeated a large segment of the radical right and provided it with a millenarian narrative in which there will be a "tribulation" consisting of an ultimate deadly struggle between godly Aryans and satanic Jews. While Christian Identity includes groups that focus on nonviolent forms of survivalism in the face of anticipated nuclear holocaust, its narrative is the sort that can lead other groups to press toward what Michael Barkun calls "a militarized apocalypse"—that is, to force the end. Mathews's own religious beliefs were apparently eclectic, involving "Odinism," with its claimed connection to pre-Christian Norse peoples, but he had some knowledge of and sympathy for the Christian Identity movement. Certainly, its believers have been among the most enthusiastic readers of *The Turner Diaries* (although Pierce has been critical of the Christian Identity religion), even if few have carried their enthusiasm for the book as far as Mathews did.

Christian Identity (along with *The Turner Diaries*) provides the far right with what Barkun calls a "philosophical center of gravity," so that what might otherwise be shifting and overlapping groupings gain a heretofore-absent "ideological coherence" in the form of an immortalizing vision of anti-Semitic and racial apocalypse. This vision, which claims to hark back to the origins of humankind and extends into an eternal white Christian future, infuses virtually every far-right paramilitary organization, including the militia movement, the Ku Klux Klan, and various neo-Nazi groups.

Even so, the guruless environment of the semimilitarized right has remained amorphous, partly under the influence of Louis Beam, an articulate former Klansman and supporter of Identity groups whose influential essay "Leaderless Resistance" appeared in the far-right journal *Seditionist* in 1992. Rejecting the Turner model of cosmic revolutionary violence as inapplicable in America, it calls instead for the creation of "phantom cells," some as small as a single person. With leaderless resistance it becomes the responsibility of each cell or person to prepare for what Beam implies are acts of terrorism and revolution, coordinating with others only in the sense that they all share a philosophy. Beam argues that the government always succeeds in infiltrating and destroying those resistance organizations with conventional command structures, while leaderless resistance would present the government with an "intelligence nightmare." Invoking the example of the committees of correspondence of the American Revolution, he does not renounce the principle of violent revolution. Rather he is giving conceptual expression to a strategy made necessary by the small numbers and limited resources of the radical right. Pierce himself, in a later novel, *Hunter,* expresses a similar doctrine, rejecting organized combat against the federal government and advocating individual acts of violence. In later denouncing the Oklahoma City bombing as "disorganized terrorism" without a plan, however, he seems to some to be looking to the possibility of groups of dedicated Earl Turners with the wherewithal to overthrow the government.

The phantom cells of Beam's leaderless resistance suggest the idea of a *phantom guru*, an invisible and nonmaterial source of compelling wisdom for movement activists. Its form of resistance, Barkun tells us, implies lawbreaking or acts of violence at a local level, as exemplified by the Oklahoma City bombing, which was accomplished by a phantom cell of two or conceivably three people moving through a larger population of like-minded individuals. Indeed, Beam's concept could have encouraged McVeigh to break out of restraints imposed by more cautious movement groups and act upon an impulse toward a dramatic display of destructive power. This kind of amorphous leaderlessness makes it difficult to mobilize any form of coordinated, large-scale operation, but it also renders the task of controlling far-right terrorism much more difficult.

In this new violent context, *The Turner Diaries* has gained the stature of a classic of the extreme right and remains a source of inspiration for its various adherents, but it has perhaps lost some of its guruistic power. There are now a plethora of small and not-so-small groups: "militias" (which can have Christian Identity influences) like the militia of Montana, the Michigan Militia, and the Citizen's Militia of Chemung County, New York; Christian Identity groups ranging from the nonviolent Church of Israel to the more aggressive Christian-Patriots Defense League to the action-prophecy-oriented Covenant, Sword and Arm of the Lord; and more traditional far-right groups like the Ku Klux Klan and the American Nazi Party—not to speak of the phantom cells of which we can know little. They all exist in a world inundated by visions of forcing some version of a racialist Armageddon and of immortalizing projects of mass murder that can be carried out with ultimate weapons.

We have seen hints of these dangers in recent years in far-right groups' acquisition of small amounts of potential agents of biological warfare. We can also observe the widespread use of the Internet by far-right groups both to inflate their size and power and to participate in national and global networking. There is no way of knowing whether or when a grouping of some sort will emerge from this confused landscape with the technological and scientific ability to act on their impulses and fantasies. We can be certain, however, that phantom gurus, whether hiding in cyberspace or issuing anonymous calls to action in some other fashion, will make their presence felt and that future phantom cells will have access to higher technology and more destructive weaponry than fertilizer bombs.

Aum's guru was anything but a phantom, but the whole of Aum could be seen as a kind of phantom cell—a few hundred hidden activists seeking to destroy the world. It is all too clear that Shōkō Asahara's impulses are in no way limited to Aum and that in our own country they have taken and can take different but related form. By examining them in relation to Aum, we may be better able to explore and contain American inclinations toward world destruction. That means probing their sources, seeking to curtail their violence, and taking steps to protect ourselves from them. Charles Manson and Jim Jones were charismatic gurus with the ability to enlist their followers in acts of murder or suicide-murder in their apocalyptic quests, but they did not imagine themselves or their groups making use of ultimate weapons to bring Armageddon about. Other gurus, like David Koresh or survivalist leaders, have armed their groups for an Armageddon struggle without themselves seeking to force the end. New groups could quite conceivably combine, as Aum did, world-ending guruism with the embrace of world-ending technology.

When we consider further the social and psychological roots of the collective urge to kill the world, we are likely to see more of ourselves in it and to begin to think of such groups as something of a dark underside or "cultural underground" of our own society. We are also likely to discover that whatever renders our society more decent and more inclusive in its benefits is likely to undermine the totalistic impulse to destroy everything. But since that impulse will not disappear, we had better continue to bring our imaginations to bear on confronting and exploring it, on finding the means to resist its lure and oppose its destructive projects.

Afterword

Although in the past I have explored behavior more successfully murderous than Aum's, this has certainly been my strangest undertaking. During the three years I have studied Shōkō Asahara and interviewed his disciples, I have been confronted at every turn by wildly bizarre fantasies converted into equally bizarre, sometimes deadly acts. Yet in my interviews I have also encountered an oddly prosaic side of Aum Shinrikyō. Here was a group whose unbounded visions led it to embrace and radically extend the most extreme of the extreme behavior I have been investigating over a professional life-time. At the same time I could not help but be struck by a familiar ordinariness to most of its members and to much of the group's every-day life, not to speak of its often bungling actions.

A researcher like myself had to be struck as well by the guru's remarkable juggling act in holding together for almost a decade the global and the local, the mystically spiritual and the concretely violent, the traditional and the New Age, the ascetic and the money-grubbing, a disciplined cult routine and the chaos of "forcing the end." A combi-nation of other-worldly strangeness and this-worldly immediacy was present in every interview I conducted and exists, I believe, in every chapter, every section of this book.

I am left with an assortment of oddly reverberating images about Asahara and Aum that, unsurprisingly, move in several directions at once. I think first of the young people I interviewed. Despite their profound Aum-related confusions, they reminded me greatly of other young Japanese I have talked with over the years—bright, thoughtful, curious, partly knowledgeable about many things, ready to enter into a dialogue, uncertain about how to combine their ideals and aspirations with everyday living. Yet former Aum disciples were very different in one overriding respect: they had encountered evil, become in some manner part of it, and were struggling either to confront or avoid that difficult truth, even as they struggled to come to terms with a guru who refused to depart from their minds.

I had to do a juggling act of my own in retaining a strong sense of Aum's evil while sympathizing with many of these intelligent young people whose spiritual quests had rendered them vulnerable to the most extreme project imaginable, that of world-ending guruism. Indeed, my own struggles during those interviews deepened my understanding of how decent young people—in fact, relatively ordinary people of all sorts, whether in Japan, the United States, or elsewhere— could be drawn to an evil that masks itself as perfect virtue. I carry away from my work with Aum Shinrikyō a stronger conviction that, even as we insist upon holding people responsible for their actions, we desperately need to explore ways in which to alter the psychological and historical conditions so conducive to the kinds of destructiveness and evil in which Aum engaged.

Images of Shōkō Asahara, a man I have never met, have also stayed with me. I think of him now—and I do continue to think of him more often than I might care to—as a self-made man whose only real talent (but a considerable talent at that) was being a guru. In discussing his emperor-centered psychology, I refer to him as a caricature of a caricature. But in considering his relationship to ultimate weapons, I came, as I wrote this book, to see him as a caricature of something else as well, something closer and more dangerous to all of us. He now seems to me to have been a caricature of present-day leaders of many countries—no longer just superpowers—who deal with ultimate weaponry and must thereby struggle with or surrender to a psychological mix of fear, control, and fantasy that could annhilate us all.

Without a state structure or official strategists and policy makers, without the "rationality" of national security explanations or efforts at weapons limitation—with only, in fact, a mad guru and his small cult—certain things become much clearer. Consider Asahara's experience with ultimate weapons: it began with Hiroshima-associated terrors and nightmares of world's end, proceeded to an embrace of weapons of mass destruction and an all-pervasive nuclearism that included omnipotent fantasies of dominating and destroying the world, led to the actual production of various versions of "the poor man's atomic bomb," and ended in dreams of ever more fantastic, as yet nonexistent annhilatory weapons. With a mad guru and a few hundred close followers, it is much easier to see how the very engagement with omnicidal weapons, once started upon, takes on a psychological momentum likely to lead either to self-implosion or to world explosion—unless there is an ultimate effort on the part of the rest of us to leave the path of nuclearism behind.

If Asahara's sequence sounds all too familiar, that is because, sad to say, his madness illuminates much about the rest of our world. This mad guru has special value for us because by scrutinizing him we can recognize the absurdity of ultimate weapons and of the world-ending projects with which those weapons inevitably become associated. In the hands of more "stable" leaders and groups, weapons-centered projects take on an illusion of sanity. A caricature can be useful for exposing such illusions, but are we capable of taking advantage of this one?

What stays with me most is a sense that Asahara and Aum have changed the world, and not for the better. A threshold has been crossed. Thanks to this guru, Aum stepped over a line that few had even known was there. Its members can claim the distinction of being the first group in history to combine ultimate fanaticism with ultimate weapons in a project to destroy the world. Fortunately, they were not up to the immodest task they assigned themselves. But whatever their bungling, they did cross that line, and the world will never quite be the same because, like it or not, they took the rest of us with them.

We can no longer pretend that such a line does not exist, that another group, even a small one, might not be capable of similar world-ending zealotry. Indeed, the next group of disciples to try might not be quite as small as Aum, or as inept, or as encumbered by its own madness. It could even be inspired by the Aum model, determined to supercede it. For that model is now abroad in the world, available to perverse imaginations of every sort—and that availability in all its threatening newness is, for me, the single most important point to come out of my exploration of Aum's world and worldview.

Ending on this somber note is by no means an expression of despair. Rather, it is a plea for awareness. We need to recognize that Asahara and Aum have changed the world for everyone. To become aware of that change marks an imaginative shift that might even prove desirable and life-affirming. One looks into the abyss in order to see beyond it. Thoughtful observers of Aum have begun to see further, as have, I would hope, readers of this book. The step taken by Aum is, and should be, profoundly troubling. But an awareness of what that step signifies, of how our world has changed, becomes in itself a step of a different kind. Part of that step should be a resistance to anyone's claim to total knowledge and ownership of our lives and deaths. "He who does not know everything," Camus tells us, "cannot kill everything." In mobilizing our imaginations to absorb the story of Aum, we may be better able to face the new danger it represents and to pursue ways of being that take into account the lives and needs of those outside our immediate groups. In such awareness lies the beginning of hope.

Notes

Many quotations and much information about Aum Shinrikyō came from the former members I interviewed, as indicated in the text. The writings of Shōkō Asahara (or those attributed to him), many of which have been translated into English, were also, of course, of great importance. Since details of Aum's behavior were emerging during the time of my research and writing, I made extensive use of Japanese newspapers, mostly from the Japanese and English Internets. These newspapers included the three main Japanese dailies—*Asahi*, *Yomiuri*, and *Mainichi*—as well as the English-language papers—the *Japan Times*, the *Asahi Evening News*, the *Mainichi Daily News*, and *Yomiuri*. In these publications there were a number of detailed series and summary articles that were especially helpful. A very important source was the prosecutorial documentation for hearings on activating the Japanese antisubversion law and for the trials of Shōkō Asahara and a number of his leading disciples, along with the court testimony of Asahara and those disciples. I drew upon the scholarly writings on Aum and Japanese religion and society of Susumu Shimazono, Manabu Watanabe, Ian Reader, and Helen Hardacre (and on extensive discussions with Shimazono, Watanabe, and Reader) and upon the journalistic accounts by the Aum specialist Shōko Egawa (and her further observations during a detailed personal discussion) and by Murray Sayle, David Kaplan and Andrew Marshall, and D. W. Brackett.

INTRODUCTION: ENDS AND BEGINNINGS

page

6   thirty thousand in Russia: Aum's remarkable presence in Russia is a story of its own, which I do not explore in this study.

9   "less a weapon of war": Edward Glover, *War, Sadism, and Pacifism* (London: George Allen & Unwin, 1946), 274.

1: The Guru and His Cult

12   "self-system" or "self-process": *Self-system* is a term used by the American psychoanalyst Harry Stack Sullivan to depict the complex interactions within the individual self; *self-process* is my own term, meant to suggest continuous movement and change.

13   a guru type: Anthony Storr, *Feet of Clay: Saints, Sinners, and Madmen: A Study of Gurus* (New York: Free Press, 1996), xii, 48. See also Margaret Thaler Singer, *Cults in Our Midst* (San Francisco: Jossey-Bass, 1994); Marc Galanter, *Cults: Faith, Healing, and Coercion* (New York: Oxford, 1989); and W.W. Meissner, "The Cult Phenomenon and the Paranoid Process," *Psychoanalytic Study of Society* (1987), 12: 69–85.

life-death dimension: See Robert Jay Lifton, *The Broken Connection: On Death and the Continuity of Life,* 1979 (Washington, DC: American Psychiatric Press, 1996), for discussion of this and other ideas and emphases in my work.

14   "magnetic attractiveness" or a "naked capacity of mustering assent": Charles Lindholm, *Charisma* (Cambridge, Mass.: Blackwell, 1990), 5–6.

16   "the head of a robot kingdom": Shōko Egawa, *Kyūseishu no Yabō* (The Ambition of a Savior) (Tokyo: Kyōikushiryo Shuppankai, 1991). See also Murray Sayle, "Nerve Gas and the Four Noble Truths," *The New Yorker,* April 1, 1996, 56–71.

18   "One day I stopped": Shōkō Asahara, *Beyond Life and Death* (Shizuoka: Aum, 1993), 25–33.

"miraculous and extraordinary happenings": Ian Reader, *Religion in Contemporary Japan* (Honolulu: University of Hawaii Press, 1991), 209, 109.

20   "the god of light": Manabu Watanabe, "Religion and Violence in Japan Today: A Chronological and Doctrinal Analysis of Aum Shinrikyō," *Terrorism and Political Violence* 10:4 (1998), 83. Much additional detail in this chapter comes from this paper, as well as from the general Aum scholarly and journalistic sources mentioned above.

22   "Father-Mother" and "human line": *The Tibetan Book of the Dead,* ed. W. Y. Evans-Wentz, 1927 (New York: Oxford, 1960), 176, 222–23.

"bring him into existence . . . lasts forever" and "an ambivalent tradition": Wendy Doniger, presentation and discussion at September 1997 meeting of the Wellfleet Psychohistory Group. See also Doniger, *The Laws of Manu,* (New York: Penguin, 1991).

25   For discussion of ideological totalism, see Robert Jay Lifton, "Cults: Religious Totalism and Civil Liberties," *The Future of Immortality and Other Essays for a Nuclear Age* (New York: Basic Books, 1987), 209–19. See also Lifton, *Thought Reform and the Psychology of Totalism: A Study of "Brainwashing" in China,* 1961 (Chapel Hill: University of North Carolina Press, 1989), 419–37.

35   "Poa Course": Shōkō Asahara, *The Law of Karma,* vol. 5 of *The Teachings of Truth* (Shizuoka: Aum, 1993), 109.

43   war on the Jews: David Goodman emphasizes the importance of Aum's anti-Semitic mind-set for its murderous acts and the influence on Aum of Japanese anti-Semites associated with such American hate groups as Liberty Lobby. See Goodman, "Antisemitism in Japan: Its History and Current Implications," *The Construction of Racial Identities in China and Japan,* ed. Frank Dikötter, forthcoming, and Goodman and Masanori Miyazawa, *Jews*

in the Japanese Mind: The History and Uses of a Cultural Stereotype (New York: Free Press, 1995).

2: IMAGINING THE END

page

45   The writings of Nostradamus: Ian Reader, "A Poisonous Cocktail? Aum Shinrikyō's Path to Violence" (Copenhagen: Nordic Institute of Asian Studies, 1996), 14; Robert Kisala, "1999 and Beyond: The Use of Nostradamus's Prophecies by Japanese Religions," *Japanese Journal of Religious Studies* 23:1–2 (1996), 143–57.

46   *Space Battleship Yamato:* See Helen Hardacre, "Aum Shinrikyō and the Japanese Media: The Pied Piper Meets the Lamb of God," Institute Reports, East Asian Institute, Columbia University, November 1995.
     Lotus Villages "would be possible": Watanabe, "Religion and Violence," 86.

47   "blind savior" with "a long beard": This characterization is emphasized in Satoshi Tamura and Kenju Komatsu, *Asahara Ossan Jigoku* (Asahara—A Dirty Old Man's Hell).
     "Day of Perishing": The Japanese title of the *manga* is *Metsubō no Hi*.

49   obscure turn-of-the-century Japanese prophet: Susumu Shimazono, "In the Wake of Aum: The Formation and Transformation of a Universe of Beliefs," *Japanese Journal of Religious Studies* 22:3–4 (1995), 381–415. Shimazono identifies the figure as Katsutoki Sakai. I have drawn upon this paper for much general information about Aum.

3: FORCING THE END

page

59–60   "The teachings of esoteric Buddhism": Watanabe, "Religion and Violence," 84–85.

60   "In order to save the world": Stella Kramrisch, *The Presence of Shiva,* 1981 (Princeton: Princeton University Press, 1992), 439.

61   "unreasonable" opposition . . . "new form of matter": Prosecutorial documents, first Asahara trial.

62   "angry emotions": Inoue statement to the court, March 21, 1996.

63   "the unity of emptiness": *The Encyclopedia of Eastern Philosophy and Religion* (Boston: Shambhala, 1994), 213.

65   "forcing the end" and Jewish criticism of "impatience": Gershom Scholem, *The Messianic Idea in Judaism* (New York: Schocken, 1971), 56–57. Scholem refers to "a deep-rooted aversion to the 'Forcers of the End,' as those people are called in Hebrew who could not wait for the arrival of the Messiah but thought to do something for it themselves."
     "It was our practice": Inoue statement.
     "Shiva wants the Tantra": Prosecutorial documents.
     "Suppose there was someone": Watanabe, "Religion and Violence," 88.
     poa as spiritual exercise for "transference" to a higher realm: *Tibetan Book of the Dead,* 85–86, and *Encyclopedia of Eastern Philosophy and Religion,* 271, 248–49.

67   The Nazis understood themselves: Robert Jay Lifton, *The Nazi Doctors: Medical Killing and the Psychology of Genocide* (New York: Basic Books, 1986).

68   "The bud of the supreme truth" . . . "*poa* the persecutors": Inoue testimony, November 8, 1996.

"So we must kill": Prosecutorial statement on Aum's chronology.

69   "no room for people other than Shōkō Asahara": Manabu Watanabe, "Salvation of the Other in Aum Shinrikyō: An Impossible Endeavor," paper presented at the 1997 meeting of the International Association for Asian Philosophy and Religion, 12.

"When can we fight seriously" . . . "dominate and reign over": Inoue testimony.

One high disciple described: Shigerō Sugimoto statement to the court, July 3, 1996.

70   "a step in the expansion": Prosecutorial statement on Aum's chronology.

88   "I will *poa* all wrongdoers": Hidetoshi Takahashi, *Aum kara no Kikan* (The Return from Aum) (Tokyo: Soushisha, 1996), 162–63.

"When you meet the guru": Watanabe, "Salvation of the Other," 11.

4: Clones of the Guru

page

94   form of doubling: Lifton, *Nazi Doctors,* 118–29.

99   *gedatsu,* or enlightenment: *Gedatsu* is usually translated as emancipation and *satori* as enlightenment, but Aum translations could alter or reverse these meanings. See Shimazono, *In the Wake* and Watanabe, *Religion and Violence.*

113   "true bliss and abundant joy": Storr, *Feet of Clay,* 185.

"joy which may result": William James, *The Varieties of Religious Experience,* 1901–02 (New York: Longmans, Green, 1952), 74, 408.

"the ecstatic merger of leader and follower": Lindholm, *Charisma,* 63.

5: The Ecstatic Science

page

116   "With the help of instruments": Shōkō Asahara, *The Bodhisattva Sutra* (Shizuoka: Aum, 1994), xi.

118   dialogues certain Nazi doctors: Lifton, *Nazi Doctors,* 278–81.

119   "destroy anything" . . . "forever end the career of man": Margaret Cheney, *Tesla: Man Out of Time,* 1981 (New York: Laurel-Dell, 1983), 246, 116. See also Nikola Tesla, *My Inventions: The Autobiography of Nikola Tesla,* 1919 (Austin: Hart Brothers, 1982).

121   Battle Cry Cultural Festival: *Asahi Shimbun* series on Aum, "*Aum Kaibō*" ("Dissecting Aum") Sept-Dec. 1995. Much of the detail about Murai's pre-Aum and Aum behavior comes from this series.

124   "a meaning, a higher purpose for life": Richard Bach, *Jonathan Livingston Seagull* (New York: Avon, 1973), 40, 81, 104.

6: Killing to Heal

page

136   Nazi medicalized killing: Lifton, *Nazi Doctors,* 1–151.

138–39   "Aum Shinrikyō upholds": Ryūzō Saki, *Aum Hōtei Renzoku Bōchōki* (The Aum Court—A Chronicle of Continuous Attendance), 2 vols. (Tokyo:

Shōgakukan, 1996), vol. 1, 40–41. Much of the material in this chapter comes from this two-volume chronicle or from prosecutorial documents.

142 "Aum Shinrikyō would not have a problem": Shōkō Asahara, *Disaster Approaches the Land of the Rising Sun: Shōkō Asahara's Apocalyptic Predictions* (Shizuoka: Aum, 1995), 188–89.

143 But in a book he wrote: Ikuo Hayashi, *Aum to Watakushi (Aum and I)* (Tokyo: Bungei Shunjū, 1998), 19.

144 "intention to achieve satori": Saki, vol. 1, 39.
"As a Doctor": Saki, vol. 1, 195–96.
He went much further: Hayashi, *Aum to Watakushi*, 114, 310.

145 "he was feeling": Toshi Maeda, *Japan Times*, May 26, 1998.
"device" . . . "useless": Hayashi, *Aum to Watakushi*, 143, 264, 309–10, 471.
"cutting-edge medical technology" . . . "in the coming final war": Asahara, *Disaster Approaches,* 168–69.

147 the work of D. Ewen Cameron: Hayashi, *Aum to Watakushi*, 287. See also Harvey M. Weinstein, *Psychiatry and the CIA: Victims of Mind Control,* introd. Robert Jay Lifton (Washington, DC: American Psychiatric Press, 1990).

148 "we were transmitting" . . . his fortieth birthday: Saki, vol. 1, 233–34; vol. 2, 148–49.
mailing packages of sarin: David E. Kaplan and Andrew Marshall, *The Cult at the End of the World* (New York: Crown, 1996), 219; D. W. Brackett, *Holy Terror: Armageddon in Tokyo* (New York: Weatherhill, 1996), 107; "Aum Planned Sarin Attacks in US Cities, Cultist Says," *Japan Times,* March 22, 1997; "Japanese Cults Said to Have Planned Nerve-Gas Attacks in US," *New York Times,* March 23, 1997.
"I wouldn't have joined the sect": Saki, vol. 1, 61.

149 On the preparation of antidotes for sarin, the use of *pam*, and Hayashi's behavior and symptoms: See Saki, vol. 2, 17–31, 52–57.

149–50 "the legacy of a murderer" . . . "irrevocably decided": Hayashi, *Aum to Watakushi,* 388–90.

150 "someone who can see" . . . "cowardly not to do it": Saki, vol. 2, 52.
"I do not want to" . . . "no more than 'not want to'": Hayashi, *Aum to Watakushi,* 388–90.

150–52 "internal conflict" . . . "used their hands to get rid of the sarin": Saki, vol. 2, 78. Quotations relating to Hayashi's conviction and sentence are from *Japan Times* reports.

152 "Ken'ichirō Katahiro is someone": Saki, vol. 2, 149.

153 "vocational truths and morals" . . . "an act of *poa*": Hayashi, *Aum to Watakushi,* 341–42, 426.
medical warriors: Nakagawa is described as a "warrior type" in Saki, vol. 2, 125.

157 "Why wasn't I arrested": Saki, vol. 2, 113.

158 "I would like Aum followers": Saki, vol. 2, 135–36.

159 "behaved as though he were pretending to be dead" . . . "absolute guru *Sonshi* Asahara": Saki, vol. 2, 128–29.
"Tsuchiya's eyes" . . . "his mental turmoil": *Japan Times,* December 9, 1997.

160 half-closed eyes and air of serenity: Saki, vol. 2, 83–84.
"Several allegations": *Mainichi Daily News,* January 25, 1995.

161 "Patient A": The account and all quoted passages, unless otherwise noted, are from prosecutorial documents for the trial of Asahara, April 25, 1996.

162 "Since he has to die anyway": Saki, vol. 2, 135.

7: Megalomania

166 "believe himself to be Christ": *Psychiatric Dictionary* (New York: Oxford University Press, 1960), 448–49.
"one of the greatest holy persons" . . . "education, etc.": *Tathāgata Abhidhamma* (The Ever-Winning Law of the True Victors) (Shizuoka: Aum, 1991), vol. 1, and *The Teachings of the Truth*, vols. 3, 4, and 5 (Shizuoka: Aum, 1992–93).

167 "the state of a Buddha": Asahara, *Bodhisattva Sutra*, 172.
the declared Christ: Asahara, *Declaring Myself the Christ* (Shizuoka: Aum, 1992), 17.

168 "Most of my close disciples": Asahara, *Teachings of the Truth,* vol. 3 (Shizuoka: Aum, 1992), 76.
previous existences in America . . . "the two are certain to unite": Asahara, *Disaster Approaches,* 299.
Visiting Egypt . . . "Instruments for *Poa*": Asahara Shōkō, *Kodai Ejiputo no Higi wo Toku* (Revealing the Mysteries of Ancient Egypt) (Tokyo: Aum, 1992)

169 "I don't think it is absurd": *Disaster Approaches,* 272.

170 In a revealing book: Tamura and Komatsu, *Asahara Ossan Jigoku.*

173 "Could a blind man like me": Brackett, *Holy Terror,* 160–61.

174 "I was deceived": Sugimoto statement, July 3, 1996.
In the fall of 1996: Accounts of Asahara's court behavior are mostly taken from *Japan Times* reports on the Internet.

8: Ultimate Weapons, Ultimate Attraction

181 it was the Nazis who first produced sarin: Sarin later came to be stockpiled by the world's major powers and was used on a large scale in the late 1980s by Iraq in the mass slaughter of its Kurdish minority and in its war with Iran. The Iraqi stockpiling of sarin may also have created a health problem for Americans, as there is some evidence that a variety of debilitating physical symptoms experienced by Gulf War veterans may have been caused by exposure to the gas when Iraqi storage buildings were blown up.

182 "Uncle Fester": U.S. Senate Permanent Subcommittee on Investigations, *Staff Statement,* Hearings on Global Proliferation of Weapons of Mass Destruction: A Case Study on the Aum Shinrikyō, October 31, 1995, 37.

183 "impure sarin was better": Brackett, *Holy Terror,* 125.

185 The songs are bizarre: The background is described in articles in *Mainichi,* May 28, 1995; Sunday *Mainichi,* June 25, 1995; and *Takarajima* (Treasure Island), August 1995.

187 extraordinary amount of peptone: U.S. Senate, *Staff Statement,* 42–43.
The contagious-disease-causing pathogens: Peter Williams and David Wallace, *Unit 731: Japan's Secret Biological Warfare in World War II* (New York: Free Press, 1989).

188   "Even for pros": Judith Miller and Sherill WuDunn, "How Japan Germ Terror Alerted World," *New York Times,* May 26, 1998.
        imitating a technique: Kaplan and Marshall, *Cult,* 235–36.

190   "make the atomic and hydrogen bombs" . . . "not so frightening anymore": Asahara, *Disaster Approaches,* 265, 305–6.

190   An Aum group: U.S. Senate, *Staff Statement,* 32–33.

191   "weapons that use light and electric waves" . . . "exterminate almost all living beings": Asahara, *Disaster Approaches,* 258, 265–66, 305.

194   "nuclearism": Robert Jay Lifton and Richard Falk, *Indefensible Weapons: The Political and Psychological Case against Nuclearism,* 1982 (New York: Basic Books, 1991), xix, 80–99.

194   "has no chance": Asahara, *Disaster Approaches,* 258–59.
        "symposia": Asahara, *Disaster Approaches,* 125–27, 131, 258.

196–99   "meditation": The quotations that follow are from Asahara, *Disaster Approaches,* 133, 140, 143–44, 185, 194. Italics added on page 199.

200   "It is unclear": This quotation and the following ones are from U.S. Senate, *Staff Statement,* 65–67, 91. See also Kaplan and Marshall, *Cult,* 192.
        forays extended to Australia: U.S. Senate, *Staff Statement,* 69–75, and Kaplan and Marshall, *Cult,* 126–33.

201   Daniel Paul Schreber: Sigmund Freud, "Psycho-Analytic Notes on an Autobiographical Account of a Case of Paranoia (Dementia Paranoides)," *Standard Edition,* vol. 12, 60–61, 72; Daniel Schreber, *Memoirs of My Nervous Illness,* ed. Ida Macalpine and Richard A. Hunter (London: William Dawson and Sons, 1955), 372–74, 379, 400; Elias Canetti, *Crowds and Power* (New York: Viking, 1962), 227, 230, 423, 433–48; Lifton, *Broken Connection,* 226–27, 230–33, 237.

9: Crossing the Threshold

203   The Hindu scholar Wendy Doniger: Presentation at Wellfleet Psychohistory Group, September 1997, and Doniger, *The Laws of Manu* .
        "is only an allusion": Kramrisch, *Presence of Shiva,* 83.

204   The concept of *poa*: Susumu Shimazono, *Gendai Shūkyō no Kanōsei: Aum Shinrikyō to Bōryōku* (A Possibility of Contemporary Religions: Aum Shinrikyō and Its Violence) (Tokyo: Iwanami Shoten, 1997).
        The Thugs of India: David C. Rapoport, "Sacred Terror: A Contemporary Example From Islam," *Origins of Terrorism: Psychologies, Ideologies, Theologies, States of Mind,* ed. Walter Reich (New York: Cambridge University Press, 1990), 121.

206   "karma" of "the Germanic world" . . . "never-to-be-written page of glory": Quoted in Felix Kersten, *The Memoirs of Doctor Felix Kersten,* ed. Herma Briffault (Garden City, NY: Doubleday, 1947), 151; Lucy S. Dawidowicz, *The War against the Jews, 1933–1945* (New York: Holt, Rinehart and Winston, 1975), 149; and in Hans Buchheim, "Command and Compliance," *Anatomy of the SS State,* ed. Helmut Krausnick et al. (New York: Walker, 1968), 366.

208   trajectory of Nazi genocide: Lifton, *Nazi Doctors,* 466–500.

211   threatening existence of nuclear weapons: Lifton, *The Broken Connection,* 335–87.

213   "need corpses": Canetti, *Crowds and Power,* 443.

10: Surviving Aum

214   they experienced many of the survivor patterns: Robert Jay Lifton, "The Concept of the Survivor," *The Future of Immortality and Other Essays for a Nuclear Age* (New York: Basic Books, 1987), 231–43.

218   former Nazis I interviewed: Lifton, *Nazi Doctors*, 6–12; Lifton, introduction to Alexander Mitscherlich and Margarete Mitscherlich, *The Inability to Mourn* (New York: Grove Press, 1975), vii–xiii.

220   "the mind of a Buddha": In *Supreme Initiation* (Tokyo: Aum, 1988), Asahara quotes the Dalai Lama as emphasizing the need to "spread real Buddhism" in Japan and adding, "You can do that well because you have a Bodhi-chitta, . . . [which] means the mind of a Buddha." He goes on to claim that because "His Holiness" is "on such a high level . . . he could perceive . . . that I was emancipated and enlightened" (10–11).

220–21   Albert Speer: Lifton, *Nazi Doctors*, 474–75.

224   softness and dependency. . . . "seek their approval and affection": Isoda and Iwai used the word *amaeru* (or its derivatives), meaning a presuming upon another's love but more generally having to do with a Japanese cultural emphasis on the dependency of children on parents. Takeo Doi, a distinguished Japanese psychiatrist, speaks of the "world of *amae*" that characterizes Japanese society. See *The Anatomy of Dependence* (Tokyo: Kodansha International, 1973).

226–27   "looking at my own face" . . . "either victims or criminals": Inoue court statements, October 1995, March 1996, and April 1996.

227   "feeling that this crazy guru": Sugimoto court statement, July 3, 1996.

228   "revered": Ishii court statement, May 16, 1997.

229   two thousand Aum members: The figures are from Manabu Watanabe, personal communication.

230–31   "I think the time will come": "Statements of Aum Members Who Believed Blindly in Matsumoto's Sermons," prosecutorial documents, hearings on the anti-subversion law, December 20, 1995. Presented back to back, the statements were meant to illustrate the continuing danger of Aum. They should not be taken to be typical of those who have had contact with the cult, but they do represent a loyalist cadre.

11: A Japanese Phenomenon?

233   Kazuaki Okazaki: Legal authorities called Okazaki's death sentence "a matter of course" and the judge spoke of him as "lacking human nature" (*Japan Times*, October 23, 1998).

234   primary school teacher: *Daily Yomiuri*, March 6, 1996.
       In the aftermath: The account of TBS's wrongdoing is from *Mainichi Daily News*, July 22, 1995; *Japan Times*, May 17, 1996; and Brackett, *Holy Terror*, 11, 17.

236   program to "destabilize Japan": *Mainichi Daily News*, June 4, 1995.

237   "thunderboltism" . . . "surfeit of change": Carol Gluck, *Japan's Modern Myths: Ideology in the Late Meiji* (Princeton: Princeton University Press, 1985), 20, 27, 17–41. See also Robert Jay Lifton, *The Protean Self* (Chicago: University of Chicago Press, 1999).

psychological price to be paid: In a study of six leading figures of modern Japan, Shūichi Katō, Michael R. Reich, and I found that all of them combined extraordinary achievement with considerable inner conflict and confusion (*Six Lives, Six Deaths: Portraits from Modern Japan* [New Haven: Yale University Press, 1979]). A similar combination was present in university students I studied in the 1960s (Lifton, "Emergent Youth: The Japanese Example," *History and Human Survival* [New York: Random House, 1970], 23–111).

237–38   "split between two opposite poles" ... ethical presence among other peoples: Kenzaburō Ōe, *Japan, the Ambiguous, and Myself* (Tokyo: Kodansha International, 1995), 105–28.

238   "imperialism of justice": Albert Camus, *The Rebel* (New York: Knopf, 1954), 203.

239   Christianity itself: Bernard McGinn, "Apocalyptic Spirituality: Approaching the Third Millennium," *The Year 2000: Essays on the End,* ed. Charles B. Strozier and Michael Flynn (New York: New York University Press, 1997), 73–80. See also McGinn's documentary collection *Apocalyptic Spirituality* (New York: Paulist Press, 1979) and his introduction to that volume.
       "millennial undertow": Norman Cohn, *The Pursuit of the Millennium,* 1957 (New York: Oxford University Press, 1970), 2–3.

239–41   Free Spirit Brethren: Cohn, *Pursuit,* 148–86, 205–22.

241   "split cosmology": Elaine Pagels, *The Origin of Satan* (New York: Vintage, 1996), 179.

242   "potential nightmare": Shimazono, *Gendai Shūkyō no Kanōsei.*

243   In recent centuries: Susumu Shimazono, presentation at the Center on Violence and Human Survival, John Jay College, May 5, 1996; discussions with Shimazono and Manabu Watanabe.

244   According to the philosopher: Yūjirō Nakamura, "Evil and Sin in Japanese Culture," paper presented at Eranos conference, 1996.
       Until the Meiji Restoration: Manabu Watanabe, personal communication; Mark R. Mullins, Susumu Shimazono, and Paul L. Swanson, *Religion and Society in Modern Japan* (Berkeley: Asian Humanities Press, 1993).

246   what could not be faced: Iris Chang, *The Rape of Nanking* (New York: Basic Books, 1997), 4; Gavin McCormack, *The Emptiness of Japanese Affluence* (Armonk, NY: M. E. Sharpe, 1996).
       early occupation years: John Dower, *Embracing Defeat* (New York: New Press, 1999).

247   The distinguished German psychoanalysts: Mitscherlich and Mitscherlich, *Inability to Mourn,* and Lifton introduction.

248   American decision to grant immunity to the emperor: McCormack's argument is similar to one made several decades ago by the distinguished historian of ideas Masao Maruyama, who refers to the emperor-centered structure as "a system of non-responsibility" (*Thought and Behavior in Modern Japanese Politics* [New York: Oxford, 1963], and personal communication).
       even greater tendency than in Germany: McCormack, *Emptiness of Japanese Affluence,* 229–34; Ian Buruma, *The Wages of Guilt: Memories of War in Germany and Japan* (New York: Farrar Straus and Giroux, 1994).
       a minority of Vietnam veterans: Robert Jay Lifton, *Home from the War* (New York: Simon and Schuster, 1973).

249   Haruki Murakami: The one-volume English translation is *The Wind-Up Bird Chronicle* (New York: Knopf, 1997).

250–52   Zen's association with force: For the discussion of Zen in these pages, I have drawn on Brian Victoria, *Zen at War* (New York: Weatherhill, 1997), 21–27, 35–37, 86–100, 116–33.

252   "psychism": Robert Jay Lifton, *Revolutionary Immortality: Mao Tse-tung and the Chinese Cultural Revolution* (New York: Random House, 1968), 32, 99–105.

254   "had overreached itself": Gluck, *Japan's Modern Myths*, 284.

255   One survivor of the atomic bombing: Robert Jay Lifton, *Death in Life: Survivors of Hiroshima*, 1968 (Chapel Hill: University of North Carolina Press, 1991, 1998), 22, 399–478.

       personal accounts: John Whittier Treat, *Writing Ground Zero: Japanese Literature and the Atomic Bomb* (Chicago: University of Chicago Press, 1995).

256   *Barefoot Gen:* Keiji Nakazawa, *Barefoot Gen: The Day After* (Philadelphia: New Society, 1988).

       "desire to express": Obituary of Tomoyuki Tanaka, *New York Times,* April 4, 1997.

257   *Godzilla:* For the film and its counterparts, see Donald Richie, "*Mono no Aware*—Hiroshima in Film," *Film: Book Two,* ed. Robert Hughes (New York: Grove Press–Evergreen, 1962), 67–86; Anderson and Donald Richie, *The Japanese Film* (Rutland, VT: Charles E. Tuttle, 1959).

258   "might laugh if they heard": Hidetoshi Takahashi, *Aum kara no Kikan* (Return from Aum) (Tokyo: Soushisha, 1996), 159.

       "apotheosis": Thomas M. Disch, *The Dreams Our Stuff Is Made Of: How Science Fiction Conquered the World* (New York: Free Press, 1998), 141–43.

       "Though Aum": Yūjiro Nakamura, "The Japanese Religious Mind Reconsidered: The Problem of Brain Death and the Aum Shinrikyō Case," ms., 12.

259–64   Japanese new religions: For consideration of Aum as a "new new religion," I have drawn on Mullins, Shimazono, and Swanson, *Religion and Society,* 221–300; Reader, *Religion in Contemporary Japan,* 194–243; and extensive discussions with Shimazono, Reader, and Manabu Watanabe, in particular with Watanabe on Aum's version of "New Age Buddhism" and on Japanese psychological man."

261   "potpourri of pursuits and effects": Michael Grosso, *The Millennium Myth* (Wheaton, IL: Quest Books, 1995), 213, 215.

265–66   Young Rebels: Robert Jay Lifton, "Emergent Youth," 40–57, 60–80, 81–103.

266–68   United Red Army: The account of the killings draws on Patricia G. Steinhoff, "Death by Defeatism and Other Fables: The Social Dynamics of the Rengō Sekigun Purge," *Japanese Social Organization,* ed. Takie Sugiyama Lebra (Honolulu: University of Hawaii Press, 1992), 195–224.

269   "the essence of Bushidō": Quotations are from the classical eighteenth-century code of the warrior, the *Hagakure,* in Lifton, *Broken Connection,* 102, 395.

       A noble failure in battle: Ivan Morris, *The Nobility of Failure: Tragic Heroes in the History of Japan,* 1975 (New York: Noonday/Farrar Straus and Giroux, 1988).

       "Jumping off Kiyomizu": Robert J. C. Butow recounts the incident in *Tōjō and the Coming of the War* (Princeton: Princeton University Press, 1961), 267.

12: FORCING THE END, AMERICAN STYLE

page

272   "melted into unity": James, *Varieties of Religious Experience,* 379.
"postmodern theories of posthistory" ... "an end without an end":
Malcolm Bull, *Apocalypse Theory and the Ends of the World* (Oxford:
Blackwell, 1995), 4–6, 207.

273   Bruce Hoffman: U.S. Senate, *Staff Statement,* 2.
"die-hard redneck bigots": John Weir, quoted in Damien Thompson, *The
End of Time: Faith and Fear in the Shadow of the Millennium* (Hanover,
NH: University Press of New England, 1996), 308.
"old gods failing": Helmut E. Gerber, quoted by Frank Kermode in Bull,
Apocalypse Theory, 258.

273   "juxtaposition of terror and bliss": Thompson, *End of Time,* 58.

274   cultic milieu: The British sociologist Colin Campbell introduced this term to
describe a network of people and practices that form around a society's
"rejected knowledge," within which groups may form, dissolve, and re-form
under different names. They can constitute a "cultural underground," whose
worldview can be a mirror image of that of the larger society (Barkun, *Religion and the Racist Right: The Origins of the Christian Identity Movement,*
rev. ed. [Chapel Hill: University of North Carolina Press, 1997], 247–78).

275   "a vision of Jesus": Nuel Emmons, *Manson in His Own Words* (New York:
Grove Press, 1986), 125.
"The Infinite One": Lindholm, *Charisma,* 129.
"a half-assed nothing" ... "yourself and the world": Lindholm, *Charisma,*
128–31.
"love, pure love" ... "smoking, eating, stabbing": Vincent Bugliosi, *Helter
Skelter: The True Story of the Manson Murders,* 1974 (New York: Bantam,
1995), 117, 107, 129.

276   "We were tuned into God": Lindholm, *Charisma,* 132.
"I became Charlie" ... "Soul or Spirit can't die": Bugliosi, *Helter Skelter,*
461, 301.
"the left-handed Tantra": R. C. Yaehner, *Our Savage God: The Perverse Use
of Eastern Thought* (New York: Sheed and Ward, 1974), 9–52.

277   "I've got a thousand faces": Lindholm, *Charisma,* 131.
"a condition of *folie à famille*": Bugliosi, *Helter Skelter,* 623.
"and with each change": Lindholm, *Charisma,* 131.
"would come out of the ghettos" ... "the black servants": Bugliosi, *Helter
Skelter,* 331, 301.

278   "One by one": Emmons, *Manson,* 199.

278–79   *White Album:* Manson's interpretations are in Bugliosi, *Helter Skelter,*
323–31.

279   "When things stop working out" ... "they needed me": Lindholm,
Charisma, 134.

280   a death taint: Lifton, *Broken Connection,* 302–50.
"The only way": Lindholm, *Charisma,* 130.

282   "many had died": Jonathan Z. Smith, *Imagining Religion: From Babylon to
Jonestown* (Chicago: University of Chicago Press, 1982), 117.

283   "any love, any understanding": Tim Reiterman, *Raven: The Untold Story of
the Rev. Jim Jones and His People* (New York: E. Dutton, 1982), 16–17.
Much of the detail in this section on Jones comes from this book.

284   "claimed the platform": John R. Hall, *Gone from the Promised Land:*

Jonestown in American Cultural History (New Brunswick, NJ: Transaction Publishers, 1987), 31.

"I am the only God" . . . "the God I could touch": James Reston, Jr., *Our Father Who Art in Hell* (New York: Times Books, 1981), 56, 25.

285   "an apocalyptic 'warring sect' ": Hall, *Promised Land,* 299.

"great desolation" . . . "no radiation coming our way": David Chidester, *Salvation and Suicide: An Interpretation of Jim Jones, the Peoples Temple, and Jonestown* (Bloomington: University of Indiana Press, 1988), 113–15.

286   "America's system" . . . "their lovely caves a year later": Chidester, *Salvation and Suicide,* 112–13, 72.

287   "revolutionary sex": Chidester, *Salvation and Suicide,* 103.

288   "Your fucking me in the ass": Reiterman, *Raven,* 177.

letter to President Jimmy Carter: Reiterman, *Raven,* 445–46.

289   "drug addicts" . . . "realize what he's doing": Reiterman, *Raven,* 428.

Jones had been taking: On Jones's drug addiction and the travels of women surrounding him to obtain drugs, see Mary McCormick Maaga, "Triple Erasure: Women and Power in Peoples Temple," dissertation, Drew University, 1996, 90.

290   "Don't kill him" . . . "too sick": Reiterman, *Raven,* 426–27.

The deified guru: Maaga argues that Jones's overall illness, his drug addiction, and his paranoia led to his becoming increasingly an "outsider in his own community, as opposed to the women around him who held leading positions in the group and were increasingly responsible for its administration." See also Maaga, "Loyalty and Freedom, a Deadly Potion: A Consideration of the Jonestown Suicides," paper presented to the New Religious Movements Group of the American Academy of Religion, November 19, 1995.

"I don't believe in anything loving in the universe": Chidester, *Salvation and Suicide,* 125.

"Dad's been saying it": Reston, *Our Father,* 265.

291   "carry out his threat": Hall, *Promised Land,* 244.

He feared the Treasury Department: Reiterman, *Raven,* 285–86.

"You people just tear me apart": Reston, *Our Father,* 267.

292   "I have failed" . . . still remain intact: Hall, *Promised Land,* 273–75.

three elements generally present in suicide: Lifton, *Broken Connection,* 239–61.

293   "immediately escalated every crisis": Chidester, *Salvation and Suicide,* 145.

"Ever since as a child" and "then always blacks": Reston, *Our Father,* 263.

293–94   "My good wife": Reston, *Our Father,* 135.

294   "to save you from jails": Chidester, *Salvation and Suicide,* 126.

"revolutionary immortality": Lifton, *Revolutionary Immortality.* See also Lifton, "The Appeal of the Death Trip," *New York Times Magazine,* January 7, 1979.

"chosen people" . . . "the day of Nazareth": Chidester, *Salvation and Suicide,* 117.

295   in Jones's case mostly women . . . "acquiescence to his bullshit": See discussion in Maaga, "Triple Erasure."

296   He would later say: Reston, *Our Father,* 275, 282.

"emerged as a proposed collective penance": Hall, *Promised Land,* 134.

"it is much easier": Reiterman, *Raven,* 370.

"The last orgasm": Hall, *Promised Land,* 135.

296   "The only fuck I want": Chidester, *Salvation and Suicide,* 146.

the writer Yukio Mishima: Lifton, Katō, and Reich, *Six Lives, Six Deaths,* 231–74.

296–300   In a rambling monologue: Quotations are from Maaga, "Triple Erasure," appendix 2, a transcript of the tape. Maaga identifies some of the people who speak and adds explanatory footnotes to this tragically valuable document.

301   "The term *genocide*": The United Nations Convention on Genocide associates the term with killing or seriously harming "a national, ethnical, racial, or religious group." See Robert Jay Lifton and Eric Markusen, *The Genocidal Mentality: Nazi Holocaust and Nuclear Threat* (New York: Basic Books, 1990), 12.

13: Inward Aum?

page

303   In March 1997: Throughout this chapter I make use of reports in the *New York Times* and the American newsweeklies. But most of what the group says about itself, and most of the quotations in the chapter, come from the Heaven's Gate Web site on the Internet.

304   "acute, generalized, total self-destruction": Karl Menninger, "Psychoanalytic Aspects of Suicide," *A Psychiatrist's World: Selected Papers of Karl Menninger* (New York: Viking, 1959), 338.

suicidal and homicidal impulses often coexist: There is evidence that an important motivation for murderers can be the prospect of execution by the state. See, for example, George F. Solomon, "Capital Punishment as Suicide and as Murder," *American Journal of Orthopsychiatry* 45 (1975): 701–11.

305   "willing to bear arms": *Time,* April 14, 1997, 44.

307   "who shared a worldview": Robert W. Balch, "Waiting for the Ships: Disillusionment and the Revitalization of Faith in Bo and Peep's UFO Cult," *The Gods Have Landed: New Religions from Other Worlds,* ed. James R. Lewis (Albany: State University of New York Press, 1995), 145.

309   False alarms . . . actually increased visionary expectation: This is in keeping with a classic study by Leon Festinger, Henry W. Riechen, and Stanley Schachter, *When Prophecy Fails* (Minneapolis: University of Minnesota Press, 1956). In that study (also of what was called a "flying saucer cult"), the failed prophecy of a particular time for an end-of-the-world event led not to disillusionment but to added proselytizing. The authors give as the reason members' inability to tolerate "cognitive dissonance," but I would emphasize the need to sustain the cultic self and the sense of transcendence and immortality associated with that self.

317   A kind of happy feeling: This pattern is described by Ludwig Binswanger in his study of Ellen West, considered a classic in existentialist psychiatry. West was long obsessed with death and suicide and, upon being released from the hospital by Binswanger (who believed he could not help her), she made a specific plan to kill herself and became "calm, happy, and peaceful" prior to carrying it out. ("The Case of Ellen West: An Anthropological-Clinical Study," *Existence: A New Dimension in Psychiatry and Psychology,* ed. R. May, E. Angel, and H. Ellenberger [New York: Basic Books, 1958], 237–64).

page

326   "the most destructive terroist act": Barkun, *Religion and the Racist Right*, 256.

"the fringe apocalypticism of the racist right": Barkun, "Racist Apocalypse: Millennialism on the Far Right," Strozier and Flynn, *The Year 2000*, 190.

327   *The Turner Diaries:* Andrew MacDonald [William L. Pierce], *The Turner Diaries*, 1978 (New York: Barricade Books, 1996).

Born in 1968 in upstate New York: Charles B. Strozier and Eric Nadler generously provided their files of newspaper and magazine articles about McVeigh and related matters. Two of the more important articles are Robert D. McFadden, "A Life of Solitude and Obsessions," *New York Times*, May 4, 1995, and Dale Russakoff and Serge F. Kovaleski, "Two Angry Men," *Washington Post National Weekly Edition*, July 24–30, 1995.

327   classic essay: Richard Hofstadter, *The Paranoid Style in American Politics and Other Essays* (New York: Knopf, 1965).

"Jesus Christ was not a pacifist": Barkun, *Religion and the Racist Right*, 275.

328   sent to fight in the Persian Gulf . . . hunger for meaning and transcendence: Charles B. Strozier, "Apocalyptic Violence and the Politics of Waco," Strozier and Flynn, *The Year 2000*, 107–08.

"all ready to go all the time": Russakoff and Kovaleski, "Two Angry Men."

329   "Do we have to shed blood" . . . "indeed a New Age": Strozier, "Apocalyptic Violence," 108, 109.

329–31   Martyrology reverberates powerfully: The details of far-right martyrology in these pages are from Barkun, *Religion and the Racist Right*, 266–68.

331   one of the centers of a "New World Order plot": Barkun, *Religion and the Racist Right*, 260.

332   "struggle and sacrifice": Foreword, *Turner Diaries*,

"holy terrorism": Brad Whitsel, " 'The Turner Diaries' and Cosmotheism: William Pierce's Theology of Revolution," *Nova Religio* 1:2 (1998), 184.

334   "We are scientific": *Turner Diaries*, 92.

335   "immense heaps": *Turner Diaries*, 122–23.

336   "dream of a White world": *Turner Diaries*, 210.

337   "I, as a free Aryan man": Barkun, *Religion and the Racist Right*, 229.

nonviolent forms of survivalism: Geoffrey Kaplan, *Radical Religion in America: Millenarian Movements from the Far Right to the Children of Noah* (Syracuse: Syracuse University Press, 1997), 47–68.

338   "philosophical center of gravity": Barkun, "Racist Apocalypse," 200.

With leaderless resistance: This account of Beam's and Pierce's doctrines draws on Barkun, *Religion and the Radical Right*, 271, 278–81.

340   "cultural underground": Barkun, *Religion and the Radical Right*, 247.

Acknowledgments

Susumu Shimazono's early and generous counsel did much to make the work possible, and he and I have engaged in a continuing lively conversation about Aum Shinrikyō, Japanese culture, and American-Japanese interactions. Manabu Wanatabe has worked closely with me, in both Japan and the United States, on virtually every aspect of the study, bringing to it his remarkable combination of knowledge, energy and insight.

At our Center on Violence and Human Survival, Charles Strozier and I extended and deepened our long-standing dialogue, along with our friendship, as we explored the nature and complexities of apocalyptic violence. Michael Flynn's incisive comments and remarkable grasp of relevant literature enhanced the study. Throughout, Cindy Ness made an invaluable contribution as a dedicated and creative research assistant. At Wellfleet meetings on psychohistory, I have benefitted from ideas expressed by Mary Catherine Bateson, Norman Birnbaum, Margaret Brenman-Gibson, Cathy Caruth, Wendy Doniger, Daniel Ellsberg, Kai Erikson, Carol Gilligan, James Gilligan, Judith Herman, Robert Holt, Sudhir Kakar, Bessel van der Kolk, John Mack, Norman Mailer, and David Tracy; and in earlier years, in ways that have lasted, by Erik Erikson. Also important have been talks with Martin Bergmann and Larry Shainberg in New York City and Wellfleet; with Shuichi Katō and Kenzaburō Ōe in various places; and with Western scholars of Japanese religion and culture, including Ian Reader, Mark Mullins, and David Goodman. Drafts of the manuscript were read by Strozier, Watanabe, and by Michael Barkun, all of whom made important suggestions.

In Japan, crucial research assistance was provided by Lico Maekawa, Kazuhiro Watanabe, and Mikimasa Maruyama; and in the United States by Yasuhiro Makimura, Nagomi Matsumoto, Reiko Tomii, Naoko Watanabe, and Ioannis E. Mentzas who also checked the manuscript for errors. Contributing to the large task of typing the manuscript were Susan Dunlap, Sandra R. Friedman, Shelly Pettigrew, Michael Schoenfeld, and especially Tamir Halaban. Lucy Silva, my assistant at John Jay College, once more coordinated everything having to do with the manuscript, and did so with her usual, but very special, combination of grace and efficiency.

For their research support I am grateful to the Japan Foundation and the International House of Japan, particularly to Mikio Katō, Ambassador Hisashi Owada, Counsul General Yoshio Karita, and Matsuo Amemiya; to the Suntory Foundation and Masakazu Yamazaki; to the New York Times Company Foundation and Arthur Gelb; and to John Jay College and President Gerald Lynch.

At Metropolitan Books, Tom Engelhardt's imaginative immersion in the manuscript was truly extraordinary; his feel for both the subject and the English language constantly enabled me to say better, and more concisely, what I wanted to say. Roslyn Schloss, in the final stages of the editing, was a beacon of clarity and accuracy. Sara Bershtel guided the overall publishing enterprise with a sure hand, applying the friendliest and most irresistible pressure one could ask for. Lynn Nesbit and Tina Bennett, my literary agents, applied their skills and sensitivity to make all things happen.

As with all of my projects, family members were inevitably affected, and they provided spiritual support in ways they might not have fully realized. That has been true of Ken and Michelle Lifton and their daughters Kimberly and Jessica; and of Natasha Karen Lifton, to whom this book is dedicated, and of Daniel Itzkovitz. Betty Jean Lifton, on the other hand, is fully aware of her support, having been with me on my trips to Japan and everywhere else, and having shared every nuance of my struggles with the work.

Index